WHEN THE BUCS WON IT ALL

WHEN THE BUCS WON IT ALL

The 1979 World Champion Pittsburgh Pirates

BILL RANIER *and* DAVID FINOLI

McFarland & Company, Inc., Publishers
Jefferson, North Carolina, and London

Frontispiece: Baserunner Omar Moreno steps over Bill Robinson, who was hit by a pitch which brought home the final run in the Pirates' 4–1 seventh game victory, as trainer Tony Bartirome looks on. (Courtesy of the Pittsburgh Pirates.)

LIBRARY OF CONGRESS CATALOGUING-IN-PUBLICATION DATA

Ranier, Bill, 1960–
    When the Bucs won it all : the 1979 world champion Pittsburgh Pirates / Bill Ranier and David Finoli.
       p.   cm.
    Includes bibliographical references and index.

    ISBN 0-7864-2050-2 (softcover : 50# alkaline paper) ∞

    1. Pittsburgh Pirates (Baseball team).   2. World Series (Baseball) (1979).   I. Finoli, David, 1961–   II. Title.
GV875.P5R36   2005
796.357'64'0974886 — dc22   2005007360

British Library cataloguing data are available

©2005 Bill Ranier and David Finoli. All rights reserved

No part of this book may be reproduced or transmitted in any form or by any means, electronic or mechanical, including photocopying or recording, or by any information storage and retrieval system, without permission in writing from the publisher.

Cover photograph: Pitcher Kent Tekulve *(Pittsburgh Pirates)*

Manufactured in the United States of America

McFarland & Company, Inc., Publishers
  Box 611, Jefferson, North Carolina 28640
  www.mcfarlandpub.com

From Dave

To my grandmothers,
Inez Fury and Maria Finoli,
who both passed away in 1979.
Thank you for the joy and
love of life you both gave me,
which I share today with
my beautiful wife Vivian
and three wonderful children:
Tony, Matt and Cara

From Bill

To my wife Marge, the
most wonderful person in my
life, who was a real
champion in our home as the
deadline for this manuscript
approached; and to my
daughter Sarah, whose birth
made 2003 more
memorable than 1979

Acknowledgments

As with any project of this nature, it was impossible to get through it without the help of many people. First off, big thank yous go to the Pittsburgh Pirates and Jim Trdinich as well as the Topps Card Company and Clay Luraschi for providing us with the wonderful photographs in the book.

The Society of American Baseball Research (SABR) has always been a valuable source for each of the projects we embark on, as they were with this one. Every time we were in need of a particular stat or fact, the SABR online community was there to help, especially Brian Mohr, Les Jackson and Pete Brewer.

Finally, researching the book brought back memories of the times we enjoyed as freshman at Duquesne University in 1979, so we'd like to acknowledge the boys of the Penthouse: Bob "Boo Boo" O'Brien, Gary Degnan, Daryl Dombeck, Mike Kraut, Shawn Christian, Bill Letrent, Rich Pipak, Pat Didiano, Joe Hershman, Ray Stefanacci (our University of Pittsburgh import), and, most of all, Leo Moga, who seemed to be a good luck charm for the Pirates whenever he watched a game, except when doing so at Three Rivers Stadium. These are the men we had the great pleasure to enjoy that magical championship season with.

From Dave

One of the things I've been lucky enough to enjoy throughout my life is the love and support of my wonderful family — my mother, Eleanor; father, Domenic; brother, Jamie, and his wife, Cindy; my sister, Mary and her husband, Matt; my nieces, Marissa and Brianna.

In spite of the Pirates' success, 1979 turned out to be as bitter as it was sweet when I lost both of my grandmothers during the course of that year. Thanks to my extended family, the Fury and Finoli clans—especially my cousins Tom A, Amanda, Claudia, Fran, Lucy, Flo, Beth, Vinny, Richard, Diane, Eddie, Pam, Debbie, Ginny Lynn, Tom D, Gary, Amy and Linda—we made it through those troubling times. Over the years they, along with my aunts Louise, Mary, Evie, Libby, Jeannie, Betty, Mary Anne and Norma and my uncle, Vince, have been a very important part of my life and show me every day the real meaning of what a family should be about.

When I married my lovely bride Vivian, I was lucky enough to become part of her family from Alliance, Ohio. Her mother, Vivian, and her father, Salvatore, have always been there to help and support us in whatever we needed. To them as well as everyone mentioned above, I give thanks for everything.

From Bill

The year 1979 was quite a good one for me. While my passion for Pirates baseball burned then as it has for most of my life, as an 18-year-old some of my other appetites were, shall I say, not quite so wholesome and led to many memorable, if not printable, moments. I would first like to thank my mother, Marcella, who certainly had a difficult time with my late adolescence and had the unenviable task of doling out the punishments that I had brought on myself. To my late father, William, who braved the cold to take me and my brothers Fran and Tim to the Pirates' 1979 opening game, I wish I still had the opportunity to say thank you for his wisdom for understanding that I was not straying too far from the path and that my indiscretions were not unusual for someone my age, even though they upset him at the time. Thanks also to Fran and his family, Josephina, Stefanie and Steven; Tim; and my sister Debbie Kazsimer, her husband Ken and their son, Matt, for their support and love. I hope our younger generation will get to experience a Pirate World Championship soon.

On a lighter note, I thank that group of "boneheads" with whom I shared wonderful misadventures: Tony Bazzo, Mark Firment, Rege Garris, Danny Horn, Mark Notarberardino, Terry Pacelli, Dan Szekely, Mike Todaro and John Toth. Good friendships, unlike great baseball teams, go on forever. By the way, Mike, thanks once again for making me miss the Pirates' triple play in '79. Things *do happen* in the third inning.

My in-laws, Raymond and Joan Borkowski, I thank once again for all the help with repair work and excellent meals they continue to provide, but most of all for all their help with Sarah. Their efforts freed up time for me to write this manuscript.

Table of Contents

Acknowledgments vii
Introduction 1

1. Prelude to a Championship 5
2. The Regular Season 11
3. The Postseason 45
4. The Fall of the Family 91
5. The Members of the Family 107

Appendix A: Team Statistics and Awards 233
Appendix B: 1979 Pirates Day by Day 245
Notes 251
Bibliography 257
Index 259

Introduction

The last year of the 1970s was not a great one for the country or Pennsylvania. The Three Mile Island nuclear power plant crisis near Harrisburg, the Iran Hostage Crisis, the Russian invasion of Afghanistan and a poor national economy — which was particularly weak through the Rust Belt — all contributed to the great "National Malaise" that President Jimmy Carter spoke of. The only thing the man on the street in an economically depressed Pittsburgh could point to with pride was sports.

And 1979 was a great time to be a sports fan in the city. The Steelers opened 1979 by winning a Super Bowl title and closed it the same way. After recruiting a young phenom quarterback from Pittsburgh Central Catholic High School by the name of Danny Marino, the University of Pittsburgh football team capped off an 11–1 campaign by winning the Lambert Trophy, awarded annually to the best college football team in the East, and finished sixth nationally in the final polls. Duquesne University won a share of the Eastern Eight basketball crown. Through it all there was a story developing in Three Rivers Stadium that summer that would eventually overshadow all others that phenomenal year.

Leading up to that final year of the '70s, the sports scene in Pittsburgh revolved around the gridiron. The Pittsburgh Steelers had been dominant throughout much of the decade; Pitt had taken the college football world by storm, winning the national championship in 1976 and becoming a perennial top ten program; and Friday night high school football, always popular in Western Pennsylvania, was made more popular still by the area's college and pro team successes; there was seemingly little room for the local sports fans to take a baseball team into their hearts.

The Pittsburgh Pirates had a tremendously successful decade, but it was also tragic. They won five National League Eastern Division crowns and the 1971 world championship, but lost the great Roberto Clemente in a plane

Dave Parker and Willie Stargell celebrate following the franchise's ninth National League championship. (Courtesy of the Pittsburgh Pirates.)

crash and pitcher Bob Moose in a car accident. By the end of the 1970s, the Pirates were a good team, but were no longer favored to win a World Series. With all the titles being captured on the football field, the Bucs got lost in the mix.

According to the experts, 1979 was to be the year of the Phillies. It was tough to argue against the prediction. After all, they were coming off three consecutive Eastern Division championships and had just added one of the greatest hitters ever, Pete Rose, to their already powerful lineup. But over the previous couple of years, Pirates general manager Harding Peterson had transformed this team from a slow power offense to one that was lightning fast but could also still smack long balls. He hoped his final few moves could put the club back on top again.

As the season developed it was apparent that the Pirates were anything but an ordinary team. Let's start with the uniforms. There were actually three different double-knit uniforms: black, gold and a very thick yellow pinstripe, which someone decided were okay to wear in combinations together. A thick yellow pinstripe shirt with gold pants? It's no wonder the '70s are the most mocked fashion decade in history. In 1976, some franchises chose to wear a 19th century-style pillbox cap — once — to celebrate the 100th anniversary of the National League. The Pirates decided they'd keep them on a permanent basis. Their aging veteran spiritual leader, Willie Stargell, awarded a gold star every time someone contributed to the team's success, stars that the players chose to adhere to these old-time caps, not unlike a college football team (such as the buckeyes that adorn the Ohio State classic helmets). The players chose a disco song, "We Are Family" by Sister Sledge, to celebrate every win. Imagine a hard rock town like Pittsburgh singing disco for every baseball victory.

On the surface, mixing all these variables in a blue-collar town wouldn't seem to be a public relations masterpiece, but somehow it all worked like a charm. Peterson added former batting champion Bill Madlock and shortstop Tim Foli to what was already a cast of characters and the Bucs, 36–33 at the time of the Madlock trade, took off. Stargell, who had been a fixture in the Pirates lineup since 1962, had been given up for dead — in terms of baseball — after the 1977 campaign, but magically found a fountain of youth and was having an MVP season. He drove the team to the top of the NL East, a spot it hadn't occupied at the end of the season since 1975.

As intriguing as the season was, it wasn't until the evening of August 25 that the Pirates faithful started to believe "it" could happen. That night, the Bucs played the Padres at San Diego. Bert Blyleven was on the mound for the Pirates against future Hall of Famer and spitball king Gaylord Perry.

Perry had mowed down Pittsburgh through eight innings, going into the ninth with a 2–0 lead. The Bucs finally got through against the 40-year-old Perry, scoring twice in the ninth to send this game into extra innings.

The game went on past midnight, both teams scoring once in the 12th, battling back and forth. Then Chuck Tanner sent in Dave Roberts, a veteran pitcher who was once a young Pirates farm hand but, nearing the end of his career, finally got a shot to pitch with the Bucs. Dave loaded the bases in the 16th and was facing Padres pitcher John D'Acquisto, at bat. Roberts tossed three straight balls. With a 3–0 count on the pitcher, another miss would give San Diego the game. At that point, the veteran lefty turned to second base to see San Diego base runner Dave Winfield giving him the choke sign. Enraged, Roberts struck out D'Aquisto, sending the game to the 17th, an inning in which the reliever once again loaded the bases with nobody out, only to strike out Jay Johnstone, get Jerry Turner to hit into a 6–2 force and Bill Fahey to end the inning with an easy grounder.

Six hours and 12 minutes later, a little after 3:00 A.M., the game ended as the Bucs scored in the 19th for a 4–3 victory.

After that contest and through the end of the season, Pirates fans, steelworkers and others, sang that disco song loud and long into the evening. Picture 300-pound men in white tanks singing Sister Sledge tunes. Who would have thought it?

The team took the Steel City by storm. After winning the Eastern Division over a very strong Montreal ball club, they defeated Cincinnati in the National League Championship Series, the same Reds team that had beaten them in the NLCS in 1970, 1972 and 1975. Pittsburgh then battled back, down three games to one in the World Series against another old nemesis, Earl Weaver and the Baltimore Orioles, winning the final three contests to capture the franchise's fifth world championship.

When center fielder Omar Moreno nestled the final out of game seven in his glove, thousands of Pirates fans took off for Market Square in the center of downtown Pittsburgh, and danced and celebrated into the wee hours of the morning. It was a scene many thought would recur over the next couple years, but it never did; 1979 represented the last title the Bucs would win to date.

Despite the Family's lack of staying power, in 1979 they did the impossible, not only winning the Series but becoming a bigger story than any of the Steel City's legendary football teams.

In the pages of this book, the story of this championship team is told. We'll watch how the 1979 world champion team was built, take a thorough look at the season and postseason, and see how the Family fell during the following campaign. There are biographical sketches of every player who appeared on the team's roster that year and, finally, a section of complete stats that tells the story of this magical ball club.

As we wrote the book many special memories came back to us, ones that we will always treasure as sports fans. We hope it will do the same for all who read it.

1. Prelude to a Championship

To understand where the Pirates ended up in 1979, one must look back almost 20 years to see how the team's philosophy towards building championship caliber teams developed.

After the Bucs won their miraculous World Series title in 1960, in which Pirates general managers Branch Rickey and Joe L. Brown used a combination of homegrown talent and adept trades to build this memorable squad, the future for this franchise looked very bright. The core of the team was very young. Series hero Bill Mazeroski was only 24. Superstar Roberto Clemente was 26. Slugging first baseman Dick Stuart checked in at 28, while MVP Dick Groat and center fielder Bill Virdon were both at the ripe old age of 30. The pitching staff was in good shape, too. Reigning Cy Young Award–winner Vern Law, 31, Bob Friend, 30, Vinegar Bend Mizell, 30, Roy Face, 33, and Harvey Haddix, 35, were on the wrong side of 30, yet all but Haddix seemed to be in their prime.[1]

The Pirates were not able to reach the heights of 1960 for the rest of the decade. Their teams were good, winning over 90 games three times: in 1962 (the year Brown introduced a young powerful slugger from Oklahoma, Willie Stargell, to the Steel City), 1965 and 1966; but they just couldn't get over the top.

Joe Brown tried to get the Bucs to the Promised Land once again in the late '60s, thinking he was only one piece away. First, he brought over the all-time single season stolen base king, Maury Wills, from the Dodgers in December of 1966, for Bob Bailey and Gene Michael; then Hall of Famer Jim Bunning in the fall of 1967 from Philadelphia, for four players including Don Money and Woody Fryman.[2] These two trades were a resounding flop: the team went a combined 161–163 over the two campaigns, seasons during which many prognosticators had picked the Pirates for first place.

While big trades did not seem to be the answer, there was hope to be

The Pirates' last world championship team as it opened its magical campaign. (Courtesy of the Pittsburgh Pirates.)

found in the Pirates' blooming minor league system. While the parent team was floundering with an 80–82 mark in 1968, the Bucs' top farm club, the Columbus Jets of the International League, was collecting a nucleus of players that would soon pay dividends. Bob Robertson, Al Oliver, Fred Patek, Richie Hebner, Manny Sanguillen, Dock Ellis, Bruce Dal Canton, Gene Garber and Dave Roberts — the man who was considered the ace of the staff but who would wait until August 25, 1979, to prove his worth to the parent organization — all were on the Jets' roster, and most would be part of Brown's plan to climb back up the baseball ladder to a championship level.[3]

Brown decided to use this group to build his team for the future rather than continuing to bring in aging stars from other franchises. The results were immediate and staggering. This collection from Columbus, when combined with the Pirates' established stars such as Clemente, Stargell and Steve Blass, won 89 games in 1969 and returned to the postseason for the first time in ten years a season later, capturing the Eastern Division crown in 1970.

Pittsburgh now had one of the most potent lineups in baseball. Although they were not the quickest collection of ball players around, they had power and a good average at just about every position. On the mound, Blass and Ellis provided the Bucs a one-two punch, and Dave Giusti became one of the best closers in the game, leading the league with 30 saves.

1971 was the crowning achievement for Brown and his team. They won that elusive World Series championship against the Baltimore Orioles in a classic seven-game ordeal, after adding a couple players via trade and bringing up Bruce Kison, Rennie Stennett and Milt May from the farm.

The sky was the limit for this franchise, as they were even better in 1972. The year began with baseball's first work stoppage in April, but by the time October rolled around, Pittsburgh was clearly thought to be the most dominant team in the sport. They led the senior circuit by a wide margin with a .274 average and .397 slugging percentage, as every starter but shortstop Gene Alley (.248) hit over .280. The bullpen was now deep and arguably the best in the game, while Blass enjoyed his best season, going 19–8 with a 2.48 ERA. By the time the Bucs entered the 1972 NLCS against the Cincinnati Reds it looked like a dynasty was very much in the making, and given the youth of the club, it looked like the '70s were going to be a Black and Gold decade in the national pastime.

The Pirates and Reds battled evenly in the first four games. Pittsburgh took a 2–1 lead into the ninth inning of the fifth and deciding contest of the NLCS and were three outs away from returning to the Fall Classic for the second consecutive season. Three outs sounded easy, especially for a team with such a dominant bullpen, but the three outs never came. When Bob Moose uncorked his infamous wild pitch that allowed a young George Foster to score the winning run, it let the air out of the team's dynastic hopes.

Although most thought the Pirates could rebound and win again in 1973, that year would turn out to be among the darkest in the annals of this proud team. First and foremost was the unthinkable, the death of their beloved leader in a New Year's Eve plane accident, when Roberto Clemente's aircraft went down in the ocean as he was on his way to deliver food and supplies to an earthquake-ravaged Nicaragua.

If that weren't bad enough, Steve Blass, their best pitcher, remarkably forgot how to pitch, and his control eluded him at only 31 years of age, right when he should have been in his prime. Blass could no longer find the plate, and he suffered his mysterious malady in a very public way, giving up 84 walks and 109 hits in only 89 innings. After he gave up five hits and seven walks a year later in five innings of work, he was out of the majors for good. The Bucs finished that disastrous '73 campaign under .500, and those thoughts of world championships were replaced by questions of how the team could rebuild.

The first step was to bring back legendary manager Danny Murtaugh, who replaced Virdon, with only 26 games left in the 1973 season. The second was to tap into their still fruitful minor league system.

Rebuilding their once powerful outfield was of the utmost importance. First Brown tabbed a young, lumbering right fielder, Richie Zisk, who became the choice to replace the great Roberto after the experiment of moving Manny Sanguillen to right failed miserably. While Zisk and speed were rarely used in the same sentence, he could consistently hit over .300 and knocked in 100 runs in 1974. The next piece was a player who eventually would turn into one of the game's premier superstars, a player who gave the Bucco faithful a talent in the right field who would develop a brightness nearly as blinding as Clemente's. Dave Parker took over in right field in 1975, allowing Murtaugh to move Zisk to left and the great Willie Stargell to first. Stargell's move to first was not only to get Parker into the everyday lineup; 1971 had proved to be the zenith of Bob Robertson's career as injuries not only cost him his once marvelous defensive prowess but also rendered him ineffective offensively. By 1974 his batting averages in the three years following the World Series were .193, .239 and .229.[4] On top of Zisk and Parker, Brown also brought center fielder Omar Moreno, catcher Ed Ott and two tall, lanky pitchers — John Candelaria and the hurler who would more than aptly replace Giusti as the closer, Kent Tekulve — up from the minors between 1974 and '75 in order to retool the team.

Although Pittsburgh now had several of the pieces to the 1979 puzzle in place, and the Pirates were able to recapture the Eastern Division crown with back-to-back championships in 1974 and 1975, they no longer had that world championship swagger.

The Dodgers and the Reds were now the best teams in the senior circuit. Fortunately for the Bucs in '74 and '75, the two best teams both resided in the Western Division. But to the club's dismay, a third team would rise from the ashes in 1976, grabbing the Eastern Division supremacy away from the Pirates: their cross-state rivals, the Philadelphia Phillies.

Instead of being the dominant team of the '70s as the Pirates had envisioned before the tragic loss of Clemente, they were now slipping down the National League ladder. Worse yet, Joe L. Brown had retired after the 1975 campaign. But before the veteran general manager faded into the sunset, he brought one last memorable player to the team, in April of 1975. It was considered at the time a minor deal, yet turned out to be a pivotal move for the franchise. Brown obtained a one-time outfield phenom, Bill Robinson, from the Phils for Wayne Simpson. Although Simpson never lived up to the promise he showed in 1970 with the Big Red Machine, Robinson finally was able to demonstrate the skills many had claimed for him when experts called him the "next Mickey Mantle" early in his career.[5] He became a super-sub for the Pirates in the late '70s and was one of the leaders of the club by the time the '79 campaign came to pass.

Filling Brown's shoes was his protégé, Harding "Pete" Peterson. Peterson had been the Bucs' minor league scouting director, helping to put together the incredibly strong system that had served the Pirates well over the previous decade. His first major job would be to replace Murtaugh at the helm of the club. Danny had led the Bucs to 1,115 wins and two World Championships over his career, but decided he would retire for good following the 1976 season. (Unfortunately, he passed away not long afterwards.) Peterson knew whom he wanted to fill Murtaugh's shoes but had to use unconventional methods to get his man.

Chuck Tanner of Oakland was the manager Pete desired. He decided that rather than haggle with A's management to get Tanner out of his contract, he would trade former All-Star catcher Manny Sanguillen (whom he eventually would reacquire in April of 1978 for Miguel Dilone and two other players) along with $100,000 to bring Tanner to the Bucs.[6]

Tanner, who was known for having his teams be very aggressive on the base paths, almost overnight took the heavy hitting offensive in a different direction. The former Lumber Company added Lightning to their nickname as Pittsburgh, who stole only 49 bases in 1975, swiped an unbelievable 260 in Tanner's first season at the helm two years later.

Peterson proved that he would be aggressive in quickly rebuilding the team into a world championship contender; to do it, he would trade the one resource the team had depended on for so long: prospects from their vaunted minor league system.

Sending Zisk to the White Sox in December of 1976, Peterson fixed his bullpen by acquiring Goose Gossage and Terry Forster in return. Pete further improved his relief core by grabbing the veteran lefty Grant Jackson from the Mariners for Craig Reynolds and Jimmy Sexton. In 1977, Gossage turned in one of the greatest single season performances out of the pen in Pirate history. He left the club the following the season by way of a new format that was taking major league baseball by storm: free agency.

Free agency was an area that Brown had never had to deal with, and it hurt the Pirates before the 1977 campaign, as the club lost Hebner to the hated Phils. Peterson would not be denied, replacing him with Phil Garner from Oakland. The price for Garner was high, costing the franchise several prospects including Mitchell Page, Tony Armas, Rick Langford and Doug Bair along with veterans Giusti and Doc Medich.

Even though free agency hurt the Bucs at first, Peterson eventually used it to his advantage by signing pitcher Jim Bibby from Cleveland before the 1978 campaign and the outfielder Lee Lacy from the Dodgers a year later.

With his bullpen now much stronger and Bibby in the fold, Peterson further strengthened his starting rotation by picking up Bert Blyleven from Texas for Al Oliver, who had been one of the most important pieces of the Pirate championships of the early part of the decade. In the trade, in which the aggressive Pittsburgh GM also gave up minor leaguer Nelson Norman, the Bucs received another important cog in the 1979 machine, John Milner. With the addition of Blyleven and 21-year-old rookie Don Robinson, who

General manager Peter Peterson made one of his finest moves when he dealt popular catcher Manny Sanguillen to the A's for manager Chuck Tanner. (Courtesy of the Pittsburgh Pirates.)

led the club with 14 wins in 1978, Harding had rebuilt the mound core into a strong unit once again.

Chuck Tanner's crew gave Pittsburgh a preview of what 1979 would be like, with a tremendous stretch run to close out 1978. After stumbling to a 51–60 record to find themselves 11½ games behind the first place Phillies prior to their August 13 contest, the Pirates rallied to win 37 of their final 50 games. Fantastic hitting by Dave Parker—who became the first player to win National League Player of the Month honors in consecutive months—led the offense, and Kent Tekulve's dominant relief work supported great starting pitching. The charging Pirates closed what seemed to be an impossible gap to come into a four-game showdown against Philadelphia with the possibility of overtaking the first place Phils. Needing to sweep the four games, the Pirates won the first two with a pair of walk-off victories in sweeping a twi-night doubleheader on September 29, but the Phillies overcame a Willie Stargell grand slam the next day to finally quiet the Bucs.

The Pirates' fantastic finish in '78 gave Pittsburghers new hope for 1979. Although Peterson would make a couple more important moves over the next 12 months, most of the pieces were now in place to finally remove the Phillies from their three-year perch atop the National League East. The stars were finally aligned for the Pirates' magical run in 1979, and the team's captain and most memorable star prepared to embark on one last great season.

2. The Regular Season

After seeing their charges finish 1978 ever so close to an Eastern Division title, Pete Peterson, Chuck Tanner and the Galbreath family began considering what areas the team needed to improve in and what amount of money the Pirates could afford to pay in order to eliminate the scant 1½-game difference between themselves and the champion Philadelphia Phillies. Although baseball's free agency system was still in its infancy, there was already a noticeable trend regarding which teams would pay big money and which would not. The New York Yankees had won the last American League pennant before free agency, but had spent large sums on the system's initial prizes, Reggie Jackson and Don Gullett, prior to 1977. In the fall of 1978, George Steinbrenner's Bronx Bombers were playing in their third straight World Series and seemed even then to have unlimited funds for buying the best talent available. The Pirates, on the other hand, had signed only one free agent, pitcher Jim Bibby, and Bibby had become a free agent later than his peers; he was able to leave Cleveland due to a contract snafu rather than filing with the majority of players. This, perhaps, had eliminated some of the competition for his services, as by the time the large right-hander had become available, most teams' rosters were fairly set. Of even bigger concern than adding a new player was locking up Dave Parker to a long-term deal. Conceded to be the best all-around player in baseball and the National League's Most Valuable Player in 1978, Parker would not be eligible for free agency until after the 1979 season, but Peterson realized the necessity of signing the Cobra before having to compete with other teams. The Pirates had been slow to lock up Rich Gossage in 1977, and the star reliever left the team for New York, as the Pirates were unable to compete with Steinbrenner's offer. During the World Series, there were rumors the Pirates would be forced to trade Parker because the Galbreaths could not afford the type of money it would take to keep him. Ownership stepped up, however, and

Even after suffering a broken cheekbone in 1978, Dave Parker continued his aggressive base running, barreling over a fallen catcher with third base coach Joe Lonnett looking on. (Courtesy of the Pittsburgh Pirates.)

Parker signed a five-year contract worth more than anything even the Yankees had paid out at the time. Hoping to add one more .300 bat to his team, Peterson also put in a strong bid for star third baseman Pete Rose. The Pirates offered Rose a package deal that, while not quite equalling the cash value of the Phillies, included a racehorse from the Galbreaths' successful Darby Dan Farms. The former Red reportedly considered the deal seriously, but in the end opted for the offer from the division champs.

Undaunted, Peterson moved away from the free agent market to the more familiar method of acquiring players, making a trade with the Seattle Mariners to strengthen the bullpen. Peterson was able to obtain Enrique Romo, a right-hander who had gone 11-7 with ten saves while pitching for a last-place ball club. Lou Gorman, the general manager of the Mariners, reportedly fielded offers from several teams for Romo, but in the end accepted the Pirates' bid of shortstop Mario Mendoza, young fastballer Odell Jones, who had spent most of 1978 pitching for AAA Portland, and Rafael Vasquez, a 14-game winner in the low minors.[1]

Although the Pirates had enjoyed a very successful decade, by the late 1970s they had decidedly taken second place to the Steelers among Pittsburgh sports teams. This was evidenced by the fact that when Peterson was able to sign a free agent, outfielder Lee Lacy, the news was almost buried on the sports pages. The timing of the transaction didn't help, though, as Peterson signed Lacy just before the Super Bowl, ensuring that the event would get little attention. It was hoped Lacy would provide the type of insurance Bill Robinson had given them a few years earlier. Lacy had some punch in his bat, as evidenced by his 13 home runs in just 245 at-bats, an excellent arm and good speed. A right-handed hitter, he was a solid backup player who, despite having deficiencies as a fielder, could fill in in the outfield or at second or third in an emergency.

The Pirates also gave invitations to several non-roster players to join them in Bradenton, Florida, for spring training.

While some players such as Larry Demery, Bart Johnson and Rick Jones had enjoyed moderate success in the majors, and young infielder Vance Law was the son of Pirate legend Vern, the only man in the group who would perform for the team in 1979 was Matt Alexander, an outfielder whom manager Chuck Tanner would often employ as a pinch runner. Still, the signing of Parker to a long-term deal and the additions of Romo to the bullpen and Lacy as a new super-sub let Pittsburghers feel the off-season was successful. With Steeler fans still wrapping themselves in their Terrible Towels to fight the cold Pittsburgh winter, the Pirates pitchers and catchers reported to spring training.

Manager Chuck Tanner and his coaches, Harvey Haddix, Bob Skinner, Al Monchak and Joe Lonnett, became reacquainted with the arms in camp. The Pirates appeared to have depth in the pitching department. Left-hander John Candelaria and right-handers Bert Blyleven and Don Robinson (1978's *Sporting News* Rookie Pitcher of the Year) were assured of starting berths. Veteran left-hander Jim Rooker, coming off a disappointing 1978 after five solid seasons as a Buc, was favored to be the fourth starter. Contending for the number five spot were right-handers Bibby (8–7, 3.54 as a swing man in 1978), Bruce Kison (who had battled a blister problem that forced him to miss over a month of the 1978 season and had required surgery), and left-hander Jerry Reuss. Reuss was once a successful pitcher for the Pirates, winning 48 games between 1974 and 1976, but after a disappointing 1977 and a poor start in 1978, he had been demoted to Tanner's bullpen. The tall left-hander returned to the rotation in late August and pitched three complete game wins. Still only 29 years old, Reuss certainly merited another shot at starting.

The bullpen was anchored by the durable Kent Tekulve, who had set team records with 31 saves and 91 appearances in 1978. Tekulve had been the National League's Pitcher of the Month in August, as he gave up only one run in 24 innings and saved nine games. The one question about Tekulve was the pitcher's ability to retire left-handed hitters. A sidearmer, Tekulve's sinker and slider were devastating against right-handers, but his pitches were not thought to be as effective against lefties. However, Tanner had the luxury of a more-than-capable southpaw setup man in Grant Jackson. Also, the newly acquired Romo, while throwing from the right side, possessed an excellent screwball that was tough for left-handers to pick up. Young Ed Whitson, who had pitched well out of the pen in '78, would probably make the team as well.

Position players reported to camp, as usual, on March 1. Much of the pre-camp thinking had centered on what the team would need to do to play more consistently in 1979. This started with the club's lead-off hitter, center fielder Omar Moreno. Moreno had led the major leagues with 71 stolen bases (a Pirates record) the year before, although he had hit only .235 and had struck out over 100 times. During the off-season, Moreno was sent to work on his hitting with former manager Harry Walker. Walker, considered one of baseball's foremost authorities on hitting, had had uncanny success in turning Matty Alou from a mediocre hitter into a batting champion when Walker ran the Pirates in the mid-1960s. The current Pirates brain trust hoped Walker could also work wonders with Moreno. Walker's strategy called for Omar to hit the ball more solidly to left field and to slap down on the ball to take advantage of the Panamanian's great speed by beating out ground balls or chopping them through the infield.

Another major area of concern was the Pirates' defense. Frank Taveras at short had fine range, but committed far too many errors. His 38 in 1978 ranked only two behind the errors made by the Cardinals' Gary Templeton — the most in the major leagues. A valuable offensive player coming off a fine season at the plate (.278, 31 doubles, 9 triples) and on the bases (his 46 stolen bases were second to Moreno in the NL), Taveras also appeared to be a moody player who did not always run out ground balls. His erratic play made him the target of the fans' wrath when things did not go well.

The Pirates had other defensive concerns as well. While newspaper reports expressed optimism that second baseman Rennie Stennett had recovered the skills lost due to a broken leg in 1977, he did not appear to be the Stennett of old.[2] His range may have improved by a few steps, but it was not up to the eye-popping form he had shown before the injury. Also, once the spring training games got started, Stennett did not hit well, batting just .210 with one extra base hit in 62 at-bats. Still, putting Stennett at second and Phil Garner at third appeared Tanner's best way to solve the team's problems in the infield.

Garner had good range for a third baseman. His problem at the hot corner was consistency. Called Scrap Iron for his rugged play, Garner's .930 fielding percentage had been last among NL third baseman in '78. Moved to second when it became obvious Stennett's injury was still hobbling him in '78, Garner proved more consistent playing second than third, but Tanner had no other player ready to play every day at third even if he had wanted to keep Garner on the keystone sack. His alternatives were Dale Berra, who contributed a few big hits late in '78 but had not shown he could consistently hit major league pitching; Lee Lacy, whose lack of defensive ability had not only cost him a shot at playing full time during his days with the Dodgers and Braves, but had moved him to the outfield; or Bill Robinson, a polished left fielder who guarded third base courageously but ineffectively.

There was no question who would be the Pirates' opening day first baseman. The question was how well the 39-year-old Willie Stargell would hold up for the entire season. Stargell had been the National League's Comeback Player of the Year in 1978 when he hit .295 with 28 homeruns in just 390 at-bats. Tanner showed skill in resting his team captain and was able to get the most out of him following the 1977 season, which he finished prematurely due to a pinched nerve. He had also been sidelined earlier in '77 with headaches and dizzy spells. Now recovered from these problems, a big season from Stargell would be necessary if the Pirates were to overtake the Phillies. He would be backed up by left-handed power man John Milner and former team hero Manny Sanguillen.

With Robinson in left, Moreno in center and Dave Parker (a Gold Glove recipient with a great arm) in right, the outfield defense was set. It was hoped Robinson would rebound from a down season in 1978 to be one of the league's better offensive players, as he had been in 1976 and 1977. Catcher Ed Ott, whose throwing had slumped early in 1978 following an injury sustained in an altercation with the Mets' Felix Millan the year before, saw his arm come alive late in 1978. He would be platooned with a former number one draft pick, rookie Steve Nicosia. Sanguillen would provide emergency services behind home plate, but it was apparent the former .300-hitting catcher would mostly pinch hit.

This particular crew of Buccaneers certainly seemed to have a balance of offensive weapons. Moreno, Taveras, Parker and Garner were all good base stealers, and just about everyone on the team was a good base runner. Parker was coming off his second straight batting title and boldly predicted a third. Stargell, Robinson and Stennett had all been .300 hitters, and Taveras had shown notable improvement at the plate the previous two seasons. Robinson gave the team a potential third player capable of hitting 20 or more home runs to join Parker and Stargell. The bench had strong veterans such as Sanguillen; Milner, who had been a regular player for the Mets and who had midrange power; and Lacy, coming off a season in which he hit 13 home runs playing only about half the time for the Dodgers. Late in spring training, Peterson balanced his bench even further by trading two minor leaguers to the Boston Red Sox to reacquire Mike Easler. Easler, a left-handed batter, had led the International League in hitting with a .330 mark while playing for the Pirates' AAA team in Columbus in 1978, but the Bucs were unable to place him on their winter roster and had sold him to the Red Sox. Easler had been unable to make the Red Sox, but had shown enough promise as a minor league hitter that Peterson believed he could fill the role of left-handed pinch hitter.

Still, most experts believed the Pirates would do no better than second and might have a struggle on their hands to accomplish that. The Phillies had certainly bolstered themselves by signing Rose and trading for Gold Glove second baseman Manny Trillo. While Rose, like Stargell, was another graybeard, he had set the National League record with a 44-game hitting streak while playing for the Cincinnati Reds in '78, and showed no signs of slowing down. He hit .302, the 13th time in 14 seasons he had hit .300, and he led the league in doubles (51) for the fourth time in five years. The flashy Trillo was also no easy out at the plate, particularly with men on base. The signing of Rose had allowed the Phillies to trade former Pirate Richie Hebner to the Mets for a talented young pitcher, Nino Espinosa, to help a pitching staff that was beginning to show some age.

While veterans Jim Kaat and Jim Lonborg were obviously nearing the end of their once stellar careers, one of the Phillie old-timers, Steve Carlton, was still one of the best pitchers on the planet and Randy Lerch, who had helped eliminate the Pirates on the second-to-last day of the season with two home runs, was only 24. Larry Christensen and Dick Ruthvan were two right-handers who had the capability to be big winners. Philadelphia also had a deep bullpen featuring Tug McGraw, Ron Reed, Rawley Eastwick and Warren Brusstar.

Rose and Trillo joined a lineup of stars featuring the powerful bats of Mike Schmidt and Greg Luzinski and spectacular defensive players Larry Bowa at short, Gary Maddox in center and Bob Boone catching. All three were good offensive players as well, as was the right fielder, Bake McBride.

Aside from the Phillies, the Pirates would also have to fight off the young but very talented Montreal Expos and a St. Louis Cardinals team with a strong offense. The Expos featured two talented all-around outfielders in Andre Dawson and Ellis Valentine. Their third outfielder was the left-handed line drive hitter Warren Cromartie. Montreal also had an All-Star behind the plate in Gary Carter, and third baseman Larry Parrish appeared ready to join him as one of the top players at his respective position. For leadership, manager Dick Williams had first baseman Tony Perez, one of baseball's most consistent RBI men. Williams did not possess a starter the quality of Carlton, but he did have a deep staff, including 20-game winner Ross Grimsley, nominal staff leader Steve Rogers, Bill "Spaceman" Lee, Woody Fryman, Rudy May, Elias Sosa, and youngsters Dan Schatzeder, David Palmer and Scott Sanderson.

In St. Louis, Ken Boyer would fill out a lineup card full of line drive hitters. Lou Brock — then the all-time stolen base leader — would still lead off more often than not, followed by fellow .300 hitters Gary Templeton, Keith Hernandez, Ted Simmons and George Hendrick. While the Cards were thought to be somewhat thin on pitching, the club had hopes for a rotation of Pete Vukovich, Silvio Martinez, Bob Forsch, Bob Sykes and John Denny. Forsch was the oldest of these hurlers at 29.

The Cubs, who had fallen out of contention in August of 1978, had some stars, such as slugger Dave Kingman, .300 threat Bill Buckner, and pitchers Rick Reuschel and Bruce Sutter, but were too thin in other areas to be given serious consideration. The New York Mets, in the third year of rebuilding, figured to be out of the race by Memorial Day. Ironically, however, the Mets had been tough on the Pirates the previous season, particularly in early September when they cooled the red-hot Bucs by beating them three games in a row.[3]

The Pirates did little on the field to convince skeptics they deserved more consideration for the number one spot during the exhibition games. A 13–11 record in Florida demonstrated uneven play. While Dave Parker had a fabulous spring, hitting .470 (31 for 66) with 10 home runs and 25 RBIs, Bert Blyleven went 4–0 with a 1.64 ERA in 22 innings, and Bruce Kison gave up only 5 earned runs in 33 innings (1.36), others did not distinguish themselves. Stargell hit only .200, Tavares .225, and the team made a horrendous 33 errors in 24 games.[4] Reuss was unhappy that his performance (26 IP, 4.50 ERA), did not win him a spot in the rotation even though Jim Rooker was placed on the disabled list as the team prepared to head north. Reuss made the trip with his teammates, but it became public knowledge that Peterson was working on a trade to send him to the Dodgers for Rick Rhoden, who was rehabilitating from off-season arm problems. The deal took a few days to be worked out and after it was, Rhoden stayed in Florida to work himself into shape. Pirates management initially believed Rhoden would be able to join the team in a week or so, but Rhoden's progress would prove to be much slower and his injury more serious than Peterson or scout Howie Haak had believed.

The Pirates hoped to erase their recent habit of starting the season slowly, then having to play catch-up to get back in contention. But the team endured their usual cold start and instead of building on their fine finish of 1978, looked more like the club that had fallen 13 games behind the Phillies

The Pirate Parrot proved a good luck charm as it debuted in 1979. The original parrot looked quite different from the current Pirates mascot. (Courtesy of the Pittsburgh Pirates.)

by mid–August of the previous year. The defensive horrors that had plagued the team throughout '78 rose from the grave, as the Bucs made five errors in losing the opening game against Montreal before a hometown crowd on Friday, April 6.[5] The Pirates got some luck of their own in the second game when the Expos' Elias Sosa threw away Willie Stargell's chopper, allowing the tying and winning runs to score. Following the play, Dave Parker had to be restrained by teammates because he believed Expos catcher Gary Carter had intentionally dropped to his knees trying to injure him. Parker, still equipped with the football-style protective helmet that he had worn in 1978 to protect his broken cheekbone, scored the winning run, but the Bucs dropped their next three games as poor relief pitching helped place the sqaud 1–4 early in the season. Newcomer Enrique Romo took two of the losses, while Bert Blyleven absorbed the third.

The Pirates returned to Three Rivers Stadium to face the St. Louis Cardinals on April 12. The Bucs temporarily righted themselves as they took the first three games of a four-game set. Don Robinson struck out nine to open the series and John Milner, subbing for the injured Stargell, had two hits and an RBI.

Milner led the team again the next day with a pair of homers and four RBIs. He also showed off some fancy glove work at first. The Pirates made it three in a row over the Cards as Milner knocked in two more runs, and Ed Ott provided four RBIs to support Ed Whitson, who pitched eight innings of strong baseball in a spot start. The Pirates' bid for a four-game sweep was denied on Income Tax Day. Frank Tavares played poorly in the field and left the game, complaining of feeling ill. Kent Tekulve had another ineffective outing and the team's hot hitter, Milner, who would be named National League Player of the Week, left the game when a ball skipped off the wet turf, injuring his knee.

Pittsburgh hoped to avenge their poor series in Philadelphia the week before, but they did anything but strike fear into the hearts of the visiting Phillies. Blyleven and Romo were again knocked around in a 13–2 loss. Greg Luzinski became the first opposing player to homer into the upper deck of Three Rivers Stadium when he homered off Don Robinson to decide a 3–2 game. The second loss left the Pirates 4–7, 4½ games behind Montreal and only half a game out of the cellar.

General manager Pete Peterson decided he needed to make a move to stop the Pirates from giving away games. He acted on April 19, making a trade that some considered a real gamble. The GM sent Tavares to the New York Mets for shortstop Tim Foli and minor league pitcher Greg Field. While no one doubted Foli's desire to win, he had been a less than impressive hitter during his eight-year career, and although he had developed into a steady fielder, the intense Foli lacked Tavaras's range and had none of his speed.

Foli couldn't have been happier with the trade. "It's something I've really wanted," he said about coming to Pittsburgh.[6] Foli had never played on a team that was a true contender. Now he was going from a backup role with the Mets — who had crowded him out of the infield picture in order to look at younger players — to being a starter on one of the favorites to win the National League East.

The immediate impact of the trade, however, was disappointing. Foli, hitting out of the number eight spot with Chuck Tanner moving Phil Garner to the number two hole, went 0 for his first 10 and committed a key error that contributed to a loss in Houston. The Pirates also lost their other two games to the Astros. The losses were painful, as they were each by a single run.

Pittsburgh rebounded for two wins in Cincinnati on April 24 and 25. In the first win, the Bucco bats pounded out 17 hits, including three each by Parker, Milner and Stennett. In the second victory, three struggling pitchers, Blyleven, Romo and Tekulve, held down the Reds' strong hitting attack until Lacy's fly ball in the 12th scored Parker for a 3–2 win. Tekulve pitched 3⅓ innings of hitless relief in what was by far his most impressive outing of the season to that point. The durable right-hander was off to a poor start, but Tanner maintained his faith in his rubber-armed pitcher, who despite an early season slump appeared in 12 of the first 16 Pirates games.

While the team took the short series from the Reds, the Pirates continued their shaky play, wasting a comeback effort to lose to the Astros 9–8 in 11 innings as former Buc and Shaler High School grad Art Howe drove in four runs. The next night, things looked bad for Tanner's men and even worse for starter Don Robinson when the pitcher — complaining of a sore shoulder — left the game after allowing a lead-off home run to Terry Puhl. But Bruce Kison pitched 7⅓ innings of one-hit relief; the top three men in the Pirate lineup, Moreno, Foli and Parker each had three hits; and Stargell drove in three runs. The 10–5 win finished off a poor April that saw the Pirates go 7–11, and except for their three wins against the Cardinals, the club's record would have been a pathetic 4–11. If the Bucs were going to contend, they would have to start playing better, and soon.

The Bucs opened May by being involved in a historic win, the 200th of Braves right-hander Phil Niekro's career. Blyleven had dueled the great knuckleballer in fine fashion through eight, but Tekulve had another bad outing, allowing three runs in the ninth. The Pirates got a spark from an unlikely source when Matt Alexander, subbing for Dave Parker, who left the game not feeling well, went 2-for-2 with a triple and Bill Robinson homered to lead the Bucs to a 10–2 win on May 2. The final game of the series, which was to feature Rick Rhoden's Pirates debut, was rained out.

Pittsburgh remained baseball's daily roller coaster ride, giving fans more ups and downs than Kennywood Park's Thunderbolt into the middle of May. The ball club, although going two weeks without winning consecutive games, went just as long without dropping two in a row. Some of the wins were exciting, such as the Pirates victory on May 5 when Stargell won a 6–5 game with a two-out-two-run single in the ninth. On May 7, Tekulve saved his first game of the year. The 1–4 Tekulve, whose ERA was near 5.00, dismissed pessimists who declared that his early season misfortunes were a sign that his excellent 1978 season had been a fluke. He pointed out that the date marked the one year anniversary of his first save of '78 when he had set the team's all-time save record.[7] The Pirates' 17–4 trouncing of Atlanta on May 9 featured not only batters hitting baseballs, but baseballs hitting batters, as the Braves' Gene Garber nailed Parker with a pitch and Tekulve retaliated by coming in close on Roland Office. Peterson supported Tekulve's retribution. "I was glad to see it," the general manager said. "You can't let other teams throw at our guys and let them get away with it."[8]

But the most memorable win during the first half of May included a controversy even more heated than the one caused by the bean ball battle in Atlanta. Major league umpires had been on strike since the start of the season and their replacements were local amateurs. Earlier in the year, Chuck Tanner had complained about poor calls costing the Pirates possible wins against the Astros, but on May 12, the hometown crowd at Three Rivers Stadium were treated to a favorable call by one of the most noted replacement umps, Harry Smail. Smail was a gargantuan man whose picture was flashed throughout the country, his girth often contrasted with the athletic build of players. He had been a famous figure in Westmoreland County sports, officiating baseball, football and basketball. On this fateful day, Smail was umpiring at third base as the Pirates trailed the Reds 2–1 in the bottom of the eighth. With two on and two out, Tanner called on his team captain, Stargell, to pinch hit. The Reds' rookie pitcher, Frank Pastore, quickly got ahead of the Pirates star 0–2. On the next pitch, Stargell appeared to swing; so much so, in fact, that Pirates play-by-play announcer Milo Hamilton started to lead into a commercial break. Home plate umpire Bob Nelson had not clearly seen the play so he deferred to the rotund man umpiring at third. Smail signaled that Stargell had not swung.

Given a second life by the only man on the field with a larger belly than his own, Stargell singled to tie the game; minutes later, Moreno singled in the game winner.

The Reds were livid. Manager John McNamara and his players were very critical of Smail and Nelson. Smail defended his call. "In my judgment, I felt he pulled back," the umpire said, but replays clearly supported the Reds' argument. The next day, Reds second baseman Joe Morgan claimed his old friend Stargell had joked with him about the call after the game. "Last night I sent him two pizzas, a half gallon of beer and a hamburger on the side. Tonight I'm going to send him a double order," Morgan quoted Stargell as saying.[9] Within a few days, major league baseball and the umpires' union settled their dispute.

As noted earlier, even with the help of Smail's bad call, the Pirates' play had been uneven. To make matters worse, Blyleven remained winless and his ERA rose to 5.62; Rhoden, after making his first appearance of the season in a 4–1 losing effort to Eddie Solomon of Atlanta, was forced back onto the disabled list, his shoulder still bothering him.

While the first streak the Pirates were able to put together was two losses, they rebounded with a six-game pick-me-up. Little-used Mike Easler started the streak with a pinch-hit home run to win in the 13th against the Mets and Skip Lockwood on May 16. The next night, Stargell launched a pair of home runs, his second a game-winning blast off Mets rookie left-hander Jesse Orosco. Pirates fans exploded in applause, and Willie was coaxed into taking what was believed to be the first curtain call by a Pirates batter since Dale Long hit his record-breaking eighth home run in eight consecutive games in 1956.[10] Steve Nicosia and Parker joined Stargell in connecting for homeruns in a 9–5 series opening win against the Cubs on May 18.

Jim Rooker came off the disabled list in time to start the Saturday afternoon game and made his first appearance of '79 an impressive one, carrying a three-hitter into the ninth. Romo and Grant Jackson provided the relief help he needed in finishing the game, with Jackson retiring tough left-handed hitter Bill Buckner to save the game.

Two more wins, including Blyleven's first of the season and featuring another Stargell homerun, capped the streak before the Expos beat the Pirates in back-to-back games.

With Don Robinson continuing to experience shoulder miseries and Kison plagued by blisters, Tanner had to adjust his starting rotation once again. Rooker and Jim Bibby were put in and Eddie Whitson was moved back to the bullpen, but to complicate the pitching, Tanner had to use up more arms in a game that was fogged out in the 11th inning on May 25. It could have been much worse, however, as the Pirates trailed going to the ninth before Easler pinch-hit another home run to tie the game. Playing conditions began to worsen in the tenth as the fog started to roll in. As the bottom of the 11th was about to get underway, left fielder Bill Robinson complained to umpire Billy Williams that visibility was quickly deteriorating in the outfield. A few minutes later, Robinson was unable to see Joel Youngblood's fly ball, which landed for a triple. The usually cool Robinson rushed in to give the umpires a piece of his mind, and the men in blue conferred and decided to hold up the game. When the fog did not lift, the umpires called the game. The decision wiped out Youngblood's triple and a likely Mets victory.

After a couple more wins against the Mets, the Bucs finally reached .500 on May 29 as Don Robinson returned to pitch eight shutout innings and Parker and Phil Garner homered to lead an 8–0 thrashing. As May was winding down, Rooker made his third straight impressive start and Stargell and Bill Robinson homered for a 9–2 win over the Cubs. The final game in May proved more dramatic as it took the Pirates ten innings to beat the Cubs 4–3. The game winner was a single by Tim Foli off an 0–2 pitch from Bruce Sutter, acknowledged as the top reliever in the National League (he would be the NL's eventual Cy Young Award Winner in '79). The hot Pirates' final four wins of the month saw them outscore the opposition 27–6, and the victories raised the Pirates' record in May to 16–10.[11] Foli's effect on the defense was being felt, as the Pirates were no longer giving away free runs. While Blyleven, Tekulve and Whitson were only a combined 4–10 with an ERA over 5.00, several Pirates were posting impressive numbers. Stargell was off to an excellent start, leading the team with a .339 average and 28 RBIs while tying Bill Robinson for the top spot on the club with ten homeruns. Parker was hitting .330 and the surprising Moreno .320, with 19 stolen bases and 22 RBIs. Rooker's three starts had netted him a 2–0 record with a 0.75 ERA, and Grant Jackson was 3–0 and 2.74. Bibby, Don Robinson and John Candelaria had ERAs in the low 3.00s to go with a cumulative 11–7 record. Still, the Bucs had moved only one game closer in the standings during the month, an indication that the National League East would not be an easy battleground in 1979.[12]

The fourth-place Pirates opened June with a fantastic comeback over San Diego. The Bucs rallied to beat the Padres 9–8 in the ninth, scoring the winning run with another great reliever, Rollie Fingers, on the mound. The Bucs trailed 8–5 going to the final frame, when Moreno and Foli singled and Parker homered against John D'Acquisto to tie the game. After Bill Robinson was retired, left-hander Bob Shirley came in to face Stargell. Stargell singled and Padres manager Roger Craig replaced Shirley with Fingers. Garner doubled, placing runners at second and third, and Ott was walked intentionally so the Padres star could face Dale Berra. Tanner sent up the more experienced Lacy to hit for the infielder, but Lacy fell behind Fingers 0–2. The pinch hitter laid off three straight curves to run the count full, then took a fastball inside for ball four to win the game.

On the next day, the Pirates would not do as well against another future Hall of Famer, as Gaylord Perry ended the Bucs' six-game winning streak with a four-hitter.

Sunday, June 3, featured another outstanding pitching performance, and one that proved more controversial than the longtime allegations of Perry's spitball. When Don Robinson was unable to pitch, Tanner called on Bruce Kison. The decision showed how thin the Pirates' pitching had been stretched; Kison had pitched an inning of mop-up relief the night before. But instead of lasting only a couple of innings, Kison hurled the team's best game of 1979. The eight-year veteran carried a no-hitter into the eighth and retired the first two batters to bring up Barry Evans, a nondescript hitter batting in the eighth spot that day. Evans hit a ball that ticked off third baseman Garner's glove. The batter ended up at second on the play. Official scorer Dan Donovan, a beat writer for *The Pittsburgh Press,* awarded Evans a double on the play. Kison was upset the play had not been ruled an error, but Donovan's decision was supported by replays, and he wrote in his column the next day that three other writers who had served as official scorers were in the press box that day and backed up his call.[13] The Pirates won the game easily, 7–0, but several of the Pirates were outspoken in their criticism and *The Press,* fearing a conflict of interest, decided not to allow its writers to score games in the future.

After Dodgers rookie Rick Sutcliffe beat the Pirates 6–4 on 6/4, the Bucs got impressive performances from three players who had not been off to good starts — Bert Blyleven, Kent Tekulve and Rennie Stennett — in a 3–1 win over Don Sutton. On June 6, the Pirates took advantage of a wild throw from old friend Jerry Reuss to rally for four runs in the eighth and a 5–4 win.

Pittsburgh followed up the last at-bat heroics two nights later for their tenth final at-bat win of the season, this time against the Giants. San Francisco starter John Curtis was working on a three-hit shutout with two gone in the eighth, when Moreno singled. With Berra, subbing for Foli, due up next, Tanner sent up his left-handed team captain to bat against the Giants' southpaw. Stargell hit a 3–1 fastball for a game-tying homerun, and Parker followed with a line drive shot almost to the exact location. Parker received a standing ovation from the crowd and responded by tipping his cap to the appreciative Pittsburghers.

San Francisco, however, proved tougher the next two games. Another venerable player named Willie, McCovey, homered to support Vida Blue's 6–2 win in the second game, and reliever Gary Lavelle picked up his seventh career victory without a defeat against Pittsburgh in the finale.

After hosting the West Coast teams, the Pirates moved on to California to face them again. The Golden State had been a difficult venue for the Pirates in recent years, and the only city in which the Bucs had held their own was San Diego, where this year's trip was to begin. But against a weak Padre team, the Bucs dropped three straight, beginning with a 6–3 loss to Perry and two tough one-run defeats, the second one coming in a 14-inning 2–1 loss.

Now on a four-game losing streak, Tanner sent Blyleven to the mound in Los Angeles. Working on a 1–0 shutout in the eighth, Blyleven retired the first two batters to bring up the Dodgers' most dangerous hitter, Steve Garvey. Blyleven missed with two curves, then signaled to catcher Ed Ott that he was going to intentionally walk Garvey to face Ron Cey. The curveball artist never got the chance as Tanner replaced him with Tekulve after Blyleven had thrown ball four to the Dodgers first baseman. Tekulve got out of the mini-jam and the Pirates broke the game open in the ninth, but Blyleven was seething after the game. To his credit, the Dutch Master admitted the move had been a smart one, since the Pirates had won the game, but he blasted Tanner's quick hook and five-man rotation, which Blyleven said resulted in him feeling "too strong" because he often had five or six days between starts.[14] Although he had signed a long-term contract prior to the start of the season, Blyleven now said he would ask for a trade at the end of the year if Tanner did not plan on using him differently.

Blyleven's displeasure did not distract his teammates. The Pirates won the next two games at Dodger Stadium, getting a complete game from Don Robinson on June 16 and a combined two-hitter from Ed Whitson and Tekulve. Matt Alexander made his first start of the season, subbing in center field for Moreno, and went 3-for-5 in the final game, scoring a pair of runs.

Moving north to San Francisco, the Bucs swept a short two-game series. Phil Garner went 5-for-5 in the opener and the Pirates got late-inning sacrifice flies from Manny Sanguillen and Lee Lacy to finally defeat Gary Lavelle, whose career ERA was 1.00 against the Pirates prior to the contest.

With the season not yet half over, the Pirates defeated the Cubs' Ken Holtzman for the third time in '79, but dropped the final two games at home against the Cubs, 4–3 and 5–0. The second loss was at the hands of All-Star Rick Reuschel, who would resurrect his career in the mid-'80s with the Pirates after several seasons of arm miseries.

Following a doubleheader split against the Mets, Bill Robinson tried to snap the Bucs out of their doldrums with a memorable birthday performance. With no fog to cloud his vision as on May 25, the Pirate left fielder robbed Joel Youngblood of an extra base hit with an over-the-shoulder catch and won the game with his 16th homerun. The blast gave Robinson two more homeruns than he had hit in 1978 when he had been bothered by a broken bone in his hand.

Robinson's performance didn't carry over the next day, though, as the normally offensively-challenged Mets exploded for a 12–9 win. With only two days left in June and a series against the first place Expos due next, Pete Peterson made a move that would turn out to be one of his best trades and which pleased even his harshest critics.

The trading deadline for years had been June 15, and in 1979 it had come and gone without the Pirates' consummating a deal. Still, the Pirates had expressed an interest in Giants infielder Bill Madlock, one of the top right-handed hitters in the game, but a player who was unhappy in San Francisco and off to a slow start. It was known that Madlock did not like playing in Candlestick Park and had differences with Giants manager Joe Altobelli. The Giants were also playing Madlock at second base, although his best position by far was third. Somehow, the Giants were able to get waivers on Madlock and on June 28, Peterson acquired him along with left-handed pitcher Dave Roberts and Lenny Randle (a two-time .300 hitter whose poor 1978 had landed him in the minor leagues) for Whitson and minor league pitchers Al Holland and Fred Breining. While Holland and Breining were solid pitching prospects and Whitson had shown flashes of good pitching with the Pirates, no one in Pittsburgh bemoaned their loss. Madlock's former teammates were not nearly so kind and almost to a man criticized the trade.

A death in his family delayed Madlock's arrival for a few days, but Enrique Romo starred in relief against Montreal to cut the Expos' lead to 5½. The Expos reclaimed their lost game by closing out June with a 5–3 win. Veteran lefty relief man Woody Fryman retired Parker with the tying run on, to save the game. Madlock's debut would be worth the wait, but the fact was the Pirates had had a lackluster 14–13 June. Another month had gone by, and the Pirates had finished it a game further out of first than they had started it.

To open July, hopes of gaining on the first place Montreal Expos were washed away with the rainout of a doubleheader. The Bucs received a shot in the arm, however, when the team's newest acquisition joined the club in St. Louis for a four-game series against the Cardinals. Although Chuck Tanner stated publicly that he would rotate Madlock, Phil Garner and Rennie Stennett, the obvious expectation that the struggling Stennett would be benched came to pass. Tanner moved Madlock back to his natural third base position and placed him sixth in the lineup, giving ample protection to his power hitting number five batter, which was usually Willie Stargell or John Milner. Garner, who had finished out both 1977 and 1978 as the Pirates' second baseman, was returned to the keystone corner.

The first game was a seesaw contest, which the Pirates won 5–4 on Tim Foli's single and strong relief pitching from lefthanders Grant Jackson and Dave Roberts. It was the newest Pirate, Madlock, who was the game's number one star, going 4-for-5 with a homerun in his new uniform. Dave Parker supplied the big hit the next night with a two-run homer to support John Candelaria and Enrique Romo, while Stargell celebrated the Fourth of July with a pair of homeruns and Madlock drove in half of the Pirates' runs in a 6–4 win. The Pirates came within inches of completing a four-game sweep in dramatic fashion as Milner's bid for a three-run homer in the ninth was hauled in by George Hendrick, saving John Fulgham's 2–0 win.

Bill Madlock was a welcome addition to the Family, hitting .328 for Pittsburgh. (Courtesy of the Pittsburgh Pirates.)

The Bucs dropped the first two of a three-game set in Cincinnati before Stargell's two-out homer in the ninth won the third game 2–1. Jackson received credit for the win.

Montreal, meantime, had been hot since leaving Pittsburgh. The Bucs headed to the Astrodome having slid into fourth place, seven games behind the front-running ball club from Canada and a game in back of the Philadelphia Phillies and the surprising Chicago Cubs.

Jim Bibby opened for the Bucs and bested Joaquin Andujar, one of three Houston pitchers named to the All-Star Team. Kent Tekulve relieved Romo in the ninth with the bases loaded but retired Reggie Baldwin to save the 4–3 win. While Andujar was a hard thrower, his fastball wasn't in the same league as that of the Pirates' next opponent, J.R. Richard. But instead of Richard's fastball exploding in on Pirates hitters, the Pirates' bats sent two of his pitches into the stratosphere as Parker and Stargell hit back-to-back homeruns. Milner, up next, didn't clear the bases, but drove a long triple and later came in to score Starter Bruce Kison finished with a six-hitter and a 5–1 win. Madlock homered again, helping Bert Blyleven and Tekulve beat Joe Niekro — the top winner in the major leagues — 5–3, as the Bucs brought a Pittsburgh broom to the Dome. After the sweep, Tanner was only too happy to point out that while Houston had some outstanding pitchers, the Pirates' overall staff, relying on excellent depth, was doing its part to keep the Bucs in contention.[15]

The older Niekro brother, Phil, beat the Pirates the next night as the Bucs moved to Atlanta to finish up the first half of the season. Jim Rooker was slaughtered for ten runs in four innings as the Braves coasted to a 13–4 win. But Candelaria was as dominating as Rooker was baffled the next night, hurling an 80-pitch complete game. Moreno had three hits and collected his 36th RBI, three more than he had totaled in 1978. Parker collected his 100th hit of the season. Bill Robinson's team-leading 19th home run and Stargell's 18th of the year led Bibby to his fifth win. The homeruns marked the seventh time in '79 that Pirates hitters had gone back to back.

Although Dave Parker, with 16 homeruns, 54 RBIs, a .297 average and 13 stolen bases, was voted in by the fans, the Cobra was the only Pirate selected for the All-Star Team. The Pirates, who had gained three games in the standings during the last two series, certainly had other players worthy of appearing in the Midsummer Classic. Most easily cited were Stargell (18–41–.306), Moreno (6–38–.305, NL leading 39 stolen bases), Robinson (19–48–.272) and Garner (.294).[16] Foli at .275 was providing clutch hits and strong, dependable defense, and Lee Lacy was hitting .295 in 95 at-bats. While no one on the pitching staff had dominating stats, Blyleven (7–3, 3.61) was on a hot streak and Tekulve was coming on as well. Romo's ERA stood at 2.55 and Bibby, Kison and Candelaria were pitching winning baseball.

Parker, though, made his teammates proud with his All-Star Game play. He had a base hit and an RBI in the game, but his excellent arm, perhaps baseball's most impressive since Roberto Clemente's, saved the National

League's 7–6 victory. After losing a fly ball by Boston's Jim Rice in the seventh, Parker quickly recovered and nailed Rice trying to stretch his hit into a triple. One inning later, his throw nailed Brian Downing at the plate as he tried to score from second on Greg Nettles' single. While National League manager Tom Lasorda credited Parker with having great instincts, the Cobra passed the credit along to Stargell and the late Roberto Clemente, both of whom Parker said had helped him develop his skills as an outfielder.[17]

The second half of the season couldn't have started with a more demanding schedule: the Pirates were faced with 24 games in 18 days. To help take some of the pressure off the pitching staff, Matt Alexander was demoted to AAA Portland and replaced by veteran pitcher Joe Coleman. Coleman, who twice won 20 games as a starter with the Detroit Tigers in the early '70s, had spent the last few years as a middle reliever and had started 1979 with San Francisco before being released early in the year. The Pirates had signed him to a AAA contract, and Coleman had pitched well in the high hitting Pacific Coast League to earn a recall.[18]

Opening with the National League West–leading Astros at home, the Pirates swept the first of what would become seven double headers over a three-week period, 9–5 and 4–2. Stargell tied Robinson for the team lead with his 19th homerun in the first game, as Dave Roberts got the win coming in for a struggling Blyleven in the fourth. In the second game, Kison bested Joe Niekro, again frustrating the knuckleballer in his quest for his 14th win.

Playing with a sore hand, Garner homered for the second night in a row — after not having hit a ball out of the park since the end of May — to lead the Pirates to their fifth strait win, 9–3. Parker added three hits as Candelaria pitched his second strait complete game, the first time the lefthander had accomplished the feat in almost three years. The Bucs moved to within 1½ games of the Expos, passing the Cubs and Phillies, and Montreal moved to bolster their team by purchasing Rusty Staub (a fan favorite during the Expos' expansion years and still a dangerous left-handed hitter) from the Tigers.

Saving their most dramatic win against Houston for the final time they would face the Astros in 1979, Garner and Robinson homered in the eighth off the seemingly invincible reliever Joe Sambito to pull out a 6–5 win. Sambito, baseball's top left-handed reliever that season, had been on a scoreless streak of 40⅔ innings before the long balls. Houston manager Bill Virdon, a former star centerfielder and manager for the Pirates, commented, "There are some pretty good hitting clubs around, but the Pirates have as many homerun threats as anybody."[19] Feeling the strain of the busy schedule, Tanner had started Roberts. While Dave had not been particularly impressive that night, Tanner again praised his 11-man

The Pirates' All-Star right fielder Dave Parker. (Courtesy of the Pittsburgh Pirates.)

pitching staff, stating that the depth of the staff, which lacked twirlers who boasted the outstanding statistics of some of the Astros moundsmen, deserved credit for keeping the Pirates in the heat of the pennant race.

With back-to-back doubleheaders scheduled against Atlanta, Tanner's pitching would certainly have to live up to its billing. To complicate matters, the first night's games were played around rain delays, but starters Don Robinson and Bibby endured the elements and the periods of inactivity. Tanner needed only Tekulve out of the bullpen; he pitched a combined four innings in the two games. The Pirates won both by a run, 5–4 and 3–2. The rain may actually have helped the Pirates in the first game, as Bobby Cox removed Eddie Solomon after the delay, replacing him with sidearmer Gene Garber. Tanner utilized the left-handed hitter Mike Easler against him, and Easler delivered a two-run single for the final scores of the game. Bibby not only starred on the mound in game two, but at the plate as well, hitting a two-run homer that provided the deciding runs.

While the doubleheader of July 22 featured two tight games, the one played on July 23 saw a pair of lopsided battles. Blyleven and Foli played Fours Are Wild in the first game, Blyleven allowing only four hits and Foli collecting the same number in a 7–1 win. Phil Niekro pitched even better than Blyleven in the second game, allowing only two hits. Although the Bucs were decidedly beaten, 8–0, the Pirates did provide a highlight with the National League's only triple play of the season. Rooker, far from 100 percent healthy, lost his fifth strait decision, and the loss left Pittsburgh one game behind Montreal.

What appeared a minor setback at the knuckles of a future 300-game winner turned into a cause for concern when the Pirates dropped three straight to the Reds. The losses were tough ones, including two one-run games (the second decided in the tenth) and a 9–7 battering of Roberts. It was certainly not the time for a prolonged slump, because the team was leaving Pittsburgh for Montreal; but despite the four strait losses, the Bucs had only lost half a game in the standings.[20]

They more than made up the gap in one night. Sore-armed Don Robinson fanned nine in 6⅓ innings, but the Pirates didn't score the game winner until the eighth, when Garner singled home Parker. The run was set up by a sacrifice bunt by Bill Robinson, the team's clean-up hitter. Garner earned several more Stargell Stars in the second contest, collecting three more hits and scoring four times. His performances in the 5–1 and 9–1 wins raised Scrap Iron's average to .315. Milner, slowly breaking out of a midseason slump, drove in four while hitting his 11th homer in the second game. The media focus, however, was on Garner, a batter who had never topped .261 in his major league career. Reporters even asked Parker — the league's two-time defending batting champion, whose average was 20 points below Garner's — if he thought his teammate could win the batting title. Parker and Garner were known for kidding each other, with Garner often needling the giant outfielder. The Cobra struck back with his own question: "Can Hell freeze over?"[21]

Mounting a 4–0 lead for Bibby the next day, the big right-hander was ably relieved by Jackson and Tekulve in a 5–3 win. Montreal won the final game of the series, reversing the score from game three. Expos ace Steve Rogers won his tenth.

Foli got his revenge against his former New York teammates with another four-hit game to spark an 8–5 Pirate comeback win, but the Pirates closed out July with a 2–1 loss. Starter Tom Hausman had to leave the game with an injury, but his relievers, Wayne Twitchell and Ed Glynn, stopped the Pirates' offense by beating Blyleven and dropped the Pirates a game behind Montreal. The tough defeat was not Tanner's main concern, though. With three more doubleheaders during the first ten days in August, he would need all of his pitchers healthy. Word came that Candelaria had been involved in an automobile accident, and thoughts about the Candy Man's availability and how the accident would affect the pitcher's fragile back may have given even the ever optimistic Tanner a second or two of worry.

August opened with two sloppy games for the Pirates against the St. Louis Cardinals. The first one went in the Pirates' favor as Mike Easler hit a pinch triple to tie the game at three and Dave Parker knocked him in a few minutes later. The Cardinals' victory on August 2 frustrated Grant Jackson, who failed to hold the Cardinals on behalf of Jim Rooker as the starter was once again denied his 100th career win. The loss to the Cardinals was played as players mourned the death of New York Yankee star Thurman Munson, who had died in a plane crash earlier that day.

While the Montreal Expos' division lead was still just one game over the Pirates, the team many felt was still the club to beat — the Philadelphia Phillies — came to Pittsburgh on August 3 for a big five-game series, featuring doubleheaders on Friday night and Sunday afternoon. With a then-rare fireworks promotion providing extra incentive, 45,309 fans, the largest Pirates crowd of the season, took in the twi-nighter.

Parker's single in the third broke an early 2–2 tie, but the Phillies knotted the game in the fourth. In the seventh, against lefty Tug McGraw, one of baseball's top relief pitchers of the 1970s, Omar Moreno and Foli singled, and the Cobra followed with a homerun for a 7–3 win. Enrique Romo retired nine strait, commenting afterwards through translator Manny Sanguillen that it was one of the biggest games he had ever pitched in, as he raised his record to 7–3 after an 0–2 start.[22]

In the nightcap, Bibby won his eighth against only two losses, 5–1. The Phillies did not score an earned run and Bibby took over the league lead in winning percentage at .800. Key hits by the two Bills, Madlock and Robinson, led the offense, but the Phillies' manager, Danny Ozark, gave most of the credit for the win to the Pirates defense, noting plays by Foli, Moreno and Garner that had kept the game in the Pirates' favor.[23]

Candelaria and Tekulve blanked the Phils 4–0 on Saturday afternoon. The next day, Pittsburgh took command of the battle for Pennsylvania bragging rights by dumping Ozark's team 12–8 and 5–2. The first game provided one of the club's most memorable wins. The Pirates fell behind 8–3 on Greg Luzinski's grand slam, and with Steve Carlton on the mound for the Phillies, the lead looked safe. The Pirates of 1979 were not a team given to conceding, however, and Lee Lacy hit a two-run homer in the fifth and Bill Robinson singled in another to make it 8–6. Steve Nicosia's third hit of the afternoon made it an 8–7 game and his fourth hit, an eighth inning double, set up Foli's game-tying hit. In the ninth, Kevin Saucier and Rawley Eastwick retired the first two Pirates hitters, but Lacy singled and stole second. The Phillies purposely passed Madlock to face Garner, but he too walked. With Nicosia due to try for his fifth hit, Tanner sent up the left-handed hitting John Milner to bat for him. Ozark countered with McGraw.

The thinking of both Tanner and Milner proved perfect: Milner drove the first pitch for a grand slam. "The plate gets small with the bases loaded," Milner was quoted as saying in the *Pittsburgh Press*. "I was looking for an inside fastball and it came in on the first pitch."[24] Tanner, for his part, had wisely realized the slumping McGraw had been reduced to relying on his famous screwball, a pitch that would effectively be removed from his repertoire by the left-handed power hitter. The dramatic win pushed the Pirates ahead of Montreal by half a game.

Pittsburgh finished up their five-game sweep against a disheartened

Phillie team to send Philadelphia eight games back in the standings. Romo and Kent Tekulve combined for 4⅔ shutout innings of relief when Don Robinson's shoulder tightened during a rain delay. Moreno and Foli each drove in a pair.

The victorious Pirates certainly had a right to celebrate, but no one was counting the Phillies out just yet. The two would meet again later in the week and this time it would be in Veterans' Stadium. The Pirates suffered two losses in three games to the Cubs in the interim, winning only the middle contest on Phil Garner's tenth inning three-run homer. Tanner planned to have Garner bunt, but changed his mind at the last second. Tanner even saw a silver lining in the Pirates' cloudy 15–2 loss to open the series, noting the way reliever Joe Coleman gutted through an extended relief performance in order to allow Tanner to rest his other relievers.[25]

The Phillies, as the Pirates had predicted, had not gone home to bury their heads. Instead, they took three games from the Expos and were ready to shove more than cheese steaks down the throats of their cross-state rivals. Another Friday twi-night doubleheader opened the series. 63,346, the largest crowd to see a baseball game in 1979, were in attendance and initially most of them felt pretty good as the Phils won the opener 4–3. Bruce Kison, though, quieted most of the cheering by carrying a one-hitter and a 3–0 lead into the eighth in the second game. The crowd started to feel some life as the thin pitcher tired. Romo allowed a pair of hits to make it a one-run affair before striking out the left-handed hitting Del Unser. With the right-handed hitting catcher Bob Boone due up, and the Bucs in need of a Kent Tekulve Special — a double-play ball — Tanner called for his ace. Teke followed his manager's request to a T, getting the catcher to hit into the ordered DP and retiring the Phils in the ninth for his 21st save.

While the Pirate-Phillies doubleheader had drawn a huge crowd, the Saturday afternoon game of August 11 provided a national audience: the contest was featured on NBC's *Game of the Week*. The Phillies quickly rocked Rooker out of the game, but Coleman helped to stabilize matters, pitching well enough to allow the Pirates' hitters to go to work. Down 8–0 in the fifth, the Pirates scored five runs. In the seventh, Garner lined a two-run double over Luzinski's head to tie the game 8–8. Fans and the media in Philadelphia sharply criticized Ozark for having kept the slow moving Luzinski in the game with a late lead. Easler contributed yet another big pinch hit to put the Pirates on top in the ninth, 9–8. With McGraw on the mound against a left-handed batter, this time Ed Ott, and the bases again loaded, Ott put the game on ice by belting another grand slam off the beleaguered pitcher. It was the fourth "granny" allowed by McGraw in 1979, a new, if unflattering, record.[26]

Sunday's rainout provided a brief respite for the Phillies, but four RBIs by Milner and another strong game by Bibby essentially took Philadelphia out of the pennant race. The high sailing Pirates' lead of 2½ games over the Expos was their top mark thus far for the year.

The Bucs moved west across the state, and the San Diego Padres came east to meet them at Three Rivers Stadium, the first of three series against the teams from California. The Pirates wasted no effort against San Diego, taking three in a row behind strong pitching by Candelaria, Blyleven and Romo, finally defeating Gaylord Perry in the last game. Roster considerations were discussed with Rooker, who had endured two straight poundings as a starter being placed on the disabled list. Fearing he could not get Matt Alexander through waivers, Peterson recalled outfield prospect Alberto Lois, whom Tanner figured to use mostly as a pinch runner. Tanner also surprised some when he said he would be interested in having Dick Allen come out of retirement to join the team as a pinch hitter in September. Allen, seen by most of his other former managers as too difficult to handle even during his years as a top hitter, had gotten along well with Tanner when the two were with the Chicago White Sox. Still, Allen had been out of baseball for over a year and a half, and Tanner admitted that due to other commitments, it was unlikely Allen would be able to return to playing baseball.[27]

One of Allen's former teams, the defending National League champion Los Angeles Dodgers, proved a much more difficult adversary than the Padres. While the Dodgers, like the Phillies, had played themselves out of serious contention, they still boasted several powerful hitters and noteworthy pitchers, and they took the first two games. Strong relief work by a couple of no-names, Dave Patterson and Bobby Castillo, outdid a combined seven hits by Ott and Madlock. Jerry Reuss won for only the fourth time against ten losses in the second contest. With another offer of fireworks after the game, another crowd in excess of 40,000 attended the finale. They were treated not to an offensive explosion but to quietly effective pitching. Candelaria and Burt Hooten matched 0's through eight before Tekulve set the Dodgers down 1-2-3 in the ninth. Hooten also easily retired the first two batters before giving up a double to Milner. With Stargell still available on the bench to pinch hit, Tommy Lasorda decided to let Hooten pitch to Madlock. Mad Dog hit a long homerun over the centerfield fence to win the game.

A lengthy rain delay of almost four hours kept the opening game against the San Francisco Giants going until 2:16 A.M., but didn't stop the Pirates from victory. Lois, pinch running for Stargell, who opened the inning with a single, scored the winning tally on a passed ball by an understandably tired Mike Sadek. Romo, after bailing out Jackson in the top of the inning, was the winner. Although the Bucs lost to Bob Knepper, 6–1, in the middle game of the series, they rallied to beat Gary Lavelle for the third time in '79 as

The ace of the bullpen, Kent Tekulve. (Courtesy of the Pittsburgh Pirates.)

Foli's fourth RBI of the game decided it. Parker collected the 1,000th hit of his career earlier in the contest.

Following a travel day, the recent hosts became visitors as Tanner's team flew to California to finish off the Western Division portion of their schedule.

On August 24, lefty sinkerballer Randy Jones, the 1976 Cy Young

Award-winner, beat the Bucs 3–2, and the Pirates fell behind the award's 1978 recipient, Perry, in the second game. With Perry in command and only the ninth inning remaining, many San Diego fans left the ballpark, missing what would be another full ballgame. Parker opened the ninth with a double. After Perry retired Stargell, he walked Milner and gave up a base hit to Madlock. Parker scored, and pinch runner Alexander (he had gotten through waivers after all) went to third. Manager Roger Craig replaced one future Hall of Famer, Perry, with another in Rollie Fingers. Fingers, in the middle of a bad year, threw a wild pitch on his first delivery to tie the game. Mark Lee relieved Fingers and stopped the Pirates from taking the lead by fanning Bill Robinson.

Both clubs scored in the 12th. Don Robinson retired Ozzie Smith to end the inning with runners in scoring position, sending the game to the 13th. With neither team scoring runs over the next three innings, Dave Roberts took the mound to start the bottom of the 16th. With two outs and a Padre on third, Roberts walked San Diego's big man, Dave Winfield, and also was ordered to pass Fred Kendall (father of future Pirates catcher Jason). Craig, out of players, was forced to stay with pitcher John D'Acquisto. The seeming mismatch was anything but, as Roberts missed with his first three pitches. The Pirates reliever turned to compose himself, only to find Winfield giving him the "choke" sign. Winfield's uncalled-for gesture did more than help Roberts compose himself: he came back to strike out his mound opponent. Showing just as much grit the next inning, Roberts loaded the bases with no one out, but pitched out of the jam against three left-handed hitters, Jay Johnstone, Jerry Turner and Bill Fahey. Finally, in the top of the 19th, Bill Robinson doubled and Foli singled him home on an 0–2 pitch. Roberts finished off the Padres in the bottom half of the final inning.

With the game ending past 3:00 A.M. Pittsburgh time and after midnight on the West Coast, one would expect the players to look a bit sluggish the next afternoon, but that was not the case. Madlock connected for four hits and Lee Lacy three, and Bruce Kison became the first Pirates pitcher since Al McBean in 1968 to hit a grand slam. The easy 9–2 win was certainly a breather compared to the night before.

After losing the first of three games in L.A. on a Dusty Baker homerun, the Pirates behind Candelaria and his sinker and a Stargell blast won 4–1. The Bucs duplicated the winning score the next day, rallying against Reuss, who carried a three-hitter into the eighth. Stargell's pinch single tied the game, and Lasorda chose to let Reuss face Garner, who was in the midst of a late August slump that had seen his average fall 20 points. Garner snapped out of his doldrums with a game-winning double.

To close out August, the Pirates opened a four-game set in San Francisco. The team, playing without Parker for the first time all year and also without Foli, who was bothered by a pulled groin, beat the Giants 6–4. Romo provided four strong innings of relief before he too left with an injury.

Although the Pirates finished August with a three-game lead in the East, Tanner could not afford to have players like Parker, Foli and Romo gone for any length of time. While the Pirates had taken care of knocking the Phillies out of the race during the month and the Cubs had faded from contention altogether, the Bucs still had to face the powerful and exuberant Expos, a team that would not disappear due to inexperience as some had predicted earlier in the season.

The baseball team the nation was by now referring to as the Family opened September in a pennant battle with Montreal. The Pirates were acknowledged to be the most balanced team in baseball, having established an excellent offense built on power and consistency at the plate and speed on the bases. The Bucs had arguably the deepest pitching in the National League as well; necessary, as Chuck Tanner had to manipulate his staff due to nagging injuries to ace John Candelaria, veteran Jim Rooker and young Don Robinson. The Expos, on the other hand, also featured a deep staff without one pitcher who was having a dominating season. Two weaknesses had become apparent for the Expos during the season's first five months. They did not play well on the road and, even though they had bolstered their bench by adding Rusty Staub, Montreal's power came almost exclusively from the right side.

General manager Pete Peterson added eight players in September call-ups and purchases on September 1. The players' identities make for a good trivia question as only one, Dale Berra, contributed to the team that season. Alberto Lois was again recalled, to give Tanner a second pinch runner, and infielder Gary Hargis made his lone major league appearance that month as an emergency set of legs. Dorian Boyland, a first base prospect, went 0-for-3 as a pinch hitter. Another addition was Rod Scurry, who would have an impact on the team in the early 1980s as a left-handed reliever and who would become one of the most tragic figures in team history, when his cocaine addiction prematurely ended his career and contributed to his early death. Pitchers Jim Willoughby and Rick Jones (both with major league experience) were recalled, but did not appear in a game, nor would catcher Harry Saferight, a left-handed hitter whose major league career was spent sitting on an exciting September bench and warming up pitchers in the bullpen. The Pirates had actually tried to call Berra up a few days before, hoping he could fill in for the injured Tim Foli, but the transaction was disallowed due to an obscure rule that was designed to prevent late season transactions from affecting minor league pennant races.

Still, Berra got a chance to play immediately upon his arrival and contributed in the Pirates' 5–3 and 7–2 doubleheader sweep of the Giants in

Candlestick Park. In the opener, the son of Hall of Famer Yogi Berra drove in the lead run, which was ably set up by Matt Alexander's speed on the bases, with a sacrifice fly. Willie Stargell hit a pair of homeruns to guide the offense. The first game is most remembered, however, for Tanner playing Kent Tekulve in leftfield. With two outs in the ninth and the tying run on base, Tanner decided he preferred to have lefthander Grant Jackson pitch to left-handed slugger Darrell Evans. As the Giants had a dangerous right-handed hitter, Mike Ivie, on deck, Tanner did not want to take Tekulve, who began the ninth on the mound, out of the game. The manager figured that if Jackson were unsuccessful against Evans, he would want Tekulve to face Ivie. Tanner conferred with his coaches regarding Tekulve's ability to shag flies during batting practice and decided to place the reliever in left, thinking it would be the most unlikely place for Evans to hit the ball. Jackson, however, put the pitch on the outside part of the plate; Evans, of course, hit the ball to the one-batter-only-outfielder; and Tekulve pulled in the "can of corn."[28]

In the second game, Berra homered and added another sacrifice fly. Lacy had three hits and three RBIs. The doubleheader saw both Bruce Kison and Jim Bibby, whose second-game performance was a complete game, each win their tenth game of the season.

Candelaria bested Vida Blue on September 2 to give the Pirates a season sweep of the Giants at Candlestick, the first time a team had performed the feat against the Giants in San Francisco.[29]

Rooker, activated from the disabled list, finally won the 100th game of his career, capturing his first victory since the end of May in the second game of a Labor Day doubleheader against Philadelphia. Berra again provided a big bat, homering and driving in three. The win salvaged the day for the Pirates, who had been beaten 2–0 by Steve Carlton in the opener.

The streaking Expos won their eighth in a row on September 4, an off day for the Pirates, to move within two of the lead. On September 5 in St. Louis, the Pirates opened a set of home-and-home series against the Cardinals and Mets. The Bucs and Cards exchanged sloppy wins. with the Pirates taking the first game of the series in the 11th when Darold Knowles' attempted pick-off of Bill Robinson hit the Pirate base runner and rolled into the bullpen allowing two runs to score. Bibby was given an early shower in an 8–6 loss the next night. The three-game set against the last-place Mets in New York also featured close games. The Pirates won 6–4 in 14 innings; Joe Coleman and Grant Jackson pitched out of a bases loaded, no-out jam in the 11th and Parker drove in Garner with the go-ahead run in the last inning; then Alex Trevino's passed ball allowed Alexander to score the team's sixth run. Tekulve helped send the game into overtime with 2⅔ hitless innings of relief. The Mets came back the next night to win an even longer marathon,

15 innings, when John Stearns drove a ball that Lacy, after a long run, was unable to hold on to, scoring the winning run. It was one of the Pirates' most frustrating games of the season because the Bucs had several chances to win the game after regulation, but could not get a clutch hit. The frustration was considerably relieved when Madlock, raising his Pirates average to .308, hustled his way around the bases to spark the team in the next day's contest. Mad dog scored from second base when Frank Taveras' throw to first on a groundball was high. First baseman Ed Kranepool was able to pull the ball in, but Madlock beat his relay to the plate. Bill Robinson followed with a game tying hit and in the ninth, Dave Parker, fighting a 3-for-27 slump coming into the game, tripled and scored on Stargell's double. The durable Tekulve again starred in relief, fanning four in two innings, but the Expos won for the 12th time in 13 games and remained only one game behind the Pirates as the Bucs returned home.

While it appeared the race would certainly go down to the wire, one advantage appeared on the schedule for the Pirates: They would have three off days over the final three weeks, while the Expos would have none. Montreal also faced having to play six doubleheaders over this span. They were playing so well, though, that the team felt confident and again pointed to its very deep staff as being a key to holding up under such strenuous conditions.[30]

On September 11, a home run by Stargell, clutch hits by Ed Ott and Mike Easler, and Dave Roberts' four shutout innings of relief for *his* 100th career win highlighted a victory over St. Louis, 7–3. Nevertheless, the Expos took first place by a few percentage points after sweeping a doubleheader from the Cubs.

On September 12, Candelaria and Tekulve continued the Pirates' strong pitching with a 2–0 gem over the offensively minded birds, and Ott and Garner drove in the team's runs. A rainout washed out the September 13 game, postponing it until September 27, and as the Pirates had an off day on the 14th, the weather gave Tanner's pitching staff some much needed rest. The Expos, however claimed another win when Staub's two-out ninth inning grounder hit a seam in the Olympic Stadium turf and bounced into the outfield for a two-run game winning hit.[31]

As the season moved into its final two weeks, Pittsburgh reclaimed a share of first with a 5–4 win over the Mets on Bill Robinson's clutch RBI; meanwhile, the Expos split a doubleheader with St. Louis. The next night, both contenders lost and only a single percentage point separated the two teams as the Bucs traveled to Montreal for a key two-game series.

The Expos had had a great season in front of their fans and boasted the best home record in the league, but the Pirates took both games, each a classic contest. Don Robinson outdid Steve Rogers 2–1 and Parker, starting to quietly surge towards .300, knocked in both runs. Robinson himself scored one of the runs after opening the fifth with a hit. The Expos had the crowd in their favor again on September 18, but the Pirates had Willie Stargell. After a long rain delay, Pops homered in the 11th as Jackson received credit for the 5–3 win.

The victories gave the Pirates a two-game lead in the pennant race, but Tanner was facing some serious questions about the health of his starters. Candelaria's back would keep him out of action for the next ten days, and both of his starters in the Montreal series, Robinson and Bruce Kison, were pitching in discomfort. The next night, supposedly healthy arms were less than effective, but the Pirates still managed to split two with the Phillies, winning 9–6 on the strength of Manny Sanguillen's pinch-hit triple after the Bucs had fallen behind 6–1. Young reliever Kevin Saucier pitched three innings to prevent another comeback in the nightcap. Omar Moreno stole two bases in the game; breaking his own club record of 71, set the previous season.

Philadelphia figured that if they could not win the division, they would certainly not allow either contender to claim the flag against them. They scored a run in the eighth to beat Tekulve 2–1. Rooker pitched six strong innings in his start, giving Tanner some hope the lefthander would be of use as the team headed for the wire. The Expos, however, had a much better couple of days, sweeping two doubleheaders from the Mets to take a half-game lead in the pennant chase.

While the Expos' next game was rained out, the Cubs' Lynn McGlothlin left some Bucs wishing that inclement weather had invaded Chicago on September 21. The right-hander shut out the Pirates 2–0, beating Don Robinson. With Tanner admitting Candelaria was in too much pain to pitch but not confident in using the September recalls, Peterson acquired Dock Ellis, a one-time Pirates All-Star, from the Mets. Ellis was happy to return to Pittsburgh, a team he been traded from under bad circumstances in 1975. Proudly proclaiming, "I'll die a Pirate," the outspoken right-hander was at the end of his career in 1979, but he had pitched well in defeating Pittsburgh on September 8 and had had another good outing against Montreal the previous weekend.[32] Ellis commented that no team in the majors had the clubhouse chemistry of the Pirates. Comparing the Bucs to the successful Yankee teams he had pitched for in 1976 and 1977, Ellis stated, "The Pirates are much closer. They don't carry grudges against each other. They don't fight each other. They're not jealous of each other."[33]

The Pirates moved back to within half a game of the lead as Kison ran his career record in September to 23–6 and Tekulve pitched 2⅓ hitless innings of relief to stop the Cubs 4–1. Madlock homered and Garner had two hits, scoring one run and driving in another, as the Expos split their doubleheader with the Phillies.

Bibby was the story for the Pirates during their last game of 1979 at Wrigley Field. He shut out the Cubs 6–0, and had two hits that contributed to the scoring. The Bucs exploded for five in the second as Stargell's double drove in two, and two bad plays by third baseman Steve Ontavaris aided the Pirates' offense. The win gave the Family a final road record of 50–31, tops in the National League, but more importantly set the team up well for its four-game series against the Expos at Three Rivers Stadium.

Tanner started Blyleven and Ellis in the Monday night twi-nighter. Blyleven pitched capably, and once again Tekulve was sharp: the two held the tough Expo lineup to two runs. Bill Robinson provided the big hits with a triple and a homerun to drive in three in the 5–2 win. Ellis and Coleman, who entered the game in the fifth, kept pitching in and out of trouble in the second game, but the Expos finally got some clutch hits late in the game against Tekulve, who surrendered a double to third string catcher John Tamargo, tying the game at five. Ellis Valentine, one of the National League's top players at that time, delivered a game winning hit against Teke after having gone 0-for-8 and stranding several runners in the two games. Some criticized Tanner for the loss, stating he should not have used Tekulve after the reliever pitched three innings in the first game, but Tekulve denied feeling tired and added that it was his job to be available to pitch anytime Tanner needed him.[34]

Pittsburgh pounded the Expos 10–4 behind Rooker and Romo, who struck out seven in four innings of relief on September 25. Stargell hit a pair of homers and Moreno ended an ugly 0-for-29 streak with two hits. Ott contributed three RBIs to the scoring, putting the Pirates back in first. Pirate hitters dominated the Expos the next night, scoring ten once again, while Kison allowed only one. Garner and Foli each drove in three and Madlock had three hits.

Both teams prepared to play makeup games on September 27. The Expos, however, had their doubleheader against Atlanta rained out. If needed, the teams would meet on October 1, the day after the season was scheduled to end. The Pirates fared worse, losing to the Cardinals 9–5. Dave Roberts, getting the start, and Candelaria, appearing as a reliever after a ten-day layoff, were knocked around as St. Louis grabbed a 5–0 lead by the game's midpoint.

The Pirates entered the final weekend of the season knowing anything could happen. The Chicago Cubs would be their opponent at Three Rivers, while the Expos would again be playing the Phillies — a team Pittsburghers generally hated, but now found themselves rooting for.

Bibby overwhelmed Chicago for the second time in less than a week, fanning 11; Parker hit a two-run homer and drove in another as the Pirates won, 6–1. Moreno had two hits to put him on a 9-for-13 streak since breaking out of his slump. Pittsburgh's new second favorite baseball team also won as the Expos' third baseman Larry Parrish was unable to come up with a groundball in the 11th of a 3–2 loss. September recall Keith Moreland provided a two-run homer.

With all eyes on the Pirates ready to clinch the National League East in a Saturday afternoon game, the player Pittsburghers had been politicking for the Most Valuable Player Award, Stargell, was suddenly being fitted for a pair of goat horns. In the top of the 13th, Stargell's throwing error allowed the Cubs to take a 7–6 lead. With a chance to redeem himself with two on in the home frame, Captain Willie struck out against Bill Caudill, whose record stood at 0–7 going into the game. Shortly afterwards, word was received that former Pirate Dave Cash had singled in the winning run for the Expos, reducing the Pirates' lead to one game, with one day remaining on the original NL schedule.

It was a tense scenario for both clubs. Stargell, a veteran of many pennant races, remained calm and was even able to joke about his miscue the day before.[35] Tanner chose Kison, one of the Pirates' all-time top pressure pitchers, to start what he hoped would be the last Pirates game of the regular season. But if the Pirates lost and Montreal won, the Expos would have to make up their doubleheader against the Braves. If this happened and the Expos split their two games with Atlanta, the Pirates, having lost a coin flip, would have to fly to Montreal for one winner-takes-all game. A decidedly worse scenario would be for the Expos to sweep the Braves. If the Expos won both games, the Pirates' 1979 season would end without them getting one last shot at Montreal.

Pittsburghers packed the ballpark for the club's annual Prize Day; ironically, the team itself was going for the largest prize of all. Opposing Kison was Lynn McGlothlin, who had shut out the Bucs nine days earlier. Stargell made sure, early on, that McGlothlin would not blank his Family again, driving in a run in the first on a sacrifice fly. Foli's walk and Parker's single had set up the run. In the fourth, John Milner surprised everyone in the ballpark by bunting for a hit. More conventional singles by Madlock and Garner made the score 2–0. Stargell won back his MVP supporters for good in the third with his 32nd homerun. Kison allowed a homerun to Dave Kingman (his league-high 48th) in the sixth, and Tanner brought on Tekulve to try to wrap things up with another extended relief appearance. The Cubs worked Tekulve for a run in the seventh, but Pirates players and fans got a quick shot of adrenaline when the electronic scoreboard in centerfield flashed, "The Magic Number Is One." Steve Carlton had defeated Montreal, clinching a tie for the Pirates by striking out 12 and giving up only three hits.

The Pirates were nearing the finish line. Against Dick Tidrow in the bottom of the inning, Moreno walked and Foli was hit by a pitch. Parker's

The Captain, Willie Stargell, floats home after a homer in the contest in which the Bucs clinched the Eastern Division crown. (Courtesy of the Pittsburgh Pirates.)

infield out advanced both runners, bringing up Stargell, who was walked intentionally. Bill Robinson — a player who had delivered many clutch hits during the season — added one more, driving in two with a base hit. The Cubs kept the game close and the tension high when they got a run back in the eighth on Kingman's double and Larry Biittner's single, but Tekulve held Chicago scoreless in the ninth, getting Bruce Kimm to foul out to Madlock to start a well deserved Family celebration.

Tanner credited his division title to the contributions of his whole squad, noting achievements from every player and reminding the media that the club went 20–10 in September while battling an excellent Montreal team. Pittsburghers hoped the harvest of September would become an Octoberfest, as the Pirates looked forward to their first postseason in four years.

3. The Postseason

The 1979 National League Championship Series

The NL Western Division Champions: The Cincinnati Reds

Pittsburgh prepared for their playoff opponents with confidence even though the Cincinnati Reds had held an 8–4 advantage over the Pirates during the regular season and, perhaps more unnerving, the Reds had three times earlier in the decade — 1970, 1972 and 1975 — prevented the Bucs from advancing to the World Series. The 1972 loss had been particularly painful, coming on a ninth inning, two-out wild pitch by Bob Moose in the final game, one of the toughest losses in franchise history.

The 1979 edition of the Big Red Machine was admittedly not as powerful as its predecessors. Pete Rose and Tony Perez were no longer with the team, and Joe Morgan and Johnny Bench, still very effective players, were no longer MVP candidates. The Reds' most dangerous hitter in 1979 was George Foster, who hit for power and average and was a deadly RBI man. Dave Concepcion was the top all-around shortstop in the game, a good enough hitter to bat third in a powerful lineup and rivaled only by young Ozzie Smith of San Diego as the best defensive player at his position. Rose's replacement at third, Ray Knight, hit .318. Speedy Dave Collins took over in right field when Ken Griffey was injured and had a career year, matching Knight's batting average. The other two regulars, centerfielder Cesar Geronimo and first baseman Dan Driessen, were good defensive players who at different points in their career had hit .300.

In 1979 Cincinnati also had one upgrade from the amazing Reds teams that won two straight World Series in the mid-70's, Tom Seaver. Seaver, the National League's top right-handed pitcher over the past decade had been

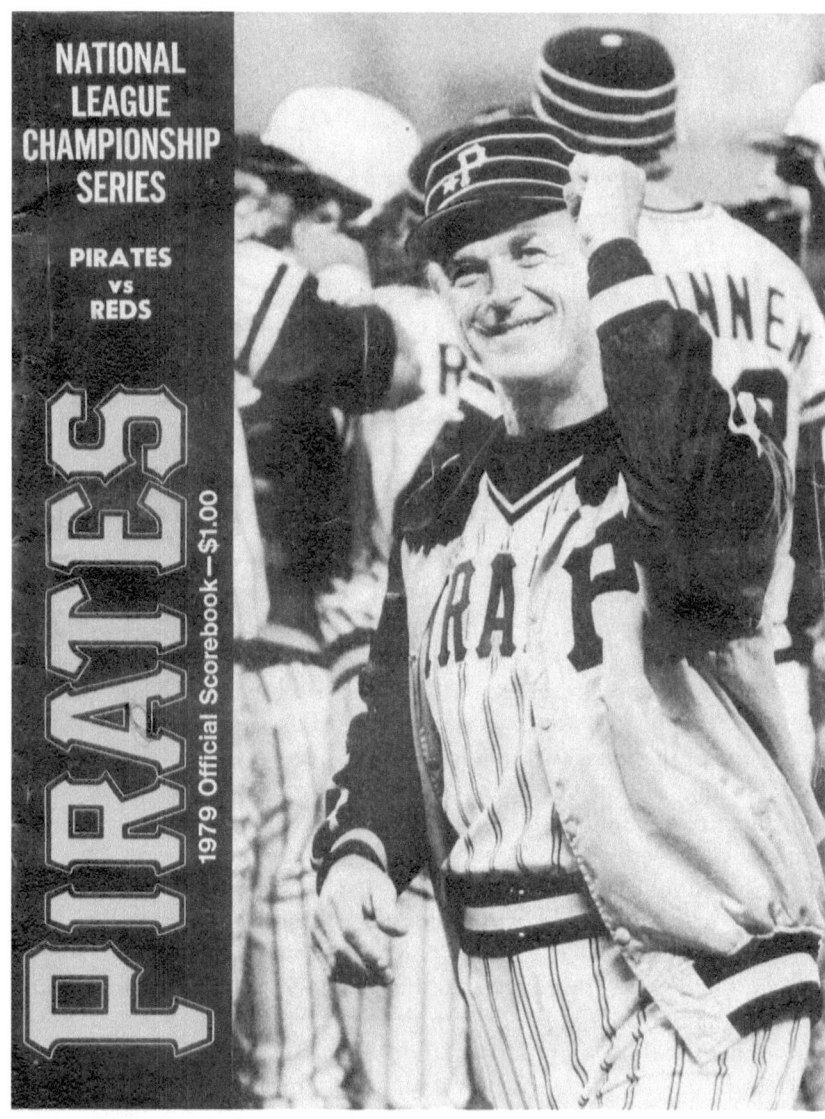

An excited Chuck Tanner adorns the cover of the 1979 NLCS Official Scorebook. (Courtesy of the Pittsburgh Pirates.)

obtained two years prior; even having fought injuries in 1979, he still won more games than any Pirates hurler. He was healthy going into the playoffs, which figured to give the Reds an edge, as manager Sparky Anderson would be able to start him twice if the National League Championship Series went five games. The rest of the Reds pitching staff could be effective, but were not considered as talented as Pittsburgh's, so it would be important for Seaver to start the Machine's engine efficiently.

Game One

In the 11 times the Pirates had faced the Cincinnati Reds in their previous NLCS encounters, they had only emerged victorious on two occasions, once in Riverfront Stadium. This was a different Bucco team, though, one that thrived on the dramatic — especially off the bat of their 38-year-old spiritual leader, Willie Stargell — and they were far from intimidated by this version of the Red Machine. By the time the game ended, Cincinnati would be reminded of that fact in a big way.

The Reds were led in this game by one of the greatest pitchers ever to grace the mound: Tom Seaver. Seaver had gotten off to a rocky start in the Queen City, but rebounded to emerge victorious in 14 of his final 15 games.[1] Cincinnati seemed to have the edge as the Bucs sent out the Candy Man, John Candelaria. This night he was making his first start after a two-week layoff due to his chronic bad back and rib cage injury,[2] but Candy had been spectacular in his only previous postseason appearance. In a 1975 NLCS game the Pirates needed to win to stay alive, Candelaria, then a 21-year-old rookie, had fanned 14 in a game the Pirates eventually lost in extra innings.

Both pitchers would be on tonight, giving up runs in only one frame each. The Bucs broke out first when Phil Garner crushed a shot to right in the second inning, giving Pittsburgh a 1–0 lead. Omar Moreno then lined one to right which Dave Collins, the Reds' right fielder, dove for and missed. The ball got past Collins, and Moreno had a triple. Tim Foli knocked him in with a sacrifice to Collins, giving Pittsburgh a 2–0 lead after the top of the second.

Cincinnati evened it up in the bottom of the fourth as Dave Concepcion singled to left before George Foster smashed a two-run homer into the second level in center, knotting the game up at two.

After Foster's big hit, both Seaver and Candelaria settled down, retiring the sides in order between the fifth inning through the top of the eighth. The only man to reach base was Foli, who singled in the fifth only to be erased by a double play.

Candy made it through seven on his return start, giving up only five hits and two runs, but the future Hall of Famer for the Reds matched Candelaria, giving up five hits and two runs in eight innings of work.

Enrique Romo replaced the Candy Man in the eighth, and the Reds almost sent the go-ahead run home. Collins singled off the Pirates reliever with one out and then stole second. Morgan walked, putting men on first and second, and Tanner went to the bullpen to call in his ace reliever, Kent

Tekulve. Teke proved his worth, getting Concepcion to bounce out into a 5–4–3 inning-ending double play.

Both teams failed to score in the ninth, and game one went into extra innings. The Bucs had a chance in their half of the tenth when Garner smacked a one-out single. Mike Easler, hitting for Tekulve, flew out to Foster before Moreno ended the inning striking out. Grant Jackson, the Bucs' veteran lefty reliever, came in and got Cincinnati in order to end their half of the tenth.

The Pirates came up in the top of the 11th and were about to show the Reds a little of the magic they had shown throughout the course of the 1979 campaign. Foli led off the inning with his second hit of the game before Dave Parker followed with an infield single, putting men on first and second. Then the man the Pirates affectionately called "Pops" came to the plate. It didn't take long for Stargell, soon to be the National League's co-MVP, to show Cincy reliever Tom Hume what '79 was all about. Stargell took Hume's first pitch over the wall, giving the Pirates a 5–2 lead.

Jackson took the hill with a seemingly safe three-run cushion and promptly got the first two Cincinnati batters out. The Big Red Machine was not dead, as Concepcion singled and was moved to second when Foster walked. The Bucs' skipper called on second-year hurler Don Robinson in hopes of shutting the door. Robinson walked Johnny Bench, loading the bases and bringing up the potential game-winning run in Ray Knight. Robinson showed his grit, bearing down and striking out Knight to end the game. The monkey was beginning to be lifted from the Pirates' backs. Beating the Reds in the opener gave them an important edge in the Series. As for Cincinnati, they got to see the magic show that the Family had been putting on all year.

BOX SCORE
October 2, 1979 (N) at Riverfront Stadium

PIT N	0	0	2	0	0	0	0	0	0	0	3	–	5	10	0
CIN N	0	0	0	2	0	0	0	0	0	0	0	–	2	7	0

Batting

Pittsburgh Pirates	AB	R	H	RBI	BB	K	PO	A
Moreno cf	5	1	1	0	0	2	0	0
Foli ss	4	0	2	1	0	0	1	5
Alexander pr	0	1	0	0	0	0	0	0
B. Robinson lf	0	0	0	0	0	0	0	0
Parker rf	4	1	1	0	1	0	4	0
Stargell 1b	4	1	1	3	1	1	18	0
Milner lf	5	0	0	0	0	0	0	0

	AB	R	H	RBI	BB	K	PO	A
Stennett 2b	0	0	0	0	0	0	0	1
Madlock 3b	5	0	2	0	0	0	0	5
Ott c	5	0	1	0	0	2	7	2
Garner 2b, ss	4	1	2	1	1	0	3	5
Candelaria p	3	0	0	0	0	2	0	0
Romo p	0	0	0	0	0	0	0	0
Tekulve p	0	0	0	0	0	0	0	1
Easler ph	1	0	0	0	0	0	0	0
Jackson p	1	0	0	0	0	0	0	0
D. Robinson p	0	0	0	0	0	0	0	0
Totals	41	5	10	5	3	7	33	19

Fielding

DP: 2.

Batting

3B: Moreno (1, off Seaver); **HR:** Garner (1, 3rd inning off Seaver 0 on, 0 out); Stargell (1, 11th inning off Hume 2 on, 0 out); **SF:** Foli (1, off Seaver); **IBB:** Garner (1, by Tomlin).

Baserunning

SB: Madlock 2 (2, 2nd base off Seaver/Bench, 2nd base off Tomlin/Bench).

Cincinnati Reds	AB	R	H	RBI	BB	K	PO	A
Collins rf	5	0	2	0	0	0	3	0
Morgan 2b	4	0	0	0	1	0	2	4
Concepcion ss	5	1	2	0	0	0	0	7
Foster lf	3	1	1	2	2	0	2	0
Bench c	3	0	2	0	2	0	7	0
Knight 3b	5	0	0	0	0	2	0	1
Driessen 1b	4	0	0	0	0	2	16	0
Cruz cf	4	0	0	0	0	1	2	0
Seaver p	2	0	0	0	0	1	0	0
Auerbach ph	1	0	0	0	0	1	0	0
Hume	1	0	0	0	0	1	0	2
Tomlin p	0	0	0	0	0	0	1	0
Totals	37	2	7	2	5	8	33	14

Fielding

DP: 1.

Batting

3B: Bench (1, off Candelaria); **HR:** Foster (1, 4th inning off Candelaria 1 on, 0 out).

Baserunning

SB: Collins (1, 2nd base off Romo/Ott); **CS:** Bench (1, 2nd base by Tekulve/Ott).

Pitching

Pittsburgh Pirates	IP	H	HR	R	ER	BB	K
Candelaria	7	5	1	2	2	1	4
Romo	0.1	1	0	0	0	1	1
Tekulve	1.2	0	0	0	0	1	0
Jackson W (1–0)	1.2	1	0	0	0	1	2
D. Robinson SV(1)	0.1	0	0	0	0	1	1
Totals	11.0	7	1	2	2	5	8

Cincinnati Reds	IP	H	HR	R	ER	BB	K
Seaver	8	5	1	2	2	2	5
Hume L (0–1)	2.1	5	1	3	3	0	1
Tomlin	0.2	0	0	0	0	1	1
Totals	11.0	10	2	5	5	3	7

IBB: Tomlin (1, Garner); **Umpires:** Kibler, Montague, Dale, Pulli; **Time of Game:** 3:14; **Attendance:** 55,006.

Game Two

Game two of the NLCS was the pivotal contest. A loss for the Reds would mean leaving their home park down two games to none, but a win would send them to Pittsburgh's Three Rivers Stadium with the series tied. Regardless, this version of the Big Red Machine had just learned that this was a different Pirates team than they had faced in the past NLCSs; this was a club that had a variety of ways to win games. "From the seventh inning on, that's our game. We have the bullpen and the hitters, and we use them. If I have 25 guys available, I may use 24," Pirates skipper Chuck Tanner confided.[3] His prediction was correct, as at some point during the season every man on his bench contributed to a win in one way or another.

In this game, the Bucs would send out veteran hurler Jim Bibby, a free agent signing out of Cleveland before the 1978 campaign, against the Reds' 22-year-old rookie Frank Pastore. Although he had spent part of 1979 in the minor leagues and finished just 6–7, Pastore had greatly helped the Reds with a couple of key victories in September. Some believed that other than Seaver, the freshman had the best stuff on the Reds' staff.

The Reds, who were hellbent on evening out this series, put Bibby in harm's way for the first three innings. In the first, Joe Morgan got a one-out walk and stole second. George Foster walked after Dave Concepcion flew out to Dave Parker, putting men on first and second. Bibby forced Johnny Bench to fly out to Parker for the inning's final out.

Cincy took their first, and only lead of the NLCS in the second inning when Dan Driessen led off the second frame with a single and was sent to

3. The Postseason

third on a Ray Knight hit. Cesar Geronimo struck out, but Pastore knocked home the game's first run with a one out sacrifice fly to center field. Knight proceeded to steal second, putting another Red in scoring position before Dave Collins struck out for the final out.

For the third time in three innings, the Reds got a man in scoring position. Bibby once again would have to bear down in order to keep the game close for Pittsburgh. Concepcion reached second on a one-out double. Foster walked once again, but Ott pegged the Cincinnati shortstop out at third, as Concepcion tried to swipe the base. Bibby got Bench for the third out once again, this time on a grounder to Willie Stargell, leaving the score 1–0.

The opposition didn't want to squander runs against the Family. But so far, the Reds had blown almost every opportunity they had had to get a comfortable lead. In the top of the fourth, the Pirates made them pay, although some questionable base running kept the Bucs out of what could have been a big inning. Tim Foli led off the fourth with a single, the first hit of the game against Pastore. Parker sent him to second with a single, as up to the plate came Stargell. Pops had relished these opportunities all season and smashed a long fly ball that bounced off the left field wall. Parker and Foli had waited to see if the ball would be caught, so they could only advance one base. In the meantime, not seeing that his teammates had stopped, Stargell came in to second for what he thought was a double. Seeing that Parker was on second, the future Hall of Famer tried to go back to first but was pegged out on throw from Foster to Morgan to Driessen at first. Pastore intentionally walked John Milner, loading the bases to induce a double play. Bill Madlock hit a grounder to Concepcion that scored Foli with the game's tying run.

Pittsburgh took the lead in the fifth after Phil Garner slashed a line drive towards center that Dave Collins dove for. Collins thought he had made a fabulous catch, but umpire Frank Pulli ruled it a trap, giving Garner a leadoff single. Bibby sacrificed the Bucco second baseman to second before Foli hit a clutch two-out double down the third base line, giving the Pirates a 2–1 lead.

Down but not out, Cincinnati fought back. First the Reds came up with a big defensive play, and then they finally collected a big hit. The Black and Gold had a chance to put an insurance run across in the seventh after catcher Ed Ott singled and moved to second on another sacrifice by Bibby. Moreno promptly singled to Foster, but the Reds' left fielder tossed out the Bucco catcher at home.

Cincinnati mounted two of their own threats. In the seventh, Knight led off the inning with a single off Bibby, then moved to second on a sacrifice before the veteran hurler got the last two outs to end the frame unscathed. The following inning, reliever Enrique Romo gave up one-out singles to

Concepcion and Foster before Tanner called on Kent Tekulve to squash the rally as he had done the night before. Teke struck out Bench before unleashing a wild pitch that sent the runners into scoring position with two outs. The Rubber Band Man then walked Driessen intentionally before getting Knight to fly out to center.

Teke was unable to close it in the ninth: Heity Cruz and Collins smacked one-out doubles off the Pirate bullpen ace to tie it up at two. Tanner called in Dave Roberts who walked Morgan to load the bases and then, again like the night before, went to Don Robinson hoping to send the game into extra frames. Robby struck out Concepcion and got Foster to ground to second, ending what eventually turned out to be the Reds' last hope in this series.

Moreno led off the tenth with a single and moved to second on a bunt by Foli. Parker singled to left. No one on the planet would have been able to throw out the speedy Moreno, who dashed across home plate with the game's winning run.

There was no steam left in Cincinnati sails after blowing so many opportunities. Robinson mowed them down one, two, three in the bottom half of the tenth, sending the Pirates home with a two-games-to-none lead. Only one victory was needed to send Pittsburgh to its seventh World Series. The sophomore pitcher's two relief performances earned comparisons to Goose Gossage from Tanner and Pirate scout Howie Haak. "That's how the Goose used to do it," said Tanner. Haak added, "Except Goose just had a slider," acknowledging Robinson's superior curveball.[4] Dan Donovan, *The Pittsburgh Press* writer who covered the team all season long, noted that Robinson's emergence as a short reliever gave the Pirates four different types of pitchers Tanner could call on with the game on the line: "… a right-handed sinkerball pitcher (Tekulve), a right-handed trick pitcher (Romo), a left-handed power pitcher (Jackson) and a right-handed power pitcher (Robinson)."[5]

The quartet's pitching had helped put the Family on the cusp of the World Series.

BOX SCORE
October 3, 1979 (D) at Riverfront Stadium

PIT N	0	0	0	1	1	0	0	0	0	1	-	3	11	0
CIN N	0	1	0	0	0	0	0	0	1	0	-	2	8	0

Batting

Pittsburgh Pirates	AB	R	H	RBI	BB	K	PO	A
Moreno cf	5	1	2	0	0	0	4	0

	AB	R	H	RBI	BB	K	PO	A
Foli ss	4	1	2	1	0	0	2	1
Parker rf	5	0	2	1	0	2	4	0
Stargell 1b	3	0	2	0	2	0	6	1
Milner lf	2	0	0	0	1	0	0	0
B. Robinson lf	2	0	0	0	0	0	3	0
Madlock 3b	5	0	0	1	0	0	1	0
Ott c	4	0	2	0	0	0	8	1
Garner 2b	4	1	1	0	0	0	1	3
Bibby p	0	0	0	0	1	0	0	1
Jackson p	0	0	0	0	0	0	0	0
Romo p	0	0	0	0	0	0	0	0
Tekulve p	1	0	0	0	0	1	0	0
Roberts p	0	0	0	0	0	0	0	0
D. Robinson p	0	0	0	0	0	0	0	0
Totals	35	3	11	3	4	3	30	7

Batting

2B: Foli (1, off Pastore); Stargell (1, off Tomlin); **SH:** Bibby 2 (2, off Pastore 2); Foli (1, off Bair); **IBB:** Milner (1, by Pastore); Stargell (1, by Bair).

Cincinnati Reds	AB	R	H	RBI	BB	K	PO	A
Collins rf	5	0	1	1	0	2	0	0
Morgan 2b	3	0	0	0	2	0	5	7
Concepcion ss	5	0	2	0	0	1	1	6
Foster lf	3	0	1	0	2	1	3	2
Bench c	5	0	0	0	0	2	5	1
Driessen 1b	4	1	1	0	1	0	13	0
Knight 3b	5	0	2	0	0	0	0	2
Geronimo cf	3	0	0	0	0	3	3	0
Pastore p	0	0	0	1	1	0	0	0
Spilman ph	1	0	0	0	0	0	0	0
Tomlin p	0	0	0	0	0	0	0	0
Hume p	0	0	0	0	0	0	0	0
Cruz ph	1	1	1	0	0	0	0	0
Bair p	0	0	0	0	0	0	0	1
Totals	35	2	8	2	6	9	30	19

Fielding

DP: 1.

Batting

2B: Concepcion (1, off Bibby); Cruz (1, off Tekulve); Collins (1, off Tekulve); **SH:** Geronimo (1, off Bibby); **SF:** Pastore (1, off Bibby); **IBB:** Driessen (1, by Tekulve).

Baserunning

SB: Morgan (1, 2nd base off Bibby/Ott); Knight (1, 2nd base off Bibby/Ott); Collins (2, 2nd base off Bibby/Ott); **CS:** Concepcion (1, 3rd base by Bibby/Ott).

Pitching

Pittsburgh Pirates	IP	H	HR	R	ER	BB	K
Bibby	7	4	0	1	1	4	5
Jackson	0.1	0	0	0	0	0	0
Romo	0	2	0	0	0	0	0
Tekulv	1	2	0	1	1	1	2
Roberts	0	0	0	0	0	1	0
D. Robinson W (1-0)	1.2	0	0	0	0	0	2
Totals	10.0	8	0	2	2	6	9

Cincinnati Reds	IP	H	HR	R	ER	BB	K
Pastore	7	7	0	2	2	3	1
Tomlin	0.2	1	0	0	0	0	1
Hum	1.1	1	0	0	0	0	1
Bair L (0-1)	1	2	0	1	1	1	0
Totals	10	11	0	3	3	4	3

WP: Tekulve (1); **IBB:** Tekulve (1, Driessen); Pastore (1, Milner); Bair (1, Stargell); **Umpires:** Montague, Dale, Pulli, Stello; **Time of Game:** 3:24 **Attendance:** 55,000

Game Three

Game three of the NLCS started late, as the rains came down before the contest began.[6] The storm just delayed the inevitable for the Cincinnati Reds. The Bucs put on an offensive display that took any suspense out of the contest early: the 1979 National League Championship Series, which had been played tooth and nail in the first two games, ended with a rout, giving the Pirates the ninth National League Championship in the history of the franchise.

Bert Blyleven, who had been critical of Chuck Tanner over the course of his time in the Steel City for the way the Pirates manager quickly went to the bullpen, threw a complete game eight-hitter, leading Pittsburgh to a spot in the 76th World Series.

Pittsburgh started early against Mike LaCoss, a 14-game winner who had struggled down the stretch for the Reds. Omar Moreno walked in the first, then stole second. Tim Foli moved him over to third, the throw by Cincinnati shortstop Dave Concepcion being too little too late to catch the National League's stolen-base king. Dave Parker proceeded to plate Moreno with a sacrifice fly to left fielder George Foster, giving the Bucs a 1-0 lead.

Phil Garner started the second with a triple and came home on a sacrifice fly, this time by Foli. It was apparent early on that LaCoss did not have it on this evening. Cincinnati manager John McNamara quickly pulled the 23-year-old hurler after he went 2-0 to Parker following the Foli sac fly.

Into the game came veteran pitcher Fred Norman; but while he stopped the Bucs in the second, he was not able to keep the lethal Pirates bats silent.

After Cincinnati failed in one of their few threats of the game, leaving Dave Collins on third and Concepcion on first in the top of the third, Willie Stargell and Bill Madlock played long ball in the bottom half of the frame, stretching the Pittsburgh lead to 4–0. An inning later Pops put the game on ice, doubling in Blyleven and Parker to give the Pirates a commanding 6–0 advantage before the game was four innings old.

The only highlight of the evening for Cincy was a sixth inning homer by Johnny Bench; it was the Big Red Machine's only run of the contest. Blyleven got tough after the clout. He gave up a single to Cesar Geronimo to open up the seventh, but choked the Reds bats the rest of the game, setting down the final nine Cincinnati batters in order.

Pittsburgh ended the scoring with an unearned run in the eighth: Garner scored as Foli reached base on an error by Geronimo, making the final 7–1 and sending the Steel City into a frenzy. The scene was incredible as the Pirates' wives danced on top of the dugouts to the team's official anthem, "We are Fam-A-Lee." They had been dancing since the seventh inning, a move that some of the players didn't like since the game still had a couple of innings to go. Others acknowledged that their wives had reason to celebrate; having gone through tough times with their husbands, they were entitled to join in on the fun.[7] Ecstatic Pirate fans to the number of 42,240 were also singing the Sister Sledge tune, and a large group stormed the field in joy after Blyleven struck out Geronimo to end the series in style.

McNamara was blunt following the contest. Asked an all too obvious question, the Reds manager replied, "What the hell can you say? Nobody likes to lose. How do I feel about it? Terrible!"[8]

Stargell was voted Most Valuable Player of the NLCS, but it was not just in modesty that he said the victory was really due to the entire team. Robinson's terrific relief, clutch hitting by Parker, Foli and Garner, and superlative pitching by the Pirates' three starting pitchers demonstrated this beyond question. Winning three games was also important, because the sweep would allow Tanner to set his pitching rotation for the biggest contest of all.

Pittsburgh had finally thrown the monkey from its back, defeating the Big Red Machine for the first time in four NLCS encounters. Pops and the Family were going back to the Fall Classic to face their old rivals from Baltimore. This magical ride was going to continue.

BOX SCORE
October 5, 1979 (D) at Three Rivers Stadium

```
CIN N   0  0  0  0  0  1  0  0  0  -  1  8  1
PIT N   1  1  2  2  0  0  0  1  x  -  7  7  0
```

Batting

Cincinnati Reds	AB	R	H	RBI	BB	K	PO	A
Collins rf	4	0	2	0	0	0	3	0
Morgan 2b	4	0	0	0	0	1	3	1
Concepcion ss	4	0	2	0	0	2	1	0
Foster lf	4	0	0	0	0	2	1	0
Bench c	4	1	1	1	0	0	5	1
Driessen 1b	4	0	0	0	0	1	6	0
Knight 3b	4	0	2	0	0	0	0	2
Geronimo cf	4	0	1	0	0	2	5	0
LaCoss p	0	0	0	0	0	0	0	1
Norman p	1	0	0	0	0	1	0	0
Leibrandt p	0	0	0	0	0	0	0	0
Auerbach ph	1	0	0	0	0	0	0	0
Soto p	0	0	0	0	0	0	0	0
Spilman ph	1	0	0	0	0	0	0	0
Tomlin p	0	0	0	0	0	0	0	1
Hume p	0	0	0	0	0	0	0	0
Totals	35	1	8	1	0	9	24	6

Fielding

E: Geronimo (1).

Batting

2B: Knight (1, off Blyleven); **HR:** Bench (1, 6th inning off Blyleven 0 on, 1 out).

Pittsburgh Pirates	AB	R	H	RBI	BB	K	PO	A
Moreno cf	2	1	0	0	2	0	1	0
Foli ss	4	0	0	1	0	0	0	2
Parker rf	3	1	1	1	1	1	3	0
Stargell 1b	4	1	2	3	0	1	9	1
Milner lf	2	0	0	0	1	0	0	0
B. Robinson lf	1	0	0	0	0	0	0	0
Madlock 3b	2	1	1	1	2	0	0	3
Ott c	4	0	0	0	0	0	9	0
Garner 2b	4	2	2	0	0	0	4	1
Blyleven p	3	1	1	0	0	1	1	1
Totals	29	7	7	6	6	3	27	8

Batting

2B: Stargell (2, off Norman); **3B:** Garner (1, off LaCoss); **HR:** Stargell (2, 3rd inning off Norman 0 on, 0 out); Madlock (1, 3rd inning off Norman 0 on, 1 out); **SH:** Moreno (1, off Norman); Blyleven (1, off Tomlin); **SF:** Parker (1, off LaCoss); Foli (2, off LaCoss).
IBB: Madlock (1, by Tomlin).

Baserunning

SB: Moreno (1, 2nd base off LaCoss/Bench); Parker (1, 2nd base off Tomlin/Bench).

Pitching

Cincinnati Reds	IP	H	HR	R	ER	BB	K
LaCoss L (0–1)	1.2	1	0	2	2	4	0
Norman	2	4	2	4	4	1	1
Leibrandt	0.1	0	0	0	0	0	0
Soto	2	0	0	0	0	0	1
Tomlin	1.2	2	0	1	0	1	1
Hume	0.1	0	0	0	0	0	0
Totals	8.0	7	2	7	6	6	3

Pittsburgh Pirates	IP	H	HR	R	ER	BB	K
Blyleven W (1–0)	9	8	1	1	1	0	9

IBB: Tomlin (2, Madlock); **Umpires:** Dale, Pulli, Stello, Quick; **Time of Game:** 2:45 **Attendance:** 42240

The 1979 World Series

The American League Champions: The Baltimore Orioles

The World Series was uncharted waters for most of the Pirates. Of the 25 men on Tanner's World Series roster, only four position players (Willie Stargell, John Milner and backups Manny Sanguillen and Lee Lacy) and two pitchers (Bruce Kison and Grant Jackson) had World Series experience. Stargell, Sanguillen and Kison remained from the 1971 Pirates postseason roster. Rennie Stennett, a hot shot rookie in '71, had not been eligible for the postseason that year; then–Pirates manager Danny Murtaugh chose Jose Pagan over him to fill out his 25-man roster.

Pittsburgh's opponents, the Baltimore Orioles, also had not been to a World Series since 1971. Likewise, most of the Orioles' players had not been on center stage before. Only the great pitcher Jim Palmer, shortstop Mark Belanger and Lee May — the team's regular designated hitter who figured to be reduced to pinch hitting appearances, since the DH would not be used in the '79 Series — had ever gotten this far before. Palmer and Belanger, however, were not the only holdovers from the great Orioles teams that had made three straight World Series appearances beginning in 1969. Earl Weaver, Baltimore's manager during their dynasty, was still guiding the Birds. Weaver was considered a master strategist and psychologist who baited the opposition and umpires, and whose tactics had been highly successful for him.

The "extended family" celebrates as fans rush onto the Three Rivers Stadium turf, following the three-game sweep of the Cincinnati Reds. (Courtesy of the Pittsburgh Pirates.)

One of the few times his team had come up short was in the 1971 World Series when the Pirates, led by Roberto Clemente's incredible play and Steve Blass's excellent pitching, upset the heavily favored Orioles.

Baltimore was a favorite going into the series and the reason, as it had been in '71, was its starting pitching. Palmer, who had battled arm problems most of '79, was an eight-time 20-game winner and was healthy once again. He had pitched well against a high-powered California Angel offence in the ALCS, which Baltimore had won in four games. The Orioles' best pitcher in '79, however, was lefthander Mike Flanagan, a 23-game winner who would be named the American League's Cy Young Award–winner later that fall. The number three man was also a lefthander, Scott McGregor, who relied on excellent control and won 13 games. A possible wild card for the Orioles was Dennis Martinez, who, some argued, had the best stuff on the staff and led the American League in starts, complete games and innings pitched, but had gone just 15–16. Weaver's bullpen was not as established as Pittsburgh's, but had been effective during the regular season. Earl figured to use his fifth starter, Steve Stone (11–7 in '79), in long relief and could turn to lefty Tippy Martinez (10–3, 2.88) and rookie Tim Stoddard (3–1,

1.71 in 29 games) to set up his enigmatic ace, Don Stanhouse (7–3, 2.84, 21 saves). For those who do not remember Stanhouse, his relief style was similar to recent Pirates closer Mike Williams. Like Williams, Stanhouse relied on his slider and was usually successful, but seldom made his saves appear easy.

The Orioles' offense had its heroes as well, but was not thought to be anywhere near the equal of Pittsburgh's. Baltimore was only ninth in the American League in scoring and scored less runs than the Pirates, despite having the benefit of the DH. Most of Baltimore's offense came from its two switch-hitters in the middle of the lineup, Ken Singleton (35–111–.295) and Eddie Murray (25–99–.295). Singleton finished second to the Angel's Don Baylor in the MVP balloting, while Murray, only 23, had just had his third straight productive year in a career that led him to enshrinement in Cooperstown in 2003. Weaver also skillfully used journeymen Gary Roenicke and John Lowenstein as a platoon in leftfield, and they combined for 36 homeruns and 98 RBIs. Al Bumbry in centerfield was a good lead-off man, boasting a .285 average and 37 stolen bases, but third baseman Doug DeCinces had an ankle injury that brought his final average down to .230. The other three positions were usually manned by steady second baseman Rich Dauer and defensive standouts Belanger (who had an embarrassing .167 batting average in 1979) and catcher Rick Dempsey (who spoke confidently of being able to stop the Pirates' running game). When seeking to get more offense into his lineup, Weaver sometimes went with Kiko Garcia at shortstop. While the Pirates Family was believed to have the strongest bench in baseball, Weaver's pinch hitting corps looked just as strong, with May (19 homers) joining Benny Ayala (6 homers in 86 at-bats) and left-handed hitters Terry Crowley (.317) and Pat Kelly (.288) as possible emergency batsmen.

Game One

While the NFL chooses to host its annual world championship in an antiseptic stadium located in a warm climate, major league baseball honors the champions of each league with home games in their own parks. When the Dodgers are in the Fall Classic the weather becomes no problem, but when an East Coast team emerges victorious in their league championship series, an October contest in the World Series becomes a very chancy prospect. In 1979 this became a big issue: torrential rains postponed the first game of the 76th version of the Fall Classic, the first time an opening game had ever been postponed.[9]

The following day was no better. First a heavy snow fell on Baltimore, then later on it turned into rain. Pat Santarone, who had been the head groundskeeper at Memorial Stadium since 1968, was given the chore of somehow saving the day so the series would not have to be put back another day. When the rain finally subsided around 1:00 PM, Santarone and his crew of 25 used hand pumps and enough sand to fill Laguna Beach trying to make the field acceptable to baseball commissioner Bowie Kuhn.[10]

There was another problem facing Santarone and his crew, the fact that the Orioles shared the field with the Baltimore Colts. Even though real turf is the field of choice in today's game, in the 1970s football and baseball teams often shared the same facility. If the playing surface wasn't artificial turf, the fields were usually ripped apart and shoddy. The Colts had played the previous two Sundays at Memorial, and the field was not in the best of shape. It was a problem that the Pirates had encountered in the past. In 1971, before the series that year, Buccos great Roberto Clemente had complained that the turf in Memorial Stadium was bad, with holes everywhere.[11] Somehow, some way, the field was deemed ready, although the less-than-perfect infield led to a combined six errors by both teams.

Despite the flawed conditions, the home team came out and came out strong: they plated five runs before the series was one inning old. The poor field came into play immediately. After Al Bumby singled and Mark Belanger walked to open up the first inning, Eddie Murray forced a one-out walk off Pittsburgh starter Bruce Kison to load the bases. John Lowenstein came up next and hit what appeared to be an inning-ending double-play ball to Phil Garner, but the cold affected Garner's grip and he threw the ball away, leading to the first two Orioles runs.

Kison then unleashed a wild pitch, scoring Murray with the game's third run. Doug DeCinces, who would commit two errors on this cold evening, smacked a homer, giving Baltimore a 5–0 advantage. Following the homer, Kison gave up a single and left the hill after a third of an inning. Jim Rooker came in, getting Rick Dempsey and Oriole starter Mike Flanagan to end the first, but the damage had already been done. Pittsburgh had spent the season battling back, but had they now dug themselves into too big a hole?

While Rooker calmed the jittery Pirates down, holding Baltimore scoreless over the next 3⅔ innings, Flanagan zipped through the Pittsburgh lineup, giving up only a first inning double to Dave Parker. The Bucs finally broke through in the fourth as Tim Foli and Parker led off with singles, moving into scoring position when Bill Robinson grounded to third. Willie Stargell knocked in the Pirates' first run, grounding out to second. For Stargell, the day had been a bad one to this point. It was reported that while the veteran slugger was at the park, his hotel room was broken into, costing the Pirates' leader $2,500 in cash, three books of checks, jewelry and some clothes.[12]

Pittsburgh inched even closer in the sixth as the infield again reared its ugly head. Parker and Robinson started the inning with singles before Flanagan retired Stargell and Madlock. Catcher Steve Nicosia hit a chopper to DeCinces. The Baltimore third baseman failed to hold on to the third out, and instead of the Orioles going into the dugout with a four-run lead, the bases were now loaded. Garner made up for his first-inning miscue with a two-run single, making the game 5–3.

Throughout the contest, the underrated heroes were the Buccos' relievers. Rooker, Enrique Romo, Don Robinson and Grant Jackson three-hit Baltimore over the final 7⅓ innings to give Pittsburgh an opportunity to come back, but they still needed two runs to do so. Stargell took care of one of them in the eighth, when the National League's co-MVP smacked a homer off a Flanagan curveball, making it just a one-run contest. The Oriole hurler decided on the sidearm curve because it was the pitch he had struck Pops out with in the second inning, but Stargell had adjusted to it.[13]

The Pirates bats had only one inning left to tie the game. Parker got things going with a one-out single and then, trying to steal second, advanced to that base when he kicked the ball out of Belanger's glove. The Cobra went to third on a ground out by Robinson, the game tying run now 90 feet away. To further complicate the Orioles' problems, Stargell was coming to the plate. Baltimore manager Earl Weaver decided to keep Flanagan in to face the future Hall of Famer who had made a hobby in 1979 out of getting clutch hits in situations just like this. Flanagan decided to throw a fastball to Willie instead of a curve like the one Stargell had deposited over the wall the inning before. Instead of leading the Pirates to an exciting first win, Starg popped up to Belanger to end the contest, sending the Bucs to their first loss of the '79 postseason.

BOX SCORE
October 10, 1979 (D) at Memorial Stadium

```
PIT N    0    0    0    1    0    2    0    1    0    -    4    11   3
BAL A    5    0    0    0    0    0    0    0    x    -    5    6    3
```

Batting

Pittsburgh Pirates	AB	R	H	RBI	BB	K	PO	A
Moreno cf	5	0	0	0	0	2	4	0
Foli ss	5	1	1	0	0	0	1	3
Parker rf	5	1	4	0	0	0	3	0
B. Robinson lf	5	1	1	0	0	1	2	0
Stargell 1b	5	1	1	2	0	2	7	0
Madlock 3b	3	0	0	0	1	0	0	1
Nicosia c	4	0	0	0	0	1	4	1
Garner 2b	4	0	3	2	0	1	3	2

	AB	R	H	RBI	BB	K	PO	A
Kison p	0	0	0	0	0	0	0	1
Rooker p	1	0	0	0	0	0	0	2
Sanguillen ph	1	0	0	0	0	0	0	0
Romo p	0	0	0	0	0	0	0	0
Lacy ph	1	0	0	0	0	0	0	0
D. Robinson p	0	0	0	0	0	0	0	0
Stennett ph	1	0	1	0	0	0	0	0
Jackson p	0	0	0	0	0	0	0	0
Totals	40	4	11	4	1	7	24	10

Fielding

DP: 1; E: Foli (1), Stargell (1), Garner (1).

Batting

2B: Parker (1, off Flanagan); Garner (1, off Flanagan); **HR:** Stargell (1, 8th inning off Flanagan 0 on, 0 out).

Baserunning

CS: Parker (1, 2nd base by Flanagan/Dempsey).

Baltimore Orioles	AB	R	H	RBI	BB	K	PO	A
Bumbry cf	4	1	1	0	0	0	3	0
Belanger ss	3	1	0	0	1	1	1	4
Singleton rf	3	0	1	0	1	0	2	0
Murray 1b	2	1	1	0	2	0	12	1
Lowenstein lf	4	1	0	1	0	1	1	0
Roenicke lf	0	0	0	0	0	0	0	0
DeCinces 3b	3	1	1	2	1	0	0	4
Smith 2b	2	0	1	0	1	0	1	3
Dauer ph, 2b	1	0	1	0	0	0	0	1
Dempsey c	4	0	0	0	0	0	7	0
Flanagan p	4	0	0	0	0	2	0	2
Totals	30	5	6	3	6	4	27	15

Fielding

E: Belanger (1), DeCinces 2 (2).

Batting

HR: DeCinces (1, 1st inning off Kison 1 on, 1 out); **SH:** Bumbry (1, off Rooker); **IBB:** Smith (1, by Romo).

Baserunning

SB: Murray (1, 2nd base off Romo/Nicosia).

Pitching

Pittsburgh Pirates	IP	H	HR	R	ER	BB	K
Kison L (0–1)	0.1	3	1	5	4	2	0
Rooker	3.2	2	0	0	0	1	2
Romo	1	0	0	0	0	2	0
D. Robinson	2	0	0	0	0	1	1
Jackson	1	1	0	0	0	0	1
Totals	8	6	1	5	4	6	4

Baltimore Orioles	IP	H	HR	R	ER	BB	K
Flanagan W (1–0)	9	11	1	4	2	1	7

WP: Kison (1); **IBB:** Romo (1, Smith); **Umpires:** Neudecker, Engel, Goetz, Tata; **Time of Game:** 3:18; **Attendance:** 53,735.

Game Two

There had been two constants to this point for the Bucs in the 1979 postseason: most of the games were exciting and most were affected by poor weather. In game two both conditions would occur again, as Pittsburgh won a thrilling 3–2 contest in the pouring rain to even the Fall Classic at one game apiece, this time with the help of a legend from the Pirates' past.

Unknown to most Pirates fans, there was another factor that would help the Bucs for the rest of the series. According to veteran hurler Jim Rooker, speaking at a SABR meeting in 2003, most of the Pirates pitchers threw out the scouting reports on the Orioles' hitters prior to game two. "I got together with Blyleven and some of the other pitchers before game two. The reports on the Oriole hitters were wrong. They were telling us to pitch to low ball hitters low and high ball hitters high. If we'd used those reports, we would have gotten killed."

In an attempt to even things up following the 5–4 loss the previous evening, the Black and Gold plated two quick runs in the top of the second as Willie Stargell and John Milner opened up the frame with singles, putting men on first and second. Bill Madlock, the former NL batting champion, laced a single on a 2–1 pitch off Oriole starter Jim Palmer, to score Pops with the game's first run. Catcher Ed Ott, up next, lofted a fly to center to put Pittsburgh up, 2–0.

Future Hall of Famer Eddie Murray smacked a homer to lead off Baltimore's half of the second, cutting the Pirates' advantage in half. At that point, Palmer and Buccos hurler Bert Blyleven settled down, silencing both offenses until the sixth inning.

Ken Singleton led off the Baltimore sixth with a single and scored when Murray knocked in his second run of the game with a double. After moving to third on a Doug DeCinces grounder, Murray was sent home by Orioles third base coach Cal Ripken, Sr., when John Lowenstein lined a ball to Pirates right fielder Dave Parker. The young star found out what so many had before him; that Parker had a gun for an arm. The Cobra, who was named MVP of the Midsummer Classic earlier in the year primarily for tossing two runners out, threw a strike to Ott nailing Murray out at home. "We're trying to force their hand, make them make the play," Baltimore manager Earl Weaver stated, when asked why Ripken sent the Oriole great.[14]

After the Pirates escaped with the score knotted at two, it was Baltimore's turn to try to escape danger in the top half of the seventh. Palmer was able to get the first batter of the inning; then Madlock reached base on an infield hit and went to second on DeCinces' third error of the series on the throw. Following a strikeout of Ott, the Hall of Fame hurler walked Garner intentionally before issuing a base on balls to pinch hitter Mike Easler, loading the bases.

Up to the plate came centerfielder Omar Moreno. Moreno had not been at the top of his game in the series to this point, prompting some to refer to him as "Omar the Outmaker." He didn't disappoint his critics this at-bat, striking out; this brought his two-game total of Pirates left on base to 11.[15]

The Orioles mounted a threat as reliever Don Robinson walked the bases loaded in the top of the seventh, only to strike out Singleton and turn Baltimore away with nothing to show for their efforts.

In the top of the ninth, Bill Robinson started off the inning with a single. Then it was time for the managerial chess game. Weaver went to his bullpen to bring in his ace Don Stanhouse, while Pirates manager Chuck Tanner pulled the speedy Matt Alexander from the bench to replace Robinson at first. Oriole catcher Rick Dempsey pegged Alexander out at second on a stolen base attempt, and then Stanhouse got Madlock to fly out to center. With two outs and nobody on, Ott singled on a 2–2 pitch. Stanhouse then walked Garner, prompting Tanner to call on an old vet to pinch hit for Robinson.

Manny Sanguillen had been a key member of the Pirates' championship clubs of the early 1970s, hitting over .300 on four occasions. Ironically, Sangy was traded to Oakland so Bucs general manager Harding Peterson could obtain manager Chuck Tanner after the 1976 campaign. Peterson retrieved Sangy in April of 1978 for three players who had not figured in the Pirates' plans, but by now the former All-Star was at the end of his career, hitting only .230 in 74 at-bats in the regular season. Manny was known as a free swinger throughout his career, and Stanhouse was trying to take advantage of that. He worked the count to 1–2, but the 35-year-old catcher kept battling back, fouling off four consecutive pitches. Finally the Baltimore hurler threw an outside slider that Sanguillen smacked into right field for a hit. "I was just trying to make contact," Manny smiled after the contest.[16]

Sangy getting a hit was only the first part of the equation; the second was for Ed Ott to make it home. Ott was not exactly Maury Wills reincarnated, and it was not a foregone conclusion that he would score. Singleton took Sanguillen's hit in right and rifled it home. Thinking it was off line, Murray cut it off at first and tossed it to Dempsey at home. Ott slid in before Dempsey could tag him, giving the Bucs a 3–2 advantage.

Kent Tekulve put the O's away one, two, three in the bottom half of the ninth for his first save of the series, tying the Fall Classic. For the game's hero, Manny Sanguillen, the only thought he had was for his close friend Roberto Clemente, who perished in a 1972 New Year's Eve plane accident. "I have him in my heart. Anything we do we're going to do for him," Sangy said afterwards.[17] It was the popular Panamanian catcher's last of many days in the sun in a Black and Gold uniform, one that Pirate fans will remember for a long time.

BOX SCORE
October 11, 1979 (D) at Memorial Stadium

PIT N	0	2	0	0	0	0	0	0	1	–	3	11	2
BAL A	0	1	0	0	0	1	0	0	0	–	2	6	1

Batting

Pittsburgh Pirates	AB	R	H	RBI	BB	K	PO	A
Moreno cf	5	0	1	0	0	2	1	0
Foli ss	4	0	1	0	0	0	0	5
Parker rf	4	0	1	0	0	0	1	1
Stargell 1b	4	1	1	0	0	1	12	0
Milner lf	3	1	1	0	0	0	3	0
B. Robinson ph	1	0	1	0	0	0	0	0
Alexander pr, lf	0	0	0	0	0	0	0	0
Madlock 3b	4	0	2	1	0	0	0	4
Ott c	3	1	1	1	0	1	6	0
Garner 2b	2	0	1	0	2	0	4	6
Blyleven p	2	0	0	0	0	0	0	0
Easler ph	0	0	0	0	1	0	0	0
D. Robinson p	0	0	0	0	0	0	0	1
Sanguillen ph	1	0	1	1	0	0	0	0
Tekulve p	0	0	0	0	0	0	0	0
Totals	33	3	11	3	3	4	27	17

Fielding

DP: 3; E: Foli (2), Parker (1).

Batting

SF: Ott (1, off Palmer); **IBB:** Garner (1, by Palmer).

Baserunning

CS: Madlock (1, 2nd base by Palmer/Dempsey); Alexander (1, 2nd base by Stanhouse/Dempsey).

Baltimore Orioles	AB	R	H	RBI	BB	K	PO	A
Bumbry cf	5	0	0	0	0	1	5	0
Belanger ss	3	0	0	0	0	0	1	2
Crowley ph	0	0	0	0	1	0	0	0
T. Martinez p	0	0	0	0	0	0	0	0
Stanhouse p	0	0	0	0	0	0	0	0
Singleton rf	4	1	1	0	0	1	1	0
Murray 1b	3	1	3	2	1	0	10	2
DeCinces 3b	4	0	0	0	0	0	0	6
Lowenstein lf	3	0	1	0	1	0	1	0
Smith 2b	4	0	0	0	0	0	3	0
Dempsey c	3	0	1	0	1	1	4	2
Palmer p	2	0	0	0	0	1	1	1
Kelly ph	0	0	0	0	1	0	0	0
Garcia ss	1	0	0	0	0	1	1	0
Totals	32	2	6	2	5	5	27	13

Fielding

DP: 2; **E:** DeCinces (3).

Batting

2B: Murray (1, off Blyleven); **HR:** Murray (1, 2nd inning off Blyleven 0 on, 0 out).

Pitching

Pittsburgh Pirates	IP	H	HR	R	ER	BB	K
Blyleven	6	5	1	2	2	2	1
D. Robinson W (1–0)	2	1	0	0	0	3	2
Tekulve SV (1)	1	0	0	0	0	0	2
Totals	9	6	1	2	2	5	5

Baltimore Orioles	IP	H	HR	R	ER	BB	K
Palmer	7	8	0	2	2	2	3
T. Martinez	1	1	0	0	0	0	1
Stanhouse L (0–1)	1	2	0	1	1	1	0
Totals	9	11	0	3	3	3	4

WP: Palmer (1); **IBB:** Palmer (1, Garner); **Umpires:** Engel, Goetz, Tata, McKean; **Time of Game:** 3:13 **Attendance:** 53,739

Game Three

In 1971, the Pirates had come back to Three Rivers Stadium down two games to none to the Baltimore Orioles, in search of a miracle to win the World Series. They found that miracle in their own home park, taking the next three contests, eventually winning the title in seven games. Eight years later they avoided such a predicament by winning game two in Memorial Stadium, 3–2, to even the series at a game apiece. To follow the logic of 1971, the Bucs could win the World Championship in their own stadium by winning the next three games. After all, on paper, the '71 Orioles team had been stronger than the one that entered the field this evening. Even though shortstop Kiko Garcia was not in the same league Brooks and Frank Robinson, as the '71 legends, he would do something that neither was able to do in the past: lead his club to a victory in the Steel City as Baltimore came from behind to crush Pittsburgh 8–4.

Garcia had wrestled playing time away from Mark Belanger during the season and had set an ALCS record by handling 11 chances at short during game two against the Angels, but he had come into this contest as the only player in the majors with more errors than RBIs, 27 to 24.[18] Furthermore, Earl Weaver, the Hall of Fame Orioles manager, decided to go with defense earlier in the series and had tabbed Belanger to start the first two games. Garcia would not let his opportunity go by, becoming only the sixth player in World Series history to reach base safely five times in a game going 4-for-4 with a walk, two runs and four RBIs, 16.7% of his entire '79 output—which it took him 417 at-bats to amass.[19]

The other hero of the contest would be the master himself, Earl Weaver. Weaver had seen his club be out-hit 22–12 in the first two games and was not going to stay pat. He changed half of his lineup, replacing lefty Al Bumbry in center with Ron Roenicke, Belanger, of course, with Garcia, left hander John Lowenstein in left with righty Benny Ayala, and switch hitter Billy Smith at second with Rich Dauer. This gave the legendary O's skipper a lineup of all right handers against the Bucs southpaw John Candelaria.[20] It was a move that, while not working out the beginning, would prove to be a genius strategy by game's end.

Pittsburgh started the contest (picking up where they left off in 1971) by dominating the Birds and threatening to make 1979 a very short Fall Classic. Omar Moreno, who had been a goat in the series so far, stranding 11 runners in the first two games, opened the Bucs' half of the first with a double off Baltimore starter Scott McGregor. McGregor balked Moreno to third, and Dave Parker brought him home with a one-out sacrifice fly to score the first run of the game.

In the next inning Willie Stargell and Steve Nicosia singled, putting men on first and second with one out. "Scrap Iron" Phil Garner came up next and doubled both runners home giving Pittsburgh a 3–0 advantage. Garner tried to take one base too many and was thrown out in a run down going to third on the hit. The miscue cost the Bucs a run as Candelaria singled to center.

Baltimore's new lineup finally awoke in the third, as rain began to fall on Three Rivers Stadium once again. Garcia walked with one out, sending up left fielder Ayala. Ayala cranked the ball over the farthest point of the Three Rivers wall in center, cutting the Pirates' lead to a single run. The O's weren't done, though; Ken Singleton singled and Eddie Murray walked, putting men on first and second with two outs when Roenicke singled to left field. Bill Robinson picked up the ball and pegged a throw to Nicosia in time to tag out Singleton at home plate, preserving the Buccos' lead for the time being.

After the Baltimore threat ended in the top of the third, a downpour began. The umpires held up the game for 67 minutes until the rain finally subsided. When the players returned to the field it was a different contest, one where the new Orioles lineup suddenly resembled Murderers' Row.

McGregor came out strong after the delay and put the Bucs down in order in the bottom half of the third. Candelaria was not so lucky: Baltimore lit him up in the top of the fourth. Dauer opened the inning with a double, going to third on Rick Dempsey's single. The Oriole pitcher bounced a chopper to Bucs shortstop Tim Foli, who couldn't handle it, loading the bases for Garcia. The game's hitting star sliced the ball to the right centerfield wall, clearing the bases with a triple. Pittsburgh manager Chuck Tanner had seen enough and brought in right handed setup man Enrique Romo to face Ayala. Weaver countered by bringing up the left handed Bumbry, whom Romo hit putting men on first and third. Singleton then singled making the game 6–3 and sending the speedy Bumbry to third. Bumbry came home on a force play after Doug DeCinces hit a ball to Foli, who threw Singleton out at second. Romo got out of the inning soon after but the damage had already been done with Baltimore now up 7–3.

The Oriole hurler had settled down, in the three innings since the rain delay, retiring all but one batter through five. Baltimore threatened in the fifth, loading the bases on a McGregor walk and singles by Garcia and Bumbry, but Romo got Singleton to fly out to Moreno, holding the O's to no runs in the inning.

Pittsburgh would finally get to the Birds' starter in the sixth when Bill Madlock knocked in Stargell, who had doubled with the Pirates' fourth run of the contest. But Baltimore ran it back up to a four-run advantage in the next frame as Garcia knocked in run number four with a single plating Dempsey, who had doubled.

The game was over at that point. McGregor retired the last nine batters, giving the Orioles the chance to play at home again in 1979. The 8–4 victory ended the hex Pittsburgh had on Baltimore in the Steel City.

BOX SCORE
October 12, 1979 (D) at Three Rivers Stadium

BAL A	0	0	2	5	0	0	1	0	0	–	8	13	0
PIT N	1	2	0	0	0	1	0	0	0	–	4	9	2

Batting

Baltimore Orioles	AB	R	H	RBI	BB	K	PO	A
Garcia ss	4	2	4	4	1	0	0	4
Ayala lf	2	1	2	2	0	0	0	0
Bumbry ph, cf	2	1	1	0	0	0	2	0
Singleton rf	5	0	2	1	0	1	4	0
Murray 1b	4	0	0	0	1	0	7	1
DeCinces 3b	5	0	0	1	0	1	0	1
Roenicke cf, lf	5	0	1	0	0	2	5	1
Dauer 2b	5	1	1	0	0	1	2	3
Dempsey c	5	2	2	0	0	1	7	0
McGregor p	3	1	0	0	1	1	0	0
Totals	40	8	13	8	3	7	27	10

Batting

2B: Garcia (1, off Candelaria); Dauer (1, off Candelaria); Dempsey (1, off Romo); **3B:** Garcia (1, off Candelaria); **HR:** Ayala (1, 3rd inning off Candelaria 1 on, 1 out); **HBP:** Bumbry (1, by Romo).

Pittsburgh Pirates	AB	R	H	RBI	BB	K	PO	A
Moreno cf	4	1	2	0	0	1	2	1
Foli ss	4	0	0	0	0	0	0	6
Parker rf	3	0	0	1	0	1	2	0
B. Robinson lf	4	0	1	0	0	2	4	1
Stargell 1b	4	2	2	0	0	1	8	1
Madlock 3b	4	0	1	1	0	1	0	0
Nicosia c	4	1	1	0	0	0	8	0
Garner 2b	4	0	1	2	0	0	2	1
Candelaria p	1	0	1	0	0	0	0	0
Romo p	1	0	0	0	0	0	0	1
Jackson p	0	0	0	0	0	0	0	0
Lacy ph	1	0	0	0	0	0	0	0
Tekulve p	0	0	0	0	0	0	1	0
Totals	34	4	9	4	0	6	27	11

Fielding

E: Foli (3), Stargell (2).

Batting

2B: Moreno 2 (2, off McGregor 2); Garner (2, off McGregor); Stargell (1, off McGregor); **SF:** Parker (1, off McGregor).

Pitching

Baltimore Orioles	IP	H	HR	R	ER	BB	K
McGregor W (1–0)	9	9	0	4	4	0	6

Pittsburgh Pirates	IP	H	HR	R	ER	BB	K
Candelaria L (0–1)	3	8	1	6	5	2	2
Romo	3.2	5	0	2	2	1	4
Jackson	0.1	0	0	0	0	0	0
Tekulve	2	0	0	0	0	0	1
Totals	9	13	1	8	7	3	7

WP: Romo (1); **BK:** McGregor (1); **HBP:** Romo (1, Bumbry); **Umpires:** Goetz, Tata, McKean, Runge; **Time of Game:** 2:51 **Attendance:** 50,848.

Game Four

It would now be up to the Bucs' Jim Bibby to see if he could quiet the suddenly hot Baltimore Oriole bats and even up the series for the Pirates. A loss would almost eliminate Pittsburgh from the World Series, as the odds of a comeback after being down three games to one were not very high. With a win, though, the Pirates would be right back in the Fall Classic.

Like the previous contest, Pittsburgh wanted to make a statement early, which they did. The hope this time, though, was that the starting pitching wouldn't fall apart as it had in both Pirates losses. After 1½ uneventful innings, the Pirates bats started swinging and with a vengeance.

Willie Stargell started off the proceedings with a 400-foot shot to straight away center. The clout was followed by a single off the bat of John Milner and a double by the Mad Dog, Bill Madlock. With men at second and third, catcher Ed Ott doubled in two runs before Phil Garner singled for the fifth straight hit off starter Dennis Martinez. Unfortunately for the Bucs, third base coach Joe Lonnett and Ott were not on the same page.[21] The Buccos' catcher had taken two steps towards second on the hit and was surprised when he saw Lonnett give him the green light to go home. Ott thought that the Baltimore centerfielder had dropped the ball, but was stunned to see that he had not. He was tagged out on a rundown between third and home.

3. The Postseason

To his credit, the Pirates third base coach took the responsibility for the unfortunate episode, explaining, "You can run on Bumbry's arm, but I'll take the blame for the play. I'm not supposed to make the first out of the inning at home plate."[22]

Orioles manager Earl Weaver decided he had seen enough from Martinez and signaled for reliever Sammy Stewart. The man they had dubbed Omar the Outmaker only two games earlier, Omar Moreno, met Stewart with a single that scored Garner and that would have also plated Ott and given the Bucs a five-run lead instead of a 4–0 advantage.

These Birds were a resilient bunch. In 1979, they came back to win 37 times after trailing in the seventh inning and beyond, so they were a team that could never be counted out.[23] They promptly responded to the Bucs' four second-inning runs by coming up with three of their own in the top of the third off Bibby. With two on and one out in the frame, the hero of the series to date, shortstop Kiko Garcia, kept up his hot hitting with his fifth hit in his last six at-bats, doubling in both O's runners to cut the Bucs' lead in half. Ken Singleton made it a one-run game with a double to left center to bring in Garcia. Bibby then bore down, striking out Eddie Murray and getting Doug DeCinces on a flyball to Milner to end the threat with the Bucs still on top, 4–3.

Not wanting to squander their early lead, Pittsburgh tried to add to their run total in the fourth, loading the bases on a single by Tim Foli, a double by Stargell and an intentional walk to Milner. Up to the plate came Bill Madlock to try and put a quick end to the game with only one out. Instead of becoming a hero, Madlock became a goat, bouncing into a 4–6–3 inning-ending double play to keep the contest a one-run game.

While Bibby had temporarily put a cap on the Baltimore offense, Pittsburgh kept the heat on, this time against Steve Stone, who had come into the game in the top of the fifth. Stone promptly walked Foli, then gave up a single to Dave Parker. After Stargell popped up to third, Milner doubled to right, scoring Foli with the Bucs' fifth run. The Oriole hurler walked Madlock to load the bases with only one out before getting Ott and Garner to end the inning with the Pirates scoring only one run. Two innings, loading the bases with less than two outs, and the Pirates had only come up with a single run. They were wasted opportunities that would soon bite back at the Black and Gold.

The Bucs added another one in the sixth on a single by Foli and a double by Parker, opening up the lead to three. The way the bullpen had been pitching during the postseason, it was a lead that seemed insurmountable.

First Bibby, then Grant Jackson, got Pittsburgh through the seventh with their 6–3 lead safe in hand. Then Pirates manager Chuck Tanner called on Don Robinson (who had adapted well to his roll in the bullpen during the postseason after spending most of the campaign as a starter) to start the eighth inning. The hot-hitting Garcia greeted Robby with a single to start the frame. Singleton then singled to left before DeCinces worked a one-out walk to load the bases. Tanner decided to go to the man he had trusted so many times during the season, side armed closer Kent Tekulve, who had saved 31 games during the season and had not given up a run in the '79 postseason so far. Ironically, this obvious move played right into Weaver's hands.

"We figured early that Tekulve would be the guy in there once the game was on the line. So we saved our three left-handed pinch hitters," Weaver stated after the contest.[24] Tekulve was not at his best against left handed hitters, and Baltimore had three lefties on the bench. Weaver's strategy once again proved to be of genius quality. First came up John Lowenstein, who doubled to right, scoring two runs to cut the three-run lead to one. Then switch-hitting Billy Smith was walked intentionally, to load the bases. Due next was the right–hand hitting catcher Dave Skaggs. Weaver went to his third consecutive pinch hitter, this time Terry Crowley, another lefty. Crowley batted only 63 times in 1979, but hit .317 in those few opportunities. The 32-year-old Crowley did not disappoint. He smacked a double to right, scoring two more runs to give the O's a 7–6 lead, their first of the game. It was at this point Weaver made a controversial move, allowing Tim Stoddard, his pitcher, to bat. An American League pitcher had not had a hit in the previous four World Series (back then the leagues alternated every other year between pitchers batting and each team getting a designated hitter). Stoddard himself had never had a hit in professional baseball, seldom getting the chance to bat even in the minor leagues. The Bucs were falling apart now, as Teke suffered the embarrassment of giving up a single to the pitcher that scored Billy Smith. Five runs in and only one out, Al Bumbry knocked in the Orioles' sixth run of the eighth when he grounded into a force that scored Crowley with the game's final run. Mercifully, Teke struck out Garcia to end the carnage.

Pittsburgh had now blown significant leads in two consecutive games, but they had gotten 14 hits in seven innings against the Oriole pitchers, and they would now have to dig deep in order to come back in the game. Moreno got a two-out single in the eighth only to be stranded, giving the Bucs only three more outs in the contest. In the ninth, Stargell got aboard on a single before Madlock singled to center, putting the tying run up to bat in Ed Ott with two outs. After allowing a long foul ball into the right field bullpen, Stoddard ended the contest by striking out Ott, giving the Orioles a superior three-games-to-one advantage.

For the Pirates, their home end of the World Series had gone horribly wrong. Their dream of ending the series in five was still a possibility, but it would not be the ending they had envisioned, with the O's only one game away from their first title since 1970. Perhaps the Pirate who was most frustrated was second baseman Phil Garner. "They kicked our butts today. I've never seen so many bullets, so many balls hit so hard, so many chinks into the holes in my whole life. They're the greatest ball club I have ever seen," said the snake bitten second baseman after the disappointing contest.[25] Their greatness was still up for debate, but they certainly appeared capable of ending the Bucs' run in 1979.

BOX SCORE
October 13, 1979 (D) at Three Rivers Stadium

BAL A	0	0	3	0	0	0	0	6	0	-	9	12	0
PIT N	0	4	0	0	1	1	0	0	0	-	6	17	1

Batting

Baltimore Orioles	AB	R	H	RBI	BB	K	PO	A
Bumbry cf	5	1	1	1	0	0	1	1
Garcia ss	5	2	2	2	0	2	6	5
Belanger ss	0	0	0	0	0	0	0	0
Singleton rf	5	0	3	1	0	1	0	0
Murray 1b	5	1	0	0	0	2	8	1
DeCinces 3b	1	1	0	0	4	0	2	0
Roenicke lf	3	0	0	0	0	1	2	0
Lowenstein ph, lf	2	1	1	2	0	0	1	0
Dauer 2b	3	0	1	0	0	0	1	2
Smith ph, 2b	0	1	0	0	1	0	0	0
Skaggs c	3	1	1	0	0	0	2	2
Crowley ph	1	0	1	2	0	0	0	0
Dempsey pr, c	0	1	0	0	0	0	3	0
D. Martinez p	0	0	0	0	0	0	0	1
Stewart p	1	0	0	0	0	1	1	2
May ph	1	0	0	0	0	1	0	0
Stone p	0	0	0	0	0	0	0	0
Kelly ph	1	0	1	0	0	0	0	0
Stoddard p	1	0	1	1	0	0	0	2
Totals	37	9	12	9	5	8	27	16

Fielding

DP: 2.

Batting

2B: Garcia (2, off Bibby); Singleton (1, off Bibby); Lowenstein (1, off Tekulve); Crowley (1, off Tekulve); **IBB:** Smith (2, by Tekulve).

Baserunning

SB: DeCinces (1, 2nd base off Bibby/Ott).

Pittsburgh Pirates	AB	R	H	RBI	BB	K	PO	A
Moreno cf	5	0	2	1	0	0	2	0
Foli ss	4	2	3	0	1	0	1	5
Parker rf	5	0	2	1	0	1	1	0
Stargell 1b	5	1	3	1	0	1	8	0
Milner lf	3	1	2	1	1	0	2	0
D. Robinson p	0	0	0	0	0	0	0	0
Tekulve p	0	0	0	0	0	0	0	0
Easler ph	1	0	0	0	0	0	0	0
Madlock 3b	3	1	2	0	2	0	0	1
Ott c	5	0	1	2	0	1	8	0
Garner 2b	4	1	2	0	0	0	5	7
Bibby p	3	0	0	0	0	1	0	0
Jackson p	0	0	0	0	0	0	0	0
B. Robinson lf	1	0	0	0	0	1	0	0
Totals	39	6	17	6	4	5	27	13

Fielding

DP: 3; E: Madlock (1).

Batting

2B: Madlock (1, off D. Martinez); Ott (1, off D. Martinez); Stargell (2, off Stewart); Milner (1, off Stone); Parker (2, off Stone); **HR:** Stargell (2, 2nd inning off D. Martinez 0 on, 0 out); **IBB:** Milner (1, by Stewart); Madlock (1, by Stone).

Baserunning

CS: Madlock (2, 2nd base by Stoddard/Skaggs).

Pitching

Baltimore Orioles	IP	H	HR	R	ER	BB	K
D. Martinez	1.1	6	1	4	4	0	0
Stewart	2.2	4	0	0	0	1	0
Stone	2	4	0	2	2	2	2
Stoddard W (1–0)	3	3	0	0	0	1	3
Totals	9	17	1	6	6	4	5

Pittsburgh Pirates	IP	H	HR	R	ER	BB	K
Bibby	6.1	7	0	3	2	2	7
Jackson	0.2	0	0	0	0	0	0
D. Robinson	0.1	2	0	3	3	1	0
Tekulve L (0–1)	1.2	3	0	3	3	2	1
Totals	9.0	12	0	9	8	5	8

IBB: Stewart (1, Milner); Stone (1, Madlock); Tekulve (1, Smith); **Umpires:** Tata, McKean, Runge, Neudecker; **Time of Game:** 3:48 **Attendance:** 50,883

In one of his most daring moves of the postseason, manager Chuck Tanner tabbed 37-year-old veteran Jim Rooker to start game five of the series, with the Bucs facing elimination down three games to one. (Courtesy of the Pittsburgh Pirates.)

Game Five

The odds were firmly against the Pittsburgh Pirates now. Down three games to one, chances were the Bucs would not join the Steelers as world champions in 1979. Only four times before in the 76-year history of the

World Series had a team battled back from such a deficit. Ironically, the Pirates had been involved in two of the four, once when they lost to Boston in 1903 (which was a best-of-nine series) and once in 1925 when they battled back to defeat the Washington Senators.

While some of the Black and Gold had to question whether this season would continue past game five, others still felt that the Bucs were superior to their counterparts from Baltimore. "We've got more talent, we've got better pitching, we've got more power and more speed," stated catcher Ed Ott after the frustrating loss in game 4.[26]

Manager Chuck Tanner put the Bucs' situation in perspective simply: "Our backs are against the wall. We have to put together a three-game winning streak or we run out of tomorrows."[27] Compounding the skipper's woes was the fact that his mother, who had suffered a stroke two weeks earlier, passed away the morning of the fifth game. Tanner's family reminded him that his mother would want him to manage the game that day.[28] With a heavy heart he went about the business of trying to figure out how to keep the Bucs afloat in the series.

It had been a World Series full of long shots coming through in a big way, such as Kiko Garcia knocking in six in the last two games after only garnering 24 RBIs the entire season, and Benny Ayala getting a surprise start in game three and responding with a long home run. In game five, Tanner would choose 37-year-old Jim Rooker, a man who had spent the better part of eight weeks on the disabled list and had won only four of eleven decisions with a 4.59 ERA, to help the Bucs stave off elimination.

Originally, Bruce Kison was scheduled to pitch after a very subpar game one performance, but a troublesome arm suffered in that contest kept him out of the lineup. "I had a reaction to the cold. After the fourth batter, I couldn't make a fist with my hand," Kison conceded.[29]

Rooker would learn of his surprise start not from Tanner but from a sportswriter: "A reporter came up to me and said Good Luck. I thought he was just saying good luck for the Series. Then he told me I would start. I hoped it wasn't a rumor."[30]

It wasn't a rumor. Tanner explained, "He's the only guy I can start. Kison had some numbness in his arm in the cold in Baltimore and it's supposed to be cold [for game five]."[31]

Things got off to a quick start. Garcia led off the first inning with a sharp liner that Rooker stabbed, making a great play. It was the beginning of complete domination for the veteran hurler over the first four innings. He gave up only a walk to Ayala in the fourth after retiring the first ten Orioles. Unfortunately, as well as the Rook was throwing, 23-game winner Mike Flanagan was almost as dominate, allowing only an infield single to Bill Madlock and a double to Bill Robinson over the same period.

After four consecutive scoreless innings, the Orioles finally broke through in the fifth, scoring the game's first run. Gary Roenicke led off the inning, doubling off Rooker, and moved to third when Doug DeCinces singled to right. The veteran lefty then got Rich Dauer to bounce into a 6–4–3 double play, but the damage had been done: Roenicke scored to make it 1–0. Rooker eventually got out of the inning, but the Bucs were down a run. They were facing the leading winner in the American League, and Flanagan was on top of his game.

In the bottom half of the fifth, Tanner sent up Lee Lacy to pinch-hit for Rooker. Even though he lifted the twirler at that point, Rooker had given the team more than they could have expected, allowing only three hits and a run in five innings. The Bucs' manager chose to bypass his usual relief pitchers and gave the ball to Bert Blyleven, the man who originally was slated to start game six. The reason Tanner made the switch at that point instead of starting Blyleven in game six was obvious: if the Pirates didn't come back and win, there would be no game six.

After five listless innings, the Pittsburgh offense finally mounted an attack in the sixth. Tim Foli walked to start the inning and moved to second on Dave Parker's single. Robinson sacrificed them into scoring position before the Bucs tied the game on Willie Stargell's sacrifice fly. Madlock put Pittsburgh ahead with a two-out single to center, scoring Parker.

Now that the Bucs had gotten to Flanagan, Weaver pinch-hit for the soon-to-be Cy Young Award–winner in the top half of the seventh after Rick Dempsey hit a two-out double to center. The O's boss put in Pat Kelly for the Baltimore starter, but Blyleven ended the threat by striking out Kelly.

In the bottom half of the seventh, Pittsburgh continued what they began an inning before with a little two-out lightning. With Moreno aboard first on a force play, Oriole reliever Tim Stoddard tried to pick him off but threw wildly, sending the NL's leader in steals to second. Foli tripled to right center, scoring Moreno. Weaver replaced Stoddard with Tippy Martinez, who gave up a double to Parker, stretching the Buccos' lead to 4–1.

Pittsburgh increased the advantage the following frame, scoring three runs on an RBI single by Phil Garner and a two-run single off the bat of Foli, making the score 7–1 after eight.

Blyleven found the emergency relief work to his liking, giving up three hits in four scoreless innings for the win. On a tough day for the Bucs' manager, his gutsy call to start the oldest man on the Pittsburgh staff paid big dividends. It also gave his team a trip to Baltimore, a trip that 24 hours before had looked very unlikely.

BOX SCORE
October 14, 1979 (D) at Three Rivers Stadium

```
BAL A   0  0  0  0  1  0  0  0  0  -  1   6  2
PIT N   0  0  0  0  0  2  2  3  x  -  7  13  1
```

Batting

Baltimore Orioles	AB	R	H	RBI	BB	K	PO	A
Garcia ss	4	0	0	0	0	0	2	1
Ayala lf	1	0	0	0	1	0	2	0
Bumbry ph, cf	1	0	0	0	1	0	1	0
Singleton rf	4	0	0	0	0	1	0	0
Murray 1b	4	0	0	0	0	0	7	1
Roenicke cf, lf	4	1	1	0	0	1	2	0
DeCinces 3b	4	0	2	0	0	2	1	4
Dauer 2b	3	0	0	0	0	0	2	1
Lowenstein ph	1	0	1	0	0	0	0	0
Dempsey c	3	0	2	0	0	0	7	0
Crowley ph	1	0	0	0	0	0	0	0
Flanagan p	1	0	0	0	1	0	0	2
Kelly ph	1	0	0	0	0	1	0	0
Stoddard p	0	0	0	0	0	0	0	1
T. Martinez p	0	0	0	0	0	0	0	0
Stanhouse p	0	0	0	0	0	0	0	0
Totals	32	1	6	0	3	5	24	10

Fielding

E: Stoddard (1), Stanhouse (1).

Batting

2B: Roenicke (1, off Rooker); Dempsey (2, off Blyleven).

Pittsburgh Pirates	AB	R	H	RBI	BB	K	PO	A
Moreno cf	4	1	0	0	1	2	3	0
Foli ss	4	2	2	3	1	0	3	7
Parker rf	4	1	2	1	1	2	1	0
B. Robinson lf	4	0	1	0	0	0	2	0
Stargell 1b	3	1	1	1	0	0	10	0
Madlock 3b	4	1	4	1	0	0	0	1
Nicosia c	4	0	0	0	0	1	5	0
Garner 2b	4	1	2	1	0	0	2	3
Rooker p	1	0	0	0	0	1	1	0
Lacy ph	1	0	1	0	0	0	0	0
Blyleven p	1	0	0	0	0	0	0	1
Totals	34	7	13	7	3	6	27	12

Bert Blyleven and Steve Nicosia congratulate each other after a convincing 7–1 game five victory, helping the Bucs escape elimination. (Photograph by Nancy Hogue, courtesy of the Pittsburgh Pirates.)

Fielding

DP: 2; E: Garner (2).

Batting

2B: B. Robinson (1, off Flanagan); Parker (3, off T. Martinez); 3B: Foli (1, off Stoddard);

SH: B. Robinson (1, off Flanagan); Blyleven (1, off Stanhouse); **SF:** Stargell (1, off Flanagan); **IBB:** Moreno (1, by Stanhouse); Parker (1, by Stanhouse).

Pitching

Baltimore Orioles	IP	H	HR	R	ER	BB	K
Flanagan L (1–1)	6	6	0	2	2	1	6
Stoddard	0.2	2	0	2	2	0	0
T. Martinez	0.1	2	0	1	1	0	0
Stanhouse	1	3	0	2	2	2	0
Totals	8	13	0	7	7	3	6

Pittsburgh Pirates	IP	H	HR	R	ER	BB	K
Rooker	5	3	0	1	1	2	2
Blyleven W (1–0)	4	3	0	0	0	1	3
Totals	9	6	0	1	1	3	5

IBB: Stanhouse 2 (2, Moreno, Parker); **Umpires:** McKean, Runge, Neudecker, Engel; **Time of Game:** 2:54 **Attendance:** 50,920

Game Six

They say pitching wins pennants. In the first four games of the 1979 World Series, the Pittsburgh Pirates' pitching had been inconsistent, putting the Bucs in a huge hole, down three games to one. It took a monumental effort in game five from their oldest starter, 37-year-old Jim Rooker, to reverse their fortunes. He gave the Pirates a breath of life, sending the Fall Classic back to Baltimore for game six and, the Black and Gold hoped, a seventh and deciding game. Pirates manager Chuck Tanner would call on 25-year-old John Candelaria to try to keep the Family's amazing '79 campaign alive for one more game. The Candy Man had not had a memorable debut in World Series, blowing a 3–0 lead in game three, lasting only three innings and giving up six runs on eight hits. He had ended the season painfully, suffering from chronic back pain and a sore rib cage, but the New York native would bear down in this contest. He and Kent Tekulve, who was coming off one of the most embarrassing performances in his career in game four, would team up to shut out the Orioles 4–0, evening up the series at three games apiece.

Facing the Candy Man was future Hall of Famer Jim Palmer. They engaged in a titanic pitching duel, each throwing shut-out ball through the first six innings. Pittsburgh threatened in the first: Omar Moreno led off the game with a single and went to third on a Tim Foli double with nobody out. But Palmer got Dave Parker to ground to third, holding the runners in place, and then got Stargell to foul out to third and caught John Milner on a grounder back to the mound to escape the first inning unscathed.

Candelaria was hot throughout the first three innings, giving up singles to only Kiko Garcia and Ken Singleton in the first and Rick Dempsey in the third. Palmer matched him after the first, giving up only a second inning two-out single to Phil Garner.

Both clubs would mount threats in the fourth, as Bill Madlock and Milner forced one-out walks while Palmer hit Garner to load the bases with two gone. Fortunately for the Oriole great, he faced Candelaria next and struck out him, to end Pittsburgh's half of the frame. Baltimore did get Ken Singleton to second after a lead-off single, but the inning ended there when Roenicke popped out to Garner.

The teams went out quietly in the fifth and sixth before the fateful top of the seventh for the unlucky Birds from Baltimore. Tanner pulled Candy in the top of the frame, pinch-hitting the right-handed Lee Lacy against the Orioles' righty. Palmer struck out Lacy, almost the only fortunate thing to happen to the Orioles that inning. Moreno, suddenly was on fire, singled to right. It appeared that the inning would be over immediately, as Foli hit a hopper towards the middle of the diamond. But the ball hit off the hurler's glove ever so slightly. Omar had been running with the pitch and shortstop Garcia was coming over to cover second on the stolen base attempt. The ball came off the tip of Palmer's glove strangely, skipped slightly off Garcia's glove (he had taken his eye off the ball for a second), and went through his legs, putting Pirates on first and second instead of ending the inning with a double play.

Earlier in the series, after game four, Garner complained that a higher power was looking over the Orioles, as they were seemingly getting every break. Game six would even out the playing field: all the breaks went in favor of the team wearing the pillbox caps. After Foli's fortuitous hit, Parker hit a line drive towards Orioles second baseman Rich Dauer. Dauer thought the ball was coming towards him as an easy line drive, but it dove down at the last second. The flight of the ball confused the O's second baseman. "It was a knuckleball. I went down on one knee to try and stop it, but once it hit the ground that was the last I saw of it," Dauer said.[32] The ball got past him, scoring Moreno to break the deadlock. Stargell hit a sacrifice fly to score Foli, giving Pittsburgh a 2–0 seventh inning lead. Rather than come out of the frame with the game still scoreless, the snake bitten Palmer was down two.

The Bucs, now fired up, could see a game seven in their sights, and added insurance in the eighth with a one-out single by Ed Ott and a ground rule double by Garner. With both men in scoring position, Bill Robinson laced a liner to left, which scored Ott and Garner, stretching the Pirates' lead to four.

Omar the Outmaker was no more. He was replaced as the most struggling batter in the series by Baltimore's Eddie Murray, who had gone hitless in 17 at-bats, stranding ten runners over that time period through game six.

Tekulve was on his game. He gave up only a meaningless seventh inning two-out single to pinch hitter Billy Smith in his three innings of work, striking out Ken Singleton and Doug DeCinces in the ninth to preserve his second save of the series.

The Baltimore offense, which Weaver had maneuvered so deftly — scoring 24 runs in the first four games including 17 in games three and four — had all of a sudden been rendered useless, plating only one over the last 18 innings. Like Ott, who spoke out after the game four debacle, DeCinces of the Orioles felt his team could reverse the momentum and bring Baltimore the title in a game seven showdown. "Not too many teams have beaten us three times in a row this season, I don't expect the Pirates to do it either," the O's third baseman stated.[33] While not many teams had beaten the Orioles three times in a row, they had never faced a club like the Bucs.

BOX SCORE
October 16, 1979 (D) at Memorial Stadium

PIT N	0	0	0	0	0	0	2	2	0	-	4	10	0
BAL A	0	0	0	0	0	0	0	0	0	-	0	7	1

Batting

Pittsburgh Pirates	AB	R	H	RBI	BB	K	PO	A
Moreno cf	5	1	3	1	0	0	4	0
Foli ss	5	1	2	0	0	0	0	5
Parker rf	4	0	1	1	1	1	3	0
Stargell 1b	4	0	0	1	0	1	8	0
Milner lf	3	0	0	0	1	0	0	0
Tekulve p	1	0	0	0	0	0	0	0
Madlock 3b	3	0	0	0	1	0	1	2
Ott c	4	1	2	0	0	0	6	0
Garner 2b	3	1	2	0	0	0	4	2
Candelaria p	2	0	0	0	0	2	0	1
Lacy ph	1	0	0	0	0	1	0	0
B. Robinson lf	0	0	0	1	0	0	1	0
Totals	35	4	10	4	3	5	27	10

Fielding
DP: 2.

Batting
2B: Foli (1, off Palmer); Garner (3, off Palmer); **SF:** Stargell (2, off Palmer); B. Robinson (1, off Palmer); **HBP:** Garner (1, by Palmer).

Baltimore Orioles	AB	R	H	RBI	BB	K	PO	A
Garcia ss	3	0	1	0	0	0	1	2
Kelly ph	1	0	0	0	0	0	0	0
Belanger ss	0	0	0	0	0	0	0	0
Ayala lf	3	0	0	0	0	0	2	0
Crowley ph	1	0	0	0	0	0	0	0
Stoddard p	0	0	0	0	0	0	1	0
Singleton rf	4	0	3	0	0	1	1	0
Murray 1b	4	0	0	0	0	0	5	1
DeCinces 3b	4	0	0	0	0	1	1	3
Roenicke cf	2	0	0	0	0	0	4	0
Bumbry ph, cf	1	0	0	0	0	0	2	0
Dauer 2b	2	0	1	0	0	0	1	1
Smith ph, 2b	1	0	1	0	0	0	0	0
Dempsey c	3	0	1	0	0	1	7	0
Palmer p	2	0	0	0	0	2	1	0
Lowenstein ph, lf	1	0	0	0	0	1	1	0
Totals	32	0	7	0	0	6	27	7

Fielding

E: Bumbry (1).

Pitching

Pittsburgh Pirates	IP	H	HR	R	ER	BB	K
Candelaria W (1–1)	6	6	0	0	0	0	2
Tekulve SV (2)	3	1	0	0	0	0	4
Totals	9	7	0	0	0	0	6

Baltimore Orioles	IP	H	HR	R	ER	BB	K
Palmer L (0–1)	8	10	0	4	4	3	5
Stoddard	1	0	0	0	0	0	0
Totals	9	10	0	4	4	3	5

HBP: Palmer (1, Garner); **Umpires:** Runge, Neudecker, Engel, Goetz; **Time of Game:** 2:30 **Attendance:** 53,739

Game Seven

It was eerie, the comparison between the two Pirates baseball legends, Willie Stargell and Roberto Clemente. While it's true that one was a defensive wizard who was a .317 lifetime hitter while the other possessed legendary power, when it came to the twilight of their exceptional careers they both used the World Series to not only show the nation what tremendous players they were, but to lift their teams with MVP performances to a world championship. They not only performed spectacularly throughout their respective series, but both hit memorable home runs in the seventh and deciding game to spur the '71 and '79 Bucs to victories in Baltimore's Memorial Stadium.

Stargell's sixth inning two-run homer, which brought home what turned out to be the Series winning run, was the cap to a perfect season. He not only finally won the National League's Most Valuable Player Award, which had eluded him in 1971 and 1973, but followed it up with MVPs in both the NLCS and World Series. It was a clean sweep for the future Hall of Famer, who went 4-for-5 in his memorable final game performance.

The seventh and final game of the World Series is always the most exciting contest in all of sports, and this one would provide the baseball world with a memorable moment. After taking a 3–1 lead in the Fall Classic, the Baltimore offense had fallen on lean times as the suddenly potent Pirates starting rotation limited the O's to one run in games five and six. Pirates manager Chuck Tanner chose Jim Bibby (who pitched decently in game four before the bullpen blew up in the eighth inning) to start, while Orioles skipper Earl Weaver named Scott McGregor, the 13-game winner who tossed a complete game victory in game three.

Pittsburgh had the first opportunities, getting men in scoring position in each of the first two innings. Omar Moreno singled to lead off the contest, going to second on a Tim Foli sacrifice. Stargell got a base hit in the second, getting into scoring position when John Lowenstein, the Oriole left fielder, bobbled the ball. On both occasions though, McGregor got out of the jams, and the game went into the third inning scoreless.

Rich Dauer led off the bottom half of the third for Baltimore and lined Bibby's pitch over the left field wall to give the O's their first lead in three games, 1–0. Had the shot turned the momentum in Baltimore's favor, or could the Family fight back and win their third consecutive game?

Pittsburgh tried in the fourth. Stargell hit a bloop double to left and went to third, Bill Madlock smacked a grounder to Kiko Garcia at short, and Garcia threw wildly to DeCinces in an attempt to get the lead runner. But with men at first and third, the Bucs wasted the opportunity once again. Catcher Steve Nicosia lined out to Dauer, and Phil Garner was called out on runner's interference after he popped up to Eddie Murray at first and collided with the future Hall of Famer inside the foul line.

Two innings later, lady luck finally started shine on the Pirates. Bill Robinson hit a grounder to Garcia that bounced off his glove into left for a single. Up to the plate next came the man who had lifted the team on his shoulders so many times, Willie Stargell. It was a moment when legends are made. Starg took full advantage, smacking a McGregor slider — that didn't slide — deep over the right field fence to put the Bucs up 2–1.

Grant Jackson, who came into the game in the fifth for reliever Don Robinson, put down all six Baltimore batters he faced in the sixth and seventh, sending the game into the eighth with Pittsburgh holding a precarious one-run lead. Pops doubled once again in the top half of the frame for his fourth hit of the game, but McGregor held firm, getting out of the inning with no damage. In the bottom half, the Orioles would make one last challenge, loading the bases as Lee May and Al Bumbry walked. Always a fan of the three-run homer, Weaver batted Benny Ayala for the singles-hitting Garcia, perhaps realizing Tanner would counter with Tekulve. When the Pirates manager did, Weaver chose the left handed hitting Terry Crowley, who had burned Tekulve with a pinch double in game four, to replace Ayala. Tekulve, the master of the inning-ending double play, got a ground ball off Crowley's bat, but it was hit too weakly to even attempt a force out. Garner threw out the pinch hitter, but both runners advanced into scoring position. Tanner put Ken Singleton aboard via an intentional walk, choosing instead to pitch to the dangerous, but slumping, Murray. "With Tekulve throwing the ball the way he was throwing it, I had to go for a force at any base. If I had pitched to Singleton and he had gotten a hit, I would've kicked myself. Besides Murray wasn't hitting well," Tanner told reporters after the game.[34] To say Murray wasn't hitting was an understatement. The O's slugging first baseman was now mired in an 0-for-21 slump, leaving 13 men on base while hitting into two double plays.

The game was up for grabs. It was a moment when Stargell again showed his real worth to the team, one that emphasized what a true leader he was. Tekulve, the tall, lanky reliever who was charged with pitching out of the jam, told the story of the situation at a recent Pirates luncheon. "I was just about ready to pitch to Murray when Stargell comes over to the mound and says, 'You know Teke, the bases are loaded ... you know Eddie Murray's the hitter ... you know Murray's a switch hitter ... you know Murray will probably bat left ... you know you have trouble getting lefties out. I'll tell you what, I'll pitch, you play first.' I lost it, standing behind the mound laughing like hell. I then got Murray out. Willie just thought I needed to forget about the situation and relax."

Get Murray out he did, although it wasn't without a little tension. The Oriole Slugger took the outside fastball to deep right field in front of the warning track where Parker, after initially stumbling, tracked it down, sending Baltimore away still behind 2–1.

The fly ball seemed to take the wind from the Orioles' sails, as Weaver sent in five pitchers—a World Series record—in the top of the ninth. The bevy of Baltimore hurlers were unable to stop the Bucs from scoring much-needed insurance runs. Pittsburgh plated two; one on a Moreno single, scoring Garner, who had doubled; and a second as Dennis Martinez hit Bill Robinson with the bases loaded, giving Pittsburgh a now comfortable 4–1 lead.

After performing well under pressure in the eighth, Tekulve sewed up his third save of the series in easy fashion, striking out Gary Roenicke and Doug DeCinces and getting Pat Kelly to fly out to center. Moreno cradled his flyball softly in his glove for the Fall Classic's final out and the end of the World Series.

With the win, the Bucs did the near impossible, becoming the fourth team in World Series history to recover from a 3–1 deficit in a seven game series to win the title. The joyful citizens of the Steel City went nuts, tens of thousands of Pirates fans celebrating in Market Square and Oakland. The disco song that had become the team's anthem, "We Are Fam-a-lee," blared loudly through the square. Fans sang and danced into the wee hours of the morning, celebrating what was to be the last world championship the team has won to date.

In Baltimore, the police who had been prepared to help control the celebration they had expected since game five went home quietly; the joyous party never would happen.

"We're not quitters, not even when we're down three games to one. Some guys are always coming in and saying a few words. Either Stargell or me or John Milner. Somehow, we always regroup and come back. But we

A leaping Willie Stargell joins his Family in celebrating the Pirates' World Series victory. (Courtesy of the Pittsburgh Pirates.)

"Crazy Horse" Foli lifts the world championship trophy over his cowboy hat. (Courtesy of the Pittsburgh Pirates.)

never change our nature," Parker said when explaining how the Family always fought back.[35]

"We scratched, we worked hard, we depended on each and every one of our 25 men," an emotional Stargell stated in the delirious Pirates' locker room.[36] There was one thing the other 24 Bucs probably wanted to tell their leader, though: that every one of the 24 men depended on him.

Pitcher Kent Tekulve and catcher Steve Nicosia embrace following the final out of the 76th World Series. (Courtesy of the Pittsburgh Pirates.)

BOX SCORE
October 17, 1979 (D) at Memorial Stadium

PIT N	0	0	0	0	0	2	0	0	2	-	4	10	0
BAL A	0	0	1	0	0	0	0	0	0	-	1	4	2

Batting

Pittsburgh Pirates	AB	R	H	RBI	BB	K	PO	A
Moreno cf	5	1	3	1	0	0	4	0
Foli ss	4	0	1	0	0	0	3	1
Parker rf	4	0	0	0	0	2	2	0
B. Robinson lf	4	1	1	1	0	0	2	0
Stargell 1b	5	1	4	2	0	0	6	1
Madlock 3b	3	0	0	0	1	0	2	1
Nicosia c	4	0	0	0	0	0	6	1
Garner 2b	3	1	1	0	1	0	1	2
Bibby p	1	0	0	0	0	0	1	0
Sanguillen ph	1	0	0	0	0	0	0	0
D. Robinson p	0	0	0	0	0	0	0	0
Jackson p	1	0	0	0	0	0	0	0
Tekulve p	1	0	0	0	0	0	0	0
Totals	36	4	10	4	2	2	27	6

Batting

2B: Stargell 2 (4, off McGregor 2); Garner (4, off Stoddard); **HR:** Stargell (3, 6th inning off McGregor 1 on, 1 out); **SH:** Foli (1, off McGregor); **HBP:** Parker (1, by T. Martinez); B. Robinson (1, by D. Martinez); **IBB:** Garner (2, by McGregor); Madlock (2, by McGregor).

Baltimore Orioles	AB	R	H	RBI	BB	K	PO	A
Bumbry cf	3	0	0	0	1	0	0	0
Garcia ss	3	0	1	0	0	0	0	5
Ayala ph	0	0	0	0	0	0	0	0
Crowley ph	1	0	0	0	0	0	0	0
Stoddard p	0	0	0	0	0	0	0	1
Flanagan p	0	0	0	0	0	0	0	0
Stanhouse p	0	0	0	0	0	0	0	0
T. Martinez p	0	0	0	0	0	0	0	0
D. Martinez p	0	0	0	0	0	0	0	0
Singleton rf	3	0	0	0	1	0	1	0
Murray 1b	4	0	0	0	0	2	11	0
Lowenstein lf	2	0	0	0	0	1	2	0
Roenicke ph, lf	2	0	0	0	0	2	1	0
DeCinces 3b	4	0	2	0	0	1	3	3
Dempsey c	3	0	0	0	0	0	3	0
Kelly ph	1	0	0	0	0	0	0	0
Dauer 2b	3	1	1	1	0	0	4	2
McGregor p	1	0	0	0	1	0	1	2
May ph	0	0	0	0	1	0	0	0
Belanger pr, ss	0	0	0	0	0	0	1	1
Totals	30	1	4	1	4	6	27	14

Fielding

DP: 1; **E:** Garcia (1), Lowenstein (1).

Batting

HR: Dauer (1, 3rd inning off Bibby 0 on, 0 out); **IBB:** Singleton (1, by Tekulve).

Baserunning

CS: Garcia (1, 2nd base by Bibby/Nicosia).

Pitching

Pittsburgh Pirates	IP	H	HR	R	ER	BB	K
Bibby	4	3	1	1	1	0	3
D. Robinson	0.2	1	0	0	0	1	0
Jackson W (1–0)	2.2	0	0	0	0	2	1
Tekulve SV (3)	1.2	0	0	0	0	1	2
Totals	9.0	4	1	1	1	4	6

Baltimore Orioles	IP	H	HR	R	ER	BB	K
McGregor L (1–1)	8	7	1	2	2	2	2
Stoddard	0.1	1	0	1	1	0	0
Flanagan	0	1	0	1	1	0	0
Stanhouse	0	1	0	0	0	0	0
T. Martinez	0	0	0	0	0	0	0
D. Martinez	0.2	0	0	0	0	0	0
Totals	9.0	10	1	4	4	2	2

HBP: T. Martinez (1, Parker); D. Martinez (1, B. Robinson); **IBB:** Tekulve (2, Singleton); McGregor 2 (2, Garner, Madlock); **Umpires:** Neudecker, Engel, Goetz, Tata; **Time of Game:** 2:54 **Attendance:** 53,733

4. The Fall of the Family

Back in the 1970s and '80s, one of the most anticipated baseball annuals that fans of the national pastime trusted was the *Complete Handbook of Baseball*, edited by Zander Hollander. In 1980 the book projected that the Pirates would not only repeat their win of the National League East, but make a return trip to the Fall Classic against the California Angels. It was not a very good year for Zander and his boys.

The book went on to claim, "The Bucs have it all, including a manager who maintains enthusiasm from the first day of the season to the last.... This is simply the best all around club in baseball."[1] While they got the part about Tanner's enthusiasm right, and while, in retrospect, this had been the best team in baseball, by the time 1980 had concluded, Pittsburgh was barely an average team.

In the offense, almost every player slumped from his 1979 performance, some drastically. There were many injuries; the foremost was the arthritic knee that the great Willie Stargell suffered throughout the campaign. On August 17, 1980, Stargell played in his 67th game of the season. His Bucs were still in first place in the East, with only a month and a half left.[2] It would be Willie's last game of 1980, and his injured knees were felt deeply in the Steel City as Pittsburgh fell drastically down to third place, a mediocre 83–79, 15 games off their championship pace of only a year before.

Worse than the hitting was the collapse of the pitching staff. The Pirates fell from third in the NL in ERA in 1979 to sixth a year later. The deepest pitching staff in the senior circuit had now become very average. Only Jim Bibby and his 19 wins in '80 improved on his world championship campaign.

This chapter will investigate, player by player, exactly what happened to suddenly end the championship days in 1980. We'll compare each of 1979's main components with that of the league average and the average by position of the senior circuit, then look at the same comparison 12 months later.

THE INFIELD

First Base 1979 Willie Stargell Age 39

Year	Totals	AB	R	HR	RBI	BB	SO	SB	AVG	OPS
1979		424	60	32	82	47	105	0	.281	.904
	Lg Average	410	55	10	51	40	55	9	.269	.738
	Pos Average	417	57	13	62	43	55	5	.279	.782

1980 Willie Stargell Age 40

Year	Totals	AB	R	HR	RBI	BB	SO	SB	AVG	OPS
1980		202	28	11	38	26	52	0	.262	.836
	Lg Average	193	25	4	23	18	26	5	.268	.724
	Pos Average	198	25	5	28	21	24	2	.281	.775

John Milner Age 30

Year	Totals	AB	R	HR	RBI	BB	SO	SB	AVG	OPS
1980		238	31	8	34	52	29	2	.244	.748
	Lg Average	240	31	5	29	22	32	6	.268	.724
	Pos Average	246	31	7	35	26	30	3	.281	.775

Bill Robinson Age 37

Year	Totals	AB	R	HR	RBI	BB	SO	SB	AVG	OPS
1980		272	28	12	36	15	45	1	.287	.783
	Lg Average	272	35	6	32	25	36	6	.268	.724
	Pos Average	278	35	8	40	30	34	3	.281	.775

First Base Analysis. As has been chronicled thousands of times in the past 25 years, Willie Stargell had a legendary 1979 campaign.

A year later Stargell's chronic knee problems, which had plagued him throughout his career, flared up once again. He was in and out of the line throughout the season and packed it in for good on August 17. At that time, Pittsburgh was 67–51 after splitting a double header with the Expos and was in first place. By the end of August the Pirates were in the midst of an eight-game losing streak that sent them into second by September 1. They floundered to a 16–28 record to end the season after the injury.[3] The loss of Stargell not only shortened the Bucco bench but deprived the club of what had given them their championship season: not just a powerful first baseman, but a leader who found a way pick the club up when they needed that extra push. That leadership on the field was obviously missed throughout the final month of the campaign.

Willie's average had fallen off significantly. In 1979 he was 12 points above the league average and two above the average NL first baseman. A year later it had fallen 19 points to .262, six under the NL mean and a full 19 under the first base average. His home run production had slipped even more, from 32 to 11. John Milner, who was Stargell's primary backup after his injury, was no better, dropping 32 points from .276 in 1979 down to .244, while his home runs were cut in half, down to eight. Bill Robinson, who split time with Milner in left the year before, played 49 of his 90 games in the field at first, as Lee Lacy and Mike Easler both hit over .330 and took over in left. Robinson was the most effective first baseman offensively, hitting a solid .287 with 12 homers in 272 at-bats. While effective when he played, injuries put a damper on Robinson's season; a bruised Achilles' heel put him on the shelf for almost a month in August.

While there were many drops in production on this club, Stargell's seemed to be the most dramatic fall of all; he went from MVP numbers in '79 to stats that were far below the NL average for a first baseman.

SECOND BASE

Phil Garner 1979 Age 30

Year	Team	AB	R	HR	RBI	BB	SO	SB	AVG	OPS
1979	Pirates	549	76	11	59	55	74	17	.293	.800
	Lg Average	518	69	13	65	50	69	11	.269	.738
	Pos Average	511	67	7	51	49	59	16	.262	.691

Rennie Stennett Age 28

Year	Team	AB	R	HR	RBI	BB	SO	SB	AVG	OPS
1979	Pirates	319	31	0	24	24	25	1	.238	.581
	Lg Average	335	45	8	42	33	45	7	.269	.738
	Pos Average	330	43	5	33	32	38	10	.262	.691

Phil Garner 1980 Age 31

Year	Team	AB	R	HR	RBI	BB	SO	SB	AVG	OPS
1980	Pirates	548	62	5	58	46	53	32	.259	.673
	Lg Average	558	71	12	67	52	75	13	.268	.724
	Pos Average	549	68	5	49	49	62	18	.260	.6721

Second Base Analysis. After the Bucs acquired Bill Madlock from the Giants, Phil Garner moved to second base, displacing Rennie Stennett, who was struggling offensively. Garner's .293 average was 55 points higher than Stennett's, so instead of having a second baseman who was 24 points under the NL average for second baseman, they had one who was 31 points higher.

Scrap Iron not only had a better average, but also provided more pop, hitting 11 homers as opposed to none for Stennett, and checking in with a .441 slugging percentage compared to .292.

Despite getting off to a great start (finishing April with a .296 average) and making the All-Star Team in 1980, Scrap Iron went in reverse. A shoulder injury in the second half of the year hampered Garner, and his batting average slumped 34 points to .259. Instead of having a dominant average when compared to the average senior circuit second baseman, he now had an inferior one. Worse yet, his homerun production was cut in half as his .441 slugging percentage dropped almost 100 points to .358. While Stargell's loss was dramatic, the fall of Garner's offense also hurt the club.

Garner's greatest season proved to be 1979: his .293 batting average was far and away the highest of his career. Only his .278 mark with the Astros in 1984 would approach that level. In slugging, Scrap's .441 was matched only in 1977. That world championship season was a career year for Garner.

SHORTSTOP

1979 Tim Foli Age 28

Year	Team	AB	R	HR	RBI	BB	SO	SB	AVG	OPS
1979	Mets	7	0	0	0	0	0	0	.000	.000
	Pirates	525	70	1	65	28	14	6	.291	.680
	Totals	532	70	1	65	28	14	6	.288	.670
	Lg Average	531	71	13	66	52	71	11	.269	.738
	Pos Average	513	63	4	44	37	57	11	.254	.641

1980 Tim Foli Age 29

Year	Team	AB	R	HR	RBI	BB	SO	SB	AVG	OPS
1980	Pirates	495	61	3	38	19	23	11	.265	.623
	Lg Average	504	64	11	60	47	67	12	.268	.725
	Pos Average	490	58	4	39	33	57	12	.254	.637

Dale Berra Age 23

Year	Team	AB	R	HR	RBI	BB	SO	SB	AVG	OPS
1980	Pirates	245	21	6	31	16	52	2	.220	.612
	Lg Average	258	33	6	31	24	35	6	.268	.724
	Pos Average	257	32	7	33	24	35	4	.266	.735

Shortstop Analysis. The Pirates dealt incumbent starter Frank Tavares to the Mets for Tim Foli to improve their defense at short, but they got more than they bargained for from Foli's offensive output in 1979.

To say Pittsburgh was surprised was an understatement. The average

4. The Fall of the Family

National League shortstop in 1979 hit only .254, a full 37 points under Foli's production. His average was also 27 points higher than his own previous output, a .264 mark with Montreal in 1976.

While it's fair to say that 1979 was in fact a career year, the Pirates shortstop still was effective in 1980, although he fell 26 points off his 1979 Pirates output. His fielding remained as solid as the year before and his average was still 11 points higher than the average shortstop (he enjoyed the second highest batting average of his major league career).

Injuries played a part in his drop-off. A spike wound suffered in April became infected, sending Foli to the disabled list by the end of May after a poor month where he hit only .225. When he returned he caught fire, hitting .320 in June and July, but a poor .185 September sealed his fate.

Yogi's boy, Dale Berra — the former first-round pick — was the club's primary utility man in the infield but hit an anemic .220 in his first full season in the bigs.

THIRD BASE

1979 Bill Madlock Age 28

Year	Team	AB	R	HR	RBI	BB	SO	SB	AVG	OPS
1979	Giants	249	37	7	41	18	19	11	.261	707
	Pirates	311	48	7	44	34	22	21	.328	.859
	Totals	560	85	14	85	52	41	32	.298	.793
	Lg Average	549	73	14	69	53	74	12	.269	.738
	Pos Average	546	72	12	64	52	67	12	.267	.724

1980 Bill Madlock Age 29

Year	Team	AB	R	HR	RBI	BB	SO	SB	AVG	OPS
1980	Pirates	494	62	10	53	45	33	16	.277	.740
	Lg Average	490	62	11	58	46	66	12	.268	.724
	Pos Average	488	61	13	63	45	66	7	.266	.735

Third Base Analysis. When Peterson traded Al Holland and Ed Whitson to the Giants for Bill Madlock, the move that put the team over the top, taking them from contenders to champions.

The Pirates were little better than a .500 team when the Bucs general manager pulled off the move with the Giants on June 28. They were 62–31 after Madlock got to Pittsburgh, so to say the move made a huge difference to the team is an understatement.[4]

The All-Star third baseman was having a poor season in San Francisco, hitting only .261 at the time of the trade, but the Steel City obviously had a good effect on him. He hit .328 for the Pirates the rest of the campaign, a full 61 points higher than the league average for third base. Better yet, his .469 slugging percentage with the Bucs was 76 points higher than the position norm.

While 1979 was not a career year for the veteran third baseman, it was much better than his 1980 season turned out to be. Injuries played a part in his decline that year. He first suffered with an injured right knee, then hurt a ligament in his left thumb later in the year, requiring off-season surgery. Madlock also received a 15-game suspension for bumping umpire Jerry Crawford with his glove.[5] Bill did rebound after his troubles to hit .306 following the All-Star break.

Mixing all the maladies together, 1980 saw Mad Dog slip to .277, 21 points under his total 1979 average and 51 under the average he turned in for Pittsburgh after the trade, despite the strong second half of the season. His .469 slugging percentage for the Bucs in the title season fell to a miserable .399, seven points less than the average third baseman turned in for 1980.

Bill rebounded after that season to win two batting crowns for the team, but 1980 went down as one of the worst campaigns in Madlock's long and illustrious career.

THE OUTFIELD
Left Field

1979 Bill Robinson Age 36

Year	Team	AB	R	HR	RBI	BB	SO	SB	AVG	OPS
1979	Pirates	421	59	24	75	24	81	13	.264	.806
	Lg Average	425	57	11	53	41	57	9	.269	.738
	Pos Average	431	61	13	60	44	62	11	.278	.780

John Milner Age 29

Year	Team	AB	R	HR	RBI	BB	SO	SB	AVG	OPS
1979	Pirates	326	52	16	60	53	37	3	.276	.848
	Lg Average	321	43	8	40	31	43	7	.269	.738
	Pos Average	325	46	10	45	33	47	8	.278	.780

Lee Lacy Age 31

Year	Team	AB	R	HR	RBI	BB	SO	SB	AVG	OPS
1979	Pirates	182	17	5	15	22	36	6	.247	.739
	Lg Average	181	24	4	23	18	24	4	.269	.738
	Pos Average	183	26	6	26	19	27	5	.278	.780

1980 Mike Easler Age 29

Year	Team	AB	R	HR	RBI	BB	SO	SB	AVG	OPS
1980	Pirates	393	66	21	74	43	65	5	.338	.979
	Lg Average	362	46	8	43	34	49	9	.268	.724
	Pos Average	370	53	10	48	35	53	15	.281	.768

Lee Lacy Age 32

Year	Team	AB	R	HR	RBI	BB	SO	SB	AVG	OPS
1980	Pirates	278	45	7	33	28	33	18	.335	.905
	Lg Average	258	33	6	31	24	35	6	.268	.724
	Pos Average	263	38	7	34	25	38	11	.281	.768

Left Field Analysis. Bright spots were few and far between for the Pirates in 1980; left field was perhaps the one area to shine.

In '79, super-sub Bill Robinson split time with John Milner patrolling left. While Robinson hit only .264, a full 14 points under the league average for left fielders, he not only provided solid defense but power and several clutch hits. Bill hit 24 homers in only 421 at-bats, many in a dramatic manner, while knocking in 75.

Milner also provided the Family a clutch bat while splitting time between first and left, platooning with Robinson. Lacy didn't exactly show the Steel City what was to come, hitting only .247 in a limited roll.

Mike Easler, a 29-year-old player who had been bouncing around the minors, finally became a regular for good in 1980, forcing Milner out of left. The Hitman hit .338 with 21 homers, in only 393 at-bats. Lacy was the other part of the two-headed left field monster that campaign, raising his average 88 points to .335. The two combined for 28 homers and 107 RBIs, giving the Bucs a much needed offensive lift in an otherwise disappointing campaign. Robinson still played some in the outfield, but he and Milner spent most of their season replacing Pops at first, after the club's spiritual leader went down for most of the campaign with an arthritic knee.

Center Field

1979 Omar Moreno Age 26

Year	Team	AB	R	HR	RBI	BB	SO	SB	AVG	OPS
1979	Pirates	695	110	8	69	51	104	77	.282	.714
	Lg Average	681	91	17	85	66	91	15	.269	.738
	Pos Average	690	98	16	82	66	99	29	.277	.752

1980 Omar Moreno Age 27

Year	Team	AB	R	HR	RBI	BB	SO	SB	AVG	OPS
1980	Pirates	676	87	2	36	57	101	96	.249	.631
	Lg Average	712	91	16	85	66	95	17	.268	.724
	Pos Average	714	100	15	77	68	108	34	.270	.726

Center Field Analysis. There was no nicer surprise in 1979 than Omar Moreno. The '79 campaign was Moreno's third full season in the majors, and up to that point he had been no better than a .240 hitter. Omar improved his average 42 points to .282, five points higher than the average center fielder.

Even though he became the first man of the century to steal over 70 bases in three consecutive seasons when he swiped a team record 96 bases in 1980, everything else in Moreno's offensive arsenal returned to its pre-1979 state. His average dropped 33 points to .249, a full 21 points behind the average center fielder, and he scored 23 fewer runs. Part of the decline could be attributed to the dislocated thumb Moreno suffered July 14, which required off-season surgery.

Like Foli and Garner, his other cohorts in the Bucs' so-called up-the-middle defense, Moreno never returned to the level he achieved in 1979, and that championship campaign proved to be Omar's career season.

RIGHT FIELD

1979 Dave Parker Age 28

Year	Team	AB	R	HR	RBI	BB	SO	SB	AVG	OPS
1979	Pirates	622	109	25	94	67	101	20	.310	.906
	Lg Average	571	76	14	71	56	77	12	.269	.738
	Pos Average	581	83	18	78	60	88	14	.279	.782

1980 Dave Parker Age 29

Year	Team	AB	R	HR	RBI	BB	SO	SB	AVG	OPS
1980	Pirates	518	71	17	79	25	69	10	.295	.785
	Lg Average	490	62	11	58	46	66	12	.268	.724
	Pos Average	496	66	14	66	47	76	9	.273	.760

Right Field Analysis. Between 1977 and 1979, there was no better all-around player in baseball than Dave Parker. On offense, he hit over .330 in '77 and '78, capturing the league MVP the latter season; while in right field he combined power and an incredibly powerful, accurate arm.

4. The Fall of the Family

Although his 1979 season was not quite as spectacular as his play the preceeding two years, he still hit .310 with 25 homers, 94 RBIs and a .526 slugging percentage, 90 points higher than the senior circuit's right fielders.

Unfortunately, the Cobra's run ended in 1980, as did that of so many of the Black and Gold players. A variety of maladies haunted Parker throughout the campaign, including a sore knee, a strained back, a bruised Achilles' tendon, a bruised shoulder, and tendonitis in his right elbow. These injuries were part of the reason his average fell under .300 to .295. Parker played through the pain, but it was apparent he was not the same ballplayer, with his homers dropping to 17 and his slugging percentage falling 68 points to .458.

CATCHERS

1979 Ed Ott Age 27

Year	Team	AB	R	HR	RBI	BB	SO	SB	AVG	OPS
1979	Pirates	403	49	7	51	26	62	0	.273	.699
	Lg Average	397	53	10	50	39	53	9	.269	.738
	Pos Average	389	45	9	49	43	55	2	.253	.709

Steve Nicosia Age 23

Year	Team	AB	R	HR	RBI	BB	SO	SB	AVG	OPS
1979	Pirates	191	22	4	13	23	17	0	.288	.799
	Lg Average	183	24	5	23	18	25	4	.269	.738
	Pos Average	180	21	4	23	20	25	1	.253	.709

1980 Ed Ott Age 28

Year	Team	AB	R	HR	RBI	BB	SO	SB	AVG	OPS
1980	Pirates	392	35	8	41	33	47	1	.260	.674
	Lg Average	394	50	9	47	37	53	9	.268	.724
	Pos Average	388	40	8	49	37	51	3	.256	.693

Steve Nicosia 24

Year	Team	AB	R	HR	RBI	BB	SO	SB	AVG	OPS
1980	Pirates	176	16	1	22	19	16	0	.216	.569
	Lg Average	191	24	4	23	18	26	4	.268	.724
	Pos Average	188	20	4	24	18	25	1	.256	.693

Catcher Analysis. The position was different but the theme was still the same: Player has best major league season, player falls flat on his face the following year, helping the team free-fall into mediocrity.

The days of Manny Sanguillen had ended for all intents and purposes, although the former All-Star still took a spot on the 25-man roster. In his place were Ed Ott and Steve Nicosia. Ott was the starter for the most part and turned in a fine .273 average, 20 points ahead of the mean for catchers in 1979, while his partner Nicosia did a bit better, coming in at .288. In slugging percentage, the two finished at .385 and .435 respectively when the average catcher only slugged at a .381 pace.

Like all good things for the Bucs that season, their performances came to an end, although not immediately for Ott. He got off to a fabulous start in 1980, hitting .304 through August 9. He suffered pulled ligaments in his foot, and he hit only .178 the rest of the way, causing his average to slip to .260, still ahead of the league catcher average. Nicosia, on the other hand, never got off to a good start. He fumbled in at a miserable .216. Worse yet for the twosome, their slugging numbers collapsed to .357 and .278 respectively.

Luckily for the franchise, catcher was one position for which the farm system could produce a replacement. A young prospect came in who would turn out to be one of the best backstops in Pittsburgh's long and illustrious history: Tony Pena.

STARTING PITCHERS

1979 Bert Blyleven Age 28

Year	Team	W	L	PCT	CG	IP	H	BB	SO	ERA
1979	Pirates	12	5	.706	4	237.1	238	92	172	3.60
	Lg Average	13	13	.500	8	237.1	240	86	127	4.00

John Candelaria Age 25

Year	Team	W	L	PCT	CG	IP	H	BB	SO	ERA
1979	Pirates	14	9	.609	8	207	201	41	101	3.22
	Lg Average	12	12	.500	7	207	209	75	111	4.00

Bruce Kison Age 29

Year	Team	W	L	PCT	CG	IP	H	BB	SO	ERA
1979	Pirates	13	7	.650	3	172.1	157	45	105	3.19
	Lg Average	10	10	.500	5	172.1	174	63	92	4.00

Don Robinson Age 22

Year	Team	W	L	PCT	CG	IP	H	BB	SO	ERA
1979	Pirates	8	8	.500	4	160.2	171	52	96	3.87
	Lg Average	9	9	.500	5	160.2	163	58	86	4.00

4. The Fall of the Family

Jim Bibby   Age 34

Year	Team	W	L	PCT	CG	IP	H	BB	SO	ERA
1979	Pirates	12	4	.750	4	137.2	110	47	103	2.81
	Lg Average	8	8	.500	4	137.2	139	50	74	4.00

Jim Rooker   Age 36

Year	Team	W	L	PCT	CG	IP	H	BB	SO	ERA
1979	Pirates	4	7	.364	1	103.2	106	39	44	4.60
	Lg Average	6	6	.500	4	103.2	105	38	55	4.00

1980   John Candelaria   Age 26

Year	Team	W	L	PCT	CG	IP	H	BB	SO	ERA
1980	Pirates	11	14	.440	7	233.1	246	50	97	4.01
	Lg Average	13	13	.500	7	233.1	235	81	125	3.84

Jim Bibby   Age 35

Year	Team	W	L	PCT	CG	IP	H	BB	SO	ERA
1980	Pirates	19	6	.760	6	238.1	210	88	144	3.32
	Lg Average	13	13	.500	7	238.1	240	83	127	3.84

Bert Blyleven   Age 29

Year	Team	W	L	PCT	CG	IP	H	BB	SO	ERA
1980	Pirates	8	13	.381	5	216.2	219	59	168	3.82
	Lg Average	12	12	.500	7	216.2	218	75	116	3.84

Don Robinson   Age 23

Year	Team	W	L	PCT	CG	IP	H	BB	SO	ERA
1980	Pirates	7	10	.412	3	160.1	157	45	103	3.99
	Lg Average	9	9	.500	5	160.1	162	56	86	3.84

Rick Rhoden   Age 27

Year	Team	W	L	PCT	CG	IP	H	BB	SO	ERA
1980	Pirates	7	5	.583	2	126.2	133	40	70	3.84
	Lg Average	7	7	.500	4	126.2	128	44	68	3.84

Eddie Solomon   Age 29

Year	Team	W	L	PCT	CG	IP	H	BB	SO	ERA
1980	Pirates	7	3	.700	2	100.1	96	37	35	2.69
	Lg Average	6	6	.500	2	100.1	101	35	54	3.84

Starting Pitcher Analysis. In the 1970s Pittsburgh was a team known for its offensive attack rather than a phenomenal pitching staff. That's not to say that they never were solid from the mound; in 1971 and 1972 they had among the deepest pitching staffs in all of baseball.

During the 1979 season their starting rotation was deep if not spectacular. It certainly was an unexpected strength of the club. Heading the list was veteran Bert Blyleven, whom the Bucs got in a trade with the Rangers for Al Oliver. Blyleven gave up a little over a hit per inning, 238 in 237⅓ innings, and walked a team-high 92 batters, but managed to strike out a club-best 172 batters and have a very respectable 3.61 ERA with a fine 12–5 mark.

Next up were two Bucco veterans of postseasons past, in 25-year-old John Candelaria and 29-year-old Bruce Kison. The Candy Man went down in Pirates lore by striking out 14 Reds his rookie campaign in a hard fought 5–3 extra inning defeat to Cincy, in the third game of the 1975 NLCS. Kison made an impression his freshman season by saving the day in a game four victory by Pittsburgh in the 1971 World Series, shutting down the Orioles after starter Luke Walker allowed three early runs.

Candelaria led the team in victories with 14, registering a 14–9 mark with an outstanding 3.22 ERA, allowing 201 hits and 41 walks in 207 innings pitched. Kison was right behind him with a 13–7 record and, even better, a 3.19 Earned Run Average. Bruce had one of his best campaigns, giving up only 157 hits in 172 innings of work.

Second-year righty Don Robinson did not quite live up to his 14-win rookie year success. Arm problems hurt the 22-year-old, and he finished a mediocre 8–8 with 171 hits and 52 walks in his 161 innings, ending the year in the bullpen.[6]

Finishing the rotation were the two grizzled veterans Jim Rooker and Jim Bibby. At 36 years old, Jim Rooker was coming to the end of his career. Rook was only 4–7 with a 4.59 ERA in 17 starts, but he kept his best for last, saving Pittsburgh's hide as they were one game away from elimination in game five of the Fall Classic. Bibby was 34 and was one of Pittsburgh's first free-agent signings. Jim split the year between the starting rotation and the bullpen, but fashioned probably the best overall season to date off the mound. He had a spectacular 12–4 mark with a sparkling 2.80 ERA, giving up only 110 hits in 138 innings.

While nobody would confuse the 1979 Pirates rotation with that of the Atlanta Braves of the '90s, it was certainly a lot more potent than their 1980 version. First off, they lost Kison to free agency as he signed with the California Angels.[7] Bibby was the only bright spot in an otherwise miserable season for the Bucco starters. The 35-year-old veteran went 19–6 with a league-best .760 winning percentage, surrendering 210 hits in 238 innings of work. He was selected to the Sporting News All-Star team as the right handed starter,[8] although a sore arm cost him a start on the last day of the season and may have cost him 20 wins. Things slid downhill from there.

Candy garnered his first losing season ever, falling to 11–14 with a plus four ERA at 4.02. Things got even worse with Blyleven. The curveball specialist openly criticized manager Chuck Tanner for the way he used him, often complaining about being pulled quickly from games. The 29-year-old said it cost him complete games and victories. He finished the season with an 8–12 mark.[9]

Injuries also would hamper the Pirates' starters. Robinson started the season on the injured reserve after off-season shoulder surgery following the World Series, which contributed to his 7–10 campaign. Rooker's shoulder gave out after his fourth start of the year, ending his career.[10]

Eddie Solomon was picked up from the Braves during spring training and did contribute with a 7–3 record and 2.70 ERA. Rick Rhoden, who was recovering from 1979 rotator cuff surgery, returned in the middle of the season to go 7–5.

Overall though, despite the fact that the starting pitching may not have been the strongest aspect of the '79 world championship run, its fall has to be considered one of the primary reasons for the collapse of the Family.

THE BULLPEN

1979 Kent Tekulve Age 32

Year	Team	W	L	G	SV	IP	H	BB	SO	ERA
1979	Pirates	10	8	94	31	134.1	109	49	75	2.75
	Lg Average	8	8		17	134.1	136	49	72	4.00

Enrique Romo Age 31

Year	Team	W	L	G	SV	IP	H	BB	SO	ERA
1979	Pirates	10	5	84	5	129.1	122	43	106	2.99
	Lg Average	7	7		6	129.1	131	47	69	4.00

Grant Jackson Age 36

Year	Team	W	L	G	SV	IP	H	BB	SO	ERA
1979	Pirates	8	5	72	14	82	67	35	39	2.96
	Lg Average	5	5		7	82	83	30	44	4.00

Dave Roberts Age 34

Year	Team	W	L	G	SV	IP	H	BB	SO	ERA
1979	Giants	0	2	26	3	42	42	18	23	2.57

	Pirates	5	2	21	1	38.2	47	12	15	3.26
	Totals	5	4	47	4	80.2	89	30	38	2.90
	Lg Average	5	5		4	80.2	82	29	43	4.00

Ed Whitson Age 24

Year	Team	W	L	G	SV	IP	H	BB	SO	ERA
1979	Pirates	2	3	19	1	57.2	53	36	31	4.37
	Giants	5	8	18	0	100.1	98	39	62	3.95
	Totals	7	11	37	1	158	151	75	93	4.10
	Lg Average	9	9		1	158	160	57	84	4.00

1980 Kent Tekulve Age 33

Year	Team	W	L	G	SV	IP	H	BB	SO	ERA
1980	Pirates	8	12	78	21	93	96	40	47	3.39
	Lg Average	5	5		15	93	94	32	50	3.84

Enrique Romo Age 32

Year	Team	W	L	G	SV	IP	H	BB	SO	ERA
1980	Pirates	5	5	74	11	123.2	117	28	82	3.27
	Lg Average	7	7		10	123.2	125	43	66	3.84

Grant Jackson Age 37

Year	Team	W	L	G	SV	IP	H	BB	SO	ERA
1980	Pirates	8	4	61	9	71	71	20	31	2.92
	Lg Average	4	4		7	71	72	25	38	3.84

Rod Scurry Age 24

Year	Team	W	L	G	SV	IP	H	BB	SO	ERA
1980	Pirates	0	2	20	0	37.2	23	17	28	2.15
	Lg Average	2	2		1	37.2	38	13	20	3.84

Relief Pitching Analysis. One of the main forces that made the Bucs champions in 1979 was the emergence of a solid, deep bullpen. The main driving force of the relief corps was the Rubber Band man himself, Kent Tekulve. Teke had a league leading 94 appearances while winning 10 games and saving 31 others, second in the circuit behind Chicago's Bruce Sutter, who had 37. The tall, gangly hurler would allow only 109 hits in 134 innings while coming in with a fine 2.75 ERA.

The setup men were solid righty Enrique Romo (10–5–3.00; 5 saves in 84 games), and 36-year-old southpaw Grant Jackson (8–5–2.96; 14 saves in 72 appearances). While Romo certainly was sharp, tossing 129 innings, Jackson was at his best, giving up only 67 hits in 82 innings of work. Also turning in solid performances in the pen were a young Ed Whitson, who was dealt to the Giants in the midseason Madlock deal, and veterans Joe Coleman and Dave Roberts (the one-time Pirates farm hand who came over from the Giants with the Mad Dog midseason). Bibby and Robinson also spent time in relief, making that area one of the Bucs' strengths in their championship run.

Although their decline wasn't as dramatic as that of the starting pitchers, the relievers nonetheless slumped the following season. Romo had very similar numbers to 1979: 117 hits in 124 innings, a 5–5 mark with 11 saves and a 3.27 ERA; as did Jackson: 8–4–2.92 and 9 saves, although he did give up a hit per inning in 1980, 71 hits in 71 innings. Solomon pitched solidly, splitting time between the bullpen and starting rotation. A young lefty named Rod Scurry, whom the Pirates kept in '80 due to the fact that he was out of options, showed promise for the future, giving up only 23 walks and 17 hits in 38 innings with a 2.13 ERA.

When comparing 1979 and 1980, the bullpen looks just fine until you throw in the superstar of the squad, Kent Tekulve. While Teke had a phenomenal '79, he slumped horribly the following season. The Rubber Band Man got off to a great start, winning his first five decisions, including three in a three-game stretch tying a major league record. He was named by Chuck Tanner to the NL All-Star squad.[11] His second half was a thing nightmares are made of, especially the last month. He lost 7 decisions, giving up 15 earned runs in 27 innings between August 26 and the end of the season. Teke won only three of his final 16 decisions, blowing 11 saves. He gave up more hits than innings pitched, 96 hits in 93 innings, as his ERA rose over a half a run per game to 3.39.

Like several other positions on the team, the performance of the bullpen in 1980 wasn't horrible, just not at the championship level it had demonstrated the year before. When a closer slumps, though, as Tekulve did, he can take the whole squad down with him.

As the team left 1980, there were several holes for Peterson to fill, holes that — after their world championship the year before — the club had figured would be filled for years to come. Unlike Joe L. Brown had had in the late sixties and Peterson had had only a couple years earlier, there would be no relief from the minor league system. Names in the system like Parker, Zisk, Oliver, Armas, and Ellis were replaced by ones such as Rick Jones, Doe Boyland and Craig Casek. The system was dry, and Harding Peterson now had very little to trade with. By 1985 the Pirates were a franchise at the bottom of the National League East, with no hope for the near future. Ironically, the deals that brought the Pirates a title in 1979 eventually helped cost Peterson his job five years later. Brown was brought back in 1985 to try and right the ship.

The Bucs enjoy a light moment during their world championship campaign. The remarkable closeness of the members of the Family was considered one of the major reasons for the team's success in 1979. Shown left to right are Kent Tekulve, Bert Blyleven, Phil Garner, Don Robinson, Ed Ott, Rick Rhoden, John Milner, Omar Moreno (kneeling), and Willie Stargell. (Courtesy of the Pittsburgh Pirates.)

Whether or not one believes Peterson was right in trading the future away for a shot at a title, he did help bring the city a world championship with those trades. This should be kept in mind when critiquing his career as the Bucs' GM.

5. The Members of the Family

The Managers

General Manager Harding "Pete" Peterson

Peterson the Player. After signing with the Bucs following his time at Rutgers University, Pete Peterson had his baseball career delayed while serving his country in the Korean War. When he came back he spent time with the Big Club as a catcher before breaking his arm in a home plate collision that helped bring his major league career to an end.

Year	Team	AB	R	HR	RBI	BB	SO	SB	AVG	OBP
1955	Pirates	81	7	1	10	7	7	0	.247	.669
1957	Pirates	73	10	2	11	9	10	0	.301	.816
1958	Pirates	6	0	0	0	1	0	0	.333	.762
1959	Pirates	1	0	0	0	0	0	0	.000	.000
	Totals	161	17	3	21	17	17	0	.273	.735
	Lg Average	169	23	5	21	18	21	2	.266	.746
	Pos Average	165	18	5	21	17	20	0	.251	.709

Peterson the Front Office Executive. After spending time as minor league manager, Peterson took over the reigns of the Bucs' minor league system in 1967 as minor league director. Peterson also attached the title of scouting director a year later, overseeing the development of one of the greatest minor league systems in baseball during his time. He helped stock the Pirates with several players who helped them win not only the 1971 World Series but five Eastern Division Championships between 1970 and 1975.

When GM Joe L. Brown retired following the 1976 campaign after 20 years in his position, Harding was the man who took over his spot. He tried to turn the Bucs back into world championship contenders, using his fruitful minor league system to make several aggressive trades.

Little by little he put the Family together. After a deal that brought Bill Madlock from the Giants in midseason during the 1979 campaign, Peterson had all the pieces in place for the team that won the franchise's fifth world championship.

Unfortunately, the Bucs were a one-year wonder, as everyone seemed to have career seasons at the same time. Injuries, among other things, ended the Pirates' run in 1980, and by that point in time, Peterson had dealt most of his top prospects, leaving a barren minor league system. Because he no longer had the personnel to trade like he did when he first took over, Pittsburgh slid from the top of the rung all the way down to the bottom in the second half of 1981 and during the abysmal 1984 and 1985 seasons.

Mired in the aftermath of a horrendous '85 season and the embarrassing Pittsburgh baseball drug trials in which many of his own players were implicated, Peterson was replaced by the man he had replaced, Joe Brown, who was given the responsibility of trying to raise the club from the depths.

On the Way In and Out

This section will look at the specific moves Pete Peterson pulled off to bring the players of the 1979 Pittsburgh Pirates together and those he made with the Family team members afterwards in an attempt to build up the ball club. Included will be each player's results after the moves were made.

11/5/76 Manny Sanguillen to the A's for Cash and Manager Chuck Tanner. Sangy went to the A's where he hit .275 with six homers in 152 games, his worst average since his rookie season. In this unusual trade, the Bucs replaced a great manager, Danny Murtaugh, with one of the hottest managerial properties in the game. Chuck had success at both Oakland and Chicago. His aggressive style on the base paths brought the team one of the best running games in the majors to go with the power they possessed. Pittsburgh won 184 games his first two seasons, and the world championship in 1979.

12/7/76 Craig Reynolds and Jimmy Sexton to the Mariners for Grant Jackson. Sexton played parts of six seasons with the Mariners, Astros, A's and Cardinals, batting only .218 in 372 at-bats. Reynolds did much better, becoming a starter at short for both Seattle and Houston. He played 13 seasons after the deal, 11 with the Astros, where he hit .256. While Jackson retired after the 1982 campaign, he was outstanding for Pittsburgh, giving them a solid left handed presence out of the pen that was pivotal in their championship run. Jackson saved 36 games and won 33 more following the trade.

5. The Members of the Family 109

3/15/77 Doug Bair, Dave Giusti, Rick Langford, Doc Medich, Tony Armas and Mitchell Page to the A's for Phil Garner, Tommy Helms and Chris Batton. The A's moved Bair to the Reds a year later, where he picked up 28 saves. He pitched until 1990, appearing the last two years of his career with the club he had originally signed with, and ending with a 55–43 mark and 81 saves. Giusti was at the end of his career and pitched only one more season, going 3–5 with 7 saves for the A's and Cubs. Langford became a solid starter for Oakland, winning 19 games in 1980 before his arm went. His final mark was 73–105–3.95. Doc Medich was 10–6 for the A's in '77 before going to Seattle and the Mets. He pitched until 1982, mostly for the Rangers, with a 67–54 mark after he left Pittsburgh. Tony Armas had a fine 13-year career. He hit 251 homers for the A's, Red Sox and Angels that included back-to-back 36 HR 107 RBI and 43 HR 123 RBI seasons for Boston in 1983 and 1984 respectively. Mitchell Page had a solid if unspectacular career after the trade, hitting 72 homers, 21 of which came in his first year in Oakland in 1977. He finished his time in the show with Pittsburgh in 1984, hitting .333 in only 12 at-bats. Tommy Helms was hitless in 12 at-bats before heading off to the Red Sox and Batton, a minor league hurler, never made the big time. Garner was obviously the key for Pittsburgh. Scrap Iron was solid at third and provided some punch as a hitter for the first two and a half seasons. Then in 1979, his career year, he was moved to second after the Madlock trade, hitting .293. Garner was a key member of the Family, helping to lead them to the world championship. He tailed off afterwards, but still made the National League All-Star Team in 1980 and 1981 before being shipped off to the Astros late in the '81 campaign.

12/8/77 Al Oliver and Nelson Norman to the Rangers for John Milner and Bert Blyleven. Oliver had been one of the greats for the Pirates in their championship run the first half of the decade and continued to be one of baseball's best hitters after the deal, hitting .311 with 1,253 hits for the Rangers, Expos, Giants, Phillies, Dodgers and Blue Jays, while Norman hit a meager .221 after the trade. 343 of his 429 at-bats after the deal came in 1979. Milner played until 1982, the last two seasons splitting time with Montreal and Pittsburgh, but had his best two seasons by far in the Steel City in '78 and '79. He hit 16 homers the latter season, many of which came in clutch situations. Bert Blyleven was one of the all-time greats and went 26–15 for the Pirates in '78 and '79, but fell apart in 1980 and was disgruntled with the way Tanner pitched him. He was shipped off to the Indians afterwards.

3/15/78 Signed Jim Bibby to a Free Agent Contract. A fabulous move by Peterson, as Bibby was one of the strengths of the Bucco starting rotation, going 31–10 in 1979 and 1980, 52–30 overall with the club. After a horrid

Starter Bert Blyleven is rewarded by one of his teammates for his nine-strikeout performance in the third and final game of the NLCS. (Courtesy of the Pittsburgh Pirates.)

1983 campaign as he tried to pitch following rotator cuff surgery in 1982, Bibby left for Texas.

4/4/78 Elias Sosa, Mike Edwards, Miguel Dilone to the A's for Manny Sanguillen. Sosa had a decent six-year career after the deal. His strongest season was in 1979, when he went 8–7 for the Expos with 18 saves and a 1.96 ERA. Mike Edwards played only three seasons in Oakland but saw significant playing time, hitting .252 in 873 at-bats. A fast runner, Edwards' defensive problems limited his opportunities after he hit just .233 in 1979. Miguel Dilone was the best of the bunch, landing with seven different clubs between 1978 and 1985. He hit .269 with 246 stolen, bases including his career season in 1980 with the Indians when he hit .341 and swiped 45 bases. The three combined made an exorbitant price to pay, as by the time the Bucs retrieved Sangy, Ed Ott had taken over and Manny was at the end of his career. He hit only .254 in 342 at-bats in three seasons, 220 of them in 1978.

10/27/78 Sold Mike Easler to the Red Sox; 3/15/79 Sent George Hill, Marty Rivas and Cash to Boston to Retrieve Easler. As peculiar as these two moves were, coming right after one another, Boston never really got anything: as Hill and Rivas never played an inning of major league ball. Pittsburgh retained a man who would be their best pinch hitter in 1979 and a solid outfielder who hit .300 for the Bucs between 1979 and 1983.

12/5/1978 Odell Jones, Rafael Vasquez and Mario Mendoza to the Mariners for Enrique Romo and Rick Jones. Over the course of six major league seasons between 1979 and 1988, Odell Jones enjoyed some success out of the bullpen for five different teams, including the Pirates in 1981. His best season was 1983 in Texas, where he saved 10 of his career 13 saves. Vasquez threw only 16 innings for Seattle in 1979, his only major league season, while

5. The Members of the Family 111

Mendoza lasted four seasons with the Mariners and Rangers, hitting 20 points over the line that bears his name. Romo became an important part of the Bucs' potent bullpen, going 10–5 in 1979 with a 2.99 ERA. Overall, he went 25–16 for the Bucs in four seasons before mysteriously leaving the game following the 1982 campaign. Rick Jones was on the roster in September of '79, but never pitched a game for Pittsburgh. In fact, Jones never appeared in the majors again.

4/9/79 Jerry Reuss to the Dodgers for Rick Rhoden. Reuss was solid member of the rotation through the middle '70s and a member of the Family as it broke camp, but the deal for Rhoden was already in the works and Reuss did not appear in a Pirates game in 1979. He pitched through 1990, winning 112 games for the Dodgers, Reds, Angels, White Sox, Brewers and finally the Pirates again, where he ended his career in 1990. Rhoden was limited to one appearance in 1979 due to an arm injury, but became one of the most reliable starters on some bad Pirates teams in the '80s. He went 79–73 through 1986, when he was sent to the Yankees, bringing, among others, Doug Drabek to Pittsburgh.

4/19/79 Frank Tavares to the Mets for Tim Foli. Taveras had been the starting shortstop for the Bucs and one of the fastest men in the game, but he was too erratic a fielder. He had a decent 1979 campaign with the Mets, hitting .263 with 42 stolen bases, but eventually faltered and was out of the game following the 1982 campaign. Foli was a backup with the Mets, which made the trade rather quizzical, but Peterson knew what he was doing: Foli was not only a drastic improvement defensively, solidifying the infield for the 1979 world champs, but was also a strong addition to the offense, hitting .291 the remainder of the season. Although Foli slumped a bit in '80 and '81, hitting .265 and .247 respectively before he left the 'Burgh, his defense remained as consistent as ever.

6/28/79 Ed Whitson, Al Holland and Fred Breining to the Giants for Bill Madlock, Lenny Randle and Dave Roberts. This was a big price to pay, as Whitson became a solid starter, winning 118 games after the deal for the Giants, Indians, Yankees and Padres. Holland saved 78 games for five teams until 1987, 54 of them coming between 1983 and 1984 for the Phils; at the time, he was considered one of the best relievers in the game. Breining had some success, winning 27 of his 47 decisions following the move to the Giants before arm problems ended his career. But it was a price worth paying. Madlock proved to be the final piece of the championship puzzle, hitting .328 after the trade and .297 for the Black and Gold through 1985. He won two NL batting titles in '81 and '83. Roberts lasted less than a year with the club, but contributed as a second left handed choice out of the pen for Tanner, going 5–2 in 1979. Randle never got a chance to play for the Bucs.

9/21/79 Purchased Dock Ellis from the Yankees. Getting the former Pirates superstar was a move intended to bolster an injured rotation through the final week of the season. He only started once and relieved twice, giving up nine hits in seven innings in what turned out to be his final major league appearances.

12/9/80 Bert Blyleven and Manny Sanguillen to the Indians Victor Cruz, Bob Owchinko, Gary Alexander and Rafael Vasquez. One of the worst trades in Pirate history. Cruz, after failing to make the team in spring training, was decent in his only season in the 'Burgh, going 1–1 in 34 games with a 2.65 ERA. Owchinko was immediately sent to the A's for Ernie Camacho. Alexander hit .213 in 47 at-bats. Vasquez, whom Peterson had traded away two years earlier in the Romo deal, never played for the Black and Gold. In the meantime, the disgruntled Blyleven won 48 games for Cleveland, including a 19–7 mark in 1984, and emerged victorious 131 times following the deal, playing with three different teams through the end of his career in 1992. Sangy left the game after 1980 and never played in Cleveland.

4/1/81 Mickey Mahler and Ed Ott to the Angels for Jason Thompson. A big win for the Bucs. Thompson hit 93 homers for Pittsburgh, giving them a power source at first that included 31 round trippers and 101 RBIs in 1982. Mahler went only 4–8 in four seasons with five teams, and Ott had seen better days hitting .217 in 258 at-bats in his last major league season before blowing out his shoulder.

8/20/81 John Milner to the Expos for Willie Montanez. Milner was definitely through, playing only two more major league seasons, hitting .217 with Montreal and then the Pirates. Montanez was also through in 1982 hitting .271 in 70 at-bats for Pittsburgh, who released him early in 1982. He signed with Philly during the stretch drive to end his career as a pinch hitter.

8/31/81 Phil Garner to the Astros for Johnny Ray, Randy Niemann and Kevin Houston. Garner had peaked with Pittsburgh, although he still remained productive for Houston before moving on to Los Angeles and San Francisco, hitting .256 through 1988, the last year of his career. Ray became one of the best young second baseman in the game, hitting .286 for Pittsburgh during the better part of his seven-season stay there and garnering 1,009 hits. Niemann was 1–2 with a 6.24 ERA in two years with the Bucs, while Houston did not play for the team.

5. The Members of the Family

9/1/81 Sold Grant Jackson to the Expos. The venerable Jackson was near the end of his career and pitched in only 21 games for the Expos and Royals. He came back to the Bucs to finish his career in 1982.

12/11/81 Doe Boyland to the Giants for Tom Griffin. Boyland was never more than just a good prospect and did not return to the major leagues after leaving Pittsburgh. Griffin, while at the end of his 14-year career, went 1–3 with Pittsburgh and had an astronomic 8.87 ERA.

12/11/81 Tim Foli to the Angels for Brian Harper. This would have been a tremendous trade for the Bucs if they had hung on to Harper, who hit .295 for his 16-year major league career and was a contributor on the '91 world champion Twins, hitting .311 in 441 at-bats. Alas, the Bucs didn't keep him, as they had their own budding superstar, Tony Pena, behind the plate, and Harper hit only .243 as a part time player between 1982 and 1984. Harper went to the Cards in the ill-fated George Hendrick deal. Foli, nearing the end of his career, hitting .252 in three seasons for the Angels and Yankees before finishing his career in the Steel City in '85 with a .189 average in 37 at-bats.

6/15/82 Bill Robinson to the Phillies for Wayne Nordhagen. This was part of a three-team deal with Pittsburgh, Philadelphia and Toronto. Robinson was done, hitting .250 with the Phils in 70 at-bats, then retiring in 1983. Nordhagen went 2 for 4 with 2 RBIs in his only appearance for the Bucs, but was sent back to Toronto a week later when it was discovered that he was injured. Pittsburgh got Dick Davis, whom the Phils sent to the Jays in the deal, but got little from him as he hit only .182 in 77 at-bats.

8/19/83 Steve Nicosia to the Giants for Milt May. Nicosia hit .267 in 251 at-bats for the remainder of his career with the Giants, Expos and Blue Jays. This included a .303 performance with San Francisco in 1984. May didn't do as well, hitting only .185 in his last year and a half in the show.

12/6/83 Mike Easler to the Red Sox for John Tudor. This was a trade that would have turned out well for both teams, if Tudor had not been part of the disastrous George Hendrick trade a year later. Easler had an outstanding '84 campaign, hitting 27 homers and 91 RBIs for a .313 average. He hit .291 in his final four seasons. Tudor was a fine 12–11 with a 3.27 ERA for a last-place Pirates team. After he was dealt to the Cards, he became one of the best in the game, going 21–8 with a 1.93 ERA the following season in St Louis.

12/20/84 Dale Berra, Alfonso Pulido and Jay Buhner to the Yankees for

Steve Kemp, Tim Foli and Cash. Berra never lived up to his potential and was erratic in the field. He hit only .221 with the Yanks and Astros in his final three major league seasons. Pulido only went one year for New York with a 1–1 mark and 4.70 ERA. Buhner, just a prospect at the time, was the big loss; he would have been a nice addition to the Bucs of the early '90s. Unfortunately for the Bronx Bombers, they didn't get a chance to take advantage of him either. They sent Jay to Seattle in 1988 where he caught on fire, hitting the bulk of his 310 career homers with the Mariners, including over 40 for three years in a row between 1995 and 1997. We know what Foli gave to the Bucs in his return to the Steel City — a .189 average in 37 at-bats — but the worst was Kemp, the one-time slugger who disappeared in Pittsburgh, hitting only .246 in a little over a season with three home runs in 252 at-bats.

4/20/85 Kent Tekulve to the Phillies for Al Holland and Frankie Griffin. It was Peterson's last trade of a member of the 1979 world champion Pirates. Tekulve was one of the key members of the club and is considered one of the top two or three relievers in team history. Teke had been off to a horrible start for the Bucs the first month of the season, but rebounded in Philly, saving 14 games the rest of the way. He did even better the next season, winning 11 while coming in with a 2.54 ERA. The Rubber Band Man stayed on until 1989 when he finished with his hometown Cincinnati Reds. During the course of his time in the show after the trade, Teke set the all-time major league mark for games pitched in relief: 1,050.

Al Holland — the one-time Pirate who was sent to the Giants in the Bill Madlock deal before becoming a star closer for the Phillies — had a decent run for the Bucs in '85 with a 3.38 ERA and a fine hits-to-innings-pitched ratio of 48 to 58⅔, but was sent to the Angels by the end of the season and left the game two years later. Griffin never played in the majors.

The Manager

#7 Chuck Tanner

Tanner the Player. Chuck Tanner homered for the Milwaukee Braves in his first major league at-bat, but after an otherwise nondescript career as an outfielder with four major league teams, his true success came as a major league manager. Tanner's best season as a player came in 1957 when he hit a combined .279 with nine homeruns for the Braves and Cubs in 117 games. Other than that campaign, the native of New Castle, Pennsylvania, played in less than 100 games in every other season and spent four years shuttling between the major and minor leagues.

5. The Members of the Family

Year	Team	AB	R	HR	RBI	BB	SO	SB	AVG	OBP
1955	Braves	243	27	6	27	27	32	0	.247	.702
1956	Braves	63	6	1	4	10	10	0	.238	.659
1957	Braves	69	5	2	6	5	4	0	.246	.674
	Cubs	318	42	7	42	23	20	0	.286	.751
	Totals	387	47	9	48	28	24	0	.279	.737
1958	Cubs	103	10	4	17	9	10	1	.262	.758
1959	Indians	48	6	1	5	2	9	0	.250	.634
1960	Indians	25	2	0	4	4	6	1	.280	.687
1961	Angels	8	0	0	0	2	2	0	.125	.425
1962	Angels	8	0	0	0	0	0	0	.125	.250
	Totals	885	98	21	105	82	93	2	.261	.711
	Lg Average	889	118	25	111	93	112	9	.266	.744
	Pos Average	902	129	34	133	101	123	8	.275	.798

Tanner the Manager. Ask most Pirates fans what they remember most about Chuck Tanner and — aside from his being manager of the 1979 world championship team, which became known as the Family — they will probably say his positive attitude. Tanner's optimism may have been questioned and criticized at times, but as an individual who struggled in the minor leagues for eight years before finally breaking into the majors, Tanner was proof that positive thinking and hard work could carry a man to his dreams.

Manager Chuck Tanner welcomes the final piece of the championship puzzle in third baseman Bill Madlock. (Courtesy of the Pittsburgh Pirates.)

Chuck had built a strong resume as a manager with the White Sox and A's, including winning the American League's Manager of the Year Award in 1972. He came to the Pirates in a trade for catcher Manny Sanguillen following Danny Murtaugh's retirement in 1976. Tanner quickly put his stamp on the team, guiding the Bucs to consecutive second place finishes in 1977 and 1978. He stressed speed on the bases and made frequent pitching changes to get the matchups he wanted. The Bucs' skipper also wasn't afraid to promote a pitcher with limited experience to the big leagues. While he was with the White Sox, had done so with Rich Gossage and Terry Forster, who both won Fireman of the Year Awards. He had great success with Don Robinson in 1978. Tanner helped Willie Stargell's comeback by sticking with the aging slugger in 1978 despite a slow start. He manipulated the lineup to make sure his grandfatherly star would get the rest he needed to stay sharp.

By 1979, Tanner was respected and well liked in Pittsburgh. He had refused to allow his players to give up after the team had fallen 13 games behind the Philadelphia Phillies the previous year, and the club put together an incredible six weeks to battle the Phils into the season's final weekend. Tanner continued to preach a positive approach in 1979. When general manager Harding Peterson acquired Enrique Romo prior to the start of the season, Chuck was able to set up his bullpen in a style suited to his strategy. Even when Romo and ace Kent Tekulve struggled at the start of the season, Tanner stayed with his plan and both relievers turned their seasons around. The two right-handers combined with lefty Grant Jackson for 28 wins, 50 saves and an ERA under 3.00, as Tanner manipulated baseball's top bullpen.

The manager was also rewarded for his patience with Omar Moreno, his fast centerfielder, who had been a weak hitter his first two full seasons in the major leagues. Tanner often said Moreno's defense was so important that he would be his centerfielder even if he hit .100. Tanner played Moreno daily despite the Antelope's frequent slumps. After working hard in the off-season with Harry Walker, Moreno improved dramatically in 1979. Tanner stuck with Moreno as his lead-off man during a terrible start in the World Series and Moreno again came up big for him by sparking the Pirates offense in the last two games.

While the Orioles' Earl Weaver won a managerial chess match against Tanner in game four of the World Series that led to Howard Cosell's seeming to go on endlessly about Weaver's genius, Tanner made several key decisions that contributed to the Pirates' series win. First, he chose Sanguillen to pinch hit with two outs and the go-ahead run at second in game two, even though Manny had only driven in four runs all year. Weaver's relief ace Don Stanhouse was on the mound, a pitcher who was effective in '79 but who often pitched outside of the strike zone. Tanner figured Sanguillen, a bad ball hitter, would be able to handle Stanhouse, and Manny did just that, singling in what proved to be the winning run. Tanner made an even gutsier decision in game five by starting Jim Rooker, who had been hurt a good part of 1979 and had gone just 4–7 with a 4.26 ERA. Even though a loss would mean elimination for Pittsburgh, Tanner had correctly surmised that Rooker, a bulldog-type veteran, could stop the Orioles; he had pitched effectively in September and had shut the Birds out over 3⅔ innings in game one. Demonstrating leadership worthy of a champion, the Pirates manager faced game five and the rest of the series after learning of his mother's passing away the morning of the pivotal game. Tanner called his players together in the clubhouse before the contest. Fighting back tears, told his charges that his mother had gone up to heaven to give them a little extra help and that she would have wanted him to continue to manage the club.

Tanner managed the Pirates a total of six more seasons after his World

Series triumph. While he never was given the Manager of the Year award during that time, he helped the team rebound from a poor 1981 season to contend again in 1982 and 1983, when few thought they would. The trophy he helped bring to Pittsburgh remains the crowning accomplishment for the western Pennsylvania boy who continues to carry himself with dignity and character some 25 years later.

Following his days with the Pirates, Tanner managed the Atlanta Braves and remains active as a scout. His son, Bruce, pitched briefly for the White Sox and is currently the Pirates' bullpen coach.

Year	League	Team	G	W	L	WP	Finish	
1970	Chicago	(AL)	16	3	13	.188	6	
1971	Chicago	(AL)	162	79	83	.488	3	
1972	Chicago	(AL)	154	87	67	.565	2	
1973	Chicago	(AL)	162	77	85	.475	5	
1974	Chicago	(AL)	163	80	80	.500	4	
1975	Chicago	(AL)	161	75	86	.466	5	
1976	Oakland		161	87	74	.540	2	
1977	Pittsburgh		162	96	66	.593	2	
1978	Pittsburgh		161	88	73	.547	2	
1979	Pittsburgh		163	98	64	.605	WS 1	
1980	Pittsburgh		162	83	79	.512	3	
1981	Pittsburgh		49	25	23	.521	4	First half of season
1981	Pittsburgh		54	21	33	.389	6	Second half of season
1982	Pittsburgh		162	84	78	.519	4	
1983	Pittsburgh		162	84	78	.519	2	
1984	Pittsburgh		162	75	87	.463	6	
1985	Pittsburgh		161	57	104	.354	6	
1986	Atlanta		161	72	89	.447	6	
1987	Atlanta		161	69	92	.429	5	
1988	Atlanta		39	12	27	.308	6	
	Atlanta		361	153	208	.424		
	Chicago		818	401	414	.492		
	Oakland		161	87	74	.540		
	Pittsburgh		1398	711	685	.509		
	Total		2738	1352	1381	.495		

The Coaches

Batting Coach   #48   Bob Skinner

Bob Skinner was a fine natural hitter who not only was a two-time All-Star in 1958 and 1960, but hit .300 on four occasions, finishing with a .277 career average while playing on two world championship clubs (1960 in Pittsburgh and 1964 in St. Louis).

After his playing career ended, Skinner managed in the minors, compiling a 116–91 record before replacing Gene Mauch in Philadelphia midway through the 1968 season. He led the Phils to a 92–123 mark before being relieved of his duties the next season.

Skinner coached in San Diego until 1973, when he returned to Pittsburgh as a batting coach and third base coach until 1977. He returned to the Padres in a stint that included one game as manager, replacing John McNamara, who had been relieved of his job. Skinner finished his tenure at San Diego with a perfect 1–0 mark.

After a year as the Angels' hitting coach, Bob came back to the Steel City, where he remained as both a hitting coach and later a third base coach until 1985. One of his biggest success stories in 1979 was helping shortstop Tim Foli to become a better hitter.

Year	Team	AB	R	HR	RBI	BB	SO	SB	AVG	OBP
1954	Pirates	470	67	8	46	47	59	4	.249	.686
1956	Pirates	233	29	5	29	26	50	1	.202	.608
1957	Pirates	387	58	13	45	38	50	10	.305	.838
1958	Pirates	529	93	13	70	58	55	12	.321	.878
1959	Pirates	547	78	13	61	67	65	10	.280	.756
1960	Pirates	571	83	15	86	59	86	11	.273	.771
1961	Pirates	381	61	3	42	51	49	3	.268	.718
1962	Pirates	510	87	20	75	76	89	10	.302	.899
1963	Pirates	122	18	0	8	13	22	4	.270	.734
	Reds	194	25	3	17	21	42	1	.253	.703
	Totals	316	43	3	25	34	64	5	.259	.715
1964	Reds	59	6	3	5	4	12	0	.220	.694
	Cardinals	118	10	1	16	11	20	0	.271	.672
	Totals	177	16	4	21	15	32	0	.254	.680
1965	Cardinals	152	25	5	26	12	30	1	.309	.853
1966	Cardinals	45	2	1	5	2	17	0	.156	.452
	Totals	4318	642	103	531	485	646	67	.277	.772
	Lg Average	4201	553	116	519	428	568	46	.264	.739
	Pos Average	4208	586	148	602	460	619	42	.271	.782

Pitching Coach   #57   Harvey Haddix

Starting out with the St. Louis Cardinals, Harvey Haddix enjoyed an outstanding two-year run in his second and third major league seasons, going 38–22 in 1953 and '54. He would entrench himself in Pittsburgh Pirates lore a few years later.

This Steel City legend came over to Pittsburgh with Don Hoak and Smoky Burgess in a trade with the Reds before the 1959 campaign. That year he pitched the greatest game in major league history, tossing a perfect 12-inning game against the Milwaukee Braves before losing it in the 13th, 1–0.

Haddix also was a prime member of the 1960 world championship club and won two games in the World Series that year.

After retiring, Haddix became a successful pitching coach, serving with the Mets, the Bucs' AAA affiliate in Columbus, Cincinnati, Pittsburgh's minor league team in Bradenton, Boston and Cleveland between 1966 and 1978. He then came back to Pittsburgh to take over the same position for Chuck Tanner and the Bucs until 1984.

Year	Team	W	L	PCT	CG	IP	H	BB	SO	ERA
1952	Cardinals	2	2	.500	3	42	31	10	31	2.79
1953	Cardinals	20	9	.690	19	253	220	69	163	3.06
1954	Cardinals	18	13	.581	13	260	247	77	184	3.57
1955	Cardinals	12	16	.429	9	208	216	62	150	4.46
1956	Cardinals	1	0	1.000	1	23.2	28	10	16	5.32
	Phillies	12	8	.600	11	206.2	196	55	154	3.48
	Totals	13	8	.619	12	230.1	224	65	170	3.67
1957	Phillies	10	13	.435	8	171	176	39	136	4.05
1958	Reds	8	7	.533	8	184	191	43	110	3.52
1959	Pirates	12	12	.500	14	224	189	49	149	3.13
1960	Pirates	11	10	.524	4	172	189	38	101	3.98
1961	Pirates	10	6	.625	5	156	159	41	99	4.10
1962	Pirates	9	6	.600	4	141	146	42	101	4.21
1963	Pirates	3	4	.429	0	70	67	20	70	3.34
1964	Orioles	5	5	.500	0	90	68	23	90	2.30
1965	Orioles	3	2	.600	0	34	31	23	21	3.44
	Totals	136	113	.546	99	2235.1	2154	601	1575	3.63
	Lg Average	124	124	.500	86	2235.1	2193	858	1204	3.90

First Base Coach   #42   Al Monchak

Like his buddy Joe Lonnett, Al Monchak was a Chuck Tanner disciple, following him from Chicago to Oakland to Pittsburgh. Also like Lonnett, Monchak enjoyed a lengthy pro baseball career, 19 years. An infielder, he suffered a major injury that perhaps cost him more time in the majors. Another thing that probably cost Monchak in his major league career was something he certainly could be proud of: a three-year stint in the military defending his country during World War II. Al also enjoyed a fine 13-year minor league managerial career, where he compiled a 923–776 mark winning four league championships. Monchak stuck with Pittsburgh until 1984.

Year	Team	AB	R	HR	RBI	BB	SO	SB	AVG	OBP
1940	Phillies	14	1	0	0	0	6	1	.143	.286
	Lg Average	16	2	0	2	2	1	0	.276	.751
	Pos Average	15	2	0	2	1	1	0	.250	.670

Third Base Coach   #32   Joe Lonnett

Where Chuck Tanner went, so did Joe Lonnett. Following a 15-year pro baseball career as a catcher and a stint as a manager in the minors with Huron in South Dakota, the Beaver Falls native hooked up with Tanner in Chicago in 1971. He followed him to Oakland and Pittsburgh, where he remained until 1984. He returned to the Pirates organization years later as a minor league coach and manager.

Year	Team	AB	R	HR	RBI	BB	SO	SB	AVG	OBP
1956	Phillies	22	2	0	0	2	7	0	.182	.432
1957	Phillies	160	12	5	15	22	39	0	.169	.566
1958	Phillies	50	0	0	2	2	11	0	.140	.347
1959	Phillies	93	8	1	10	14	17	0	.172	.499
	Totals	325	22	6	27	40	74	0	.166	.505
	Lg Average	371	49	10	46	37	48	4	.266	.742
	Pos Average	362	37	10	46	36	49	1	.248	.699

The Players

#2   Gary Hargis

Pos: PR; Age: 22; Batted: Right; Threw: Right; Year in Major Leagues: 1st

Pre-1979. Hargis was selected in the second round of the Pirates' free agent draft in 1974. He made a gradual climb up the Pirates' minor league system, hitting .295 with 20 stolen bases in Niagara Falls in 1974, then moving up to Salem, then Shreveport in AA. When he got the call in 1977, he was with the Bucs' AAA affiliate in Columbus.

His best season in AAA was his second, 1978 when the infielder not only hit .283 with 105 hits, but showed a flash of power he never had in the past; he hit 10 homers, compared to a total of 11 in his previous four year of minor league ball.

1979: In a career like that of the legendary Moonlight Graham, Hargis played in one major league game, never getting a chance to bat. His entire major league experience came on September 29, when he pinch ran for Tim Foli. It was the bottom of the 13th inning, the next to last game of the season against the Cubs. Chicago had scored in the top of the frame to take the lead. With two out, Foli singled to right and Tanner replaced him with Hargis. Parker then singled, sending the young rookie to second with the tying run. Willie Stargell struck out to end the game and, with it, Gary Hargis' career. Despite the brevity of his time in the majors, he earned a world championship ring for his moment in the sun.

1979 Postseason. Hargis was not on the postseason roster.

Post-1979. That game in 1979 was it for the Minneapolis native, who failed to make the Pirates in 1980.

Year	Team	AB	R	HR	RBI	BB	SO	SB	AVG	OBP
1979	Pirates	0	0	0	0	0	0	0		
	Lg Average	0	0	0	0	0	0	0		

#3   Phil "Scrap Iron" Garner

Pos: 2b–3b; Age: 30; Batted: Right; Threw: Right; Year in Major Leagues: 7th

Pre-1979. General manager Pete Peterson's trade for Phil Garner during spring training, 1977, demonstrated the Pirates' willingness to acquire championship caliber talent, no matter the cost in terms of players given up. Garner had established himself as a hustling infielder with the Oakland A's in the mid-1970s. A third baseman in the minor leagues, Garner moved to second base to replace Dick Green upon the longtime A's second baseman's retirement following the 1974 World Series. Phil immediately became a regular, and although he committed the high total of 26 errors as a rookie, he displayed enough skills by his sophomore season of 1976 to be named to the All-Star Team. Garner stole a career high 35 bases that year and drove in 74 runs, despite usually hitting eighth in Chuck Tanner's lineup.

When Tanner came to the Pirates after the season and found he was not satisfied with any of the candidates who were available to take over Richie Hebner's old hot corner job, Peterson reunited the skipper with one of his favorite players. There was no doubt Garner was expensive. Peterson had to give up minor league prizes Tony Armas, who would one day lead the American League in homeruns; pitchers Rick Langford, Doug Bair and outfielder Mitchell Page; and

Phil Garner (courtesy of the Topps Company, Inc.).

two well-established major league pitchers, Dave Giusti and Doc Medich. The Pirates also received utility man Tommy Helms and minor league pitcher Chris Batton in the trade.

Garner got off to a slow start with the Pirates in '77 and was struggling to stay above .200 in early June.[1] He continued to hustle and worked hard to improve his stroke. He caught fire in midseason, finishing the year at .260 with 17 homeruns and 77 RBIs, also stealing 32 bases. Moved to second base following Rennie Stennett's season-ending leg injury on August 20, Phil also filled in at short on occasion and committed just 17 errors. He became very popular in Pittsburgh; as the town appreciated not only his hard play but his candor and sense of humor. His nickname, Scrap Iron, was recognizable to fans not only in Pittsburgh but across the country, and described the never-give-up attitude he showed on the field.

Off to another slow start in '78, Garner again had a second-half surge and hit eight of his ten homeruns following the All-Star break. Two of his blasts were grand slams that he hit on back-to-back days, becoming the first player since Jimmy Sheckard of the Brooklyn Robins in 1901 to accomplish the feat.[2] He topped his '77 average by one point, and while he had some defensive difficulties at third (18 errors in 81 games), his fielding was more solid at second. He appeared in the same number of games at both positions, a move necessitated by the fact that Stennett's leg had not healed well enough to allow Rennie to return to his former star quality play.

1979: With the Pirates still hopeful of a return to form by Stennett in 1979, Garner again opened the season as the club's third baseman. Unlike in his previous years, Scrap Iron got off to a strong start in 1979. Some felt it was a good omen for the Bucs, but as the author notes in *The New Bill James Historical Baseball Abstract*, Garner's hot streak was assisted by the fact he had been hit on the hand by a pitch early in the season; this caused him to grip the bat differently, preventing him from over-swinging.[3] He hit .294 prior to the All-Star break, including a five-hit performance on June 19. Nine days later, the Pirates acquired Bill Madlock, and Garner was permanently moved to second base. Scrap Iron increased his power numbers as the season went along, again hitting eight second-half homeruns for a second year in a row. Three of his shots came during a mid-July spurt which saw him hit .409 and claim National League Player of the Week honors. His hitting in the second half remained consistent. He hit just one point lower than in the first, and his overall mark of .293 placed him 15th in the league. Clutch down the stretch as he had been all year, Garner ended the season on a 14-game hitting streak.

1979 Postseason. Garner starred during the 1979 postseason for the Pirates. He opened the scoring in the National League Championship Series with a third inning homerun off Tom Seaver in game one. Then he singled and scored the Bucs' second run in the team's 3–2 ten-inning win in game two. In game three, Garner went 2-for-4 with a triple and two runs scored. He finished the NLCS with a .417 average. It was highly unlikely Garner could improve on such an impressive mark in the World Series, but after a costly error on the first ball hit to him in game one, Garner excelled.

Hitting safely in all seven games, Garner totaled 12 hits for a .500 average, which tied Pepper Martin's record for the highest batting percentage in a seven-game series. The 12 safeties tied Willie Stargell's figure for the series lead and were only one short of the all-time series record. Garner drove in five runs and collected three walks, giving him a series OBP of .556. His hits included four doubles. Scrap Iron also redeemed himself in the field by participating in nine double plays at second base, a series record Bill Mazeroski would have been proud of. World Series MVP Stargell told sports writers before the seventh game that Garner was the outstanding player of the series. "If you guys don't make Garner MVP, I'm going to have to slap some heads," the Pirate team captain kidded.[4] The award, of course, eventually went to Stargell, but few players ever had as big a postseason as the rough-and-tumble second baseman of the Family.

Post-1979: Garner played well with the Pirates over the next year and a half, but did not duplicate his 1979 heroics. A full time second baseman in 1980, Phil played better in the first half of the season, when he hit .273 and was named by Tanner as a backup on the National League All-Star Team. Garner, speaking candidly about his selection, said he felt at that point he was the best second baseman in the NL, because the starter in the Mid-summer Classic that year, Davy Lopes, was hitting below .250. When asked to compare himself to the Phillies' Manny Trillo, who was hitting .300 at the time and was known for his outstanding defense, Garner stated, "I drive in more runs and score more runs than Trillo."[5] With a shoulder injury bothering him, Garner's hitting fell off during the second half of the season. He finished 1980 with 19 less hits, including 13 less extra base hits, than he had in 1979. The shoulder problems worsened for Garner the next spring and he began 1981 on the disabled list. When he returned to action, Garner hustled his way to an All-Star selection for the second consecutive year.

Garner was 32 years old, though, and the Family had deteriorated from a world championship to a cellar dweller by the second half of the 1981 split season. Changes had to be made. On the final day for him to be eligible for postseason play, Garner was traded to the Houston Astros for top second base prospect Johnny Ray, pitcher Randy Niemann and minor league outfielder Kevin Houston. Garner hit just .239 for the Astros down the stretch, but rebounded with one of his best years in 1982 and hit 14 homeruns. He drove in 79 in 1983 after being moved back to third base. He helped the Astros to a division title in 1986, platooning with Denny Walling at third. He moved from the Astros to the Dodgers and Giants over the next two years, retiring from playing following his release from San Francisco in 1988.

Using his skills with people and his knowledge of the game, Garner became a coach for the Astros in 1989 and in 1992 took over as manager of the Milwaukee Brewers. He led an undermanned Brew Crew to a surprise second place finish in the American League West, but the small market Brewers were unable to furnish him with enough talent to finish .500, let alone contend again. Still, Garner's skill as a pilot was evidenced by the fact that Milwaukee ownership kept him on for six and a half more seasons. He was hired by the Detroit Tigers, another small market team trying to rebuild, prior to 2000, but lasted in the Motor City just over one year. Taking over a disappointing Astros team in midseason 2004, Garner helped turn the veteran team around, guiding it to a wild card playoff birth.

While it is true that several members of the Family, including Garner, overachieved during the 1979 season, Garner did so for his entire career. Lanny Frattare was asked at the 2004 Piratefest which Pirates player — from his many years as a broadcaster for the team — he would recommend that a young player emulate. "Phil Garner," Frattare responded. "He had only slightly above average ability, but he worked hard, studied the game and got the most out of his talent that he could." Frattare went on to say that it came as no surprise to him that Garner became a manager following his playing days. Fratare had previously noted that Scrap Iron was also one of the most approachable players he has dealt with during his time in Pittsburgh. He named Garner the top Pirates second baseman he has covered during his 29 years as the Voice of the Pittsburgh Pirates.

Year	Team	AB	R	HR	RBI	BB	SO	SB	AVG	OBP
1973	A's	5	0	0	0	0	3	0	.000	.000
1974	A's	28	4	0	1	1	5	1	.179	.421
1975	A's	488	46	6	54	30	65	4	.246	.641
1976	A's	555	54	8	74	36	71	35	.261	.707
1977	Pirates	585	99	17	77	55	65	32	.260	.766
1978	Pirates	528	66	10	66	66	71	27	.261	.745
1979	Pirates	549	76	11	59	55	74	17	.293	.800
1980	Pirates	548	62	5	58	46	53	32	.259	.673
1981	Pirates	181	22	1	20	21	21	4	.254	.653
	Astros	113	13	0	6	15	11	6	.239	.609
	Totals	294	35	1	26	36	32	10	.248	.636
1982	Astros	588	65	13	83	40	92	24	.274	.743
1983	Astros	567	76	14	79	63	84	18	.238	.679
1984	Astros	374	60	4	45	43	63	3	.278	.743
1985	Astros	463	65	6	51	34	72	4	.268	.717
1986	Astros	313	43	9	41	30	45	12	.265	.744
1987	Astros	112	15	3	15	8	20	1	.223	.616
	Dodgers	126	14	2	8	20	24	5	.190	.569
	Totals	238	29	5	23	28	44	6	.206	.592

1988	Giants	13	0	0	1	1	3	0	.154	.368
	Totals	6136	780	109	738	564	842	225	.260	.712
	Lg Average	6218	796	145	744	604	888	140	.264	.723
	Pos Average	6178	782	113	661	582	782	150	.262	.701

#4   Dale Berra

Pos: SS–3B; Age: 22; Batted: Right; Threw: Right; Year in Major Leagues: 3rd

Pre-1979. Being the son of a Hall of Famer gave Dale Berra big shoes to fill, but he was nonetheless considered a great prospect coming out of Montclair High School in New Jersey. The Bucs gambled that this Berra could be as successful as Yogi and drafted him in the first round of the 1975 free agent draft, 20th overall.

Dale would admit later, "It was a rude awakening that first year in the minors. I was hitting .550 in high school. When you face college pitching and other first-round picks, you realize how difficult the game really is. I hit .260 there. I had never hit less than .400."[6] While the adjustment was difficult, he led the New York–Penn League in RBIs and was voted as the player who would go furthest in baseball, receiving the Stedler Award.

Berra showed much better than average power for a shortstop at the time, cracking 16 homers in 1976. Then he made the leap from A ball to AAA, where he showed he belonged by hitting .290 with 18 homers for Columbus, getting his first call to the majors that season. He collected his first hit and RBI against the Dodgers on September 4.

Dale had another solid campaign at Columbus the following year. He got a much closer look with the Bucs in '78, getting 135 at-bats, mostly at third base, although mustering up only a .207 average, which included his first major league homer, against Tom Dixon of Houston.

1979: Berra began the year with the Pirates, but was sent down in midseason (after the Bucs acquired Bill Madlock and Dave Roberts) to the club's new AAA

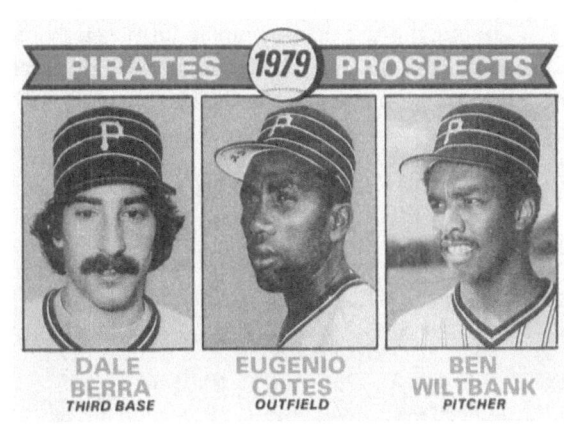

Dale Berra (courtesy of the Topps Company, Inc.).

affiliate in Portland. He had a very impressive .324 average in 56 games before once again getting the call to join the Family. Berra played equally between third and shortstop, 22 games at each, but even though he contributed some big hits in early September, filling in for the injured Tim Foli, he was still not completely ready for the Show. He hit only .211, while defensively he registered a poor .940 fielding percentage at short and an even worse .879 at the hot corner.

1979 Postseason: Berra did not participate in the postseason for Pittsburgh.

Post-1979: After a couple years as a utility infielder, Dale finally took over the spot at short on a full time basis in 1982. For two years he showed he was a decent offensive player, combining with second baseman Johnny Ray to give Pittsburgh the best offensive double play combination in the senior circuit. Unfortunately, his defensive prowess still remained suspect, as he committed 30 errors a year each season between 1982 and 1984.

In 1984, Berra's offense also suffered; he slumped to .221 and became one of the most criticized Pirates.

Following the dismal campaign, Berra was shipped to the Yankees with Jay Buhner and Alfonso Pulido in the forgettable Pete Peterson trade for Steve Kemp and Tim Foli. In New York, Dale was reunited with his father Yogi, who was manager of the Bronx Bombers. The reunion lasted only 16 games. then the elder Berra was fired.

Dale's time in the Big Apple lasted only two seasons; then he was little more than a utility player. Berra's reputation took a hit off the field as well during this time: he was among the players mentioned in baseball's drug trials in 1985. After being released by the Yanks in July of 1986, Berra signed with Houston, where he played only 19 games in 1987, his final major league season.

Despite the fact that his career didn't exactly go the way he had planned, Berra did finish his time in the majors with one record of note. He and Yogi held the father-son all-time home run record of 407 in a career, until a family by the name of Bonds broke it two years later.

Year	Team	AB	R	HR	RBI	BB	SO	SB	AVG	OBP
1977	Pirates	40	0	0	3	1	8	0	.175	.395
1978	Pirates	135	16	6	14	13	20	3	.207	.641
1979	Pirates	123	11	3	15	11	17	0	.211	.597
1980	Pirates	245	21	6	31	16	52	2	.220	.612
1981	Pirates	232	21	2	27	17	34	11	.241	.621
1982	Pirates	529	64	10	61	33	83	6	.263	.692
1983	Pirates	537	51	10	52	61	84	8	.251	.685
1984	Pirates	450	31	9	52	34	78	1	.222	.591
1985	Yankees	109	8	1	8	7	20	1	.229	.597

1986	Yankees	108	10	2	13	9	14	0	.231	.646
1987	Astros	45	3	0	2	8	12	0	.178	.540
	Totals	2553	236	49	278	210	422	32	.236	.638
	Lg Average	2642	337	62	316	252	379	60	.264	.723
	Pos Average	2600	311	41	268	215	339	57	.256	.674

#5 Bill "Mad Dog" Madlock

Pos: 3B; Age: 28; Batted: Right; Threw: Right; Year in Major Leagues: 7th

Pre-1979: A prototypical line drive hitter, Bill Madlock was the final piece needed to turn the 1979 Pittsburgh Pirates from contender to world champion. He not only provided the high average hitting Pete Peterson expected of him — the general manager sent three of the team's top pitching prospects to San Francisco for Madlock, pitcher Dave Roberts and veteran utility infielder Lenny Randle — but played solid defense at third and ran the bases fearlessly.

Bill was selected by the Washington Senators on the 99th pick in the secondary phase of the 1970 winter draft. His first two minor league seasons produced so-so numbers. He hit .269 with six homeruns for Geneva in 1970 and just .234 with 10 homeruns for AA Pittsfield in 1971. Madlock's bat began to show life in 1972, as he returned to Pittsfield and hit .328 in 42 games. By 1973, the stocky infielder had developed into a blue chip prospect. Playing for Spokane in the Pacific Coast League, Madlock led the circuit in runs (119) and total bases (270) while finishing second in batting (.338) and hits (166). The third baseman also drove in 90 runs and his knocks included 22 homers. A September promotion to the big leagues with the Texas Rangers gave him 77 at-bats and he hit .351. Although Texas did not want to part with the blossoming star, the Chicago Cubs insisted on Madlock as the man who would replace Ron Santo at third when Texas sought to acquire Ferguson Jenkins.

Bill Madlock (courtesy of the Topps Company, Inc.).

Madlock had a fine rookie year, batting .313 for the Cubs. In 1975, he posted a career high .354 average to win his first batting title. His second came the very next season, and Madlock captured it in style. Needing to get at least four hits in the final game of the season to pass the Reds' Ken Griffey, Mad Dog went wild at the plate, going 4-for-4.[7] He also increased his power numbers in '76, hitting a career high 36 doubles and establishing new personal highs with 15 homeruns and 84 RBIs.

Despite his consecutive batting titles, Cubs management felt Madlock missed too many games with injuries and decided to trade him to San Francisco for a player with more homerun pop, Bobby Murcer, and Steve Ontavaris, who took over Madlock's position in the field at Wrigley. Madlock had been outspoken, sometimes critical of ownership during his time in Chicago, and this probably hastened his exit from the Windy City. The Cubs agreed to pay Murcer, who was five years older than Madlock, $500,000 more than the contract Madlock had signed.[8]

The change of scenery didn't help much. The Giants moved him to second base, a position for which the stocky infielder was ill-suited. Also, Candlestick Park was known as a difficult field for hitting for average. Madlock, while not adding any batting titles, was able to battle the Candlestick winds to hit .300 in both 1977 and 1978. However, Madlock was not happy. He admitted he did not like playing second[9] and it became public knowledge that he and Giants' manager Joe Altobelli did not get along.

1979. San Francisco had been a surprise contender in 1978, but the team got off to a poor start in '79 and Madlock was ice cold. Instead of finding his name listed among the league leaders in April, the former batting champion was struggling to reach .200. His hitting returned to respectability by June, but his displeasure with Altobelli did not change. The Giants, realizing their run at the Western Division title in 1978 had been a fluke, made Madlock expendable. It was rumored prior to the trading deadline that he would be heading to Pittsburgh, but the deal could not be worked out in time. Still, San Francisco had been able to get waivers on Madlock, and the trade was completed on June 28. Pittsburghers were exuberant about the Pirates adding Mad Dog's considerable skills to Chuck Tanner's lineup. Madlock's former teammates, particularly Darrell Evans and Jack Clark, criticized the trade, and Altobelli was fired in September.

Madlock didn't disappoint his new fans. His debut quickly silenced whatever critics he may have had in Pittsburgh as he went 4-for-5 with a homerun and two RBIs. He stayed hot through the All-Star break, batting .389 in his first 54 at-bats with the Bucs. Turning the dog days of summer into the Mad Dog days of summer, Bill continued to surge the rest of the season, finishing the year on a 10-game hitting streak, batting .421 through the most pressured games of the Pirates' season. Overall in September, Madlock batted .342 and scored 25 runs in 30 games. He stole 12 bases and committed only one error in the season's final month. Additionally, Bill continued to take opposing fielders out of plays with his football-style takeouts. In a city full of Steeler fans, Madlock's aggressiveness was understood and appreciated. Despite having been placed in the sixth spot in the Family's impressive batting order, Madlock's combined season statistics showed new highs for games played, at-bats, runs, RBIs and stolen bases. And although he missed out on hitting .300 for the first time in his major league career, Bill's .298 mark was 14th in the league and one hit short of putting him in the charmed circle of batsmen.

1979 Postseason. Madlock homered against Fred Norman in game three of the NLCS to give the Pirates a 4–0 lead in the game, and went 3-for-12 in the NLCS with a pair of stolen bases. His glove work, however, was even more important in the Pirates' victory, as he played fine defense in the three-game sweep. "He has soft hands," commented Reds scout Ray Shore. "He makes the plays."[10]

An even larger audience got to see Bill at his best during the World Series. He hit .375, going 9-for-24 and he also drew five walks, putting him on base in just under 50 percent of his plate appearances. Madlock's biggest game came in the fifth contest, when he tied what was then a World Series record by going 4-for-4 and driving in the game winning run. Following his record-tying performance against the Orioles, Baltimore's Earl Weaver compared the Pirates star to the American League's perennial batting champion, Rod Carew.

"They told me Madlock was a high ball hitter and then someone told me he was a low ball hitter," Weaver lamented. "What Madlock is, he's a high ball, low ball hitter."[11] Although Orioles pitching stopped Mad Dog in games six and seven, his hitting in game five made those contests necessary.

Post-1979. Pittsburghers hoped to see Madlock battle Dave Parker for a batting crown in 1980, but he got off to a poor start, his sweet swing affected by a thumb injury. Madlock was then suspended for an altercation with umpire Jerry Crawford following what most observed to be a bad call on May 1. Vehemently arguing his point, the third baseman waved his glove in Crawford's face, accidentally hitting the umpire. The action cost Madlock a 15-day suspension and a $5,000 fine. Although he returned to the lineup later in the month, it wasn't until August that his bat got hot. His final .277 average was a disappointment to all concerned.

Mad Dog came back strong the next three seasons, winning batting titles in 1981 (.341) and 1983 (.323). In between, he had his most productive year by adding to his .319 average (second in the league), 33 doubles, 19 homeruns, 92 runs scored and 95 driven in. By this time the Pirates' number three hitter, Madlock had returned to his status of one of baseball's elite batsmen. Injuries, however, reduced his playing time during both of his Silver Bat seasons with the Bucs. He barely got in enough plate appearances to capture his third and fourth batting championships. Some of his critics assert that he would pick and choose when he would play based on how easy the opposing team's starting pitcher was to hit,[12] but in 1983 he played with a torn tendon in his calf the final month of the season, which greatly reduced his availability.[13]

Other facts seem to weaken the argument that Madlock was interested more in winning batting titles than playing. Following Willie Stargell's retirement in 1982, Tanner thought enough of Mad Dog to appoint him team captain. Also, in 1983, the Pirates were fighting the Phillies for the Eastern Division title into September. Considering the drive Madlock always played with when his team had a chance for the postseason (a point even his critics have agreed with), it would have been out of character for him to sit out important games if he was not truly hurt.

The next season, problems with Madlock's right shoulder and elbow greatly reduced his effectiveness, and he had season-ending surgery on August 14.[14] By 1985, the Pirates and the stocky third baseman were struggling to regain old glories. Several teammates became involved with drugs. Madlock became more and more frustrated with the team and his own play. He again was fighting to keep his average above .250. He openly criticized the club's play and resigned as team captain. Madlock himself was criticized for being overweight and he did nothing to hide the fact that he wanted out of Pittsburgh. Joe L. Brown had returned as general manager earlier that season after Peterson had been fired. He granted Madlock his wish by sending the disgruntled player to the Dodgers for three young players: Sid Bream, R.J. Reynolds and Cecil Espy. Madlock responded to the trade by playing great ball for L.A. down the stretch, hitting .360 in 34 games, and he added a .333 performance with three homeruns in a losing cause in the NLCS. Madlock again suffered from injuries in 1986, although he managed to hit .280 before being released in early 1987. No longer having the range to play third on a regular basis, the veteran signed with the Detroit Tigers and appeared mostly as a designated hitter. Again moving to a contender brought his bat alive, as Madlock hit .279 for Detroit with 17 homeruns. However, he was not offered a contract to return in 1988. He moved on to play in Japan for a season before retiring with a career .305 major league average.

Although Mad Dog's final two seasons in Pittsburgh were discouraging, and fans became disenchanted with him due to his lack of success on the field and as Stargell's successor as team captain, Madlock's earlier performances with the team were outstanding. He helped balance the Family's lineup, giving Tanner a second experienced right-handed bat to go with Bill

Robinson in the middle of the Pirates' order. At the time of Mad Dog's arrival in Pittsburgh, the third baseman had the highest batting average (.325) of any active National Leaguer. His new teammate, Dave Parker, possessed the second highest mark, something of an oddity in the history of the league. Madlock was initially very popular in the 'Burgh. He shared what was seen as a blue collar approach to playing sports, and even had the same nickname as one of the city's favorite sports heroes of the day, Steeler Dwight White. He made Pittsburghers forget Peterson's failed attempt to sign Pete Rose.

Although Rose had expressed interest in joining the Pirates prior to 1979, he eventually signed with the Phillies. This left the Pirates again starting the season with Phil Garner at third and Rennie Stennett, still not fully recovered from his 1977 leg injury, at second. Had the Pirates signed Rose, it is likely he would have taken over third base and, barring a trade, Garner probably would have remained as second, where he had finished 1978 as the team's regular. Rose was still a great hitter in 1979, batting .331 with 40 doubles and 95 walks. Although the Phillies played him at first base, he probably could have played third for another couple of seasons. But Rose was not a middle-of-the-order hitter. He was a great lead-off man, but Tanner had two men at his disposal, Omar Moreno and Frank Taveras, who had finished 1–2 in the league in stolen bases in 1978. Would Tanner have hit Rose third? Possibly, but this would have meant his top three hitters in the lineup would have combined for only 10 homeruns the year before. And what about after Taveras was traded? Moreno was hitting well, so Rose could have hit second, with Tanner turning to Garner as his number six hitter and Tim Foli batting eighth. Would this lineup have been as effective, however, as the one that had Madlock and his line drive power batting sixth? Probably not. It would have lacked the balance Madlock helped to provide, and the Pirates' number five hitters (usually Stargell or John Milner) would not have been so well protected. Also, while Rose hit .331 with plenty of walks, Madlock batted .328 after coming to Pittsburgh with more homeruns, RBIs and stolen bases.

What would the impact of having Rose instead of Madlock have been, over the time Madlock played in Pittsburgh? Rose was a better player than Madlock in 1980, but hit only one homerun all year; the Pirates needed power. In 1981, Madlock won the batting crown, but Rose was the runner-up and played 25 more games and collected 45 more hits. Madlock, though, easily outdistanced the future all-time hits king in extrabase hits. Also, Rose turned 40 years old in 1981. One has to wonder if he still would have been able to guard third base. While Madlock's range was beginning to decline, he was still an adequate fielder at the hot corner. By 1982, Rose was down to being a .271 hitter with only 32 extra-base hits. Madlock, as noted above, had an excellent all-around season and followed it up by winning his third batting title while Rose dropped all the way down to .245 with just 14 doubles and three triples in 493 at-bats.

The signing of Pete Rose would have grabbed national headlines and sold a few more tickets before the 1979 season; but over the next five years, *not* signing Rose probably helped the Pirates win many more games than they would have if Pete Peterson had been successful in bringing the most famous Red into the Black and Gold.

Year	Team	AB	R	HR	RBI	BB	SO	SB	AVG	OBP
1973	Rangers	77	16	1	5	7	9	3	.351	.944
1974	Cubs	453	65	9	54	42	39	11	.313	.816
1975	Cubs	514	77	7	64	42	34	9	.354	.881
1976	Cubs	514	68	15	84	56	27	15	.339	.912
1977	Giants	533	70	12	46	43	33	13	.302	.786
1978	Giants	447	76	15	44	48	39	16	.309	.859
1979	Giants	249	37	7	41	18	19	11	.261	.707
	Pirates	311	48	7	44	34	22	21	.328	.859
	Totals	560	85	14	85	52	41	32	.298	.793
1980	Pirates	494	62	10	53	45	33	16	.277	.740
1981	Pirates	279	35	6	45	34	17	18	.341	.908
1982	Pirates	568	92	19	95	48	39	18	.319	.856
1983	Pirates	473	68	12	68	49	24	3	.323	.830
1984	Pirates	403	38	4	44	26	29	3	.253	.620
1985	Pirates	399	49	10	41	39	42	3	.251	.711
	Dodgers	114	20	2	15	10	11	7	.360	.869
	Totals	513	69	12	56	49	53	10	.275	.747
1986	Dodgers	379	38	10	60	30	43	3	.280	.740
1987	Dodgers	61	5	3	7	6	5	0	.180	.609
	Tigers	326	56	14	50	28	45	4	.279	.811
	Totals	387	61	17	57	34	50	4	.264	.779
	Totals	6594	920	163	860	605	510	174	.305	.807
	Lg Average	6304	808	148	756	614	907	141	.264	.723
	Pos Average	6306	806	161	775	628	895	102	.263	.729

#6   Rennie Stennett

Pos: 2B; Age: 28; Batted: Right; Threw: Right; Year in Major Leagues: 9th

Pre-1979: Signed by superscout Howie Haak out of Panama in 1969, Rennie Stennett burst onto the Pittsburgh scene in 1971 after hitting a sparkling .344 in the first half of the season at the Bucs' top farm club in Charleston. Stennett was brought up to replace Dave Cash, who was out fulfilling his military obligations, and hit a career best .353 his freshman campaign. Unfortunately for the young second baseman, he was left off the Pirates' '71 postseason roster in favor of the veteran Jose Pagan.

5. The Members of the Family

After Cash enjoyed two decent seasons the following two campaigns, general manager Joe L. Brown shipped him out to the Phillies for pitcher Ken Brett, paving the way for Stennett to be the starting second baseman in 1974.

Stennett not only succeeded offensively but was strong defensively leading the National League in fielding percentage, put outs and total chances on two occasions each over the next few seasons. He had 59 consecutive errorless games in 1974.

The highlight of the Panamanian second baseman's career came in 1975 in a game against the Chicago Cubs on September 16 in Wrigley Field: the 24-year-old Pirate became the first player in the 20th century to get seven hits in a nine-inning game when he went 7-for-7 in a 22–0 demolition by the Bucs. Stennett would stretch his string to nine in a row by getting hits in his next two at-bats during the following game against the Phils.

Rennie Stennet (courtesy of the Topps Company, Inc.).

The year 1977 marked both the high and low points of Stennett's career. The second baseman was battling with teammate Dave Parker for the NL batting crown and was hitting a tremendous .336 when the Pirates took on the Giants in Candlestick Park on August 21. While sliding into second base, he broke his leg horribly, disfiguring it in a manner such as catcher Jason Kendall did 22 years later in 1999. Stennett was out the remainder of the season, falling only 12 plate appearances short of qualifying for the batting title (which was won by Parker with a .338 mark).

Stennnett came back in 1978 but was a shell of his former self, batting only a dismal .243. It was hoped that with some off-season rest, he would be able to come back strong for the 1979 campaign.

1979. Unfortunately for Stennett and the Bucs, their hopes were not realized. He started the season at second base with Phil Garner at third, but with Stennett still not performing up to par, general manager Pete Peterson pulled the plug on a trade with the Giants, bringing over third baseman Bill Madlock. While the move was the final piece in Pittsburgh's championship puzzle, it turned out to be the end for the nine-year vet as a Pirate. Manager Chuck Tanner moved Garner to second to make a place for Madlock, leaving Stennett out of the mix. He finished the year with only 76 hits and a .238 average, his lowest marks since joining the Pirates in 1971. Although he was only 29, it was the beginning of the end for his baseball career.

1979 Postseason. His position now lost, Rennie was but a bit player for the Bucs in the 1979 post season, appearing for only one inning in the NLCS as a defensive replacement in game one.

Rennie got his only at-bat of the postseason in game one of the World Series, singling to right off Mike Flanagan while pinch hitting for Don Robinson. The hit would be his last in a Pirates uniform and it would be the only action Stennett saw in the series.

Post-1979. Rennie Stennett was granted free agency after the 1979 campaign and signed a contract with San Francisco. The Giants thought he could turn his career around, but he unfortunately could not. He batted .241 in two seasons before being released in April of 1982.

While the end of his career came prematurely at 31 years of age, the Panamanian will be remembered in the Steel City as a player who gave his all. Brown summed up Stennett's time in the 'Burgh best when he said, "There hasn't been a player in baseball, not even Pete Rose, who hustled more than Rennie Stennett."[15]

Year	Team	AB	R	HR	RBI	BB	SO	SB	AVG	OBP
1971	Pirates	153	24	1	15	7	9	1	.353	.835
1972	Pirates	370	43	3	30	9	43	4	.286	.683
1973	Pirates	466	45	10	55	16	63	2	.242	.623
1974	Pirates	673	84	7	56	32	51	8	.291	.696
1975	Pirates	616	89	7	62	33	42	5	.286	.707
1976	Pirates	654	59	2	60	19	32	18	.257	.618
1977	Pirates	453	53	5	51	29	24	28	.336	.806
1978	Pirates	333	30	3	35	13	22	2	.243	.583
1979	Pirates	319	31	0	24	24	25	1	.238	.581
1980	Giants	397	34	2	37	22	31	4	.244	.588
1981	Giants	87	8	1	7	3	6	2	.230	.528
	Totals	4521	500	41	432	207	348	75	.274	.665
	Lg Average	4442	553	97	515	437	622	90	.262	.712
	Pos Average	4390	534	46	396	393	486	123	.258	.664

#8 Willie "Pops" Stargell

Pos: 1b; Age: 39; Batted: Left; Threw: Left; Year in Major Leagues: 18th

Pre-1979: Rising to the major leagues despite facing strong prejudice and even death threats while playing minor league ball in the South, Willie

5. The Members of the Family

Stargell established himself as a budding star by his second full season with the Pirates in 1964. A year later, he was acknowledged as one of baseball's top power hitters, smashing 27 homeruns and driving in 107 in the heat of a pennant race. In 1966, Stargell upped his homerun total to 33, the most yet hit by the left-handed hitter, who played half his games in Forbes Field and hit a career high .315. Stargell continued to be a productive hitter throughout the 1960s, but his power numbers were greatly reduced by his home ballpark.

That changed when the Pirates moved into Three Rivers Stadium during the 1970 season. Stargell hit .500 against the Cincinnati Reds in the Bucs' loss in the 1970 NLCS. The first Pirate to homer at Three Rivers, he hit a major league high 48 homeruns in 1971, the first full season the Pirates called the new facility home. He also drove in a career high 125 homeruns while hitting .295. Knee problems, however, greatly reduced the Hall of Famer's power late in the season and he was only a shadow of himself in the Pirates' postseason victories against the San Francisco Giants and Baltimore Orioles.

Willie Stargell (courtesy of the Topps Company, Inc.).

The hard turf at Three Rivers Stadium complicated the knee problems and forced Stargell, who possessed one of baseball's strongest arms—perhaps second only to Roberto Clemente's in the early 1970s—from leftfield to first base in 1972. Stargell had another All-Star season in '72, and in 1973 not only moved back to left field, but almost single-handedly carried the Pirates into the playoffs by leading the league in homeruns (44), doubles (43), RBIs (119) and slugging (.646) while missing hitting .300 by a single point. Stargell had two more strong years in 1974 and 1975, although he did not statistically match his performance of the first four years of the decade. In 1976, the future of his career came into question for the first time.

Now 36 years old and an everyday first baseman, the Pirates' team captain faced personal tragedy when his wife Delores was diagnosed with a life threatening blood clot on her brain. Willie, playing under great stress and battling an assortment of nagging injuries, managed only 20 homeruns and a .257 average. His homerun total tied his lowest mark since becoming an everyday player, and his batting average was his worst since 1968. Willie's 65 RBIs were also his fewest since his rookie season. Although his wife recovered and Stargell looked forward to a big comeback season in 1977 under his new manager, Chuck Tanner, the prolific slugger's season was cut short. Battling dizzy spells early in the year, Stargell nonetheless hit 13 homeruns and batted .274 in 186 at-bats before suffering a pinched nerve. The injury came a few days after Stargell had hit his 400th career homerun, while he broke up a fight between Bruce Kison and the Phillies' Mike Schmidt. The Captain's comeback year would have to wait until 1978.

Once '78 began, however, Stargell had trouble hitting. Tanner decided to stick with him, noting the 38-year-old's bat speed remained as good as anyone's in the league. Stargell made his manager look like a genius by rebounding from his slow start to make the All-Star Team for the seventh time in his career. He finished with 28 homeruns and 97 RBIs, his highest totals in both categories since 1973. He not only quieted critics who said he was washed up, but helped lead the Pirates to an almost miraculous drive that nearly netted them the Eastern Division title after having fallen 11½ games behind the Phillies in mid-August. Following the season, Willie was named the National League's Comeback Player of the Year.

1979. The year 1979 was when Stargell finally received recognition from the national media for his achievements. The charismatic leader of the Pirates led the team in homeruns and contributed seemingly countless clutch hits. Pops, who had finished a disappointing second in the Most Valuable Player voting in 1971 and 1973, finally was rewarded with the MVP Award following the season, sharing the honor with Keith Hernandez, the St. Louis Cardinals batting champion. Stargell's totals of 32 homeruns and 82 RBIs were far from league-leading tallies, but he mattered as much or more to his team's success in 1979 as any player in sports. Eight of his homeruns, including four hit in September, won games.[16] His blasts included one in extra innings against the Pirates' chief rival, the Montreal Expos, on September 18, and a homerun in the final game of the season to help the Pirates clinch the East.

The year 1979 also demonstrated to the world the growth of Stargell as a human being. Early in his career, he had been known for his playfulness, keeping late hours and even as a young player battling weight problems, but by the 1970s he had become a soft spoken man who was involved in philanthropic activities. Outside of Pittsburgh, however, Stargell's charitable contributions were not well known. Although the media usually gave the Captain positive press, he was often overlooked despite being one of baseball's most feared hitters for over a decade.

It had taken Stargell a few years to grow into the role of leader, a responsibility thrust on him following the death of Clemente and retirement of

Bill Mazeroski in 1972. By the late 1970s, however, Stargell had become the man younger players turned to for advice and counsel. He had faced adversity on and off the field. He had heard boos as well as cheers and knew how to keep his demeanor even, his manner professional. Players, on both the Pirates and other teams, genuinely liked the man playing first base for Pittsburgh. His teammates came to refer to him as Pops, the unquestioned leader of the team known as the Family. Stargell was still playful, even in his patriarchal role. He encouraged good natured rivalry among his teammates, passing out felt stars, much as teachers used to pass out gold star stickers, as rewards for something a player had done to help the Bucs to victory.

Stargell Stars became hot commodities among the Pirates, who began sewing them onto their caps as badges of honor. Willie's outlook on life (he was fond of saying, "The umpire says 'play ball, not work ball'") and his humor helped keep the Pirate ship steady in what was uncharted waters for many of his crew — baseball's postseason, especially when the Pirates fell behind the Orioles, 3–1, in the World Series.

1979 Postseason. In the National League Championship Series, Stargell won the opening game with a three-run homer off the Reds' Tom Hume in the tenth inning. His homerun in game three put the Pirates in position to sweep the Reds. Willie went 5-for-11 overall for a .455 average and was named the NLCS Most Valuable Player. Still, it was the World Series where Stargell's star shone the brightest. He hit .400 (12-for-30) with a record-setting seven extra-base hits, which included three homeruns and four doubles. Pops also tied World Series records with 25 total bases and four hits in one game. Most memorable though, was his two-run homerun in the sixth inning of game seven, which gave the Pirates the 2–1 lead that they would not again relinquish. He was named the World Series MVP, chosen despite a record-tying .500 batting average by Phil Garner and excellent performances by Tim Foli, Dave Parker, Bill Madlock, Bert Blyleven and Kent Tekulve. Stargell's performance focused new attention on the old star from the small market team in Western Pennsylvania, and undoubtedly helped him into Baseball's Hall of Fame on his first try in 1988.

Post-1979. Although there were those who argued that Stargell should have gone out on top and announced he was retiring following the World Series, Pops knew what he meant to his Family and still enjoyed playing the game. He got off to a strong start in 1980, but suffered a hamstring pull in late May, then severely injured his knee in mid-August, ending his season. Not coincidentally, the Pirates, who were in first place at the time of Stargell's knee injury, uncharacteristically slumped in September and finished in third place. Pops returned in 1981, but the Pirates were all too aware of his advancing age and knee problems and traded for slugger Jason Thompson in spring training. Stargell spent the last two years of his career mostly pinch hitting.

He appeared in just 17 games in the field in 1981 and 1982 combined. His last homerun came off Tom Hume, the same pitcher he had taken deep to win game one of the 1979 NCLS, on July 21, 1982, about six weeks short of the 20th anniversary of his first major league at-bat.

Following his playing career, Stargell briefly worked in broadcasting, announcing Pirates games on cable with Bob Prince and Steve Blass. He later worked as a minor league instructor for the club, and in 1985, with the Pirates in desperate need of anything which would remind fans of happier times, joined Tanner's coaching staff. When the manager's contract was not renewed following the season, Stargell moved with him to be a coach with the Atlanta Braves. He worked in Atlanta's front office as well, before returning to the Pirates as a special assistant to the general manager in 1997. By this time, however, Stargell's health was starting to fail him. His weight had ballooned following his playing career, and although he had dropped significant poundage by the time he came back to the Pirates, the returning hero did not look well. The media respected Stargell's privacy, but when diabetes and renal problems began to take a greater toll a few years later, his battle became public knowledge when he was unable to continue in his duties for the Pirates.

Still, Stargell made one last, memorable appearance in Pittsburgh, returning for the closing ceremonies at Three Rivers Stadium. Amid a standing ovation, the now frail Stargell lobbed a ball which bounced to catcher Jason Kendall. It was the final pitch at the stadium where Willie had hit more homeruns than any man. Earlier that weekend, a model of a statue being built to honor Stargell outside PNC Park (soon to be the Pirates' new home) was unveiled. Sadly, Pops never got to see the finished product. He was too ill to travel to Pittsburgh when the statue was dedicated, and he passed away the morning of the ballpark's first regular season game, April 9, 2001.

An interesting question emerges about Stargell and his career. At what point did the Pirates hero start to merit consideration for election to Baseball's Hall of Fame? During the 1960s, Stargell's power numbers were affected by playing in spacious Forbes Field, and while he had big seasons, particularly in 1965, 1966 and 1969, he was overshadowed by contemporary sluggers such as Hank Aaron, Willie Mays, Orlando Cepeda and Willie McCovey when power hitters of the National League were discussed. On his own team, Roberto Clemente was a bigger star, and despite some healthy batting averages, Stargell also posted unimpressive marks such as his .243 as a rookie in 1963 and .237 in 1968.

The Captain's home run numbers were expected to go up with the team's move to Three Rivers Stadium, and Stargell was one player who openly admitted he would not miss "Lady Forbes."[17] His wife Delores one season estimated that if Stargell had been playing in the still-to-be-finished stadium instead of the old ballpark, he would have added over 20 homeruns to his season total. Willie did not disappoint the prognosticators. He enjoyed his biggest home run year in 1971, the first full season Three Rivers Stadium was open. He followed this up with another excellent year in 1972 and an MVP caliber year and homerun championship in 1973, his second of each in three years. However, the major league's top power threat saw his homerun totals decline in both 1974 and 1975. At this point, Stargell had hit 368 homers in his career. He hit only 33 homeruns combined in 1976 and 1977, due to the above mentioned personal hardship and injuries. While as individual seasons they did nothing to endorse Willie's candidacy, they did allow him to eclipse the 400 homerun mark.

Some have argued that without Stargell's MVP trifecta season of 1979, he would not have been voted to the Hall of Fame.[18] Although there is merit to the argument that Stargell would not have been a first-ballot Hall of Famer if his career had continued to decline or even if he had ended it following the 1977 season, it seems he would have been elected at some point by the baseball writers. He had too many achievements for the voters to ignore him during his time of eligibility.

By hitting his 400th homerun on June 29 off Eric Rasmussen, Stargell joined an elite club of just 16 other players. At the time, all of those players with 400 homeruns who were eligible for Cooperstown were elected to the Hall of Fame. Those 400 HR Club members not yet eligible included Hank Aaron, Willie Mays, Frank Robinson, Harmon Killebrew, Willie McCovey and Billy Williams. Aaron, Mays, Robinson and McCovey were all first-ballot Hall of Famers. Killebrew was voted in on his fourth try and Williams his sixth. By the year Willie would have become eligible if he had retired following 1977, only one other player, Carl Yastrzemski, had joined the ranks. Yaz was elected in his first year of eligibility. As it was, Stargell played through 1982 and his name did not appear on the ballot until 1988. By that time, the first generation of players who would not be voted into the Hall of Fame had arrived with Dave Kingman and Darrell Evans. Stargell, however, was a far superior player to both. Neither hit for impressive averages and Kingman was an atrocious fielder. Evans, a better all-around player than Kingman, was helped by playing most of his career in two ballparks that boosted power numbers, Atlanta's Fulton County Stadium and Detroit's Tiger Stadium. Like Kingman, though, he hit under .250 for his career. Adding to the argument that Pops would have been voted into the Hall of Fame is the fact that two sluggers of his generation who did not hit 400 homeruns and who were not standout defensive players, Tony Perez and Orlando Cepeda, have been added to the hall in recent years. While it is true Cepeda made it through the Veterans' Committee, he was probably denied the necessary 75 percent votes by the baseball writers because of a drug charge that followed his playing days.

Stargell, although handicapped by playing in Forbes Field for a number of prime seasons, enjoyed (given the era he played in) seven standout years, which would be expected of a Hall of Fame power hitter. A simple way of looking at this without getting too scientific is to count the years Willie had superior numbers in two of the three triple crown categories, categories generally acknowledged as representing a hitter's greatness. These three are, of course, homeruns, RBIs and batting average. For players of the 1960s and 1970s, hitting 20 or more homeruns, knocking in 100, and batting .300 were target numbers that people generally agreed represented a star caliber season for a middle-of-the-lineup hitter. It was particularly true of players who played in ballparks with deep power alleys. Stargell eclipsed two of these three categories in 1965, 1966, 1969, 1971, 1972, 1973 and 1974. Players like Aaron and Mays certainly had many more years in which they could boast of such achievements, but the topic here is not whether Willie was as good a player as they were, but whether he would have made the Hall of Fame without 1979.

Stargell's two best seasons, 1971 and 1973, rank among the two most potent years by a player in during the '70's. Only George Foster in 1977 enjoyed a bigger homerun year than Stargell did in 1971. It is true Pops did not win the Most Valuable Player Award in either year, but there were certainly arguments in Stargell's favor against the choices of Joe Torre in 1971 and Pete Rose in 1973.

Speaking of Rose: During the 1970s, he may have been the only player in baseball who was more media friendly than Stargell. While popularity with reporters should not be a factor in Hall of Fame voting, it obviously can help an individual's chances of being elected to Cooperstown. Stargell also was involved in humanitarian causes. Most noteworthy was his work to help those afflicted with sickle cell anemia.

In 1979, Stargell's magnificence as a hitter and team leader was put on center stage and earned him national appreciation. He was named Man of the Year by the *Sporting News* and shared *Sports Illustrated's* Sportsman of the Year award with the Steelers' Terry Bradshaw. Willie Stargell was worthy of the Hall of Fame long before he became the only man in baseball history to accept three MVP trophies in one year.

Year	Team	AB	R	HR	RBI	BB	SO	SB	AVG	OBP
1962	Pirates	31	1	0	4	3	10	0	.290	.805
1963	Pirates	304	34	11	47	19	85	0	.243	.718
1964	Pirates	421	53	21	78	17	92	1	.273	.805
1965	Pirates	533	68	27	107	39	127	1	.272	.829
1966	Pirates	485	84	33	102	48	109	2	.315	.962
1967	Pirates	462	54	20	73	67	103	1	.271	.830
1968	Pirates	435	57	24	67	47	105	5	.237	.756

1969	Pirates	522	89	29	92	61	120	1	.307	.938
1970	Pirates	474	70	31	85	44	119	0	.264	.840
1971	Pirates	511	104	48	125	83	154	0	.295	1.026
1972	Pirates	495	75	33	112	65	129	1	.293	.931
1973	Pirates	522	106	44	119	80	129	0	.299	1.038
1974	Pirates	508	90	25	96	87	106	0	.301	.944
1975	Pirates	461	71	22	90	58	109	0	.295	.891
1976	Pirates	428	54	20	65	50	101	2	.257	.797
1977	Pirates	186	29	13	35	31	55	0	.274	.931
1978	Pirates	390	60	28	97	50	93	3	.295	.949
1979	Pirates	424	60	32	82	47	105	0	.281	.904
1980	Pirates	202	28	11	38	26	52	0	.262	.836
1981	Pirates	60	2	0	9	5	9	0	.283	.683
1982	Pirates	73	6	3	17	10	24	0	.233	.729
	Totals	7927	1195	475	1540	937	1936	17	.282	.889
	Lg Average	7504	920	176	857	729	1111	126	.258	.708
	Pos Average	7620	987	231	1005	787	1202	120	.267	.752

#10   Tim "Crazy Horse" Foli

Pos: SS; Age: 28; Batted: Right; Threw: Right; Year in Major Leagues: 10

Pre-1979. Tim Foli reached the major leagues as a teenager after shooting through the New York Mets' minor league system in less than two years. In his first full season, 1971, Foli held his own as the Mets' top utility man, and despite not always displaying a cool head, impressed scouts so much that the Montreal Expos insisted he be part of a huge trade the following season that sent star outfielder Rusty Staub to Gotham.

Tim immediately became the Expos' everyday shortstop, and quickly became known for his outbursts on the field. Gene Mauch, his manager with the Expos, was quoted as saying that Foli's problems with control stemmed from his "constant search for perfection."[19] Others weren't as generous in their appraisals. The shortstop's tempestuous behavior on the field

Tim Foli (courtesy of the Topps Company, Inc.).

seemed to the casual observer to reflect immaturity, which might also explain why he showed little improvement in his hitting until 1976, when he batted .264 with 36 doubles. His fighting with the opposition and teammates, blasting umpires, and on-field tantrums led to the nickname "Crazy Horse." Although Foli's defense had been fairly steady and sometimes spectacular, when he got off to a .175 start in 1977 he was traded to San Francisco for Giants shortstop Chris Speier.

Tim spent the remainder of the season in San Francisco, but the Giants were so unimpressed that they sold him to the Mets in December. Injuries limited Foli to 113 games in 1978, his fewest since his rookie season in 1971. He continued to play consistent defense and rebounded offensively to hit .257, but the following spring Mets manager Joe Torre decided to move another glove man, Doug Flynn, to shortstop in order to play Kelvin Chapman, a rookie, at second.

1979. Spending most of the first two weeks of the season on the Mets bench, Foli was not surprised when New York general manager Joe McDonald told him he was traded. He became ecstatic to learn he had been dealt to the Pirates. Foli was quick to point out that he had always played for poor teams before coming to Pittsburgh: "The best team I had ever played on was the Mets my first year. The Pirates [have] been a great team since I had come into the league."[20] Now in his ninth season in the major leagues, Tim blamed his low emotional boiling point on his frustration over losing. Although he credited Mauch with helping him play within his limits, the shortstop admitted he was "plenty hard-headed then."[21]

Pirates general manager Harding Peterson had made the trade to tighten the Pirates' shaky defense. Although Foli was not thought to have the range of the man he was replacing, Frank Taveras, he had long demonstrated fine instincts for the position and knew as well as anyone in the league how to play hitters. Peterson assessed his new player's skills: "He's a good defensive shortstop. He's been involved in making a lot of double plays. I don't consider him an out man at the plate."[22] Pittsburghers had soured on Tavares' lack of hustle as well as his erratic play at shortstop. While Foli's flareups were well documented, Peterson dismissed them, noting, "If he plays well and has an outgoing personality, I think he will be a crowd-pleaser. He plays hard."[23]

Initially, Tanner moved Phil Garner into Tavares' number two spot in the batting order and hit Foli eighth, but his first few games in black, gold and pinstripes were frustrating for everyone. He got off to a 0-for-10 start and made an error that cost the Bucs a game in Houston.

Foli broke out of the doldrums with three hits the next night, but the Pirates continued to play below expectations. Batting coach Bob Skinner worked with Foli, adjusting his stance to help him focus on making contact. Skinner had Foli hold the bat parallel to the ground and then choke up on the bat handle more than any of his teammates. In May, Tanner decided to move Foli, who had become a tough man to strike out, to the second spot in the order behind speedster Omar Moreno. Although the shortstop did not walk much, he was an excellent bunter and hit-and-run man and could afford the league's top base stealer ample protection. Foli closed out May with a game winning hit off Bruce Sutter (later to win the Cy Young Award). His defense gave the Steel City its most consistent play at shortstop since Gene Alley was in his prime, over a decade before.

Still playing with great intensity, Foli was contributing offensively as never before. At the All-Star break, he was hitting .282,[24] finally summing up his talents in a manner that suited his abilities and pleased his employers. While Pittsburghers were cautiously optimistic Foli would continue this pace, the now-solid all-around player improved his average to .301 in the second half.[25] His final .288 average and 65 RBIs were career highs. He struck out only 14 times all season, making the Family's number two batter the toughest man in the National League to strike out in '79. His ability to cover the plate was spectacular late in the season; Tim did not strike out at all after August 17. Defensively, Foli was everything Peterson had hoped for. His .978 fielding percentage with Pittsburgh trailed only the record-setting mark of .991 by Phillies' Larry Bowa. Foli committed just 15 errors, again trailing only Bowa, whose six errors established a new major league low for an everyday shortstop. Taveras, in contrast, had made 38 errors in 1978 and committed 28 in '79. Foli had also outhit the man he replaced by 26 points for the season.

1979 Postseason. If Pirates fans delighted in Foli's play during the regular season in 1979, they were elated by it during the postseason. He hit .333 in both the National League Championship Series and World Series and drove in three runs in each of the championship sets of games.

In the opening game of the NLCS, Foli started the Pirates' game winning rally in the 11th with a leadoff single, and he started the Pirates on the right path in game two. With the Bucs trailing 1–0 in the fourth, he singled and eventually scored the tying run on Bill Madlock's infield grounder. In the fifth, he singled in Garner for the go-ahead run. The Reds tied the game in the ninth, but Foli was again involved with the Pirates' scoring an extra-inning victory as he sacrificed Moreno to second in the tenth, setting up Dave Parker's game winning hit. Foli added an RBI in game three on a deep fly ball to centerfield to cap the Pirates' 7–1 win. Foli's fielding against the Reds was flawless; as he handled a dozen chances without an error during the three-game sweep. Foli finished second to Willie Stargell in the Championship Series MVP voting.

Although Foli made a surprising three errors in the World Series, his overall play was outstanding. He started a heads-up double play in the second game, scored the tying run in game five. He was in the middle of the Bucs' initial scoring in game six when his single put two men on base for Parker in the seventh. The Cobra's wicked shot off second baseman Rich Dauer led to the Pirates' first run, and Foli scored the second on Stargell's sacrifice fly. The formerly weak hitter finished the World Series with 10 hits to his credit and a place in Pittsburgh sports history.

Post-1979. Foli played well in 1980, but not as well as in 1979. He did win his first fielding title, becoming the first Pirates shortstop since Rabbit Maranville in 1923 to lead the league in fielding, but his batting average fell to .265 and his RBIs from 65 to 38. Foli also missed 35 games due to assorted injuries.

The physical pounding the shortstop took began to further affect Foli's range. After he hit .247 in 1981 he was traded to the California Angels for hitting prospect Brian Harper, amid talk that he could no longer cover shortstop on a turf field. Reunited with Mauch and healthier in 1982, Foli had the luxury of playing on a slower grass surface in Anaheim and performed well, winning his second fielding title in three years with a .983 mark and driving in 56 runs. His play helped the Angels win the American League West.

In 1983, Foli played only 74 games at shortstop, giving way to young Dick Schoefield, the son of another former Pirate by the same name, who possessed much greater range. Tim went back to New York a third time in 1984, but this time as a utility player for the Yankees. With Foli still having the sure hands that helped make him a fan favorite in 1979, the Pirates reacquired him along with Steve Kemp for Dale Berra and two minor leaguers: Jay Buhner, who later became a star for the Mariners, and Alfonso Pulido whose major league career never took off. Tanner hoped publicly that Foli could play the majority of games at shortstop for the Pirates in 1985, but he was injured early in the season. After going just 7-for-37, he decided to retire as a player when the Pirates realized he could no longer play every day. Since then, Foli has served at times as a major league coach, including a stint with the Milwaukee Brewers under his former double play partner from Pittsburgh, Phil Garner.

Tim was a player one had to watch daily to appreciate. When Peterson traded Taveras for Foli, there were many — among them Peterson's former mentor, Joe L. Brown — who did not agree with the move. Taveras had more range in the field than Foli and was one of baseball's most dangerous base stealers. He had also hit .278 in 1978, a figure higher than Foli's best mark. Tavaras' offense and sometimes spectacular defense led to some articles' placing him below only Larry Bowa and Dave Concepcion as the National League's top shortstops,[26] even though Tavaras annually ranked among the league leaders in errors, topping the National League in that negative category in 1978. More frustrating to fans were his mental lapses and occasional lack of hustle. He did not always run out ground balls and at times seemed to openly sulk. Pittsburghers were divided over their feelings towards the shortstop, and while debates raged over whether or not the Pirates should trade him, most fans were unimpressed that the player Peterson settled on in exchange for Taveras was, a shortstop who had lost his regular job on the last-place Mets.

Perhaps, it was argued, the real key to the trade was minor league pitcher Greg Field, whom the Pirates had obtained as well. Surely it wasn't Foli, perceived by many in the 'Burgh as a hot tempered loudmouth who had spent his mediocre career with lousy teams.

Field, however, never played for the Pirates. Foli became, as Peterson predicted, a fan favorite, arguably second only to Stargell among members of the Family. After playing poorly for a few games, Foli's competitiveness and consistency in the field won over the city. He shied away from no one when making the double play and did little things that annoyed the opposition but entertained fans and helped the Pirates win. Foli used to fall on top of opposing base runners when a teammate's throw got away. Choking up on the bat, the Pirates shortstop dumped little hits into the outfield and protected his teammates on the bases by expanding his strike zone to the point of even tossing his bat at balls on pitchouts. At least twice during the season, Foli actually singled on such plays. Reining in his emotions, Tim became something of a middle-class (he played too well to be called a poor man's) Dick Groat for the 1979 world champions.

It is true Foli's career reached its pinnacle in 1979, but it is likely that his hard style of play contributed to his decline. Without it, though, it's unlikely that the season of the Family would have been more than a footnote in the history of Pirates baseball.

Year	Team	AB	R	HR	RBI	BB	SO	SB	AVG	OBP
1970	Mets	11	0	0	1	0	2	0	.364	.728
1971	Mets	288	32	0	24	18	50	5	.226	.553
1972	Expos	540	45	2	35	25	43	11	.241	.561
1973	Expos	458	37	2	36	28	40	6	.240	.561
1974	Expos	441	41	0	39	28	27	8	.254	.590
1975	Expos	572	64	1	29	36	49	13	.238	.578
1976	Expos	546	41	6	54	16	33	6	.264	.647
1977	Expos	57	2	0	3	0	4	0	.175	.470
	Giants	368	30	4	27	11	16	2	.228	.570
	Totals	425	32	4	30	11	20	2	.221	.558
1978	Mets	413	37	1	27	14	30	2	.257	.603
1979	Mets	7	0	0	0	0	0	0	.000	.000
	Pirates	525	70	1	65	28	14	6	.291	.680

	Totals	532	70	1	65	28	14	6	.288	.670
1980	Pirates	495	61	3	38	19	23	11	.265	.623
1981	Pirates	316	32	0	20	17	10	7	.247	.582
1982	Angels	480	46	3	56	14	22	2	.252	.581
1983	Angels	330	29	2	29	5	18	2	.252	.563
1984	Yankees	163	8	0	16	2	16	0	.252	.584
1985	Pirates	37	1	0	2	4	2	0	.189	.457
Totals		6047	576	25	501	265	399	81	.251	.592
	Lg Average	6240	780	139	728	609	877	128	.262	.714
	Pos Average	6070	687	52	515	473	731	142	.248	.629

#10   Frank Tavares

Pos: SS; Age: 29; Batted: Right; Threw: Right; Year in Major Leagues: 8th

Pre-1979. Frank Tavaras played three years of A ball after being inked by the Bucs as a free agent in 1968. He finally made a jump in 1971. That year he flew from AA to AAA Charleston before getting one at-bat with the world champion Pirates. Tavaras spent the next two seasons in Charleston, being named to the International League All-Star Team the latter season. The Dominican Republic native made the majors for good in 1974 and was named the Pirates' Rookie of the Year by the Pittsburgh baseball writers.

He was an exciting fielder yet an extremely erratic one; a player who was subpar offensively. But once Pirates manager Danny Murtaugh moved the fleet-footed shortstop to the top of the order in 1976, Tavaras gave the Steel City the most exciting running it had seen on the base paths since the days of Honus Wagner and Max Carey. He swiped 58 bases that season before smashing Carey's all time mark the following year with a league-leading 70.

In 1978 he combined with center fielder Omar Moreno to give the Bucs a double stolen base threat. Tavares garnered 46 with a then-career-high .278 average,

Frank Taveras (courtesy of the Topps Company, Inc.).

5. The Members of the Family 147

while Moreno broke Frank's one-year team mark with an NL high 71. Tavares showed some power, smashing his previous lifetime mark in doubles with 31.

1979. Although Tavares was exciting, his fielding at short was not what championship clubs were built on, so general manager Pete Peterson pulled off a surprise deal, sending the former stolen base champ to the Mets for New York's back-up shortstop, Tim Foli. While on paper the move seemed quizzical, prompting former general manager Joe Brown to wonder why such a deal had been made, it certainly turned out to be a gold mine. Foli settled the infield defensively and hit a surprising .291 with 65 RBIs while Taveras hit only .262 for the season, which included a .244 average in 45 at-bats with the Bucs.

1979 Postseason. Tavaras was, of course, in the Big Apple when the Bucs won the world championship.

Post-1979. The Mets felt Taveras was a team leader, so they gave him a five-year extension after playing well for New York in '79.[27] Unfortunately, after hitting a career best .279 in 1980, Frankie proved the Mets wrong, and he was out of the game two years later after a one-year stint with the Expos. The Pirates discussed having Tavaras join the team as a non-roster invitee in spring training, 1983, but Tavaras changed his mind and did not report.

Year	Team	AB	R	HR	RBI	BB	SO	SB	AVG	OBP
1971	Pirates	0	0	0	0	0	0	0		
1972	Pirates	3	0	0	0	1	1	0	.000	.250
1974	Pirates	333	33	0	26	25	41	13	.246	.570
1975	Pirates	378	44	0	23	37	42	17	.212	.541
1976	Pirates	519	76	0	24	44	79	58	.258	.618
1977	Pirates	544	72	1	29	38	71	70	.252	.637
1978	Pirates	654	81	0	38	29	60	46	.278	.666
1979	Pirates	45	4	0	1	0	2	2	.244	.555
	Mets	635	89	1	33	33	72	42	.263	.638
	Totals	680	93	1	34	33	74	44	.262	.633
1980	Mets	562	65	0	25	23	64	32	.279	.635
1981	Mets	283	30	0	11	12	36	16	.230	.553
1982	Expos	87	9	0	4	7	6	4	.161	.462
	Totals	4043	503	2	214	249	474	300	.255	.614
	Lg Average	4137	524	91	489	402	568	91	.264	.719
	Pos Average	4023	460	31	335	304	468	99	.251	.632

#12 Dock Ellis

Position: P; Age: 34; Batted: Both; Threw: Right; Year in Major Leagues: 12

Pre-1979. One of the Pirates' top starters during the late 1960s and early 1970s, Dock Ellis was traded from the Pirates following a 1975 season in

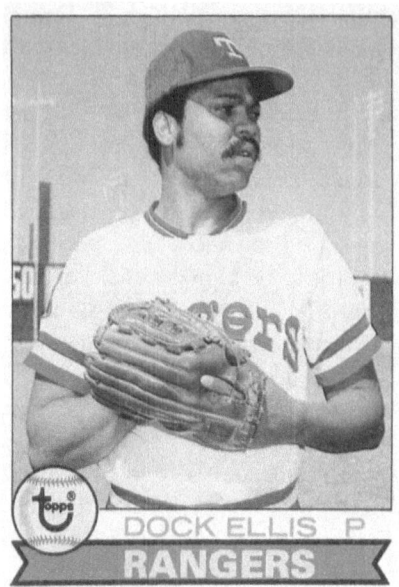

Dock Ellis (courtesy of the Topps Company, Inc.).

which he first refused to pitch out of the bullpen, then berated manager Danny Murtaugh and some of his teammates in what he claimed to have been a meeting in which he hoped to clear the air. He was suspended for a couple of weeks after the incident, before being traded. He returned to the Steel City after Harding Peterson picked him up in September 1979 to help the Bucs in their push for a division championship.

Ellis was considered a fine prospect and had pitched well for the Pirates as a rookie in 1968. He became a regular starter in 1969, but had a bad luck 11–17 season. In 1970 he won 13 games to help Pittsburgh into the playoffs. The year 1970 also saw Dock pitch a no-hitter against the San Diego Padres, an achievement he later claimed he made while under the influence of LSD. Ellis pitched shutout ball through nine innings of the NLCS as well, but the Cincinnati Reds scored three times in the 10th as Dock absorbed the loss.

Ellis used his 1970 success as a springboard for 1971. He was the National League's best pitcher the first half of the season and used his bravado to help force Sparky Anderson and the National League to use him as the starting pitcher for the All-Star Game. With Vida Blue, another African American, the foregone conclusion as the American League starter, Ellis stated "They'll never start a brother against a brother."[28] Ellis later said his comment was a play; by voicing it he believed baseball would fear being criticized for racism if he was not chosen to start. Ellis had elbow problems the second half of the season, which decreased his effectiveness. Still, the outspoken pitcher finished the season with a career high 19 wins.

Dock picked up a victory in game two of the NLCS, surviving 10 base runners in five innings, but allowing only two runs. He was not as lucky in the World Series. Named to pitch the opening game, he lasted just 2⅓ innings and his elbow prevented him from appearing again in the series.

Ellis continued to battle arm problems in 1972, but when able to pitch, did quite well, going 15–7 with a 2.70 ERA. He did not allow an earned run in the NLCS, but left after five innings in game four trailing 3–0, a victim of poor support in the field and at the plate by his teammates.

As it did in that postseason encounter, lack of offense hounded Ellis during 1973 as well. He went 12–14 despite posting a fine 3.05 ERA. Like several of his fellow Buccos, Ellis got off to a poor start in 1974, going just 3–8, but afterwards he was the Pirates' best pitcher, fashioning a 9–1 record with a 1.87 ERA. His season was ended when he took a Willie Montanez line drive off his pitching hand.

Appearing healthy in spring training, Ellis had a great camp, but sputtered once the season started. When Murtaugh asked him to pitch in relief, the hurler balked. As stated above, Ellis later called a clubhouse meeting. Murtaugh believed Ellis was going to apologize to his teammates, but when Dock's speech became critical, the Pirates manager turned livid. Coaches and players intervened and Ellis was suspended without pay. Although he was reinstated in time for the NLCS, Ellis's time as a Pirate was clearly over, and he was traded to the New York Yankees with Ken Brett and Willie Randolph for Doc Medich on December 11.

Ellis had a fine year for the Yankees in 1976, winning 17 games and pitching an impressive playoff win over Kansas City. The Reds, however, pounded the familiar opponent in the World Series and Ellis didn't last long in the Bronx Zoo. After three starts in 1977, Ellis was headed to Oakland, where he pitched very poorly (1–5, 9.69) to earn a quick ticket to the Texas Rangers. Again a change of scenery helped the colorful pitcher, who finished the year by going 10–6 with a 2.91 ERA for Texas.

By 1978, Ellis was pitching more on guile and control than ever before. He finished the year 9–7 but had an ERA over 4.00 for the first time in his career. He was nearing the end of his yellow brick road in the major leagues, but not even the Wizard of Oz would have predicted its final destination.

1979: Off to a 1–5 start with the Rangers, Ellis was shipped to the last-place New York Mets. He went just 3–7 for the Mets, posting an ERA over 6.00, but late in the year pitched well in an extended relief appearance against the Pirates and had an effective performance against the Montreal Expos. With Don Robinson and John Candelaria battling arm problems, Peterson bought Ellis's services with a little over a week remaining in the season. Proudly proclaiming, "I'll die a Pirate,"[29] Ellis responded with three workmanlike performances over the final nine days, allowing just two runs in seven innings.

1979 Postseason: Ellis was ineligible for postseason play.

Post-1979: Ellis retired following 1979. After seeking help for substance abuse problems, he became an addictions counselor and worked to help others battle the same problems.

As fine a pitcher as Ellis was, winning 138 games in his career including 96 as a Pirate, he is more remembered for the controversies he involved himself in than his stellar work on the mound. Aside from the above mentioned incidents, Dock also raised eyebrows by wearing pink hair curlers during practice; complained about the size of the bed in his hotel room; and once, in order to show the Reds and his teammates he refused to be intimidated by Cincinnati's Big Red Machine, hit the first three batters of a game with pitches, then narrowly missed beaning the next two before Murtaugh removed him.

Dock, though, had another side to his personality as well. During a radio talk show on KDKA, a fan once called in to say Ellis had been the only player kind enough to sign his son's cast. Dock was the only former teammate of Willie Stargell's to attend Pop's Hall of Fame induction in 1988. Once finding his own sobriety, Ellis not only helped other ballplayers struggling to maintain recovery, but worked with the poor as well.

Upon trading the veteran hurler to the Yankees, Joe L. Brown spoke about Ellis in favorable terms. "He's a good guy," Brown told Bob Smizik, "We wouldn't have kept him around so long if he wasn't. We don't keep bad apples. He's said a lot of things in his time, but they've never had a bad effect on the team. His teammates understood him. He's a big-hearted guy and he's no dummy. Sometimes he let his emotions control his intellect. But he's a good guy."[30]

In the end, Ellis was smarter than anyone realized. While he is remembered today as a successful pitcher from the 1970s, his name would not be recalled nearly as often had it not been for all of the controversies he was involved in.

Year	Team	W	L	PCT	CG	IP	H	BB	SO	ERA
1968	Pirates	6	5	.545	2	104	82	38	52	2.51
1969	Pirates	11	17	.393	8	218.2	206	76	173	3.58
1970	Pirates	13	10	.565	9	201.2	194	87	128	3.21
1971	Pirates	19	9	.679	11	226.2	207	63	137	3.06
1972	Pirates	15	7	.682	4	163.1	156	33	96	2.70
1973	Pirates	12	14	.462	3	192	176	55	122	3.05
1974	Pirates	12	9	.571	9	176.2	163	41	91	3.16
1975	Pirates	8	9	.471	5	140	163	43	69	3.79
1976	Yankees	17	8	.680	8	211.2	195	76	65	3.19
1977	Yankees	1	1	.500	1	19.2	18	8	5	1.83
	A's	1	5	.167	0	26	35	14	11	9.69
	Rangers	10	6	.625	7	167.1	158	42	90	2.90
	Totals	12	12	.500	8	213	211	64	106	3.63
1978	Rangers	9	7	.563	3	141.1	131	46	45	4.20
1979	Rangers	1	5	.167	0	46.2	64	16	10	5.98
	Mets	3	7	.300	1	85	110	34	41	6.04
	Pirates	0	0		0	7	9	2	1	2.57
	Totals	4	12	.250	1	138.2	183	52	52	5.84

Totals		138	119	.537	71	2127.2	2067	674	1136	3.46
Lg Average		118	118	.500	81	2127.2	2042	781	1250	3.64

#14   ED "Otter" OTT

Pos: C; Age: 28; Batted: Left; Threw: Right; Year in Major Leagues: 6th

Pre-1979. The last thing Ed Ott ever imagined was that he would be the starting catcher of the 1979 world champion Pittsburgh Pirates. He began his athletic career at Muncie High School in Pennsylvania. They didn't offer baseball so Ott instead would star in football, lettering three times while being named to the All-East and All-Conference teams, and wrestling, where he also lettered.

Despite not playing in high school, Ott was chosen by the Bucs on the 23rd round of the 1970 free agent draft as an outfielder. The Allentown native enjoyed some offensive success in the minors, leading the Carolina League in triples with 10 in 1972 and finishing fifth in batting with a .304 mark. Ed also showed he had a fine arm, topping the International League with 21 assists in 1974 for the Bucs' top farm club in Charleston.

The only kind of players Pittsburgh had an abundance of in the mid-1970s were outfielders, so Ott was moved behind the plate in spring training of '75. He learned his trade quickly, leading the IL in putouts for a catcher and being named to the All-Star Team.

After hitting .308 in 39 at-bats with the big club in 1976, Ott forced his way into the starting lineup, splitting time with Duffy Dyer for the '77 campaign. The Bucs' new backstop was stocky and tough, both physically and mentally. He was described in a recent article by Ed Eagle of MLB.com as "Jack Lambert in catcher's gear."[31] Ott's most famous moment in Pirate lore occurred on August 12 of that season when an enraged Ott picked up Mets second baseman Felix Millan and tossed him down, breaking Millan's collarbone; it ended the infielder's career.

The ex–football star got off to

Ed Ott (courtesy of the Topps Company, Inc.).

a miserable start in 1978, and a sore arm didn't help things much. "My arm bothered me ... and it really hurt my defense. And I let my defense hurt my offense," Ott confided.[32] He eventually worked things out and hit .326 in August and September, smacking three homers with 17 RBIs.

Dyer left following the season and Ott, a left-handed hitter, would platoon with rookie Steve Nicosia in 1979.

1979: Still young as a catcher, Ott worked hard on his defense, particularly his handling of balls in the dirt, framing the pitches, and calling the game, in preparation for what he thought would be his first season as the Bucs' number one catcher.[33]

While it turned out that the position wasn't his alone (since he platooned with Nicosia), the hard work paid off, as "Otter" would have the finest season of his career, hitting .273 with 51 RBIs. Ed also had some fine moments individually that season, smacking a grand slam against the Phillies reliever Tug McGraw in August, which propelled the Bucs to a 14–11 victory. The Muncie High alum also knocked in a career-high five RBIs that day. His four-hit game against the Dodgers six days later also represented a career high for the former wrestler.

1979 Postseason: Ott would be the only catcher whom manager Chuck Tanner would use in the NLCS against the Reds, going 1-for-5 in game one with a fourth inning single, before singling twice in the second contest. In the 3–2 victory, which put Pittsburgh up two games to zero, Ott was tossed out at home plate when George Foster pegged one home to Johnny Bench in time, tagging out the backstop who was trying to sprint home from second on an Omar Moreno single.

Ed went hitless in four at-bats in the final game, but would get his opportunity to play in the Fall Classic as Pittsburgh crushed the Reds 7–1 to complete the three-game sweep.

Nicosia got the call in game one of the World Series against the Orioles lefty Mike Flanagan, but Ott saw his first action the following day, which provided the Bucs catcher with his most memorable moment in a Black and Gold uniform. After hitting a sacrifice to center in the second for his first postseason RBI, scoring John Milner, Ed got his first World Series hit in the ninth, a clutch two-out single with the score tied at two. Phil Garner then walked, sending the stocky base runner to second with Manny Sanguillen coming to the plate. Sangy sent one to right field and Ott hustled home. Ken Singleton rifled the ball home. First baseman Eddie Murray cut off the throw, tossing it to catcher Rick Dempsey. As Dempsey turned to tag Ott at the plate, Ed slid his left foot across the plate ahead of the throw for the game-winning run, tying the series at one apiece.

The former All-Conference gridiron star once again got the start in game four, doubling home two runs in the second inning to give Pittsburgh a temporary 3–0 advantage. Garner came to the plate next and singled. Ott and third base coach Joe Lonnett got their signals mixed up as Ed got caught in a rundown and was tagged out, costing the Bucs an all-important run.

Ott singled twice in game six, his final performance of the '76 Fall Classic, ending his only excursion into the World Series with a .333 average and three RBIs. He got one RBI per every four at-bats, the second best figure in the history of the Fall Classic among batters who had more than ten at-bats in a series.

Post-1979: Ott got off to a fiery start in 1980, hitting .304 though August 8. It was at that point that injuries took their toll. Pulled ligaments in his foot caused the ex-grappler to hit only .178 during the remainder of the campaign.

At the beginning of the 1981 season general manager Pete Peterson made an astute trade, dealing Ott to the Angels with Mickey Mahler for Jason Thompson so he could make room for a young catcher by the name of Tony Pena.

Hitting only .217 in 1981, Ott would tear his rotator cuff, an injury he was never able to come back from. The man from Allentown never made it on a major league diamond again, finally being released by California in 1984.

Since then Ed Ott has carved a career out as a coach and minor league manager. While he spent time in the majors as a coach, most recently with the Tigers as a bullpen coach, Ott's claim to fame is as Barry Bonds' first professional manager, when Ott headed Woodbridge in 1985. Currently he's the skipper for his hometown Allentown Ambassadors in the independent Northeast League. When discussing why he chooses to spend his time in the lowest form of professional baseball, he said, "I've fulfilled my dream. What I'm here for is to help these young guys fulfill their dreams."[34] Nothing could illustrate the attitude Ott had as a player better than that.

Year	Team	AB	R	HR	RBI	BB	SO	SB	AVG	OBP
1974	Pirates	5	1	0	0	0	1	0	.000	.000
1975	Pirates	5	0	0	0	0	0	0	.200	.400
1976	Pirates	39	2	0	5	3	5	0	.308	.708
1977	Pirates	311	40	7	38	32	41	7	.264	.729
1978	Pirates	379	49	9	38	27	56	4	.269	.724
1979	Pirates	403	49	7	51	26	62	0	.273	.699
1980	Pirates	392	35	8	41	33	47	1	.260	.674
1981	Angels	258	20	2	22	17	42	2	.217	.545
	Totals	1792	196	33	195	138	254	14	.259	.679
	Lg Average	1782	228	40	213	171	243	39	.265	.723
	Pos Average	1756	189	39	215	183	240	11	.253	.698

#15 Enrique Romo

Pos: P; Age: 32; Batted: Right; Threw: Right; Year in Major Leagues: 3rd

Pre-1979. Following the 1978 campaign, Pete Peterson sought to add depth to the Pirates bullpen. In December the general manager was able to trade for one of the American League's most underrated relievers, Enrique Romo.

Listed as 31 years old at the time of the trade, Romo had begun pitching professionally in the Mexican League in 1966.[35] His brother, Vicente, had had some success in the late '60s and early '70s pitching for the Dodgers, Red Sox, White Sox and Padres. Like Vicente, Enrique was a right-handed hurler. Enrique had helped the Mexico City Reds to league championships in 1973, 1974 and 1976, posting victory totals of 11, 17, 13 and 20 during this span.[36] His 20 wins in '76 came against only four losses, and Romo held Mexican League offenses to a scant 1.89 earned runs per game while striking out 239 batters in 233 innings that season. The newly created Seattle Mariners invited him to spring training in 1977 and officially purchased his contract from Mexico City just before the start of their introduction to the AL. Used primarily as a reliever, Romo won eight games, saved 16 others and posted a fine 2.84 ERA during his rookie year in the States. He followed that up with 11 relief wins, pitching for a weak Seattle team in 1978.

1979: Enrique came to the Pirates with a reputation of having an outstanding screwball among his vast pitching arsenal and a temper, which he did not hide, on the field. With a reputation as a strikeout pitcher, Romo was expected to be the perfect complement to groundball machine Kent Tekulve. Peterson and Chuck Tanner figured Romo's screwball, tough on left-handed batters, would also take some of the load off Grant Jackson, who opened 1979 as the Pirates' only left-handed reliever. Early in the season, only his temper was evident; Romo's pitching earned few accolades.

Enrique Romo (courtesy of the Topps Company, Inc.).

He was tagged with losses in the Bucs' third and fourth games of the year. Then, like his temper, Romo's pitching started to smoke. By midseason, he was pitching very effectively, posting a 1.29 ERA in 15 games in June. In 12 appearances between July 27 and August 11, Romo was automatic, pitching 19⅔ consecutive scoreless innings.[37] Between July 1 and August 24, the reliever won seven in a row. He went 10–3 following the first week of the season, finishing with an even 3.00 ERA. Romo's 84 games ranked second only to Tekulve in the National League, and he pitched 129 innings of relief, a career high. He also saved five games. Enrique proved to be a big part of Tanner's bullpen strategy after all. The Pirates skipper would use him in spots that called for a strikeout, and Romo k'd 106 men in '79.

1979 Postseason. Romo came into the postseason battling a minor hamstring injury and did not fare well. He appeared in games one and two of the NLCS, but retired just one of the five men he faced. His performances were uneven early in the World Series, so Tanner elected to go with Don Robinson, during the latter stages of the series situations Romo would previously have pitched.

Post-1979. Enrique pitched well again in 1980, saving 11 and posting a 3.27 ERA. In 1981, he led the club with nine saves, but his pitching was less effective overall. Profiting from an excellent offensive team that lacked starting pitching in 1982, the Bucco setup man went 9–3 in his final major league season, but for the second year in a row posted an ERA above 4.00.

Although his strikeouts per innings pitched had declined noticeably during the three years following the Bucs' championship season, the Pirates kept Romo on the roster heading into spring training, 1983; but he never joined the team. There were several rumors why this was so. Some said he just wanted to pitch in Mexico, but there was also a story that Romo had been having a relationship with a woman who was involved with a mob figure and was told not to return to Pittsburgh. To date, Romo has never appeared at any 1979 Pirates reunions or autograph shows.

Enrique Romo certainly was the most unusual character on the 1979 Pittsburgh Pirates, a team noted for its individual personalities. From his on-field outbursts, to his need for a Spanish speaking teammate to translate for him during interviews, to his wide variety of pitches and deliveries and finally to his strange disappearance from the major league baseball scene, Romo was the closest embodiment to a "Wild Thing" the Family had to offer.

Year	Team	W	L	PCT	CG	IP	H	BB	SO	ERA
1977	Mariners	8	10	.444	0	114.1	93	39	105	2.83
1978	Mariners	11	7	.611	0	107.1	88	39	62	3.69
1979	Pirates	10	5	.667	0	129.1	122	43	106	2.99
1980	Pirates	5	5	.500	0	123.2	117	28	82	3.27
1981	Pirates	1	3	.250	0	41.2	47	18	23	4.54

1982	Pirates	9	3	.750	0	86.2	81	36	58	4.36
	Totals	44	33	.571	0	603	548	203	436	3.45
	Lg Average	34	34	.500	1	603	601	216	329	3.86

#16   Steve Nicosia

Pos: C; Age: 24; Batted: Right; Threw: Right; Year in Major Leagues: 2nd

Pre-1979: Unlike Ed Ott, the man he platooned with in 1979, Steve Nicosia had some baseball pedigree coming out of high school. Nicosia was the Baseball MVP and Athlete of the Year at North Miami High before being selected in the first round, 23rd overall, of the 1973 free agent draft.

The Patterson, New Jersey, native had some success in his minor league career, hitting .305 at Salem in 1974 and being selected to the Carolina All-Star Team that campaign. While at Shreveport the following year, he was selected for Texas League honors.

Injuries crept up on Nicosia in 1977; he had knee issues that would eventually lead to surgery, limiting him to only 25 games for the AAA Columbus Clippers. After the knee healed, Nicosia had his best minor league campaign, hitting .322 for the Clippers in 1978 — second in the International League — prompting a call up to the Show where he went 0-for-5 in his short time up.

1979. 1979 would be Nicosia's official rookie campaign and he would not disappoint. He worked himself into a platoon system, starting against lefties, and had a fine freshman season, hitting .288 in 191 at-bats with four homers. The latter two stats would turn out to be career highs for the former soccer and football star.

One of Nicosia's highlights of that year was his first major league hit on April 7, which also proved to be his first homer and RBI; he spanked a one-out second inning shot off Expos starter Ross Grimsley to give the Bucs a 2–0 advantage in what would turn out to be a 7–6 win. The memorable home run would come on Nicosia's second at-bat of the season and the seventh in his major league career. The 24-year-old catcher would also smack a then-career-high four hits against the Phillies on August 5.

1979 Postseason. After not appearing in any of the NLCS games against the Cincinnati Reds, Nicosia got his first opportunity in the postseason, going 0-for-4 in game one against the Orioles. He got his first postseason hit two games later, a second inning single off the O's Scott McGregor, then scored on a Phil Garner double. He also showed some defensive prowess that game, taking a throw from left fielder Bill Robinson and applying a tag on Baltimore's Ken Singleton at home plate, preserving what was then a 3–2 Pirates lead.

Nicosia went hitless in four at-bats in game five before being given the honor of starting the seventh and deciding game. Going 0-for-4, he ended his one and only postseason excursion with one hit in 16 at-bats for a miserable .063 average. While he struggled at the plate, Nicosia was given credit for hit pitch selection. Jim Rooker said after game five, "You've got to give a lot of credit to Nicosia. He called for the fastball on right-handed hitters and it ran in on them."[38]

Post-1979. The former first round selection of the Bucs platooned once again with Ott in 1980, having much less success. While he made most of his 38 hits count, registering 22 RBIs, he batted only .216 even though he did not give up a passed ball all season.

After garnering only a .231 average in 1981, Nicosia rebounded a little in 1982, hitting .280 in 100 at-bats. He was not long for the Steel City, though, and was dealt in August of 1983 for former Bucs backstop Milt May of the Giants.

Nicosia had some success with the Giants offensively, gaining a .333 average in 33 at-bats for the remainder of the '83 campaign, then coming in with a .303 mark the following year which included a Giants record of eight consecutive hits.

Like his fellow backstop Ott, injuries prematurely ended Nicosia's career. He was out of the game at age 30 following a .186 debacle for the two teams north of the border, Montreal and Toronto in 1985.

Year	Team	AB	R	HR	RBI	BB	SO	SB	AVG	OBP
1978	Pirates	5	0	0	0	1	0	0	.000	.167
1979	Pirates	191	22	4	13	23	17	0	.288	.799
1980	Pirates	176	16	1	22	19	16	0	.216	.569
1981	Pirates	169	21	2	18	13	10	3	.231	.623
1982	Pirates	100	6	1	7	11	13	0	.280	.688
1983	Pirates	46	4	1	1	1	7	0	.130	.388
	Giants	33	4	0	6	3	2	0	.333	.722
	Totals	79	8	1	7	4	9	0	.215	.531
1984	Giants	132	9	2	19	8	14	1	.303	.798
1985	Expos	71	4	0	1	7	11	1	.169	.441
	Blue Jays	15	0	0	1	0	0	0	.267	.534
	Totals	86	4	0	2	7	11	1	.186	.456
	Totals	938	86	11	88	86	90	5	.248	.655
	Lg Average	965	123	22	115	92	135	22	.265	.722
	Pos Average	948	100	22	115	92	134	6	.251	.689

#17   Lee Lacy

Pos: LF; Age: 31; Batted: Right; Threw: Right; Year in Major Leagues: 8th

Pre-1979. It took Lee Lacy a long time to develop into the major league

Lee Lacy (courtesy of the Topps Company, Inc.).

hitting machine Dodgers fans of the early 1970s had expected. A graduate of the same high school that had produced baseball superstars Frank Robinson, Vada Pinson and Curt Flood, Lacy was the Dodgers' second round pick as an infielder in the winter draft of 1969. After 3½ years in their minor league system, Lacy appeared ready to become the next star in a long line of talented ballplayers developed by the Dodgers. He reached the major leagues in midseason, 1972.

Lee had hit so well in the minors that despite fielding percentages of .866 and .879 (with 66 errors) his first two professional seasons, he appeared certain to be a star for years to come. Before his recall in 1972, Lacy had reduced his errors to just seven in 68 games at AA El Paso and in those games had batted .372. He carried his hot bat to the big leagues with him, hitting safely in 12 of his first 13 games as a Dodger, and was named co–player of the week with the Pirates' Manny Sanguillen.

The young second baseman held his own for Walter Alston's team and fielded at a .973 rate, but a terrible slump in 1973 and the emergence of Davy Lopes pushed Lacy onto the bench. He remained a backup player for the next two years, performing well at the plate in 1975 when he hit .314 in 306 at-bats. Traded to the Braves in the trade that brought Dusty Baker to Los Angeles, the infielder began the season as Atlanta's regular second baseman, but struggled defensively and was traded back to the Dodgers with Elias Sosa for Mike Marshall in midseason. The next two years, Lacy again was an all-purpose utility player for the Dodgers, playing almost every position, but his best spot remained in the batter's box. In 1978, Lee belted a healthy .382 (13-for-34) as a pinch hitter with five homeruns and ten RBIs. His grand totals for the season included a career high 13 homeruns while batting less than 250 times.

1979. Lacy was signed as a free agent by the Pirates in late January. Pete Peterson and Chuck Tanner hoped he would take over the super-sub role Bill Robinson had filled so well in 1976 and 1977 before becoming a regular in 1978. Although the Pirates could not be certain Rennie Stennett was completely healed from his ankle injury two seasons before, Lacy's failures as an infielder with the Dodgers and Braves made it unlikely he would see extended time at second or at third if Tanner decided to keep Phil Garner at second. When Stennett's play showed only minimal improvement over his rehab year of 1978, the Pirates chose to trade for Bill Madlock rather than play Lacy in the infield.

Lacy's contributions in 1979 were limited. He batted only 182 times, many fewer than anticipated. The lack of playing time was indicative, however, of the health and fine years enjoyed by the Pirates outfielders and Willie Stargell, rather than a lack of ability on his part. The free agent signee batted .295 during the first half of the season before a second half slide dropped him down to .247.[39] He had a poor season as a pinch hitter, going just 6-for-33 (.182) and not homering in that role all season. The ex-Dodger hit much better when playing in the field: he batted .265 with five homeruns in 144 at-bats.

1979 Postseason. Lacy appeared in four World Series games as a pinch hitter, getting one hit. Tanner did not use him in the NLCS.[40]

Post-1979. A spare part in 1979, Lacy became one of the few members of the Family to have a big season in 1980. A very valuable man to have around when injuries and slumps afflicted his teammates, Lacy took over as Tanner's right-handed hitting left fielder, platooning with Mike Easler. He hit a career high .345 and stole 18 bases. Tanner used him in similar roles over the next three seasons, and Lacy responded with solid play.

Despite his semiregular status, Lee's 24 stolen bases in 1981 ranked eighth in the league, and his 40 thefts in 1982 were good for seventh place. He also hit over .300 in 1982 and 1983, and his play helped the Pirates contend in both seasons. Still, Lacy had to continue to hit before getting a chance to play every day in 1984. Although the Pirates had traded Easler and Dave Parker had left via free agency, the Bucs decided to begin the season with aging free agent Amos Otis in left, defensively oriented Marvell Wynne in center and minor league slugger Doug Frobel in right. When only Wynne held up, Lacy finally became a regular, eventually settling into right field. He hit .321, second in the NL to Tony Gwynn's .351. However, the Pirates finished last and Lee, now 36 years old, was allowed to leave as a free agent following the season. George Hendrick filled his spot in right field the next year in a truly demoralizing experience for Pirates fans.

Lacy's signing with the Pirates was illustrative of the team's lack of public relations timing in the 1970s. He joined the Pirates just two days before the Steelers' Super Bowl XIII matchup against the Dallas Cowboys, so the news of his joining the Bucs got little notice. This is truly an irony as, 25 years later, Lacy remains one of the team's best free agent acquisitions. Met with much less fanfare than the signings of Derek Bell, Mike Kingery or Walt Terrell, he was one free agent who eventually exceeded fan expectations and gave Pittsburghers several fine years — although one might never have predicted it based on his 1979 season.

Year	Team	AB	R	HR	RBI	BB	SO	SB	AVG	OBP
1972	Dodgers	243	34	0	12	19	37	5	.259	.625
1973	Dodgers	135	14	0	8	15	34	2	.207	.509
1974	Dodgers	78	13	0	8	2	14	2	.282	.652
1975	Dodgers	306	44	7	40	22	29	5	.314	1.459
1976	Braves	180	25	3	20	6	12	2	.272	.666
	Dodgers	158	17	0	14	16	13	1	.266	.653
	Totals	338	42	3	34	22	25	3	.269	.660
1977	Dodgers	169	28	6	21	10	21	4	.266	.720
1978	Dodgers	245	29	13	40	27	30	7	.261	.853
1979	Pirates	182	17	5	15	22	36	6	.247	.739
1980	Pirates	278	45	7	33	28	33	18	.335	.905
1981	Pirates	213	31	2	10	11	29	24	.268	.692
1982	Pirates	359	66	5	31	32	57	40	.312	.784
1983	Pirates	288	40	4	13	22	36	31	.302	.758
1984	Pirates	474	66	12	70	32	61	21	.321	.826
1985	Orioles	492	69	9	48	39	95	10	.293	.752
1986	Orioles	491	77	11	47	37	71	4	.287	.725
1987	Orioles	258	35	7	28	32	49	3	.244	.725
	Totals	4549	650	91	458	372	657	185	.286	.749
	Lg Average	4425	563	105	527	432	649	97	.262	.720
	Pos Average	4456	599	115	550	428	675	124	.269	.740

#18   Omar "The Antelope" Moreno

Pos: CF; Age: 27; Batted: Left; Threw: Left; Year in Major Leagues: 5th

Pre-1979. The Pirates of the early-to mid-1970s were a slugging brigade of batsmen who relied on their hitting skills to produce a fearsome offense for Pittsburgh. But one ingredient missing from these teams, as successful as they were, was that when the batters were not swinging successfully, the Bucs could do little to manufacture runs. Aware of this, as well as of the effect artificial turf surfaces were having on speeding up the game, the Pirates began to groom jackrabbit quick ballplayers in the minor leagues. The two most noted greyhounds were a pair of outfielders, Miguel Dilone and Omar Moreno. Dilone — perhaps the more celebrated of the two after stealing 95 and 84 bases in Class A ball in 1973 and '74 and hitting .331 in '74, and following up with a .335 average with 61 more steals at AAA Charleston in '75[41] — never saw much playing time with the Pirates. He was traded to Oakland prior to 1978 in the trade that brought Manny Sanguillen back to Pittsburgh. Moreno, on the other hand, became the first Pirates rookie since the stellar class of 1969 to be counted on for regular duty in his first full season, after Harding Peterson traded Richie Zisk to the White Sox in December 1976.

The Antelope was just 16 years old when he signed with the Pirates in '69. He had some success as a hitter and base thief, coming through the organization usually a year behind Dilone. Omar hit .284 with a league high 72 stolen bases at Class A Salem in 1973. He then batted .300 while capturing a second consecutive stolen-base title, playing for AA Thetford Mines in 1974. After a cup of coffee with the Bucs in 1975, Moreno was called up to stay in August 1976, when regular Pirates centerfielder Al Oliver was suffering from vertigo.

Omar Moreno (courtesy of the Topps Company, Inc.).

At the time, the rookie had been hitting .315 with 55 steals for the Pirates' top farm club. Moreno did well enough — hitting .270 with 15 stolen bases in 48 games and displaying excellent range in centerfield — that the Bucs felt comfortable tabbing him as the team's regular centerfielder as Chuck Tanner took over command of the team for 1977. With veteran hitters Richie Hebner and Sanguillen joining Zisk on the list of former Pirates, the *Pittsburgh Press's* Bob Smizik wrote that the Pirates were counting on Moreno more than any rookie "since perhaps Bob Bailey" some 14 years earlier.[42]

Omar struggled at the plate but did not disappoint on the bases during his first two major league seasons. He hit just .240 in his first full year, but also stole 53 bases (fourth in the NL), and his speed allowed him to run down balls no Pirates center fielder in recent memory could get to. In 1978, Moreno's average and modest extra-base hit numbers declined, but he more than doubled his walks and led the National League with 71 stolen bases, setting a new Pirate record that eclipsed Frank Tavares' year-old mark by one.

1979. Even with his daring base-running and fine defense, Moreno's hitting was a weakness in Tanner's lineup. The Pirates turned to Harry Walker (the team's manager in the mid-1960s), who had helped another quick outfielder, Matty Alou, become not only a .300 hitter but a batting champion as well. The Bucs hoped Walker, considered one of baseball's foremost authorities on hitting, could do the same for Moreno.

As he had with Alou, Walker worked to get the speedy center fielder to hit the ball more solidly to leftfield and to take advantage of his speed by hitting the ball on the ground. The Hat's tutelage paid off, particularly during the first half of 1979, when Moreno hit .305.[43] Walker, according to Moreno, corrected a flaw in his swing that had the left-handed hitter popping out to leftfield too often.[44] Once the season started, Tanner had hitting coach Bob Skinner continue to work with Moreno to make sure Omar would not fall back into bad habits. The Antelope's hot first half included a 15-game hitting streak that saw him bat .379 with 11 RBIs, equaling a third of his grand total from 1978. Several of his Pirates teammates felt Moreno was slighted when he was left off the All-Star Team, and some even considered him the club's MVP for the first half of the season.

Moreno ended up playing in 162 games in 1979. Near the end of the year, his hitting trailed off. His final average was .282. Still, the Antelope led the league in at-bats and stolen bases, and he increased his extra-base hit total from 24 in 1978 to 41 in '79. His eight homeruns and 69 RBIs would be his career highs. The RBI total was an especially impressive figure for a lead-off man prior to the hitting currently seen in major league baseball. Although he struck out over 100 times for the third year in a row, Moreno was on base enough to score 110 runs, second in the National League to batting champion Keith Hernandez of St. Louis. Defensively, Omar had more putouts and total chances than any other outfielder. If not for his late season slump, Moreno probably would have been a solid MVP candidate. Even with his average sagging, Omar still contributed to the Bucs' offense in September, stealing 13 bases without being caught between September 3 and September 30.[45]

1979 Postseason. Omar hit .250 in the NLCS, scoring three runs in the Pirates' three-game sweep of Cincinnati, including the game winner in the tenth inning of game two. He was also credited with scoring the game winning tally in the Bucs' game three romp to the pennant. Proving what a catalyst Moreno was to the Pirates offense, the lead-off man struggled early in the World Series.

Through the first three games, the young outfielder was just 3-for-14 and failed to hit at all in the clutch. Pittsburgh fell behind two games to one. He did collect two hits in his team's game four loss, but went hitless as the Family stayed alive to win game five, making him just 5-for-23 (.218) as the clubs headed back to Baltimore. Orioles pitchers were striking him out with regularity, and he had been a nonfactor on the bases as well. The media had taken to calling him Omar the Outmaker. Moreno quieted his critics in the final two games by going 6-for-10 with three hits in each game, raising his final series average to .333 and tying Bucky Harris' mark with 33 World Series at-bats. Although Earl Weaver's hurlers and catcher Rick Dempsey stopped Moreno from stealing, the champion base thief used his speed to set up the first Pirates run in their 4–0 game six win, and his base hit in the eighth finished the scoring. Omar also knocked in a big insurance run in the ninth inning of game seven against Cy Young Award–winner Mike Flanagan to complete his revival at the plate.

Post-1979. Moreno's 1980 season was an odd one statistically. He returned to some of his bad hitting habits and saw his average decline by 33 points, yet he destroyed his own club record for steals in a season by running off with 96 for the year. Even stranger, Moreno did not win the stolen base title, because Montreal's Ron LeFlore stole 97, including one on the final day of the year when it appeared Moreno might tie or surpass him. The Antelope set a career high with 13 triples, but his RBI total fell all the way down to 36 and his OBP to just .309. Still, Moreno's speed made it nearly impossible for Tanner to take him out of the lineup, and he led the league again in put outs with 479.

The Antelope's hitting came back in 1981 to .276, and he again finished second in the National League in steals, this time with 39 during the strike-shortened season. For the third year in a row, Moreno led all National League outfielders in putouts. Around this time, however, opposing base runners were starting to take more liberties with his arm. Certainly adequate earlier in his career, Moreno's throwing started to lose some zip in his late 20s. Still able to cover more ground than just about any centerfielder in the league, Tanner continued to play him almost daily in 1982, penciling Omar into his lineup 158 times even though Moreno's batting dropped once again into the .240s and his OBP fell below .300. Still the Antelope's biggest supporter, even Tanner had to relent, occasionally dropping Moreno to the eighth spot in the lineup. Peterson and Tanner hoped Omar would agree to remain a Pirate after the outfielder filed for free agency at the season's close, but Moreno chose to sign with Houston instead. Peterson felt angry about him leaving Pittsburgh, but Moreno's agent, Tom Reich, called the Houston deal substantially better than what the Pirates had offered.[46]

Moreno's career fizzled after he left Pittsburgh, and he lasted less than a full season in Houston. His playing time decreased as he became a utility outfielder, playing the rest of his career with the Yankees, Royals and Braves. He was out of the major leagues by the end of 1986. He was a player who ran his way into the hearts of Pirates fans (his 412 stolen bases with the Pirates remain third on the team's all-time list behind Hall of Famers Max Carey and Honus Wagner). For one grand season, Omar Moreno hit his way there as well.

Year	Team	AB	R	HR	RBI	BB	SO	SB	AVG	OBP
1975	Pirates	6	1	0	0	1	1	1	.167	.453
1976	Pirates	122	24	2	12	16	24	15	.270	.726
1977	Pirates	492	69	7	34	38	102	53	.240	.653
1978	Pirates	515	95	2	33	81	104	71	.235	.642
1979	Pirates	695	110	8	69	51	104	77	.282	.714
1980	Pirates	676	87	2	36	57	101	96	.249	.631
1981	Pirates	434	62	1	35	26	76	39	.276	.681
1982	Pirates	645	82	3	44	44	121	60	.245	.607
1983	Astros	405	48	0	25	22	72	30	.242	.608
	Yankees	152	17	1	17	8	31	7	.250	.630
	Totals	557	65	1	42	30	103	37	.244	.614
1984	Yankees	355	37	4	38	18	48	20	.259	.655
1985	Yankees	66	12	1	4	1	16	1	.197	.542
	Royals	70	9	2	12	3	8	0	.243	.709
	Totals	136	21	3	16	4	24	1	.221	.628
1986	Braves	359	46	4	27	21	77	17	.234	.627
	Totals	4992	699	37	386	387	885	487	.252	.649
	Lg Average	5135	658	120	616	493	726	116	.265	.724
	Pos Average	5159	719	118	585	472	799	208	.269	.731

#19 Jim "The Rook" Rooker

Pos: P; Age: 36; Batted: Right; Threw: Left; Year in Major Leagues: 12th

Pre-1979. Pitching was not Jim Rooker's first aspiration after signing with the Detroit Tigers in 1960. He was an outfielder in the system his first four seasons, then became a pitcher with Duluth-Superior in 1964. It would be a few more years before Rooker showed he had the talent to make it.

Following a couple failed attempts to pitch with the Tigers' AA affiliate in Montgomery, Rooker went 12–5 with a 2.05 ERA in A ball at Rocky Mount, and he never looked back. The southpaw finally made it in AAA with a 14–8 mark for Toledo in 1968, earning him a shot with the '68 world champions. The Oregon native was sold to the Yankees after the season and two weeks later was selected by the Kansas City Royals in the sixth round of the expansion draft.

With Kansas City, Rooker finally got a chance to pitch full time in the majors. He had a decent rookie campaign, despite what his 4–16 record might suggest. His offensive talent showed through those first two seasons. On July 7 of 1969, he became the first Royal to hit two home runs in a game,[47] smacking four homers with eight RBIs that year.

Winning ten in 1970 while getting five RBIs in a game, Rook spent the next two seasons between Kansas City and their AAA team in Omaha. Pirates general manager Joe L. Brown saved him, sending reliever Gene Garber to the Royals for the 31-year-old veteran.

In the Steel City, the red-headed hurler thrived, winning in double digits from 1973 through 1977 while finishing with sub-3.00 ERAs in each of his first three Pirates seasons. He ended 1974 and 1975 with the eighth lowest figure in the senior circuit.

Rooker was on the verge of having back-to-back 15-win seasons when he fractured his arm in a car accident in September 1977. Although he recovered in 1978, Rooker had his worst season in the Black and Gold, going 9–11; but he pitched better ball the second half of the season.

1979. To say 1979 was a disappointing year for Jim Rooker would be an understatement. He suffered his worst ERA since joining Pittsburgh, twice ending up on the disabled list for an inflamed elbow.

Rooker actually got off to a good start. He had two victories while allowing only two earned runs in his first three starts, one of which was a two-hit complete game win against the Cubs. Things went south from there; he lost his next six decisions before breaking the streak against the Phils on September 3. During the losing streak, Rook's ERA rose from 0.74 to 4.65, and he was repeatedly frustrated in his attempt to win career victory number 100.

1979 Postseason. His season had been a bust, and he didn't get a chance to pitch in the NLCS against the Reds. Not even the most astute gamblers would have bet on Jim Rooker to earn a place in Pirates history during the 76th Fall Classic.

The 37-year-old southpaw got his first taste of a World Series in game one after Baltimore chased starter Bruce Kison with five first-inning runs. Rooker held the Birds at bay over the next 3⅔ innings, giving up only two hits and a walk.

After Baltimore took two of the next three games to hold a seemingly insurmountable lead of 3 games to 1, Pittsburgh manager Chuck Tanner made a surprise announcement: he named Rooker the starting pitcher for the fifth game — and what could be the final one for the Bucs if they lost. Kison seemed to be the odds-on choice to start the all-important contest, yet before the game he told Tanner that his arm wasn't feeling right. Enter the Rook. When questioned about the move Tanner said, "I don't care what people think, I have confidence in Rooker. When he's healthy, he can beat any club."[48] Jim Rooker was certainly healthy that day.

The 11-year vet mowed down the first 10 Oriole batters and 12 of the first 13 before giving up a lead-off double to Gary Roenicke in the fifth inning. Doug DeCinces followed with a single sending Roenicke to third, then Roenicke scored on a 4-6-3 double play. The run gave the Orioles a 1–0 lead at the end of four and a half innings. Tanner pinch-hit for Jim on the bottom half of the frame, but after two successive poor pitching performances by his teammates, the wily veteran had found a way to silence the

Baltimore bats. Pittsburgh eventually caught fire, taking Rooker off the hook and giving the Bucs a 7–1 win.

Without Rooker's clutch performance, his team would have been no more than a footnote in baseball annals. While it is hard to compare it to the game seven performances of Babe Adams and Steve Blass, it has to go down as one of the single most important clutch pitching performances in Pittsburgh's World Series history. There were few non-seventh games to compare with it. One would be the game one six-hit masterpiece by the then-little-known Adams in the 1909 series, which gave the Bucs an advantage against the strong American League champs from the Motor City. (Adams' performance was a taste of things to come; he won three games during the series.)

There was also a 6–3 complete game victory in a similar situation on game five of the 1925 fall classic, with the Senators up 3–1. Vic Aldridge held the potent Washington offense to eight hits in the victory that, like 1979, saw Pittsburgh come back from being down 1–0 in the contest. Aldridge, however, was one of the Pirates' better pitchers that year, going 15–7, while Rooker was having his worst campaign since his days in KC. In 1960, Cy Young Award–winner Vern Law, who had been the Bucs' stopper all season, stopped the Yankee tide in game four, 3–2, after the Black and Gold had been outscored 26–3 in the preceding two games.

It also would be tough to forget the three-hit, 5–1 win over the Orioles in 1971 by Blass, the Birds having won the first two games, or Nellie Briles' two-hit shutout two games later to give Pittsburgh an unexpected three-games-to-two advantage.

In all of these situations, the pitcher who came through in the clutch was one of the leaders of the staff. Only Aldridge's game in 1925 was similar, in the sense that the Pirates were facing elimination. But in that contest, despite being down by a run after the first inning, Pittsburgh scored two in the third and was tied at two going into the seventh. While Aldridge's situation was tough, it was not quite as tough as Rooker's; he was behind by one when he left in the fifth inning.

Rooker's performance was not only memorable because of the surprise circumstances in which it came about, but because it was probably his finest moment in a Black and Gold uniform, and one of his last. Arm problems ended his career only a year later.

Post-1979. In 1980 Rooker hurt his arm once again. This time it cost him his career after only four starts. He retired after being released by the club following the campaign and began a 13-year stint as the Bucs' knowledgeable color man. In probably his most memorable moment behind the mike, he boasted — after Pittsburgh took a 10–0 lead in the first inning of a game at the Vet against the Phils in 1989 — that he would walk home from

Philadelphia if the Bucs blew the game. Unfortunately, 16 runs later, the Pirates had in fact blown the lead, losing 15–11. The Rook made good on his promise after the season, walking from Philadelphia to Pittsburgh for charity. While it certainly was a time Bucco fans would remember, it could never supersede that moment in 1979 when Rooker saved the Bucs' hide on that perfect day in game five.

Year	Team	W	L	PCT	CG	IP	H	BB	SO	ERA
1968	Tigers	0	0		0	4.2	4	1	4	3.86
1969	Royals	4	16	.200	8	158.1	136	73	108	3.75
1970	Royals	10	15	.400	6	203.2	190	102	117	3.54
1971	Royals	2	7	.222	1	54	59	24	31	5.33
1972	Royals	5	6	.455	4	72	78	24	44	4.38
1973	Pirates	10	6	.625	6	170.1	143	52	122	2.85
1974	Pirates	15	11	.577	15	262.2	228	83	139	2.78
1975	Pirates	13	11	.542	7	196.2	177	76	102	2.97
1976	Pirates	15	8	.652	10	198.2	201	72	92	3.35
1977	Pirates	14	9	.609	7	204.1	196	64	89	3.08
1978	Pirates	9	11	.450	1	163.1	160	81	76	4.24
1979	Pirates	4	7	.364	1	103.2	106	39	44	4.60
1980	Pirates	2	2	.500	0	18	16	12	8	3.50
	Totals	103	109	.486	66	1810.1	1694	703	976	3.46
	Lg Average	101	101	.500	64	1810.1	1756	673	1045	3.71

#22 Bert "Dutchman" Or "Dutchmaster" Blyleven

Pos: Starting Pitcher; Age: 28; Batted: Right; Threw: Right; Year in Major Leagues: 10th

Pre-1979. Although he was born in Zeist, Holland, on April 6, 1951, Rik Aalbert Blyleven was helping the Minnesota Twins capture the American League Western Division title by the time he was 19 years old. Drafted by the Twins in the third round of the June draft just one year earlier, Blyleven went a combined 11–4 in his brief minor league career.[49] By his sophomore season in the big leagues and still short of his 21st birthday, Bert had become the best pitcher on a team that included veteran stars Jim Perry and Jim Kaat. However, most of the players who had helped the Twins to championship seasons in 1969 and 1970 were aging or being overtaken by injuries, and Minnesota became a mediocre to poor team for the rest of Blyleven's tenure.

The Dutchmaster was a very durable performer, however. Featuring the best curveball in the major leagues, Blyleven proved very effective, if not always victorious. In 1973, his most successful year with the Twins, he won 20 games and finished second in the league in both ERA and strikeouts, while topping the junior circuit with nine shutouts. Critics, however, rather than

Bert Blyleven (courtesy of the Topps Company, Inc.).

focusing on his excellent overall season, noted that he had also lost 17 games. Some fans felt he worried more about personal stats than the team's success.[50] No one could argue with his stamina, however. When he got off to a slow start in 1976 despite calling for a large contract, cost conscious owner Calvin Griffith traded his pitching star to the Texas Rangers with a career record of 99–89. He immediately impressed his new fans by pitching a pair of 1–0 shutouts in his first two starts, the first being a one-hitter.[51] The following season, Blyleven went 14–12 with his usually low ERA of 2.72, capping off his season with a no-hitter on September 22, 1977, his final start for the Rangers. Texas, with a chance to acquire one of baseball's best hitters, Al Oliver, gave up Blyleven to the Pirates as part of a four-team trade, the first in the history of the major leagues.[52] His first season in the National League was successful; he went 14–10 and finished fourth in the league with 182 strikeouts.

1979. Expected to give the Pirates a formidable 1–2 punch at the top of the rotation with lefthander John Candelaria, Blyleven started poorly in 1979. At the end of May, his record stood just 1–2 and his ERA approached 5.00. He became vocal in his criticism of manager Chuck Tanner's insistence on a five-man rotation and of his frequent use of relief pitchers. The outspoken hurler prided himself on being able to give his team a lot of innings and wanted the chance to start more often and be allowed to pitch out of trouble. He argued that he felt "too strong" when his scheduled starts were disrupted due to rainouts and that he often pitched better as the game went along. Tanner, however, had a more talented group of relievers at his disposal than any of Blyleven's previous managers and never hesitated to turn to his bullpen.

Tensions boiled over on June 15. Pitching against the Dodgers that night, Blyleven carried a 1–0 shutout into the eighth inning. After retiring the first two batters, he fell behind Steve Garvey, the Dodgers' best hitter, 2–0. At that point, the pitcher decided to intentionally walk Garvey to face the powerful but less consistent Ron Cey. After he threw two more intentionally wide pitches, Tanner took Blyleven out of the game and replaced him with Kent Tekulve. Blyleven voiced his anger to the media and, although he had signed a lucrative contract extension the previous winter, stated that if the way he was pitched did not change, he would ask to be traded following the season. The start, however, was Blyleven's second strong performance in a row, and he began turning his season around. He went 8–1 between May 21 and July 30 and with Candelaria having physical problems was the Pirates' most effective starter during this stretch; Pittsburgh moved from fourth place, six games out, to second place and only half a game behind Montreal.[53]

After losing to Wayne Twitchell and the New York Mets as July closed, Blyleven continued to pitch well down the stretch. Tanner, however, relied as much as ever on his relievers and the starter recorded only four more decisions the rest of the year, going 3–1. His final victory of '79 was a 5–2 win over the Expos on September 24 that momentarily put the Bucs in first place by half a game. One piece of forgotten trivia from Blyleven's 1979 season was that at the time his 20 no-decisions set a major league record; he finished 12–5 in a club-high 37 starts.

1979 Postseason. Blyleven was well rested for his game three start in the National League Championship Series. While his teammates John Candelaria and Jim Bibby had given Tanner strong starts which helped put the Family up two games to nothing, Blyleven completely dominated the Big Red Machine. He struck out nine, and the only run the Reds scored came on a solo homer by Johnny Bench. Naturally, the pitcher showed a rush of adrenaline, pumping his fist in the air after his pennant-clinching strikeout of Cesar Geronimo to end the game.

Although Candelaria and Bibby had more rest, neither was completely healthy when the World Series opened in Baltimore. After Bruce Kison started the series opener, Tanner went back to Blyleven to try to even the series. Again, the Dutchmaster was tough. Although Eddie Murray knocked him for a homerun and a run scoring double, Blyleven handled the rest of the Oriole batters before he was removed for a pinch-hitter in the seventh with the game tied at two. His performance came against all-time great Jim Palmer, who matched Blyleven's effectiveness. The Bucs of course won the game on a ninth inning pinch hit from Manny Sanguillen, and once again, the Dutchmaster gained only a no-decision, but it was his second strong postseason performance. His third would come three days later.

Tanner surprised just about everyone with his game five choice of Jim Rooker as starter. Rooker pitched extremely well, but with the Bucs trailing 1–0 in the fifth, Tanner again chose to hit for his starter. This time, however, the man called from the bullpen was Blyleven, who, in his first relief work since his rookie season, held Baltimore scoreless over the final four innings. He was credited with the win, and his slugging teammates broke the game open, scoring in three straight innings. While Pirates hitters received most of the credit for the Family's World Championship, Blyleven was one of the mound stars in the series, giving up just two runs in ten innings of work for a 1.80 ERA.

Post-1979. While it was hoped by Pittsburgh fans that having earned a World Series ring and posting a two year record of 26–15 would ease Blyleven's feelings about being removed earlier from games than he preferred, 1980 saw Blyleven not only continue to express his discontentment, but pitch less effectively. While the vast majority of the Family fell off their championship season performances, Blyleven fell to 8–13. He dropped his first four decisions, although his opening game loss to the St. Louis Cardinals and Pete Vukovich was by a 1–0 score. The curveball artist pitched better in the middle of the year, but went just 1–5 after August 16 as the Pirates faded from the race.[54] In fairness to Blyleven, it seemed his teammates played particularly poorly when he was pitching early in the year, so much so that at the time there was a column written in which a sports psychologist was asked if his teammates subconsciously could be reacting to Blyleven's demands to be traded.

Everyone realized Pete Peterson would grant the Dutchmaster's wish following the season. The only question was who the Pirates would receive in return. There was a rumor that the California Angels were offering 1979 American League MVP Don Baylor in return for Blyleven and Ed Ott, but when Peterson made his move, he sent his unhappy player along with Manny Sanguillen to the Cleveland Indians for pitchers Bob Owchinko, Victor Cruz, Rafael Vazquez and utility man Gary Alexander, who had excellent power but struck out at an alarming rate. Critics wondered if Peterson's choice of the Indians was actually his attempt to punish the pitcher by sending him to what many considered the most hopeless franchise in baseball. The trade proved an immediate bust; only Alexander made the Pirates out of spring training and he was seldom used.

After a couple of lackluster and injury-plagued seasons, Blyleven rebounded in 1984 with what was actually his best overall year, winning 19 games while losing only 7 for a team that went 75–87. With his first team, the Minnesota Twins, being desperate for pitching to help a possible title run in 1985, the Indians swapped him back to the Twin Cities in a trade that included future Buc Jay Bell. Blyleven remained a workhorse and pitched $293\frac{2}{3}$, $271\frac{2}{3}$, 267, 207 and 241 innings from 1985 through 1989.

Although he set a record by allowing 50 homeruns in 1986 and would end his career holding the record for long balls given up, he was pitching in the stadium comfortably nicknamed the Homerdome at the time. In 1986,

Bert won 17 games before garnering 15 more the following year for the world champions. A fine postseason followed once again: Blyleven won three more games, two in the ALCS and game two of the World Series. After a league-leading 17 losses and 5.43 ERA in 1988, Blyleven was traded to the Angels. Once again he rebounded with an excellent year, going 17–5 while cutting his ERA in half to 2.73. But arm problems again took their toll on Blyleven as he was closing in on 300 wins.

He missed all of 1991 following rotator cuff surgery, and although he battled back in 1992, he would go only 8–12. The eight wins gave Blyleven 287 for his career. He hoped to catch on one more time with the Twins, who offered him a shot as a non-roster player in 1993. Failing to make the team, Blyleven moved to the booth as an announcer for the ball club instead.

Blyleven ranks high in several major league categories. Although Roger Clemens passed him on the strikeout list in 2002 and Randy Johnson the following year, Bert remains fifth all-time in K's with 3,701, ninth in shutouts with 60, and 24th all-time in victories.

Eligible for baseball's Hall of Fame since 1998, Blyleven has gotten luke-warm support from voters but has become a favorite candidate for people to write about, noting his high standing for achievements.[55, 56] Bill James named him to his all-decade team of the 1980s despite an average record of 15–13 for the decade and rates him as the 39th greatest pitcher of all time.[57]

Certainly, Blyleven was a great pitcher, but a ranking of 39th all-time seems a bit high. No doubt Blyleven could absorb a lot of innings. Even during his years with the Pirates, Bert led the team twice, in a span of three years, in innings pitched. His 1979 postseason was excellent, as were his 1987 playoff and World Series showings. Prior to 1978–1979, however, Blyleven had not had two winning seasons in a row since his rookie and sophomore years; and in both of those years, he won just one more than he lost. He didn't have back-to-back winning campaigns again until 1984–1985, and once again he was on the positive side of the ledger by just one victory in 1985.

Obviously, this was not all Blyleven's fault. The Twins were an aging team when the Dutchmaster joined them. As Harmon Killebrew declined and Tony Oliva's career was derailed by a knee injury, the offense sputtered, relying heavily on Rod Carew's high average (but low power) hitting. The teams he pitched for following 1970 during his first go-around with Minnesota were mediocre at best, but Blyleven went just 14–12 for a Texas team that won 94 games in 1977 and then deemed him expendable. However, following his 1979 World Series performances, Jim Palmer spoke favorably of Blyleven after the Orioles legend lost game six. "Everybody knocks Bert Blyleven," Palmer said, "They say he can't win the big one, but how about me? That happened to me tonight. It happens to everybody. When he was in the American League, I used to beat him 2–1 all the time and people said he just couldn't win."[58]

Over his 22-year career, Blyleven posted a .534 winning percentage, compared to his teams' .502, and that is certainly a significant difference. However, he won 20 games only once (although he missed out on a chance to win 20 in 1984 due to a broken bone). Looking then at Blyleven's seasons individually, he seems to have been one of the most consistently unlucky pitchers in baseball history. But how much of that bad luck did Blyleven create? Did he, as Jose DeLeon would do later for the Pirates, tend to make a mistake at a critical time after having dominated the opposition for most of the game? Was he unable to rebound if a teammate committed an error in back of him? He rubbed fans the wrong way as a young player at times; could he have had the same effect on his teammates?

Another question about Blyleven is how many times he was one of the top five starters in his league. He certainly was in 1984, and probably in 1973. In 1971, he was surpassed by Vida Blue, Mickey Lolich, Wilbur Wood, Andy Messersmith and Palmer and possibly by a few others. In 1972, Lolich, Wood and Palmer were again more effective; so were Luis Tiant, Catfish Hunter and Nolan Ryan. He may have cracked the top five based on his secondary statistics in 1974, but he was only a .500 pitcher. His 15–10 in 1975 represented his best winning percentage to date (.600), but the next year he went just 13–16 for teams that went a combined 161–163. He would not have been considered one of the top five pitchers in the American League that year despite his durability. Again pitching well in 1977, Blyleven's winning percentage of .538 paled in comparison to the Rangers' .580 mark.

Coming to the perennially contending Pirates in 1978, 20-win seasons were expected by Pittsburghers. Blyleven pitched well his first two years in Pittsburgh, but despite not having to face designated hitters and pitching in larger ballparks, the Dutchman's ERA rose each year. In none of his three seasons in Pittsburgh was he one of the National League's five best starters. His complaints about Chuck Tanner's use of him were met with disgust by the fans. This was particularly true in 1980; people realized the Pirates had several older players who would be hard pressed to repeat their 1979 seasons, but Blyleven, coming off his big postseason and still only 29 years old, figured to be a man who could take up the slack. His voiced discontentment earned him the nickname "Cryleven."

Back in the American League with Cleveland the next season, Blyleven again posted a sub-3.00 ERA. One could argue that in the strike-shortened season of 1981, he was one of the AL's best pitchers. He missed most of 1982 with injury, and 1983 became a rehab year. In his excellent 1984 campaign he was the best starter in his league and deserved the Cy Young Award over reliever Willie Hernandez of the Detroit Tigers. Blyleven pitched for two

5. The Members of the Family

poor teams in 1985, and tied for fifth in the league in wins (17); his 3.16 ERA netted him the fifth spot in the circuit as well. Throw in his league leading innings pitched and Bert makes the top five once again, despite his unimpressive 17–16 mark.

It is difficult to argue for Blyleven's placement in the top five the next two years. His numbers, particularly his homeruns allowed and ERA, were greatly affected by pitching in the Metrodome, but his overall numbers seem to fall short behind the likes of Roger Clemens, Jack Morris, Tom Candiotti, Teddy Higuera, Mike Witt and Kirk McCaskill in '86. Clemens, Morris, and Higuera would be joined by Jimmy Key, Brett Saberhagen, Charlie Liebrandt, Dave Stewart, Mark Langston, Floyd Bannister, Charlie Hough and his own teammate, Frank Viola as being rated ahead of Blyleven during Minnesota's championship season. Following a horrible 1988 season, Blyleven came back to have one more big year in 1989, a season in which he was probably one of the American League's five best pitchers.

So, tallying up Blyleven's career, there is one year when he was the best starting pitcher in his league, another (1973) when he was clearly in the top five. In five other years (1974, 1975, 1981, 1985 and 1989) he was probably one of the top five pitchers in the American League. While it's still very questionable that Blyleven was the 39th greatest pitcher of all time, there still is a good argument, given his career totals, to honor him in Cooperstown, particularly when adding in his postseason stats. One of the strongest cases against Blyleven's enshrinement is that his winning percentage of .534 is well below the usual standards for a Hall of Famer. The irony is that his best winning percentage over a two-year period of good health came during his first two years pitching for Chuck Tanner. If Blyleven had been able to maintain anything close to his .634 mark of 1978–79, even if it had meant fewer victories, there would be no argument against his enshrinement.

Year	Team	W	L	PCT	CG	IP	H	BB	SO	ERA
1970	Twins	10	9	.526	5	164	143	47	135	3.18
1971	Twins	16	15	.516	17	278.1	267	59	224	2.81
1972	Twins	17	17	.500	11	287.1	247	69	228	2.73
1973	Twins	20	17	.541	25	325	296	67	258	2.52
1974	Twins	17	17	.500	19	281	244	77	249	2.66
1975	Twins	15	10	.600	20	275.2	219	84	233	3.00
1976	Twins	4	5	.444	4	95.1	101	35	75	3.12
	Rangers	9	11	.450	14	202.1	182	46	144	2.76
	Totals	13	16	.448	18	297.2	283	81	219	2.87
1977	Rangers	14	12	.538	15	234.2	181	69	182	2.72
1978	Pirates	14	10	.583	11	243.2	217	66	182	3.03
1979	Pirates	12	5	.706	4	237.1	238	92	172	3.60
1980	Pirates	8	13	.381	5	216.2	219	59	168	3.82
1981	Indians	11	7	.611	9	159.1	145	40	107	2.88

1982	Indians	2	2	.500	0	20.1	16	11	19	4.87
1983	Indians	7	10	.412	5	156.1	160	44	123	3.91
1984	Indians	19	7	.731	12	245	204	74	170	2.87
1985	Indians	9	11	.450	15	179.2	163	49	129	3.26
	Twins	8	5	.615	9	114	101	26	77	3.00
	Totals	17	16	.515	24	293.2	264	75	206	3.16
1986	Twins	17	14	.548	16	271.2	262	58	215	4.01
1987	Twins	15	12	.556	8	267	249	101	196	4.01
1988	Twins	10	17	.370	7	207.1	240	51	145	5.43
1989	Angels	17	5	.773	8	241	225	44	131	2.73
1990	Angels	8	7	.533	2	134	163	25	69	5.24
1992	Angels	8	12	.400	1	133	150	29	70	4.74
	Totals	287	250	.534	242	4970	4632	1322	3701	3.31
	Lg Average	277	277	.500	138	4970	4842	1813	2929	3.76

#23   Grant "Buck" Jackson

Pos: P; Age: 37; Batted: Both; Threw: Left; Year in Major Leagues: 16th

Pre-1979. Buck Jackson, given the moniker because it was thought he moved around like a cowboy, was signed by the Philadelphia Phillies as an amateur free agent in 1961. After four years in the minors, the most successful of which was a 12–8–3.89 campaign in 1963 with Bakersfield, he made his major league debut with the Phils in 1965.

He was used sparingly with Philadelphia in '65 and '66 before returning to their AAA team in San Diego, where he went 10–8.

Jackson spent the next two years in the Philly bullpen, used sometimes as a spot starter, and then was inserted into the starting rotation in 1969 where he showed promise, going 14–18 while being selected to represent the Phillies in the All-Star Game. Grant's bright prospects as a starter were dashed the next season when he tumbled to 5–15 with a horrendous 5.29 ERA. It would be the low point in the Fostoria, Ohio, native's career. After four consecutive losing campaigns and the highest ERA he would endure until his final major league campaign, he was dealt to the Baltimore Orioles with two players for minor league star Roger Freed. Jackson would never again suffer a losing season in the majors.

Earl Weaver turned Jackson into a reliever and the results were staggering. Buck became the best left-handed man in the bullpen of those great Orioles teams of the early seventies. He would enjoy solid seasons in '71 and '72, pitching in his first World Series against Pittsburgh in 1971. Later he became the only player to play on both sides in the 1971 and 1979 Fall Classic rivalries. His career year came in 1973 when the southpaw was undefeated with an 8–0 record, saving nine contests and posting a miniscule 1.90 ERA. Jackson also had a successful postseason that year, winning game four against Oakland in the ALCS while tossing three hitless innings in two games.

Buck had two more decent seasons in Baltimore, going 10–7 with 19 saves in 1974 and 1975. He was dealt to the New York Yankees early in 1976 as part of a ten-player deal that gave the Orioles five players, three of which, Tippy Martinez, Scott McGregor and Rick Dempsey, were important cogs of the 1979 O's squad that played the Bucs in the '79 World Series.

Jackson enjoyed the Big Apple, finishing the '76 campaign by going 6–0 with the Bronx Bombers with a 1.69 ERA. He got a chance to pitch in another Fall Classic that year, but the 1976 postseason was not kind to the 33-year-old reliever; it was the only time in five postseasons he would give up an earned run, allowing five between the ALCS and World Series.

Grant Jackson (courtesy of the Topps Company, Inc.).

Despite his fabulous stint with the Yanks, Jackson was not protected in the expansion draft and was selected by Seattle in the 11th round. He did not last with the Mariners long. He was dealt to the Bucs before he ever had a chance to suit up for Seattle, and came to the Pirates only a month after the draft for Craig Reynolds and Jimmy Sexton. It was a fortuitous move for the Bucs, who later obtained left-hander Terry Forster that off-season. After Forster left following the '77 campaign, Jackson was almost manager Chuck Tanner's only choice when he needed a lefty out of the bullpen. Although he was a fine 12–8 between '77 and '78, it was only a prelude to the great 1979 he would turn in.

1979. Grant Jackson had a couple good seasons in the Steel City before showing Pittsburgh that he was one of the finest left-handed relievers in the game. Buck was a four-ball pitcher. While his fastball was his bread and butter, he was also proficient at the slider, curveball and change and used them all to thwart National League batters to the tune of allowing only 67 hits in 82 innings of work. Until the Bucs acquired Dave Roberts in June, he was still Tanner's only left-handed choice out of the pen, but Jackson was confident that he could get any one out, no matter what side the of the plate they batted.[59]

In the early part of the season when Bucco closer Kent Tekulve was struggling, Jackson came up big to pick up the pieces. "Jackson did a helluva job, it's a good thing because I wasn't going good," Teke said.[60]

His solid campaign included eight wins in relief and 14 saves, good for tenth in the senior circuit. Buck's 72 appearances not only set a club record for southpaws but was the third best in the NL, as well as on the team, just behind Tekulve and Enrique Romo.

While the 1979 regular season would be a solid one, it was during the postseason that Jackson's star really rose.

1979 Postseason. To defeat the powerful Cincinnati Reds and Baltimore Orioles in the 1979 postseason, Tanner would have to rely on his bullpen heavily, and Buck would be a huge part of the formula. In game one of the NLCS, Jackson entered the contest in the tenth inning. He put the Big Red Machine down in order in his first frame of work. Then he gave up a single and a free pass with two outs in the bottom of the 11th, after the Bucs took a 5–2 lead. Tanner called on Don Robinson to finish things up at that point, but Jackson ended up with the victory, giving the Pirates the advantage in the series.

In his second and final performance of the '79 NLCS, Tanner would use Jackson only situationally, getting the great left handed Joe Morgan to ground out to Phil Garner at second.

The World Series would be the third for Buck, having placed each with a different team. He was only the third player at the time (the other two being Andy Pafko and Vic Davalillo) to have done so.[61]

After Bruce Kison gave up five runs in the top of the first inning to Baltimore, Jackson would be part of the impressive bullpen performance of Pittsburgh the remainder of the game. The Pirates relievers gave up only three hits and no runs in the final 8⅔ innings of work, including Jackson's ninth inning in which he gave up only a lead-off single to Rich Dauer; but it was too little too late, as the Bucs could only muster up four runs in the 5–4 defeat.

In game three, he got another situational appearance, this time stopping an Orioles rally by getting the left handed centerfielder Al Bumbry to fly out to left. Jackson would put the fire out once again in the next contest, prompting Pat Kelly to ground into a 6–4–3 double play to end the seventh and preserving the Bucs' momentary three-run advantage.

As the Pirates starting rotation finally showed some success in games five and six, Jackson got a break. Tanner would not call the Bowling Green alum until the seventh and deciding game, with Pittsburgh behind 1–0. The Pittsburgh manager batted for starter Jim Bibby in the fifth and, after Robinson allowed two on with two out in the bottom half of the frame, called on the southpaw to try and keep the Bucs' disadvantage to a mere run. Jackson

5. The Members of the Family

got Bumbry once again to end a threat, this time on a foul out to Madlock. It would be the beginning of Buck's longest performance in the postseason. He retired the next six batters he faced, then turned the game over to Tekulve in the eighth after walking two with only one out. Teke loaded the bases but got out of the jam, preserving a 4–1 win. It was Jackson's second victory of the postseason, the victories being in the first game the Bucs played and in the last. In the NLCS and World Series, the 15-year vet was outstanding, giving up no runs and only two meaningless hits in 6⅔ innings of work.

His sparkling performance in the postseason was the norm for the southpaw. In the five postseasons in which he appeared, he was 3–0 with a 2.55 ERA, allowing but 11 hits in 17⅔ innings of work. In fact, Jackson was perfect in four of his five seasons, giving up all five runs in 1976 for the American League champion Yankees.

Post-1979. Buck was one of the few Pirates to enjoy a successful 1980 campaign. He went 8–4 after a phenomenal start and gave up only six earned runs in his first 31 innings of the season.

The year 1980 was the beginning of the end for Jackson; Pittsburgh dealt him to the Expos in the middle of 1981. Jackson fizzled with Montreal and was traded to the Royals in the off-season for Ken Phelps. Kansas City cut him in July of 1982 following a poor start when he accumulated a 5.17 ERA. Pittsburgh picked him up in September, and Jackson ended his major league career giving up a run in ⅔ of an inning of work. After failing to make the Pirates as a non-roster player in 1983, Jackson signed on as a bullpen coach and in 1985 served as Chuck Tanner's last pitching coach in Pittsburgh. He later coached with the Cincinnati Reds.

Year	Team	W	L	PCT	CG	IP	H	BB	SO	ERA
1965	Phillies	1	1	.500	0	13.2	17	5	15	7.24
1966	Phillies	0	0		0	1.2	2	3	0	5.40
1967	Phillies	2	3	.400	0	84.1	86	43	83	3.84
1968	Phillies	1	6	.143	1	61	59	20	49	2.95
1969	Phillies	14	18	.438	13	253	237	92	180	3.34
1970	Phillies	5	15	.250	1	149.2	170	61	104	5.29
1971	Orioles	4	3	.571	0	77.2	72	20	51	3.13
1972	Orioles	1	1	.500	0	41	33	9	34	2.63
1973	Orioles	8	0	1.000	0	80.1	54	24	47	1.90
1974	Orioles	6	4	.600	0	66.2	48	22	56	2.57
1975	Orioles	4	3	.571	0	48.1	42	21	39	3.35
1976	Orioles	1	1	.500	0	19.1	19	9	14	5.12
	Yankees	6	0	1.000	1	58.2	38	16	25	1.69
	Totals	7	1	.875	1	78	57	25	39	2.54
1977	Pirates	5	3	.625	0	91	81	39	41	3.86
1978	Pirates	7	5	.583	0	77.1	89	32	45	3.26
1979	Pirates	8	5	.615	0	82	67	35	39	2.96
1980	Pirates	8	4	.667	0	71	71	20	31	2.92

1981	Pirates	1	2	.333	0	32.1	30	10	17	2.51
	Expos	1	0	1.000	0	10.2	14	9	4	7.59
	Totals	2	2	.500	0	43	44	19	21	3.77
1982	Royals	3	1	.750	0	38.1	42	21	15	5.17
	Pirates	0	0		0	0.2	1	0	0	13.50
	Totals	3	1	.750	0	39	43	21	15	5.31
	Totals	86	75	.534	16	1358.2	1272	511	889	3.46
	Lg Average	76	76	.500	20	1358.2	1302	497	810	3.65

#24 Mike "The Hit Man" Easler

Pos: PH; Age: 28; Batted: Left; Threw: Right; Year in Major Leagues: 6th

Pre-1979. Mike Easler's career proves that if you're persistent, good things can happen. He was selected in the sixth round of the 1969 draft by Houston, but despite getting a few cups of coffee with the Astros, he could never stick with the parent club, going 1-for-27 between 1973 and 1975.

Easler moved to the Cardinals Angels organizations. He continued to hit successfully in the minors, leading the American Association with a .352 at Tulsa, but could never make it in the Show. The Bucs obtained him from California in 1977. The Hit Man continued to dominate minor league pitching, hitting .302 in 1977 and reaching an International League high .330 in 1978, both with Columbus. In between, he came up 18 times for Pittsburgh in 1977, accumulating eight hits including his first major league home run. The Pirates were unable to add Easler to their winter roster following his IL batting championship so, rather than risk losing him in the Rule Five draft, they traded him to the Red Sox. Easler was unable to make the hitter-laden Sox in spring training and Pete Peterson, realizing that the Pirates needed a left-handed bat off the bench, traded two lesser prospects, George Hill and Martin Rivas, to reacquire him.

1979. After strong campaigns with the Bucs' top farm team, Easler stayed up with the Pirates for the entire 1979 campaign, becoming the Pirates' most used pinch hitter. Line-Drive, as he was known back then, only played two games in the field. Easler contributed several big hits as an emergency batsman, tying one game with a homerun and blasting a game winning shot against the Mets on May 16.

1979 Postseason. The Hit Man did get a chance to see some action in the postseason, although not much. In the NLCS, he pinch-hit in the tenth inning, and flew out to George Foster in left for his only appearance in the NLCS.

Easler did it one better in the 76th Fall Classic, walking in the seventh inning of game two after he came up for Bert Blyleven, then flying out to left in the last frame of the 9–6 game four loss.

5. The Members of the Family

Post-1979. The wait was finally over for the Cleveland native. Ten years of ripping apart minor league pitching and not much more came to an end for Easler. He worked his way into the rotation in left field after hitting two homers against the Expos on April 22, 1980. He replaced John Milner, showing the baseball world he truly belonged with 21 homers, a sparkling .338 average and .583 slugging percentage. Now dubbed "the Hit Man," Easler's batting average was higher than that of Bill Buckner, the NL's official batting champion, and his slugging percentage was surpassed only by Mike Schmidt's .624 mark. Unfortunately, Easler lacked the necessary plate appearances to qualify for the titles. During the season he was named as the NL's player of week on June 10 after hitting for the cycle against the Reds. Following the campaign, he was named the Roberto Clemente Award–winner.

The Hit Man proved his '80 campaign was no fluke with an All-Star selection in 1981, but was never again able to reach the lofty levels he had that season, although he did break the .300 barrier his final season in the Steel City in 1983. Following that year, the Bucs sent Easler back to the Red Sox for John Tudor. Easler was never the most able defensive player in baseball. Boston turned him into a DH which Mike found to his liking, smacking a career high 27 homers with 91 RBIs.

The 35-year-old DH was sent to the Bronx for Don Baylor, hitting over .300 in 1986 before ending his major league career the following season in 1987, playing for the Phils and then the Yanks once again.

While getting up in age, Easler — who was as natural a hitter as there was — still was strong, hitting .282, 11 points under his career .293 mark. The Hit Man didn't leave the majors for good; he took his knowledge of the bat with him to Milwaukee, Boston and St. Louis as a coach. He unsuccessfully interviewed for the Pirates' managerial position following the 2000 season.

Year	Team	AB	R	HR	RBI	BB	SO	SB	AVG	OBP
1973	Astros	7	1	0	0	2	4	0	.000	.222
1974	Astros	15	0	0	0	0	5	0	.067	.134
1975	Astros	5	0	0	0	0	1	0	.000	.000
1976	Angels	54	6	0	4	2	11	1	.241	.555
1977	Pirates	18	3	1	5	0	1	0	.444	1.143
1979	Pirates	54	8	2	11	8	13	0	.278	.815
1980	Pirates	393	66	21	74	43	65	5	.338	.979
1981	Pirates	339	43	7	42	24	45	4	.286	.759
1982	Pirates	475	52	15	58	40	85	1	.276	.773
1983	Pirates	381	44	10	54	22	64	4	.307	.790
1984	Redsox	601	87	27	91	58	134	1	.313	.892
1985	Redsox	568	71	16	74	53	129	0	.262	.737
1986	Yankees	490	64	14	78	49	87	3	.302	.811
1987	Phillies	110	7	1	10	6	20	0	.282	.661

Yankees	167	13	4	21	14	32	1	.281	.726
Totals	277	20	5	31	20	52	1	.282	.701
Totals	3677	465	118	522	321	696	20	.293	.803
Lg Average	3498	450	85	422	338	519	80	.263	.724
Pos Average	3491	471	115	481	377	575	81	.263	.754

#25   Bruce "Buster" Kison

Pos: P; Age: 29; Batted: Right; Threw: Right; Year in Major Leagues: 9th

Pre-1979. Selected in the 14th round of the 1968 draft, Bruce "Buster" Kison made a rapid rise through Pirates organization, going 30–9 (which included a 10–1 mark with AAA Charleston in 1971) before being brought up for the stretch run of the world champs that season.

The 21-year-old hurler also developed a reputation for throwing inside in his minor league odyssey, leading no fewer that three different minor leagues in hit batsmen. Once in the Steel City, Kison was immediately put in the rotation to replace Bob Moose, who was fulfilling a military commitment. Buster did not disappoint with a 6–5 mark, but it wasn't until the postseason that he made his real mark in Pirates history. He won the fourth and deciding contest of the NLCS against the Giants with 4⅔ shutout innings, then threw his real masterpiece in the '71 Fall Classic. It was the fourth game once again, with the Pirates down two games to one. It also happened to be the first nighttime World Series contest in the history of the game. Pittsburgh had fallen behind in the top of the first, 3–0, when manager Danny Murtaugh replaced starter Luke Walker with the young rookie. Bruce was at his absolute best, mowing down the potent Orioles bats one after another, giving up only one hit in 6⅓ innings, leading the Bucs to a dramatic 4–3 victory. Following the Pirates' World Series triumph a few days later, he was whisked away by helicopter after game seven and taken to the Baltimore airport, flying to Pittsburgh for his wedding that evening.

Kison stuck with the big club in '72, then spent most of the following campaign in Charleston as he was bothered by arm problems that started in spring training. When promoted, Buster won all three decisions and never looked back, going 26–20 over the next two seasons.

A persistent problem reared its ugly head for the first time in 1977 and plagued the right hander throughout the next couple years with Pittsburgh: a blister on his finger. It troubled him to the point that his ERA rose to a career worst 4.90. Buster was demoted to the bullpen in 1978 after the problem reappeared. It sent him to the disabled list by the end of May. He had surgery on the problematic blister and when he came back, he finally seemed to have conquered the problem. He made it back into the starting rotation, starting nine games over the last two months of the season including a 2–1 mark in September with a 1.97 ERA.

1979. Buster began the 1979 campaign going back and forth from the bullpen. He had started five of his first six games and was sent to the pen with a 1–1 mark on May 22, spending the next couple of weeks there. After six consecutive games in relief, Tanner finally gave Kison another shot on June 3 against the Padres, when Don Robinson was unable to pitch. Through 7⅔, Bruce had been awesome, giving up only two walks and no hits. Barry Evans came to the plate with Kison needing only four more outs for a no-hitter and hit a smash down the third base line that hit off Phil Garner's glove. The ball was ruled a hit, irritating Kison (although Garner admitted afterwards that it was in fact a hit).[62] Kison got his emotions together, retiring the final four Padres to complete the one-hitter.

Bruce Kison (courtesy of the Topps Company, Inc.).

The gem secured Kison a spot in the rotation the rest of the season, although after a 5–3 loss against the second place Expos on July 29, the nine-year veteran stood only at 6–6. Through 1978, Buster had owned September, going 19–6. This year was to be one where he definitely saved the best for last.

Kison went on a roll, winning three of his next four starts, losing only to the Giants on August 21, 6–1. The 29-year-old hurler then did August one better, winning all four decisions in September. He finished with a sparkling 13–7 mark while lowering his ERA from 3.53 all the way down to 3.19 the final month of the season.

1979 Postseason. New York had Reggie Jackson; in the Steel City, Bruce Kison was Mr. October. Though 1974, Kison had not given up a run in 20 innings, going 4–0 while allowing a mere six hits in the process. Finally in the eighth inning of game two in the 1975 NLCS, he surrendered a run, hitting Joe Morgan with a pitch and allowing a run-scoring single to Tony Perez.

Kison didn't get a turn in the '79 National League Championship, but got the call to pitch in the opener of the Fall Classic against Baltimore. The air was cold and Buster had nothing, as his arm went numb from the elbow on down; he finally had a poor postseason performance. He allowed five runs, four earned, on three hits and two walks in ⅓ of an inning, then was removed by Tanner before the Bucs got out of the first frame. The Pirates rallied but fell short 5–4, giving Kison the first postseason loss of his career.

He was due to get another chance for revenge in game five with the O's up three games to one, but his arm was still sore from his game one debacle and he couldn't grip the ball well. Jim Rooker would have to save the day. Game one proved to be Kison's final performance for the Bucs; he became a free agent following the series.

Post-1979. Buster signed on with the California Angels after the World Series, becoming the first member of the Family to depart. He had his worst season as a pro, going 3–6, although he had another brush with greatness, taking a no-hitter into the ninth against the Twins (a game that Ken Landreaux ruined with a one-out double).

Kison split the '82 and '83 campaigns between starting and relief, winning 22 of his 33 decisions. He had one last postseason performance, going 1–0 in two starts of the 1982 ALCS; this gave him a 4–0 record in league championship series with a 1.21 ERA. After one more year in California, Kison signed a free agent contract with the Red Sox, retiring following the 1985 season. A master at pitching inside and using intimidation as part of his repertoire, Kison has since worked as a pitching coach with Kansas City and Baltimore.

Year	Team	W	L	PCT	CG	IP	H	BB	SO	ERA
1971	Pirates	6	5	.545	2	95.1	93	36	60	3.40
1972	Pirates	9	7	.563	6	152	123	69	102	3.26
1973	Pirates	3	0	1.000	0	43.2	36	24	26	3.09
1974	Pirates	9	8	.529	1	129	123	57	71	3.49
1975	Pirates	12	11	.522	6	192	160	92	89	3.23
1976	Pirates	14	9	.609	6	193	180	52	98	3.08
1977	Pirates	9	10	.474	3	193	209	55	122	4.90
1978	Pirates	6	6	.500	0	96	81	39	62	3.19
1979	Pirates	13	7	.650	3	172.1	157	45	105	3.19
1980	Angels	3	6	.333	2	73.1	73	32	28	4.91
1981	Angels	1	1	.500	0	44	40	14	19	3.48
1982	Angels	10	5	.667	3	142	120	44	86	3.17
1983	Angels	11	5	.688	4	126.2	128	43	83	4.05
1984	Angels	4	5	.444	0	65.1	72	28	66	5.37
1985	Redsox	5	3	.625	0	92	98	32	56	4.11
	Totals	115	88	.567	36	1809.2	1693	662	1073	3.66
	Lg Average	101	101	.500	57	1809.2	1768	655	1022	3.73

#26   Jim "Big Jim" Bibby

Pos: P; Age: 35; Batted: Right; Threw: Right; Year in Major Leagues: 8th

Pre-1979. Jim Bibby, a six foot five, 235 1b. Vietnam veteran, was the Family's most successful starting pitcher in 1979, based on his league-high

.750 winning percentage and his team-leading figures of 7.17 hits allowed per nine innings and 2.80 ERA. But if not for a mistake by the Cleveland Indians' front office, the pitcher Chuck Tanner chose to start game seven of the 1979 World Series might never have become a Pirate.

Bibby was signed by the New York Mets but never pitched for them in a major league game. It took him eight years to reach the major leagues because his career had been interrupted for two years by his tour of duty with the army and for another due to a back injury. In 1971, Bibby tied for the International League lead with 15 wins, but he had problems with control. Since the Mets were extremely well stocked with a pitching nucleus that featured Tom Seaver, Jerry Koosman, Nolan Ryan, Gary Gentry, Tug McGraw, Ray Sadeki and a young Jon Matlack, New York included him in an eight-player trade with the Cardinals that October. Bibby struck out 208 AAA batters the next season before getting a late season call-up to St. Louis.

Jim Bibby (courtesy of the Topps Company, Inc.).

He pitched well, but got off to a terrible start in 1973 and was dealt to the Texas Rangers in June after making just six appearances during the season's first two months. The pathetic Rangers were going nowhere, so Bibby got a chance to pitch and accorded himself quite well. A power pitcher all the way, he overwhelmed the world champion Oakland A's on July 30, pitching the first no-hitter in Rangers history. He finished the season with a 9–10 record for the Texas club, which lost 105 games, and struck out 155 batters in 180 innings. Still struggling with control, Bibby walked 106 men in those 180 innings as well. Billy Martin took over as manager near the end of 1973 and gave the sophomore plenty of work in 1974; Bibby started 41 games. Breaking even at 19–19, Big Jim's performances were uneven as evidenced by his 4.74 ERA and 113 walks. Seeking more consistency, Texas traded Bibby to Cleveland midway through the next season for future Hall of Famer Gaylord Perry.

The Vietnam vet pitched well in Cleveland over the next 2½ years, but the Indians were also a weak team and his record with the Tribe was a cumulative 30–29. Some of the blame for the Indians' problems lay in the front office; this was painfully demonstrated to Cleveland fans when the Indians failed to pay Bibby an incentive bonus on time for the second straight year. Bibby and his agent, Richard Hull, sought free agent status for the pitcher, and an arbitrator ruled in their favor.[63] Although Hull said he had received offers from 10 or 15 teams on Bibby's behalf, Big Jim narrowed his choices to Pittsburgh, Philadelphia and Baltimore, deciding on the Pirates when Harding Peterson agreed to slightly increase the club's offer in spring training.

At the time, Frank Robinson, who had managed Bibby in Cleveland and was coaching for the Orioles, expressed regret at the right-hander's decision, calling Bibby a late bloomer. The irony of the Pirates' bounty would not be lost on Robinson and the Baltimore organization a year and a half later.

Bibby joined a veteran Pirates staff and split his time between starting and relieving in 1978. Although Tanner compared his fastball to Goose Gossage's, Bibby seldom closed out games for the Pirates, but pitched well in his assigned roles.

1979: Jim displayed a willingness to pitch whenever he was needed during 1979. He had stated upon his signing with Pittsburgh that he preferred starting, but added that he was willing to do whatever was "most helpful to the team."[64] The hurler began the season in the bullpen, and while he made a few spot starts early in the season, Bibby didn't become a regular starter until July 10. The powerful pitcher showed he belonged there by winning six strait games. His seven wins during the second half of 1979 tied Bruce Kison for most by a Pirates starting pitcher.

Bibby pitched two dominating wins over the Cubs during the season's closing juncture. He shut out Chicago on September 23 and five days later fanned 11 Bruins in the Pirates' 6–1 victory. Prior to these wins, Big Jim, noting he had never pitched for a contender, had wondered aloud whether he would prove to be a money pitcher.

1979 Postseason. Bibby pitched effectively in all three of his postseason starts, even though he did not get credit for a victory. The Pirates came away with two wins in the three games. Getting a crick in his neck, Bibby left game two of the NLCS with a 2–1 lead, but the bullpen allowed the Reds to tie the game before Dave Parker singled in the winning run in the tenth. In his first World Series start, game four, Jim fanned seven, pitching into the seventh inning and allowing only two earned runs, but Earl Weaver's pinch hitters did in Kent Tekulve after a shaky performance by Don Robinson. After using his usual starting pitchers (Jim Rooker, Bert Blyleven and John Candelaria) in the next two games, Tanner gave the ball to Bibby for game seven.

Jim made it no secret that he planned to come after the Orioles with his fastball. "You try to go to a player's weakness," he said before game seven.

5. The Members of the Family

"I'll think about their weaknesses. But you have to go with your strength, too. I'm going out there and throw my fastball. That's my strength."[65]

For the most part, Bibby's strength kept the Baltimore batters at bay. He allowed only a homerun to Rich Dauer and two other meaningless singles in his four innings of work, but with the Pirates trailing 1–0 in the fifth, Tanner lifted him for a pinch hitter. Bibby, though, had done his job. After Pirates relievers Robinson, Grant Jackson and Tekulve shut out the Birds the rest of the way, Bibby could certainly answer the question he had posed to himself a few weeks earlier about whether or not he would prove to be a money pitcher. With his 3–1 September and fine postseason pitching, Big Jim had proven to be a very valuable one indeed.

Post-1979. Bibby continued dominating batters early in 1980. He made the All-Star Team with an 11–1 record and finished the season 19–6. His 19th win of the year was the 100th of his career, and he was named the *Sporting News'* right-handed pitcher on its postseason National League All-Star Team. Jim got off to another blazing start in 1981. On May 19, he retired 27 straight batters after giving up a leadoff single to Terry Harper in a win over the Braves. Following the player's strike, Bibby began experiencing shoulder problems and pitched only four times after play resumed. The following spring, he was diagnosed with a torn rotator cuff. Bone fragments had to be removed from his shoulder, which shelved him for the season.

Big Jim came back in 1983, but his control was poor. His ERA shot up to a horrid 6.69 to go with a 5–12 record, while pitching for a team that was in contention into mid-September. Not offered a contract by the Pirates following the season, Bibby signed with Texas and made eight relief appearances in 1984 before retiring. After his playing days, the hurler served as a minor league pitching coach in the Pirates organization. Bibby finished his pitching career with 111 victories, joining 11 teammates from the 1979 Bucs in winning over 100 games. Below is a list of those pitchers and their career victory totals:

Pitcher	*Career Victories*
Blyleven	287
Reuss	220
Candelaria	177
Rhoden	151
Coleman	142
Ellis	138
Whitson	126
Kison	115
Bibby	111
Robinson	109
Roberts	103
Rooker	102

None of the above, however, was as intimidating as the tall bulky hurler. A large man who would perspire profusely on hot days, Bibby was a slow worker, but once he cut the ball loose, he could blow it by the best hitters in the game. He threw all of his pitches hard, but once he mastered command of his pitches with the Pirates, he was one of baseball's toughest pitchers to hit. Only his shoulder giving out on him prevented him from finishing with a higher win total. During the Family's run at the top in 1979, no Pirates pitcher proved more effective.

Year	Team	W	L	PCT	CG	IP	H	BB	SO	ERA
1972	Cardinals	1	3	.250	0	40.1	29	19	28	3.35
1973	Cardinals	0	2	.000	0	16	19	17	12	9.56
	Rangers	9	10	.474	11	180.1	121	106	155	3.24
	Totals	9	12	.429	11	196.1	140	123	167	3.76
1974	Rangers	19	19	.500	11	264	255	113	149	4.74
1975	Rangers	2	6	.250	4	68.1	73	28	31	5.00
	Indians	5	9	.357	2	112.2	99	50	62	3.20
	Totals	7	15	.318	6	181	172	78	93	3.88
1976	Indians	13	7	.650	4	163.1	162	56	84	3.20
1977	Indians	12	13	.480	9	206.2	197	73	141	3.57
1978	Pirates	8	7	.533	3	107	100	39	72	3.53
1979	Pirates	12	4	.750	4	137.2	110	47	103	2.81
1980	Pirates	19	6	.760	6	238.1	210	88	144	3.32
1981	Pirates	6	3	.667	2	93.2	79	26	48	2.50
1983	Pirates	5	12	.294	0	78	92	51	44	6.69
1984	Rangers	0	0		0	16.1	19	10	6	4.41
	Totals	111	101	.524	56	1722.2	1565	723	1079	3.76
	Lg Average	96	96	.500	58	1722.2	1694	627	956	3.75

#27 Kent "Teke" or "The Rubber Band Man" Tekulve

Pos: P; Age: 32; Batted: Right; Threw: Right; Year in Major Leagues: 6th

Pre-1979. The story of Kent Tekulve is not one that would invoke memories of *The Natural*. He was a tall, lanky, bespectacled hurler standing six foot four while weighing only 175 pounds. He had been described as a "plucked chicken" or "as thin as the center field foul pole."[66] To go along with his physical impression, Teke employed a sidearmed delivery that had most scouts skeptical. "People thought I wouldn't do much in this game. I didn't have the right build and I had a funny, almost underhand motion.... They always wanted me to switch to overhand, but that was my natural motion. Nevertheless, they thought I was just a gimmick pitcher," Tekulve confided.[67] Despite the fact that he didn't exactly look like the second coming of Roy Hobbs, Teke was signed by the Pirates as a free agent in 1969 out of Marietta College in Ohio.

He toiled in the minors for a while, getting a shot at the Bucs' AAA club in Charleston in 1972, then was sent down to AA Sherbrooke the following season after a below-average campaign. At Sherbrooke he finally showed the parent club he might have a future in the majors, with a league-high 12 wins and 57 appearances. In an age where assignment as a relief specialist was still not a common way for major league teams to groom a prospect, Tekulve broke the mold, starting only 18 of his 265 minor league appearances.

After his breakthrough season in AA, Kent was promoted to Charleston once again and this time didn't disappoint. His 6–3 mark and 2.25 ERA finally prompted a call-up from the Bucs at 27 years of age.

Kent Tekulve (courtesy of the Topps Company, Inc.).

The lanky reliever began 1975 in Charleston once again, but his second chance in the Steel City would be the one that kept him there; he had a fine 2.25 ERA in 34 games, allowing only 43 hits in 56 innings. He got his first chance to pitch in the postseason, giving up three hits and a run in one inning of work against the Reds.

Tekulve became the team's ace reliever during the 1976 stretch run, but 1977 saw the Rubber Band Man as the main setup man to the newly signed Goose Gossage. The sidearmer went 10–1 in 102⅔ innings. When Gossage left following the season, Teke returned to being the Pirates' main man out of the pen as the club's closer.

Showing that the move wasn't a mistake, Tekulve responded with a fabulous 8–7 season, saving an NL second-best 31 saves — a Pirates record — while leading the circuit in games pitched with 91. His breakout major league campaign landed him a fifth place finish in the league's Cy Young Award voting, and he missed being named the Rolaids Relief Man of the Year by one point; the award went to Hall of Famer Rollie Fingers. As the '79 season approached Kent Tekulve was considered a star.

1979. In 1978, Kent Tekulve established himself as one of the top relievers in the game. In 1979, he took it to the next level, becoming one of the most recognizable figures in baseball. Teke tied his one-year-old team mark of 31 saves, again finishing second in the circuit, and once again led the National League in games pitched and games finished. Impressively enough, Tekulve also finished the season with another double digit win total, ten, while compiling another sub-3.00 ERA, 2.74, allowing only 109 hits in 134 innings.

Probably the most unexpected event in Kent's world championship campaign happened during the second game of a doubleheader against the Giants. The Rubber Band Man came into the game for Bruce Kison in the top of the eighth with the Bucs up 5–3. Teke put the Giants away in the eighth and had two out in the ninth, when Jack Clark singled. Up to the plate came lefty Darrell Evans, so Tanner decided to go to his pen and bring in southpaw Grant Jackson, since Teke was not at his best against left-handed hitters. With the right-handed Mike Ivie coming up next, Tanner employed a strange strategy, moving the slender Tekulve to left field in place of John Milner, so he could bring back his closer to face Ivie if he had to. Oddly enough, Evans lofted a fly to the one place Chuck Tanner didn't want him to, toward Tekulve in left field. Teke settled under it and made the catch to end the contest.

So fine was Tekulve's season, and so respected was he by others for his leadership, that the man who some of the scouts thought would have no future finished eighth in the voting for senior circuit MVP.

1979 Postseason. Winning a world championship requires having a solid bullpen, and Tekulve would be counted on heavily if Pittsburgh were to bring a title home for the Steel City.

The Rubber Band Man got his first postseason experience in 1979 under fire, coming into a game one jam against the Reds in the NLCS. With two on and two out in the eighth inning of a 2–2 game, Teke entered the contest for Enrique Romo and promptly got Dave Concepcion to bounce into a 5-4-3 double play. He got the Reds out in order, although he walked Johnny Bench—who then was pegged out trying to steal second—in the ninth, keeping the score tied.

In the second contest, Teke once again came into a trouble in the eighth and once again was able to render the Cincy threat fruitless, this time with Pittsburgh up 2–1. Needing only three more outs to all but ensure the Bucs a spot in the 76th World Series, the Ohio native was not up to the challenge, giving up back-to-back doubles to Hector Cruz and Dave Collins, allowing his hometown club to tie the score. Luckily his team was able to bail him out, winning 3–2 in ten innings to come back to Pittsburgh with a 2–0 lead.

Bert Blyleven pitched a complete game in the third contest of the NLCS, holding off Tekulve's next postseason appearance to game two of the World Series against Baltimore. In that game Teke was given the ball with a one-run lead in the ninth. He promptly set the O's down in order, striking out two for his first postseason career save.

Tekulve followed that up with two perfect innings in the game three loss to the Orioles, putting down all six men he faced. He got the chance to get another save in the next contest. Being put in a jam was commonplace for the Bucco ace; getting out of jam was his specialty. Don Robinson had loaded the bases with one out and Tekulve was called in to hold a 6–3 lead. Baltimore manager Earl Weaver hoped to expose Teke's weakness in the face of left handed hitters by sending up his three lefties off the bench. The Rubber Band Man had held right handed hitters to only a .190 average in 1979, but left handers hit almost 100 points better at a .287 clip. Weaver first pinch-hit John Lowenstein, who doubled in two runs, cutting the lead to one. Then the switch-hitting Billy Smith entered the game. Teke intentionally walked him, loading the bases to try and set up a force. Lefty Terry Crowley entered the contest and poked a two-run double to give the Birds a one-run lead. The Pirates' all-time saves leader gave up two more singles to complete the destruction, turning a three-run lead into a three-run deficit.

With the Bucs on the brink of extinction down three games to one, Tekulve would have hoped that his teammates came up big to give him an opportunity to make amends for his poor outing. Luckily, they did. The 6–4 hurler made up for it and then some, pitching three scoreless innings in game six and striking out four to earn his second save in the 4–0 victories.

Finally came the seventh and deciding contest. With Pittsburgh up 2–1 in the eighth, Jackson walked two with only one out. Tanner called on his closer in hopes of avoiding a repeat of the game four debacle. After getting Crowley out on a grounder to second, the Bucs chose to walk the switch-hitting Ken Singleton (to load the bases with two out) and to pitch to the young slugger Eddie Murray, who was struggling mightily in the Fall Classic. But Murray was also a switch-hitter, so he would bat left against Teke. Willie Stargell went to the mound to calm the Bucs' ace down. When Tekulve finally pitched to Murray, the future Hall of Famer hit a long shot to right, which found its way into Dave Parker's glove for the final out. Pittsburgh tacked on two insurance runs in the ninth. Tekulve would have the honor of finishing the seventh game of a World Series, putting the Birds away 1-2-3 to win the World Championship, and gaining his third save of the series.

Post-1979. Like the most of the Family, Kent Tekulve struggled in 1980, losing 12 of his final 16 decisions (although he did save 21, sixth best in the NL).

Some thought that batters had finally solved his strange delivery and that this would be the death knell of his career, but Teke would right the ship. By 1982 he was at his best once again, winning 12 with 20 saves and a 2.83 ERA, then saving 18 the next year with a career low 1.64 ERA.

After he struggled a little in 1984, the Pirates sent their legendary hurler to the cross-state Philadelphia Phillies for Al Holland. Tekulve stayed with the Phils for three seasons, enjoying some success, including an 11–5 mark in 1986 when he finished tenth in the National League with a .688 winning percentage, and the following season when he led the senior circuit for the fourth time in appearances.

He was released by Philadelphia a year later and ended his career for his hometown team in 1989. That season Teke set the all-time record for relief appearances, breaking Hoyt Wilhelm's record with 1050. Tekulve's mark was broken by Jesse Orosco in 1999. Kent retired midway in the season, falling short of Wilhelm's record for total games pitched by 20.

To look at Tekulve's career, you must look at the time period during which he played, not compare him against relievers from other eras. The relief pitcher is the one position that has changed dramatically in the annals of baseball. Before 1970 teams used mainly a four-man rotation, and the relief pitcher was an afterthought. In the 20 years that followed relievers became a specialty, but closers would often go more than one inning — not come in just for three outs when their team is ahead in the ninth inning, as happens today. In fact, the term "closer" wasn't used much until the late 1980s, when the one-inning relief star came into vogue. During Tekulve's time, the pitcher to whom managers turned to finish games was referred to as a "relief ace." In the 21st century, relief pitchers are microspecialists, rarely pitching more than an inning. Eric Gagne, the 2003 Cy Young Award–winner tossed 82⅓ innings in 77 games, while in his prime seasons, 1978 and 1979, Tekulve pitched over 50 more innings.

In comparson to the relievers of his time period, Teke rates very well. Obviously, no one pitched more games between 1974 and 1990 than Tekulve. He tossed 1050 games, 187 more than the next highest, Gene Garber; and he finished 638 games, 30 more than former teammate Goose Gossage. He was in the top ten in appearances in the National League for 12 consecutive years and still holds the senior circuit's all-time mark for games pitched.

In the all-important save category, Kent falls off, finishing his career at 184; a fine mark and 39th on the all-time list, but only tenth in the time period; far behind Goose Gossage, who had the most between 1974 and 1990 with 305. While Tekulve is certainly not a candidate for the Hall of Fame, he can be talked about in the same category as some of the best relief pitchers to play the game.

When you talk about the greatest relievers of the Black and Gold, the conversation begins and ends with only three names: Roy Face, Tekulve and Dave Giusti. In team history the Rubber Band man is second to Face in both saves, with 158, and games pitched, with 722.

Following his major league career, Tekulve spent time as an announcer for the Phillies, then became the director of baseball operations for the Frontier League's Washington Wild Things, a position he retired from prior to the 2004 season. The former Pirates great also has the honor of having named after him the award for pitcher of the year in the Ohio Athletic Conference — the league he pitched for with Marietta College so long ago, when nobody knew just how great this submarine pitcher would turn out to be.

Year	Team	W	L	PCT	CG	IP	H	BB	SO	ERA
1974	Pirates	1	1	.500	0	9	12	5	6	6.00
1975	Pirates	1	2	.333	0	56	43	23	28	2.25
1976	Pirates	5	3	.625	0	102.2	91	25	68	2.45
1977	Pirates	10	1	.909	0	103	89	33	59	3.06
1978	Pirates	8	7	.533	0	135	115	55	77	2.33
1979	Pirates	10	8	.556	0	134.1	109	49	75	2.75
1980	Pirates	8	12	.400	0	93	96	40	47	3.39
1981	Pirates	5	5	.500	0	65	61	17	34	2.49
1982	Pirates	12	8	.600	0	128.2	113	46	66	2.87
1983	Pirates	7	5	.583	0	99	78	36	52	1.64
1984	Pirates	3	9	.250	0	88	86	33	36	2.66
1985	Pirates	0	0		0	3.1	7	5	4	16.20
	Phillies	4	10	.286	0	72.1	67	25	36	2.99
	Totals	4	10	.286	0	75.2	74	30	40	3.57
1986	Phillies	11	5	.688	0	110	99	25	57	2.54
1987	Phillies	6	4	.600	0	105	96	29	60	3.09
1988	Phillies	3	7	.300	0	80	87	22	43	3.60
1989	Reds	0	3	.000	0	52	56	23	31	5.02
	Totals	94	90	.511	0	1436.1	1305	491	779	2.85
	Lg Average	80	80	.500	0	1436.1	1			

#28 Bill "Blinky" Robinson

Pos: Lf, 1b; Age: 36; Batted: Right; Threw: Right; Year in Major Leagues: 12th

Pre-1979. When a player begins his career tabbed as the next Mickey Mantle, that generally means trouble. Most young prospects aren't able to handle such pressure. After all, didn't Mantle himself fail when he first came up to the big leagues tabbed as the next Joe DiMaggio? But good or bad, that's exactly what was thought of Bill Robinson after the New York Yankees traded Clete Boyer to the Braves for the young prospect.[68]

While the comparison might have been a bit outrageous, there was reason for optimism. Robinson hit a league-leading .348 with 18 homers and 81 RBIs for Yakima in 1964. In AAA with Richmond two years later, he hit .312, smacking 20 long balls while playing in the outfield, second and third base, a sign of things to come with the Pirates.

Coming to the Yankees in 1967 with so much hope, Robby fell flat on his face, hitting a combined .206 in 906 at-bats for the Bombers between 1967 and 1969, adding a paltry 16 home runs in the process. The player, who had had the hopes of the legendary franchise on his shoulders, was sent to the White Sox for a pitcher named Barry Moore after spending a year with the Yankees' AAA team in Syracuse.

Robinson never made it to Chicago, being sent to the Phillies a year later for catcher Jerry Rodriguez. He rebounded with the Phils' Eugene club, hitting .304 with 20 homers in only 240 at-bats. This prompted a call-up back to the Bigs in midseason. Robby finally showed his potential in Philadelphia with a .288 average, striking 25 long balls in 1973.

Robinson could not maintain the level he had set in '73. He was sent to the Steel City before the 1975 campaign for another disappointing former superstar by the name of Wayne Simpson, who had dominated hitters for Cincinnati in 1970 before shoulder injuries disrupted the remainder of his career.

Going to the Bucs was the best thing that could have happened to Robinson, who was from nearby Elizabeth, Pennsylvania. "To come home was great. The whole local man returns home storyline meant a lot to me. It got me closer to my father, a man who worked in the Glassport Steel Foundry all his life until it killed him," the former Buc recalled for a recent story in *The Pirates Report*.[69] Despite having no set position, Robby led the club in homers with 21 in 1976, hitting three in one game against the Padres on June 5, while hitting .303 and being named the team MVP. He was promised by manager Danny Murtaugh that he would be the everyday third baseman in 1977, but Murtaugh retired and then passed away; and new skipper Chuck Tanner put Phil Garner there.[70] Even though he again had no set position until becoming the team's first baseman when Willie Stargell was injured, Robinson had his career year in 1977, when he led the team in homers and RBIs with 26 and 104 respectively, finishing eighth in the NL in the latter stat.

Finally assigned an everyday position in left field following the trade of Al Oliver, Robinson was hampered by a fractured thumb, which he injured on opening day in 1978, throughout that season. He hit only .246, although he finished 11th in the league with 80 RBIs.

1979. The 1979 campaign began with some questions for the Elizabeth native. While he had considered surgery in the off-season, instead he and his doctor had decided Robinson would lay off batting practice in hopes the thumb would heal by the spring.[71] Luckily for Bill the thumb felt better, and he entered the season as the team's left fielder, although a fine start by John Milner forced Robinson to give up some of his playing time.

Bill Robinson (courtesy of the Topps Company, Inc.).

5. The Members of the Family

After a two-homerun-game in a June 5 5–4 win against the Dodgers, Robinson led the team in homers and RBIs. He went into the All-Star break as the club's leader in homeruns, while trailing only Dave Parker in RBIs. Pulling off two home runs in a game was a feat he performed two more times during the regular season.

Bill also played 28 games at first, backing up Willie Stargell. He finished the year with 421 at-bats, 24 homers, 75 RBIs (finishing third on the team in both categories), and 13 stolen bases for the world champions. In researching this book, one of the forgotten facts to come to light was the unusual number of clutch hits Robinson collected for the team. When in the lineup, Bill's name was mentioned prominently in accounts of the Bucs' winning rallies, indicating that his overall value to the club exceeded his statistics. A fine defensive outfielder, Robinson often entered games he did not start, to fill in for Milner in the latter stages of contests.

1979 Postseason. Robinson began slowly in the NLCS, going 0-for-2 in the first two games. He came in as an 11th inning defensive replacement in game one and during the sixth of game two. He grounded up and popped out in his only two at-bats. Game three was no better. Robinson replaced Milner in the fifth, popping up to Bench in the seventh for his only time up in the contest.

Despite playing little against the Reds, Robinson went for the ride with the rest of the Bucs, going on to face the Orioles in the World Series. He got his first start in game one against the O's left-handed Cy Young Award–winner, Mike Flanagan. The former Philly finally broke out of his 0-for-5 slump in the postseason, singling to right in the sixth inning, scoring the Bucs' third run of the contest in a 5–4 game-one loss.

Milner got the start in game two, but Robinson made the most of his only at-bat, singling in the ninth in a pinch hit appearance. Bill had a one-out single in the third inning of game three, then struck out in his only time up in a 9–6 game four loss that put the Bucs down 3–1.

Limited to a double in a 1-for-4 performance against Flanagan in the fifth contest, the one-time super-sub finally got his first RBI of the postseason in the next game with a one-out eighth inning sacrifice fly to center in his only time to the plate.

Bill finished a rather disappointing postseason with a bang in the seventh and deciding contest at Baltimore's Memorial Stadium. After popping out his first two times against Scott McGregor, Robby smacked a one-out single to left and then watched the league MVP Willie Stargell smack a majestic two-run shot. Robinson came across the plate with the tying run on the hit that put the Bucs ahead for good, 2–1.

Robinson got an insurance RBI in the ninth in a peculiar manner, after he was hit by Tippy Martinez with the bases loaded, scoring Omar Moreno.

While he hit a meager .227 in 22 at-bats in his first postseason effort, he was an integral part in the Bucs' drive to the world title.

Post-1979. Injuries took their toll on Robinson after 1979; a bruised Achilles' heel cost him 29 games in an otherwise fine .287 campaign in 1980. It would be his last good season. He only had a combined 159 at-bats in 1981 and 1982 before Bucs GM Pete Peterson sent him back to Philadelphia for Wayne Nordhagen in a three-way deal with the Blue Jays. (The Pirates eventually got Dick Davis after it was discovered Nordhagen suffered from a bad back.) Bill hit .261 in 69 at-bats for the Phils to finish the '82 campaign, before closing out his career with a one for seven swansong in 1983.

Since retiring, Robinson has won three more World Series rings, one with the Mets as a first base coach in 1986, one with the Yankees as a roving hitting instructor, and one in 2003 when he was a hitting coach for the Florida Marlins. During the 2003 series Bill made a statement about Florida, saying, "Willie [Stargell] used to say all the time to respect everyone but fear no one. We're not supposed to be here. But we're a very confident team, a very relaxed team."[72] It sounded strikingly like the description of the 1979 club he starred for so many years before.

Year	Team	AB	R	HR	RBI	BB	SO	SB	AVG	OBP
1966	Braves	11	1	0	3	0	1	0	.273	.728
1967	Yankees	342	31	7	29	28	56	2	.196	.540
1968	Yankees	342	34	6	40	26	54	7	.240	.674
1969	Yankees	222	23	3	21	16	39	3	.171	.505
1972	Phillies	188	19	8	21	5	30	2	.239	.684
1973	Phillies	452	62	25	65	27	91	5	.288	.855
1974	Phillies	280	32	5	29	17	61	5	.236	.626
1975	Pirates	200	26	6	33	11	36	3	.280	.763
1976	Pirates	393	55	21	64	16	73	2	.303	.863
1977	Pirates	507	74	26	104	25	92	12	.304	.862
1978	Pirates	499	70	14	80	35	105	14	.246	.707
1979	Pirates	421	59	24	75	24	81	13	.264	.806
1980	Pirates	272	28	12	36	15	45	1	.287	.783
1981	Pirates	88	8	2	8	5	18	1	.216	.576
1982	Pirates	71	8	4	12	5	19	0	.239	.737
	Phillies	69	6	3	19	7	15	1	.261	.799
	Totals	140	14	7	31	12	34	1	.250	.767
1983	Phillies	7	0	0	2	1	4	0	.143	.393
	Totals	4364	536	166	641	263	820	71	.258	.738
	Lg Average	4422	546	99	508	429	636	85	.260	.710
	Pos Average	4485	593	123	568	452	670	87	.269	.748

#29 Harry Saferight

Pos: C; Age: 30; Batted: Left; Threw: Right; Year in Major Leagues: 1

Pre-1979. The Pirates traded former major league infielder Tommy

Matchick for Saferight, a backup catcher in the Phillies organization, on June 17, 1974. Saferight's hitting improved during his 2½ years at AA Shreveport. He capped his stay with a .336 mark and five homeruns in 107 at-bats before being promoted to Columbus, where he hit .295 with 10 homers in 261 at-bats. Not viewed as a strong defensive catcher, Saferight was a designated hitter and played 13 games in the outfield during a disappointing 1978 when he hit .247 in AAA. He was, however, seen as a strong enough hitter to be added to the Pirates' winter roster for 1979.

1979: Saferight was added to the big league club on September 1 after batting .265 with 11 homers and 81 RBIs in Portland, but was used only to warm up pitchers in the bullpen.

1979 Postseason. He was ineligible for postseason play.

Post-1979. The Pirates dropped Saferight from the roster after the 1979 season to make room for brighter prospects than the 30-year-old career minor leaguer. Although there were also three pitchers — Jim Willoughby, Rod Scurry and Rick Jones — who did not appear in a game for the World Champions in 1979 after being added to the roster on September 1, Saferight was the only member of the 1979 team never to appear in a major league game.

#29   Rick Rhoden

Pos: P; Age: 26; Batted: Right; Threw: Right; Year in Major Leagues: 6th

Pre-1979. Nothing Rick Rhoden could have done would be more impressive than the first 12 years of his life. Rhoden survived many leg ailments, including osteomyelitus, which caused him to wear a brace until he was 12.

He battled back, becoming a two-sport star in high school in both basketball and baseball, then breaking into the majors in 1974 with the Dodgers.

Rhoden's best start came in 1976 when he won his first 9 decisions en route to a 12–3 mark. The campaign was a prelude to a fine 1977, a season when he won 16, pitched four scoreless innings against Phillies in the NLCS, and then backed it up with a fine World Series performance versus the Yanks, giving up only four hits in seven innings.

The year 1978 brought a sign of things to come; the Florida native suffered arm injuries that sent him to the bullpen after his return.

1979: A trade saw Rhoden go from Los Angeles to the Steel City as general manger Pete Peterson sent southpaw Jerry Reuss to the Dodgers the day after the Bucs' opening game. Rhoden had been nursing a tender shoulder, but the Pirates believed he would be able to recuperate after a few weeks in extended spring training. This did not happen. After an unsuccessful start against Atlanta on May 5, the right-hander went on the disabled list for the rest of the season. He eventually underwent rotator cuff surgery in the off-season.

1979 Postseason: Rhoden was on the disabled list for the postseason.

Post-1979: After spending the first half of the 1980 campaign at the Bucs' AAA team in Portland rehabbing his shoulder, the veteran, who had the reputation throughout his career of doctoring the baseball, finally lived up to Peterson's hopes. He became the best pitcher on some bad Pirates teams in the mid–1980s; his best two campaigns, in '84 and '86, were during particularly poor seasons for the Bucs. A hot commodity on the market, the new GM Syd Thrift, in need of a harvest of young talent to turn around the club, traded Rhoden to the Yankees for three pitchers: Brian Fisher, Logan Easley and a hurler by the name of Doug Drabek.

Rhoden — who was also a great hitting pitcher, winning the Silver Slugger Award on three occasions; as well as a good fielder, with only six lifetime errors — had two fine seasons in the Big Apple, winning 28 games. He ended his career in Houston in 1989.

Rhoden had a passion for golf, eventually becoming the best player on the fast growing celebrity golf tour.

Year	Team	W	L	PCT	CG	IP	H	BB	SO	ERA
1974	Dodgers	1	0	1.000	0	9	5	4	7	2.00
1975	Dodgers	3	3	.500	1	99.1	94	32	40	3.08
1976	Dodgers	12	3	.800	10	181	165	53	77	2.98
1977	Dodgers	16	10	.615	4	216.1	223	63	122	3.74
1978	Dodgers	10	8	.556	6	164.2	160	51	79	3.66
1979	Pirates	0	1	.000	0	5	5	2	2	7.20
1980	Pirates	7	5	.583	2	126.2	133	40	70	3.84
1981	Pirates	9	4	.692	4	136.1	147	53	76	3.89
1982	Pirates	11	14	.440	6	230.1	239	70	128	4.14
1983	Pirates	13	13	.500	7	244.1	256	68	153	3.09
1984	Pirates	14	9	.609	6	238.1	216	62	136	2.72
1985	Pirates	10	15	.400	2	213.1	254	69	128	4.47
1986	Pirates	15	12	.556	12	253.2	211	76	159	2.84
1987	Yankees	16	10	.615	4	181.2	184	61	107	3.86
1988	Yankees	12	12	.500	5	197	206	56	94	4.29
1989	Astros	2	6	.250	0	96.2	108	41	41	4.28
	Totals	151	125	.547	69	2593.2	2606	801	1419	3.59
	Lg Average	145	145	.500	68	2593.2	2552	937	1522	3.84

#30 Jim Willoughby

Pos: P; Age: 30; Batted: Right; Threw: Right; Year in Major Leagues: 9th

Pre-1979. After being taken in the 11th round of the 1967 free agent draft, Jim Willoughby rose through the Giants' farm system with 45–32 mark in five minor league seasons. He debuted with San Francisco in 1971, and had a fine rookie season the following year in the Giants' rotation. That campaign, the California native had his best major league season, going 6–4 in 11 starts with a 2.35 ERA.

Tailing off in 1973, his first full season in the show, Jim returned to the Giants' AAA team in Phoenix the following year, then finished 1974 in the San Francisco pen.

The reliever was sent to the Cardinals after the season, but was traded to the Red Sox for Mario Guerrero before ever appearing for St. Louis. Willoughby went 5–2 down the stretch for the pennant-winning Sox, pitching in his one and only Fall Classic. He limited the Big Red Machine to only three hits and no earned runs in 6⅓ innings, although he gave up an unearned run in the tenth inning of game three after three fabulous innings of relief, losing his only career post season decision.

In 1976, despite losing 12 games, the 27-year-old hurler saved ten games, good for eighth in the junior circuit, and posted a fine 2.82 ERA. Following one more season in Boston, Jim was purchased by the White Sox before the '78 campaign, a season in which he finished 47 games, third in the AL, saving a career-high 13 contests.

1979: After the 1978 season ended, the Cards once again traded for the veteran hurler only to quickly let him go, marking the second time St. Louis dealt for Jim only to never use him in a game. The Cubs organization inked Willoughby afterwards, sending him to Wichita where a 2–1 mark with a dismal 5.82 ERA prompted his release. Pittsburgh eventually picked him up, assigning him to their AAA team in Portland. There, Willoughby was a little more successful, compiling a 3–2 record with five saves in 24 appearances and sporting a 2.85 ERA. With his decent performance in the minors, the Pirates made him a late season call-up, although Jim never got into a game for the Bucs.

1979 Postseason. Willoughby was, of course, not included on the postseason roster.

Post-1979. Jim's venture with the White Sox in 1978 would prove to be the last time he ever played in the majors

Year	Team	W	L	PCT	CG	IP	H	BB	SO	ERA
1971	Giants	0	1	.000	0	4	8	1	3	9.00
1972	Giants	6	4	.600	7	88	72	14	40	2.35
1973	Giants	4	5	.444	1	123	138	37	60	4.68
1974	Giants	1	4	.200	0	41	51	9	12	4.61
1975	Redsox	5	2	.714	0	48	46	16	29	3.56
1976	Redsox	3	12	.200	0	99	94	31	37	2.82
1977	Redsox	6	2	.750	0	55	54	18	33	4.91
1978	Whitesox	1	6	.143	0	93	95	19	36	3.87

Totals	26	36	.419	8	551	558	145	250	3.79
Lg Average	31	31	.500	8	551	532	201	313	3.63

#31   Ed Whitson

Pos: P; Age: 24; Batted: Right; Threw: Right; Year in Major Leagues: 3rd

Pre-1979. Considered by many to be the Pirates' top pitching prospect in the mid- to late 1970s despite uneven success in the minor leagues, Eddie Whitson enjoyed 126 major league victories, 118 after being traded in the deal that brought Bill Madlock to the Pirates. Whitson's finest minor league campaign was in 1976, when he tied for the Carolina League lead with 15 wins and topped the Class A circuit in strikeouts (186), innings pitched (203) and complete games (16).

A victim of nonsupport in 1977, Whitson was called up to the Pirates in September after an 8–13 season for AAA Columbus.[73] He looked good in his brief stay that fall and the next season, after striking out 55 batters in 51 innings for the Clippers, was recalled in late June. After never having relieved in his minor league career, Whitson spent his rookie season pitching exclusively in that role for the Pirates, and proved to be effective, posting a 3.28 and allowing only 66 hits in 74 innings pitched, while striking out 64 men.

Eddie Whitson (courtesy of the Topps Company, Inc.).

1979. Ticketed for double duty in 1979, Whitson began the year in Chuck Tanner's bullpen, but made seven starts. He struggled with his control, but was dominant in a start against the Dodgers in mid-June, allowing only two hits to the defending National League champions. The Giants considered him one of the better young pitchers in the game and required him in exchange for their disgruntled .300 hitting infielder when Pete Peterson called. Whitson, only 2–3 with a 4.34 ERA at the time of the trade, was placed directly into the Giants' rotation by Joe Altobelli. The hurler's control improved with regular work, but his 5–8 mark with a 3.96 ERA demonstrated continued need for development.

Post-1979. Whitson lowered his

5. The Members of the Family

ERA to 3.10, pitching well despite showing a losing record for 1980. He was not as effective in 1981 and was traded after the season for second baseman Duane Kuiper. Pitching mostly in relief for the Tribe, Whitson did well in Cleveland, and bigger things were expected of him when he was traded to the Padres for 1983. He lapsed back into mediocrity in '83, but helped San Diego to the National League pennant the following year with 14 wins. Whitson pitched a fine game against the Cubs in the NLCS that fall, but the Tigers knocked him out in less than an inning in his game two World Series start.

One of the top free-agent pitchers available following the series, Ed was signed to a longterm contract by the New York Yankees. The move proved a terrible one for all involved. Whitson was hit hard early in the year, starting 1985 0–6.[74] He was hounded by fans in New York, and things got so bad that he was harassed at his home. The frustrated pitcher even got into a fight with his manager, Billy Martin, breaking his skipper's arm in a barroom battle. When Lou Piniella took over as Yankees manager, he decided against using Whitson in games at Yankee Stadium. Freely expressing his contempt for the city, Whitson asked to be traded and was shipped back to San Diego halfway through his second year in the Big Apple.

Out of the New York pressure cooker, Whitson won 50 games over the next four seasons, including a career best 16 in 1989. After winning 14 more and posting a career low ERA of 2.60 in 1990, Ed suffered arm problems that led to his retirement in 1991.

Year	Team	W	L	PCT	CG	IP	H	BB	SO	ERA
1977	Pirates	1	0	1.000	0	15.2	11	9	10	3.45
1978	Pirates	5	6	.455	0	74.1	66	37	64	3.27
1979	Pirates	2	3	.400	0	57.2	53	36	31	4.37
	Giants	5	8	.385	2	100.1	98	39	62	3.95
	Totals	7	11	.389	2	158	151	75	93	4.10
1980	Giants	11	13	.458	6	211.2	222	56	90	3.10
1981	Giants	6	9	.400	2	123	130	47	65	4.02
1982	Indians	4	2	.667	1	107.2	91	58	61	3.26
1983	Padres	5	7	.417	2	144.1	143	50	81	4.30
1984	Padres	14	8	.636	1	189	181	42	103	3.24
1985	Yankees	10	8	.556	2	158.2	201	43	89	4.88
1986	Yankees	5	2	.714	0	37	54	23	27	7.54
	Padres	1	7	.125	0	75.2	85	37	46	5.59
	Totals	6	9	.400	0	112.2	139	60	73	6.23
1987	Padres	10	13	.435	3	205.2	197	64	135	4.73
1988	Padres	13	11	.542	3	205.1	202	45	118	3.77
1989	Padres	16	11	.593	5	227	198	48	117	2.66
1990	Padres	14	9	.609	6	228.2	215	47	127	2.60
1991	Padres	4	6	.400	2	78.2	93	17	40	5.03
	Totals	126	123	.506	35	2240.1	2240	698	1266	3.79
	Lg Average	125	125	.500	51	2240.1	2206	809	1339	3.87

#31 Rod Scurry

Pos: P; Age: 23; Batted: Left; Threw: Left; Year in Major Leagues: 1st

Pre-1979. Rod Scurry was the Pirates' first round selection in the June 1974 free agent draft after leading Hugh High School in Reno, Nevada, to the state AAA baseball championship. He posted an unimpressive 32–46 minor league record through 1978, but developed an excellent curveball, which the Pirates believed could be an effective strikeout pitch. He was added to the team's 40-man roster in 1977.

1979. Scurry posted only so-so numbers with AAA Portland (5–5, 4.13 with 94 Ks and 72 walks in 122 innings). Again looking at Scurry's curveball as a potentially devastating pitch against lefthanders, the Beavers used him in 20 relief appearances. He showed enough to be recalled when the rosters expanded on September 1, but not enough for Chuck Tanner to call on him to pitch during the pressure packed final month of the season.

1979 Postseason. Scurry was ineligible for the 1979 postseason.

Post-1979. Out of options in 1980, Scurry came north with the Pirates out of spring training. Tanner moved Scurry along slowly as a rookie, using him very effectively in 20 relief appearances, a total that was limited by a groin pull. The reliever allowed only 23 hits in 38 innings while striking out 28 and posting a 2.13 ERA.

In 1981, Scurry got a few starting assignments, but when Grant Jackson was traded in late August, the southpaw assumed the role of left-handed setup man and pitched well, foreshadowing his excellent 1982 season. Still occasionally struggling with control, Scurry's numbers in 1982 included 14 saves and a 1.74 ERA in 74 games. He allowed just 79 hits in 103⅔ innings pitched and struck out 94. One poll of major league scouts concluded Scurry had the best curveball in baseball.

Unfortunately, cocaine addiction would soon begin sucking away Scurry's career and later his life. He had a horrible 1983 season, but pitched better in 1984 after seeking help through Gateway Rehabilitation. While his control numbers suffered in 1985, he was still fairly effective. But Scurry's troubles with substances continued to haunt him. Following a trade to the New York Yankees near the end of 1985 and pitching for the Bronx Bombers in 1986, Rod was out of the major leagues in 1987, having been released in spring training following a drunken driving charge that was later dropped.[75] After pitching that year for the Giants' AAA Phoenix club, Scurry got a chance to hurl again in the major leagues with the Seattle Mariners in 1988. The Mariners released the reliever on December 21 that year, and the following morning, Scurry was arrested for buying two rocks of crack cocaine in Reno.

On October 29, 1992, Rod's neighbors called the authorities, saying he was acting strangely. When sheriff's deputies arrived, they reportedly found Scurry complaining that he was being bitten by snakes. When the deputies tried to calm him, the former pitcher became agitated and violent and stopped breathing as the deputies tried to handcuff him. Doctors later said Scurry had collapsed due to a lack of oxygen to the brain, the result of cardiopulmonary arrest. He was placed on life support at a nearby hospital, but died a week later.[76]

Although Scurry's presence on the Pirates' 1979 roster is largely forgotten, since he did not appear in any games, his story is certainly the saddest of any member of the Family. He was not the only member of the team to be seduced by drugs, but he was the man who paid the highest price.

Year	Team	W	L	PCT	CG	IP	H	BB	SO	ERA
1980	Pirates	0	2	.000	0	37.2	23	17	28	2.15
1981	Pirates	4	5	.444	0	74	74	40	65	3.77
1982	Pirates	4	5	.444	0	103.2	79	64	94	1.74
1983	Pirates	4	9	.308	0	68	63	53	67	5.56
1984	Pirates	5	6	.455	0	46.1	28	22	48	2.53
1985	Pirates	0	1	.000	0	47.2	42	28	43	3.21
	Yankees	1	0	1.000	0	12.2	5	10	17	2.84
	Totals	1	1	.500	0	60.1	47	38	60	3.13
1986	Yankees	1	2	.333	0	39.1	38	22	36	3.66
1988	Mariners	0	2	.000	0	31.1	32	18	33	4.02
	Totals	19	32	.373	0	460.2	384	274	431	3.24
	Lg Average	26	26	.500	1	460.2	453	164	265	3.82

#34 John "The Hammer" Milner

Pos: LF-1B; Age: 29; Batted: Left; Threw: Left; Year in Major Leagues: 9th

Pre-1979. It was hoped that John Milner would become the New York Mets' first homegrown power hitter when he arrived in the major leagues in 1971. While he did provide enough long balls in the Big Apple to help the Mets to the National League Pennant in 1973, he never quite developed into the top-notch homerun threat New Yorkers had envisioned. Milner's best power numbers in New York were 23 homeruns during the Mets' "Gotta Believe" year and 20 in 1974, but injuries had, at times, greatly reduced his effectiveness, as in 1975 when he batted just .191. The Mets gave up hope that Milner would someday develop into one of the game's elite sluggers and by December 1977 included him in a trade with the Texas Rangers as part of a four-team deal that brought the Mets Willie Montanez and Ken Henderson. Texas, which also received pitcher Jon Matlack from New York, immediately packaged Milner with right-hander Bert Blyleven, sending the two to Pittsburgh for outfielder Al Oliver and shortstop prospect Nelson Norman.

Although Blyleven was the major acquisition in the trade from the Pirates' standpoint, adding Milner to the team was extremely important. The trade of the .300 hitting Oliver meant Bill Robinson would become the Pirates' everyday leftfielder, and this meant the Bucs needed someone to replace Robinson's power off the bench. Also, Willie Stargell had spent most of the second half of 1977 on the disabled list with a pinched nerve; and at the age of 37, the status of their team captain's health caused reasonable concern for the Pirates brass. Milner, it was figured, could provide not only a homerun threat off the bench, but would be a valuable insurance policy should Stargell not rebound.

Stargell enjoyed a huge comeback season in 1978, but Chuck Tanner was able to get Milner 295 at-bats as the Pirates' number two leftfielder and first baseman. The left-handed hitter's .271 average equaled his career high, set in 1976; and, although he lifted only six balls out of the yard all season, Milner provided enough offense for the Bucs to hope for bigger things in 1979.

1979. Expected to fill a similar role to the one he played in 1978, Milner got off to a great start in 1979, forcing his way into the lineup more often than expected. The Hammer was named National League Player of the Week for his performance between April 10 and April 15 when he blasted two homeruns, drove in eight, had a pair of game winning hits and batted .571. Although injured shortly thereafter, Milner finished April with a .469 average. He then slumped all the way to .248 and added just 10 more RBIs during the first half of the season.[77]

John Milner (courtesy of the Topps Company, Inc.).

The Hammer's bat caught fire again shortly after the All-Star break. He provided one of the memorable moments of 1979 when he hit a ninth inning grand slam to beat the Phillies on August 5. It was the second grand slam of the season for Milner, who had also connected off the Braves' Phil Niekro on May 9.[78] Milner batted .301 during the second half of the year, reclaiming a spot as Tanner's leftfielder against right-handed pitching. He struggled a bit in September, but his final average of .276 would be his lifetime high. John also finished with 16 homeruns and 60 RBIs in just 326 at-bats. His RBI ratio of one run batted in every 5.4 at-bats was second on the team behind only Stargell and was the eighth best mark in the National League.

1979 Postseason. Milner's late-season slump continued into the National League Championship Series. He started all three games in leftfield, but went 0-for-9. Always a streaky hitter, Milner's struggles led to some discussion about whether or not Tanner should bench his left-handed bat and play Robinson, a much better defensive player against both left- and right-handed pitching in the World Series. Tanner, however, was not involved in this fan debate, and decided to play the cards that had been a winning hand throughout the season. Milner responded with a .333 performance in the World Series, going 3-for-9 and drawing a pair of walks. He scored twice, including the tally which tied game two and knocked in a run in a losing cause in game four.

Post-1979. Milner's hitting tailed off in 1980, and an early season hitting barrage by Mike Easler pushed the Hammer back into Tanner's tool box. He played only 11 games in the outfield that season as opposed to 64 appearances in 1979. Milner did see more action after Stargell was injured, and played 70 games at first base, which was his best defensive position.

By 1981, one of the shining stars of Pop's Family just two years earlier had become primarily a pinch hitter, going to bat only 59 times in 34 games before being traded again in a deal involving Willie Montanez. Milner went to the Expos, but returned to the Pirates the following season after going just 3-for-28 and garnering his release from Montreal. Pete Peterson signed the Hammer in late July after Dave Parker was placed on the disabled list.[79] The final 25 at-bats of Milner's career came as a pinch hitter to finish out the season. He drove in eight runs with his six pinch hits, including a grand slam off Steve Mura of St. Louis on August 15. John was let go in spring training 1983, finishing his career with a .249 average, 131 homeruns and a World Series ring from 1979. He passed away from cancer on January 4, 2000.

Fans old enough to remember the glorious 1979 season will never forget Milner's contributions to the Family. Always dangerous with the bases loaded (he finished his career with ten grand slams), his game winning blast against the Phillies that year demonstrated to all of baseball that the Pirates, and not the reigning division champions, were Pennsylvania's team to be reckoned with in 1979.

Year	Team	AB	R	HR	RBI	BB	SO	SB	AVG	OBP
1971	Mets	18	1	0	1	0	3	0	.167	.389
1972	Mets	362	52	17	38	51	74	2	.238	.763
1973	Mets	451	69	23	72	62	84	1	.239	.761
1974	Mets	507	70	20	63	66	77	10	.252	.745
1975	Mets	220	24	7	29	33	22	1	.191	.638
1976	Mets	443	56	15	78	65	53	0	.271	.809
1977	Mets	388	43	12	57	61	55	6	.255	.768
1978	Pirates	295	39	6	38	34	25	5	.271	.732
1979	Pirates	326	52	16	60	53	37	3	.276	.848
1980	Pirates	238	31	8	34	52	29	2	.244	.748
1981	Pirates	59	6	2	9	5	3	0	.237	.648
	Expos	76	6	3	9	12	6	0	.237	.762
	Totals	135	12	5	18	17	9	0	.237	.713
1982	Expos	28	1	0	2	4	2	0	.107	.319
	Pirates	25	5	2	8	6	3	1	.240	.966
	Totals	53	6	2	10	10	5	1	.170	.629
	Totals	3436	455	131	498	504	473	31	.249	.757
	Lg Average	3445	429	76	400	338	484	70	.262	.712
	Pos Average	3501	457	102	474	377	514	54	.271	.758

#35 Manny "Sangy" Sanguillen

Pos: C; Age: 35; Batted: Right; Threw: Right; Year in Major Leagues: 12th

Pre-1979. Manny Sanguillen established himself as one of the finest all-around catchers in baseball during the early 1970s, but the biggest hit of his career came at a time when he was a little used pinch hitter nearing the end of his playing days.

Sanguillen arrived in the majors in 1967, called up to the Pirates when injuries felled regular backstops Jerry May and Jim Paglarioni. He hit a respectable .271, but while displaying a strong arm and raw talent, needed to refine his abilities. He spent 1968 in the minor leagues after a broken finger cost him a shot at the Bucs. Sangy hit .316 in AAA that season, including an unbelievable .387 performance over his final 87 games. Manny opened 1969 as May's backup, but soon won the catching job and hit .303. Manny followed this up with .325, .319 and .298 the next three seasons. His defense improved to the point that most observers rated him behind only Johnny Bench as a catcher. Some, in fact, including base stealing champion Lou Brock, rated Sangy higher. "He always seems to make a perfect throw on me," Brock commented. "It comes in straight and low, and I'd have to say he throws a little better than Bench."[80]

Sanguillen's longtime battery mate, Steve Blass, agreed. "Other than the homeruns and RBI's, Sangy was as good a catcher as Bench."[81]

As a hitter, the Panamanian was as undisciplined as he was successful.

Danny Murtaugh stated, "I've seen him hit doubles off pitches that seemed headed for his head."[82] Flashing an ever-ready smile, Sanguillen became extremely popular in Pittsburgh even if he seldom walked. In 1971, Sangy drew only six unintentional walks all year. His free-swinging style earned him the title of "baseball's best bad ball hitter since Yogi Berra." During the 1971 World Series, Manny hit a robust .379, second only to Roberto Clemente in the Series. Manny collected 11 hits, but did not drive in a single run in the Pirates' victory.

Manny Sanguillen (courtesy of the Topps Company, Inc.).

When Sanguillen's average fell just below .300 in 1972, there began to be concern that his duties as a catcher were starting to age his skills prematurely. Manager Bill Virdon began experimenting with him as an outfielder to lessen the catcher's workload behind the plate and to get more at-bats for Milt May, a strong left-handed hitter who had been considered a blue chip prospect in 1971 but was stuck playing caddie to Sanguillen. When his close friend Roberto Clemente died on New Year's Eve, 1972, Virdon chose to accelerate his plan and Sanguillen, who possessed fine running speed, was named to open 1973 as the team's right fielder. The experiment failed. Sangy struggled in right, and with the team playing below expectations, he was moved back to his catching position in midseason.

Sanguillen continued to be the Pirates' number one catcher through 1976. He hit a career high .328 in 1975, but had a difficult NLCS when the Cincinnati Reds ran wild against him and the Pirates' mounds men. In '76, injuries limited him to 114 games, and while Sanguillen hit .290, he was seen as expendable enough to be traded to the Oakland A's for their manager, Chuck Tanner.

After hitting .275 during his one season in Oakland, Sanguillen was reacquired by Pete Peterson near the end of spring training, 1978, for Miguel Dilone, Mike Edwards and Elias Sosa. Peterson, however, did not bring Sanguillen back to Pittsburgh for his old job. Instead, he returned as a role player and spent 1978 subbing at first base, catching only occasionally and pinch hitting.

1979. With the Pirates' signing of Lee Lacy, Sanguillen's role was even further reduced in 1979. He caught eight games, played five at first base, and batted just 74 times, collecting 17 hits for a .230 average. Manny drove in only four runs all year, but two of those came on a game-winning pinch hit on September 19.

1979 Postseason. After not appearing against the Reds in the National League Championship Series, Sanguillen unsuccessfully pinch hit in game one of the World Series. With the score tied in the ninth inning of the second contest and Ed Ott on second base with two outs, Tanner called on the man whom the Pirates had once given up to put Chuck in the black and gold. Sanguillen singled to right against Don Stanhouse to win what was the most exciting game of the World Series. Tanner, remembering Sanguillen's ability to handle pitches off the plate, had picked the veteran as his weapon against Stanhouse's pitches that often ran out of the strike zone. Sanguillen dedicated his hit to the memory of Clemente and was greeted with a standing ovation when his name was announced before game three in Pittsburgh. Ironically, his one hit in the 1979 World Series will always be remembered more than the eleven he drilled in the 1971 Fall Classic.

Post-1979. Sanguillen spent one last season for the Pirates in 1980, primarily pinch hitting. Traded with Bert Blyleven to Cleveland following the season, Sanguillen retired after the Indians released him in spring training.

Sanguillen remains a popular figure in Pittsburgh. He continues to flash the broad smile that helped make him a fan favorite during his first go-around with the team. While never as powerful a hitter as Willie Stargell or even teammates Dave Parker or Al Oliver, Sangy was a more popular player with Pittsburghers prior to Stargell's final few seasons. Pirates fans loved his work ethic, his hustle and positive attitude. Even in the 1970s, many players would have balked at moving from a position where they were acknowledged as one of the best in the game, as Sanguillen was asked to do in 1973. Some would have grumbled at coming back to a team they had starred with only a season or two before, to find their role lessened by a player with only one year's experience as a platoon catcher (Ott) and a career backup catcher (Duffy Dyer). Not Manny. When asked about the difficulty of accepting these changes during Piratefest, 2004, Sanguillen simply responded, "I just did my job. I did what they paid me to do."

That's an attitude Pittsburghers relate to. The current Pirates management wisely chose Sanguillen to host a barbeque stand at PNC Park in 2002. The barbequed pork and roast beef might tantalize the taste buds of Pirates fans, but nothing could ever be as sweet as his single to right off Don Stanhouse on a cold October night in 1979.

Year	Team	AB	R	HR	RBI	BB	SO	SB	AVG	OBP
1967	Pirates	96	6	0	8	4	12	0	.271	.613
1969	Pirates	459	62	5	57	12	48	8	.303	.731
1970	Pirates	486	63	7	61	17	45	2	.325	.788
1971	Pirates	533	60	7	81	19	32	6	.319	.771
1972	Pirates	520	55	7	71	21	38	1	.298	.726
1973	Pirates	589	64	12	65	17	29	2	.282	.712
1974	Pirates	596	77	7	68	21	27	2	.287	.684
1975	Pirates	481	60	9	58	48	31	5	.328	.842
1976	Pirates	389	52	2	36	28	18	2	.290	.716
1977	A's	571	42	6	58	22	35	2	.275	.656
1978	Pirates	220	15	3	16	9	10	2	.264	.632
1979	Pirates	74	8	0	4	2	5	0	.230	.598
1980	Pirates	48	2	0	2	3	1	3	.250	.607
	Totals	5062	566	65	585	223	331	35	.296	.724
	Lg Average	4826	601	111	559	485	699	87	.260	.713
	Pos Average	4752	500	110	563	492	718	26	.247	.685

#36 Matt "The Scat" Alexander

Pos: OF-PR; Age: 32; Batted: Both; Threw: Right; Year in Major Leagues: 7th

Pre-1979. Chuck Tanner loved the running game, and because he valued speed so much, Matt Alexander got to play in a World Series.

Always a fast runner, Alexander starred in football and basketball as well as baseball in high school. The Scat pitched as well as playing in the field in high school, and not only hit over .400 as a senior but won two games in the state championship, including one against future major league star Vida Blue.[83] He was signed by Negro Leagues legend Buck O'Neil for the Chicago Cubs in 1968.

Alexander progressed up to AA San Antonio by his second season, but spent 1970 and 1971 in the United States Navy. Returning to AA baseball in 1972, Matt hit .270 and stole 38 bases for Midland. The Cubs moved him up to AAA Wichita in 1973, and Alexander topped .300 before getting a late season call-up to Chicago. The switch hitter split 1974 between AAA and the big league, but hit only .204 in 45 games with the Cubs. He began 1975 back in AAA, but was traded to the Oakland A's for a player to be named later on April 28. Oakland owner Charles O. Finley had always pushed for his team to have a man on the roster whom his manager could use as a type of "designated runner" and had gone so far as to employ world class sprinter Herb Washington as a member of his ball club. Washington, though, had no experience in baseball and his only skill was his speed. Some argued he lacked baseball instincts, and his teammates resented his taking up a spot on the roster.[84]

In Alexander, the A's obtained a player who could replace Washington and could fill in in the field if needed. In addition to his speed, Matt knew how to run the bases, knowledge most felt Washington lacked. Still, Alexander's appearances in the field were relatively few. In three seasons, playing for three different A's managers, he batted just 72 times while appearing in 213 games. However, during these years Alexander stole 17, 20 and 26 bases respectively.

The pinch running specialist spent most of 1978 out of baseball. When the rosters were expanded on September 1, Tanner, one of his former bosses in Oakland, remembered him, and the Pirates signed him to pinch run for the team. He appeared in seven games, scored two runs and stole four bases.

1979. Invited to spring training as a non-roster player, Alexander was such a long shot to make the team that his picture was not included in the Pirates' yearbook. Regardless, Matt the Scat spent most of 1979 with the Bucs. As usual, he seldom appeared at the plate, but when he did, he was uncannily successful, going 7-for-13 with a triple. More important was his success as a base stealer; he went 13-for-14 in his primary role. Matt spent the middle of the year playing for AA Buffalo, where he batted .313 with five homeruns and ten doubles in 32 games. He was recalled on August 21 and spent the remainder of the year on the big league roster.

1979 Postseason. Alexander made one appearance in each postseason series. He scored the game winning run as Tim Foli's legs in game one of the NLCS, then was thrown out on a close by Orioles catcher Rick Dempsey in game two of the World Series.

Post-1979. Matt appeared in 52 games for the Pirates the next two seasons, going 5-for-14 while stealing 13 bases. He was released following the 1981 season.

Alexander's career line in baseball record books is one of the oddest in history. He finished his major league career with 374 appearances, but just 168 at-bats. Even stranger are his other ratios. He collected only 36 major league hits, yet stole 103 bases and scored 111 runs while driving in just four.

Matt the Scat had a definite flair about him as a player. He would sometimes jog in backwards to score a run when assured there would be no play on him. While this amused some Pirates fans, it did not sit particularly well with the opposition. Pirates broadcaster Bob Walk recalled that when he joined the Phillies in 1980, Alexander's ballet was scorned by the Phils. If other teams around the league shared the Phillies' collective opinion, perhaps it was a good thing for Matt that he seldom was in the line of fire from an enemy hurler.

Year	Team	AB	R	HR	RBI	BB	SO	SB	AVG	OBP
1973	Cubs	5	4	0	1	1	1	2	.200	.533
1974	Cubs	54	15	0	0	12	12	8	.204	.636
1975	A's	10	16	0	0	1	1	17	.100	.282
1976	A's	30	16	0	0	0	5	20	.033	.066
1977	A's	42	24	0	2	4	6	26	.238	.566
1978	Pirates	0	2	0	0	0	0	4		
1979	Pirates	13	16	0	1	0	0	13	.538	1.23
1980	Pirates	3	13	0	0	0	0	10	.333	1
1981	Pirates	11	5	0	0	0	1	3	.364	.728
	Totals	168	111	0	4	18	26	103	.214	.556
	Lg Average	233	29	5	27	23	33	5	.263	.713
	Pos Average	232	30	5	27	24	34	6	.262	.718

#37 Alberto Lois

Pos: LF; Age: 23; Batted: Right; Threw: Right; Year in Major Leagues: 2nd

Pre-1979. Alberto Lois was signed by the Pirates in 1974 and was a fine minor league hitter. His best season was 1976, when he hit .323 with a league-high 12 triples for the Pirates' AA squad in Shreveport. He was then promoted to their top farm team at Charleston, hitting .300 in 110 at-bats.

Hamstring injuries bothered Lois in 1977, limiting him to only 142 at-bats. When he fully recovered the next season, he played a full season at Columbus before being a September call-up. He collected his only major league hit, a triple, in his only major league start on October 1.

1979. The speedy Dominican native scored six runs in 11 games for the Bucs in 1979. He never got a chance to bat, being used as a designated runner.

1979 Postseason. Lois was not on the postseason roster.

Post-1979. An auto accident impaired Lois' vision and he never played in the majors after 1979.

Year	Team	AB	R	HR	RBI	BB	SO	SB	AVG	OBP
1978	Pirates	4	0	0	0	0	1	0	.250	1
1979	Pirates	0	6	0	0	0	1	1		
	Totals	4	6	0	0	0	1	1	.250	1
	Lg Average	5	1	0	1	0	1	0	.263	.720
	Pos Average	4	1	0	1	0	1			

#39 Dave "The Cobra" Parker

Pos: RF; Age: 28; Batted: Left; Threw: Right; Year in Major Leagues: 7th

Pre-1979. Dave Parker came to Pittsburgh at a time when the team had suffered its most debilitating blow in the long illustrious history of the franchise, the death of one of its superstars, Roberto Clemente. Parker did not pale in comparison. He not only replaced their fallen leader in right, but continuing the team's excellence in right field and became one of the greatest players ever to grace the Steel City.

Parker was from Cincinnati, and was selected in the 14th round of the 1970 free agent draft. Many thought he would be picked earlier, but the two-sport star (Parker rushed for 1,300 yards in football) ripped up his knee his senior year. He also had a reputation for having a bit of an attitude, so much so that according to superscout Howie Haak, his home town Reds laughed at the Bucs when they drafted him.[85]

While the laugh would eventually be on the rest of the league, there were times in his minor league career when Parker flashed that attitude in a big way. After being told by then–minor league director Harding Peterson that he was going to be sent to the team's class A affiliate following a spring training in 1972 when he hit .400, Parker tossed a bat to home plate in anger. An incensed Peterson screamed at him, ordering Parker to retrieve his bat. When the Cobra didn't jump to attention, Peterson moved to grab him. Parker spouted, "You grab me, give me a reason to punch you."[86]

Another altercation came in 1973, when Parker wasn't called up despite the Bucs' troubles on the field. He had been a .300 hitter in every minor league season, including the ill-fated year in Salem where he led the league in hitting, .310, with 101 RBIs, and was on his way to a .317 season at their AAA team in Charleston. So angry was Parker that he left the Charlies, not understanding why he wasn't given the call. His parents talked him into returning, and he smoothed over his rocky relationship with the team.

Dave Parker (courtesy of the Topps Company, Inc.).

Parker eventually did make it with the Pirates in '73, hitting .288 in 54 games. He got a shot in the Bigs full time the following season. That year he continued to show his potential, although hamstring injuries limited him to only 220 at-bats.

Finally, Parker began to make a name for himself in a big way in 1975. He led the league in slugging with a .541 mark, and finished fifth in both homers and RBIs, resulting in a fifth place finish in the MVP vote.

Although his power numbers suffered a little in '76, the Cobra not only added to his reputation as the best all-around Pirate, but as one of the game's premier superstars. He won his first batting title with a .338 mark (the first one won by a Pirate since Clemente turned the trick ten years earlier) and a league best 215 hits. He also led the circuit with 41 doubles, got to start in right field in the All-Star Game, and captured his first Gold Glove, primarily for the incredible arm he displayed in right. He also had two 22-game hitting streaks during his stellar season.

Despite his impressive run, Dave finished third in the MVP vote, behind George Foster and Greg Luzinski. It was something he would correct the next campaign, when he enjoyed his best major league season. Parker continued to exhibit his excellence, winning his second consecutive batting title as well as second Gold Glove, and emerging on top of the slugging percentage race with a .585 mark. His power numbers were up with 30 homers and 117 RBIs, good for third and second in the senior circuit respectively. The most impressive things about his campaign were the way he played through pain and the way he led his team in the clutch. Before the All-Star Game, the behemoth was involved in a collision at home plate that broke his jaw, forcing him to miss 11 games and the Midsummer Classic. Instead of suffering all season on the disabled list, Parker attached a football mask to his batting helmet to protect his jaw. He would prove his worth as a team leader late in the season, after his club had seemingly fallen off the pennant race. Parker stepped it up a notch, hitting .398 in August and September knocking in 60 runs, single-handedly bringing the Bucs back to life as the team cut an 11½ game deficit to the Phils to only half a game within three weeks. For his efforts, the Cobra not only became the first player ever to win back-to-back NL Player of the Month Awards, but also captured the most important prize, the league's Most Valuable Player. General managers as well as the baseball writers recognized Parker's greatness. In an off-season poll, the GMs voted him baseball's most coveted talent. Parker's brashness and confidence came to life afterwards, when he exclaimed that he thought the general managers were right in selecting him.[87]

1979. After his award winning campaign, Parker was coming into the last season of his contract. Free agency would soon be a reality. The Cobra said that he didn't want negotiations with the Pirates to go on past the beginning of spring training; he wanted to concentrate on nothing but baseball after that point. If he didn't ink a deal with the Bucs, baseball's best player could be gone, with the Pirates getting nothing in return. The Galbreaths and Peterson didn't want things to get to that point, so they not only signed one of the game's greats at the time, but they made him the first million-dollar man in professional team sports history, inking the superstar to a five-year, $7 million deal.

While the Cobra's 1979 campaign was not as impressive as the one a season before, Parker nevertheless lived up to his deal with a fine year. Perhaps the highlight of the season was his performance in the All-Star Game. Although his offense was not at its best, mustering up only an infield single in three at-bats, his arm became the star of the game. In the seventh inning, Dave lost a fly ball off the bat of Jim Rice in the lights at the Kingdome, but when Rice tried to stretch his hit into a triple, Parker pegged a line drive to third into the glove of Pete Rose, who tagged him out. An inning later, the Cobra put his cannon on display once again, tossing Brian Downing out at home after a single by Greg Nettles with what would have been the AL's go-ahead run, to end the inning. For his impressive defensive performance, Parker was named the MVP of the Midsummer Classic.

Dave did have some fine performances during the year, such as his 3-for-4 day against the Phillies in August with four RBIs and his 18th homer of the year; and the five singles he collected on the next to last day of the season versus the Cubs. Again shining the last two months of the season, Parker hit .336, including a .365 mark in September, helping to take the Pirates to their first division title in four years. He destroyed opposing pitchers the last week of the season, hitting over .500.

Whereas his power numbers were down a little for the season (25 homers and 94 RBIs), and his average slipped to .310 after a poor June and July when the reigning MVP hit only .282, Parker still was one of the game's best, leading the circuit with 77 extra-base hits that included 45 doubles, third in the NL. He finished in the top ten in voting for the NL's MVP for the fourth time in five seasons, finishing tenth, third among the Family behind teammates Willie Stargell (first) and Kent Tekulve (eighth).

1979 Postseason. The Cobra put on display his clutch bat in the postseason, knocking in the winning run in three of the Bucs' seven postseason victories. In a 1-for-4 performance in game one, Parker singled in the 11th, scoring on Pop's game winning three-run round tripper. He had two hits in game two: a tenth inning single that knocked in Omar Moreno with the deciding run in a 3–2 triumph; and a sacrifice fly to left in the third contest, scoring Moreno once again with a first inning tally that put the Bucs ahead for good in a 7–1 shellacking of the Western Division champs.

Over all, Parker hit .333 in his third venture into the NLCS, scoring two and knocking in two runs in the sweep against the hated Reds. Parker vaulted into his first Fall Classic.

Pittsburgh once again faced the Baltimore Orioles in the 76th World Series, the same foe they defeated eight years earlier. The Cobra got off to a spectacular start, doubling in the first inning of game one against Mike Flanagan. Dave singled three more times, scoring an unearned run in the sixth on a Phil Garner single. His World Series debut was certainly impressive, as he finished the game 4-for-5.

Parker followed up that initial performance with a sixth inning two-out single in the Bucs' 3–2 game two victory. He went hitless in game three, although he knocked in his first run of the series with a first inning sacrifice, scoring Omar.

After getting out his first two at-bats in the next contest, the Cobra broke out of his mini 1-for-9 slump with two game four hits, a fifth inning single followed by a double a frame later, which scored Tim Foli. Despite his decent game, Pittsburgh was now down three games to one and in danger of being eliminated from the Fall Classic. As the team got hot the next game, the Cobra kept his bat going with two more hits that included another double and RBI, which came in the seventh inning with two out, scoring Foli once again, and putting the Bucs up 4–1 in a contest they eventually took 7–1.

Two days later, Parker broke a scoreless seventh inning tie with a one-out shot to right, scoring Moreno once again with his third game-winning RBI of the postseason. It led the Bucs to a 4–0 victory, tying the series at three.

Although Parker wore the collar in game seven, going 0-for-4, Pittsburgh emerged triumphant 4–1, winning the franchise's fifth world championship. Even though game seven wasn't one of the Cobra's best efforts, Parker hit .345 for the series, with ten hits and four RBIs.

Post-1979. With the end of the seventies came the end of Parker's dominance in Pittsburgh. Injuries that appeared first in 1980 included a flareup of his knee injury, problems with his Achilles' tendon and lower back, tendonitis in his elbow, and a bruised knee and shoulder suffered on July 3. He missed 27 games that season and played through the pain the rest of the time. His average dipped below .300 for the first time as a regular, although he still ended up with a respectable .295 mark.

On top of the injuries and a knee operation following the '80 campaign came a battle with weight. His average continued to slip. Pirates fans became disenchanted with the million-dollar man. One fan whipped a 9-volt battery at his head during a game. What people didn't know at the time was that Parker had begun experimenting with cocaine, a fact that came out in the Pittsburgh drug trials a few years later. The discovery cost the Cobra $120,000 (10 percent of his salary), a fine he chose to pay in lieu of a year-long suspension by the commissioner's office.

Meanwhile, Dave had gotten himself back in shape and signed with his hometown club, the Cincinnati Reds. Parker regained his stroke and, by the time the news broke about his involvement with drugs, was once again among the game's elite players, leading the league in doubles with 42. He hit 34 homers, had an NL-high 125 RBIs, and ran 350 total bases while hitting over .300 for the first time since the world championship season of 1979. He finished second in the MVP race in a close vote to the Cardinals' Willie McGee.

Showing '85 was not a last gasp, he knocked over 100 once again in '86 with 31 homers — second best in the senior circuit — and garnered another top-five MVP finish. After another decent season in Cincinnati, Parker was sent to the A's for Jose Rijo. With his defense no longer what it was, he became the perfect DH, overcoming a thumb injury that put him out for seven weeks. He helped the A's to back-to-back World Series appearances including his second world title in 1989. That year, he hit not only two homers in the ALCS — the first two postseason round-trippers in his illustrious career — but a homer and a double in the Fall Classic triumph over Oakland's rivals from San Francisco.

Parker made $2.8 million over the two years, following the series. He signed a free agent contract with the Brewers, hitting 21 homers before ending his career in 1991 with the Angels and Blue Jays.

Parker eventually made peace with the city of Pittsburgh and the Pirates organization. He came to the Bucs' spring training facility in Bradenton before the 2003 and 2004 campaigns and helped some of the club's young hitters. More important than that, while in Bradenton in 2004, Parker removed the hex he had placed on the Pirates following his departure in 1983. "I think I said they wouldn't win anything when I left in '83, so it's time to lift that and let them go on. It's something I said, and I thought about it coming down here. Lift that hex off Pittsburgh now."[88]

So now that the Cobra's baseball life has come full circle and he's been welcomed back into the Pirates' fold, how do we look at Dave Parker's career? Let's start with where he ranks on the all-time lists. As of the end of the 2003 season, Parker's 2,712 hits were 52nd in the history of the sport. Bill Buckner, Rusty Staub, Al Oliver, Vada Pinson and Andre Dawson are the only eligible players ahead of him not in the Hall of Fame. He has the 41st-most RBIs in history, with 1,493, only 16 behind Mickey Mantle. Here only Dawson stands above him as an eligible player not yet enshrined. The Cobra is 39th in total bases, 41st in at-bats, 29th in doubles and 36th in extra-base hits.

Bill James, the famous baseball statistician, has a formula that predicts whether or not a player is eligible for the Hall of Fame, called the Hall of Fame monitor. It assigns points for eclipsing certain statistical achievements. An average Hall of Famer is 100, a sure shot ranks with 130 or above. Parker comes in with a 125.5 rating, far above the average and ahead of such notables as Willie Stargell, Pie Traynor and Jackie Robinson. James' *New Baseball Abstract* rates Parker as the 14th-best right fielder of all time. Not surprisingly, James projected Parker to be elected by 2003.[89] That obviously didn't happen, as Parker has never been close, garnering only 54 votes in the 2004 election; only 10.5 percent of the vote, far below the 75 percent needed. Whether it is his past problems with the press, his part in the drug trials or just that the electorate doesn't think he's worthy, the chances that the Cobra will enter Cooperstown via the Baseball Writers are small at best.

That doesn't mean others don't think he's worthy, although they understand his omission. In an article for the *Baseball Online Library*, Paul White writes that while he would vote for both Dawson and Parker, because of Parker's off-field antics, he wouldn't blame the writers for keeping him out.[90]

Scott Miller of *CBS Sportsline* confides that while Parker can be considered one of the greats, he would be left on "Cooperstown's Porch" instead of being invited inside because the Cobra and a few others who may be worthy "were sensational at their peaks, but the peaks were not sustained over a long enough time."[91]

Confident as ever, Parker feels he belongs in the Hall of Fame. "I won two batting titles, should have won two MVPs, was in three World Series, was the MVP of the All-Star Game, DH of the Year twice and won the RBI crown. I did everything that you could possibly do in baseball, and I'm not in the Hall? I should be in the Hall of Fame. Ain't no doubt about it."[92]

Whether or not Dave Parker belongs in Cooperstown is a debate that will be decided by the Veterans Committee, years down the road when his eligibility is placed in their hands. Regardless of the outcome, there is no doubt that he's one of the best ever to wear the Black and Gold.

Year	Team	AB	R	HR	RBI	BB	SO	SB	AVG	OBP
1973	Pirates	139	17	4	14	2	27	1	.288	.761
1974	Pirates	220	27	4	29	10	53	3	.282	.731
1975	Pirates	558	75	25	101	38	89	8	.308	.898
1976	Pirates	537	82	13	90	30	80	19	.313	.824
1977	Pirates	637	107	21	88	58	107	17	.338	.928
1978	Pirates	581	102	30	117	57	92	20	.334	.979
1979	Pirates	622	109	25	94	67	101	20	.310	.906
1980	Pirates	518	71	17	79	25	69	10	.295	.785
1981	Pirates	240	29	9	48	9	25	6	.258	.741
1982	Pirates	244	41	6	29	22	45	7	.270	.777
1983	Pirates	552	68	12	69	28	89	12	.279	.722
1984	Reds	607	73	16	94	41	89	11	.285	.738
1985	Reds	635	88	34	125	52	80	5	.312	.916
1986	Reds	637	89	31	116	56	126	1	.273	.807
1987	Reds	589	77	26	97	44	104	7	.253	.744
1988	A's	377	43	12	55	32	70	0	.257	.720
1989	A's	553	56	22	97	38	91	0	.264	.740
1990	Brewers	610	71	21	92	41	102	4	.289	.781
1991	Angels	466	45	11	56	29	91	3	.232	.637

BlueJays	36	2	0	3	4	7	0	.333	.844
Totals	502	47	11	59	33	98	3	.239	.653
Totals	9358	1272	339	1493	683	1537	154	.290	.810
Lg Average	8944	1147	213	1073	873	1336	202	.263	.722
Pos Average	9040	1207	283	1224	939	1536	166	.268	.759

#41 Joe Coleman

Pos: P; Age: 32; Batted: Right; Threw: Right; Year in Major Leagues: 15th

Pre-1979. A two-time 20-game winner with the Detroit Tigers in the early 1970s, Joe Coleman saw himself pitching in AAA in 1979. A midseason recall to the Pirates helped him finally contribute to a world champion.

Coleman, whose father and namesake pitched in the American League for ten years, tossed two complete game shutouts for the Washington Senators as an 18-year-old late season call-up in 1965. Like his father, the younger Coleman was stuck pitching for poor ball clubs while with the Senators, but after being included in a blockbuster trade to the Tigers following an 8–12 campaign in 1970, Joe came into his own. Taking the place of Denny McLain (the 1968 American League Cy Young Award–winner and 1969 co-winner of the award) in the Tigers' rotation, Coleman starred for Detroit over the next three seasons. After suffering a fractured skull in spring training, he returned to start 38 games and won 20 during his initial season with the team. Continuing to show durability the next three years, Coleman started 39, 40 and 41 games from 1972 to 1974 while recording 19–14, 23–15 and 14–12 records. He also set a Championship Series record in 1972 by striking out 14 Oakland A's, pitching a shutout as his Tigers faced elimination. However, Coleman's ERA rose each year during this time and in 1975, the bottom fell out: he went 10–18 with a 5.55 ERA. He was traded to the Cubs in the midst of a 4–13 season in 1976. The Cubs sent him to the A's, who had been depleted by free agency, in 1977. Relieving and spot starting, Coleman pitched well, lowering his ERA to back under 3.00. He was generally effective pitching in setup roles for the A's and Toronto Blue Jays in 1978.

1979. Pitching for his third team in two years, Coleman opened the season in the San Francisco Giants' bullpen. Although he was unscored-on in five early season appearances, the Giants released him, and the hurler signed with the Pirates' AAA Portland team on May 7.[93] When the Bucs needed an extra arm due to a backlog of doubleheaders following the All-Star break, Coleman was recalled after going 5–1 with a 2.65 ERA. Coleman, who relied more than ever on his forkball and control by 1979, gave the Pirates several good outings. His statistics with the Bucs were severely affected by having to endure a pounding at the hands of the Chicago Cubs after Jim Rooker was knocked out a game early on August 8. Chuck Tanner needed to rest his bullpen, and Coleman became the sacrificial lamb in the 15–2 laugher.

1979 Postseason. Coleman ended up being the odd man out in the numbers game when the postseason rosters were set and was not included.

Post-1979. Released following the World Series, Joe retired from baseball with 142 big league wins. He has since served as a pitching coach with several organizations, including the Cardinals, Orioles and Angels.

Joe Coleman's brief time with the Pirates reminds one of how player transactions have changed over the years. Before multi-year million-dollar contracts, teams almost never were able to trade for a star player during the season. Even with the major leagues changing the trade deadline from June 15 to July 31, there would not be the wholesale movement of stars if not for the huge money involved and teams' fears of losing players without compensation. Prior to the late 1990s, deadline deals and in-season pickups usually saw journeyman types or fading stars moved to contenders, but never players the caliber of Randy Johnson, who was dealt from the Mariners to Houston in 1998. Moves the Pirates made in the late 1970s included buying veteran pinch hitters Cito Gaston and Dave May in 1978, resurrecting Coleman and purchasing a fading Dock Ellis in 1979. Pete Peterson's trade for Bill Madlock, which came after the June 15 deadline, was an aberration for its era, but it too brought two players into the organization, Dave Roberts and Lenny Randle, who fit the usual definition of players added during a pennant race at the time. Coleman and Ellis, who also retired after 1979, and Roberts, who was near the end of his career as well, had all been stars during the Pirates' previous World Series run in 1971. While Roberts was on the team's postseason roster in 1979, none of the three appeared in the World Series.

Joe Coleman (courtesy of the Topps Company, Inc.).

Year	Team	W	L	PCT	CG	IP	H	BB	SO	ERA
1965	Senators	2	0	1.000	2	18	9	8	7	1.50
1966	Senators	1	0	1.000	1	9	6	2	4	2.00
1967	Senators	8	9	.471	3	134	154	47	77	4.63

1968	Senators	12	16	.429	12	223	212	51	139	3.27
1969	Senators	12	13	.480	12	248	222	100	182	3.27
1970	Senators	8	12	.400	6	219	190	89	152	3.58
1971	Tigers	20	9	.690	16	286	241	96	236	3.15
1972	Tigers	19	14	.576	9	280	216	110	222	2.80
1973	Tigers	23	15	.605	13	288	283	93	202	3.53
1974	Tigers	14	12	.538	11	286	272	158	177	4.31
1975	Tigers	10	18	.357	6	201	234	85	125	5.55
1976	Tigers	2	5	.286	1	67	80	34	38	4.84
	Cubs	2	8	.200	0	79	72	35	66	4.10
	Totals	4	13	.235	1	146	152	69	104	4.44
1977	A's	4	4	.500	2	128	114	49	55	2.95
1978	A's	3	0	1.000	0	19.2	12	5	4	1.37
	BlueJays	2	0	1.000	0	60.2	67	30	28	4.60
	Totals	5	0	1.000	0	80.1	79	35	32	3.81
1979	Giants	0	0		0	3.2	3	2	0	0.00
	Pirates	0	0		0	20.2	29	9	14	6.10
	Totals	0	0		0	24.1	32	11	14	5.18
	Totals	142	135	.513	94	2570.2	2416	1003	1728	3.69
	Lg Average	143	143	.500	89	2570.2	2435	934	1546	3.55

#41   Jerry Reuss

Pos: P; Age: 26; Batted: Left; Threw: Left; Year in Major Leagues: 6th

Jerry Reuss (courtesy of the Topps Company, Inc.).

Pre-1979. Jerry Reuss, a St. Louis native, had a decent four-year run with the Cardinals and Astros through the 1973 campaign. He was traded to the Bucs for Milt May, the hero of game four of the 1971 World Series.

With the Pirates, Reuss became one of the best southpaws in the senior circuit, winning 16 games in 1974 and emerging victorious 18 times in '75 with 2.54 ERA, both fourth in the league. For his efforts he was named the starting pitcher in the 1975 All-Star Game.

Jerry had a decent 1976 before slumping in the next two seasons. He reached a low point in '78, when he spent half of the season out of the pen, his ERA ballooning to 4.90.

1979. Reuss had the shortest tenure of the Family, lasting exactly one day. On

April 7, one day after opening day, general manager Pete Peterson pulled off a deal with the Dodgers bringing Rick Rhoden over to the Bucs.

1979 Postseason. Reuss of course did not participate in the postseason.

Post-1979. After getting off to a poor start with the Dodgers, Reuss rebounded to go 18–6 in 1980, being named the NL Comeback Player of the Year; he also etched his name in major league history by tossing a no-hitter. He finished second in the Cy Young Award voting.

Jerry finally got a chance to pitch in the Fall Classic in 1981 and made the most of it, with a complete game win in game five of the series.

Reuss won 18 games once again in 1982 before suffering injuries. He went on to pitch seven more years with five different clubs, including one final shot with the Bucs in 1990, ending his career as the second pitcher in baseball history to win 200 games without winning 20 in a season.[94]

Year	Team	W	L	PCT	CG	IP	H	BB	SO	ERA
1969	Cardinals	1	0	1.000	0	7	2	3	3	0.00
1970	Cardinals	7	8	.467	5	127.1	132	49	74	4.10
1971	Cardinals	14	14	.500	7	211	228	109	131	4.78
1972	Astros	9	13	.409	4	192	177	83	174	4.17
1973	Astros	16	13	.552	12	279.1	271	117	177	3.74
1974	Pirates	16	11	.593	14	260	259	101	105	3.50
1975	Pirates	18	11	.621	15	237.1	224	78	131	2.54
1976	Pirates	14	9	.609	11	209.1	209	51	108	3.53
1977	Pirates	10	13	.435	8	208	225	71	116	4.11
1978	Pirates	3	2	.600	3	82.2	97	23	42	4.90
1979	Dodgers	7	14	.333	4	160	178	60	83	3.54
1980	Dodgers	18	6	.750	10	229.1	193	40	111	2.51
1981	Dodgers	10	4	.714	8	152.2	138	27	51	2.30
1982	Dodgers	18	11	.621	8	254.2	232	50	138	3.11
1983	Dodgers	12	11	.522	7	223.1	233	50	143	2.94
1984	Dodgers	5	7	.417	2	99	102	31	44	3.82
1985	Dodgers	14	10	.583	5	212.2	210	58	84	2.92
1986	Dodgers	2	6	.250	0	74	96	17	29	5.84
1987	Dodgers	0	0		0	2	2	0	2	4.50
	Reds	0	5	.000	0	34.2	52	12	10	7.79
	Angels	4	5	.444	1	82.1	112	17	37	5.25
	Totals	4	10	.286	1	119	166	29	49	5.97
1988	Whitesox	13	9	.591	2	183	183	43	73	3.44
1989	Whitesox	8	5	.615	1	106.2	135	21	27	5.06
	Brewers	1	4	.200	0	33.2	36	13	13	5.35
	Totals	9	9	.500	1	140.1	171	34	40	5.13
1990	Pirates	0	0		0	7.2	8	3	1	3.52
	Totals	220	191	.535	127	3669.2	3734	1127	1907	3.64
	Lg Average	204	204	.500	116	3669.2	3581	1333	2128	3.76

#43 Don "The Caveman," "Mountain Man Don" or "Disco Don" Robinson

Pos: P; Age: 22; Batted: Right; Threw: Right; Year in Major Leagues: 2nd

Pre-1979. Selected in the third round of the 1975 free agent draft by the Pirates, Don Robinson hurt his elbow late in the 1977 campaign while still in the minors, which made him wonder if he would have a career in the big leagues.[95] Robby rehabbed the arm and had a successful stint in the Puerto Rican winter league that earned him an invitation to spring training in 1978.

The 21-year-old hurler, who had an unspectacular minor league career, going 22–18 in three seasons, made the most of his opportunity. He showed the Bucs a devastating curveball and a mid-90s fastball, securing himself a spot on the opening day roster. The Caveman, as he was called, was spectacular, going 14–6 with a 3.47 ERA. His efforts earned him the *Sporting News'* Rookie Pitcher of the Year as well as a spot on the All-Rookie Teams in both *Baseball Digest* and *The Baseball Bulletin*; he also finished eighth in voting for the National League's Cy Young award.

1979. Although a suddenly bright future had been on the horizon, a black omen appeared early in the 1979 campaign. The Caveman's shoulder began to stiffen and hampered him throughout the season. Despite the pain, Robinson started 25 contests and appeared in four more out of the bullpen, finishing with a disappointing 8–8 mark and 3.87 ERA.

Mountain Man Don completed only four games during 1979, but one couldn't have come at a more important time; he allowed only six hits in a 2–1 victory against the Montreal Expos, the team that was battling with the Bucs for first place in the National League East on September 17. At the time, Pittsburgh was one game out, but Don's complete game gem moved them into the catbird seat.

Even though injured for most of the campaign, Robinson did manage to match his career strikeout high to date on two occasions. He K'd nine against St. Louis on April 12 and matched the feat in 6⅓ innings against the Expos July 27.

Don Robinson (courtesy of the Topps Company, Inc.).

1979 Postseason. The Caveman was relegated to the bullpen for the 1979 postseason, and for the most part pitched with much success.

In the exciting game one of the NLCS against Cincinnati, Robinson came into the contest with two on and two out in the bottom of the 11th. The Bucs were nursing a 5–2 lead on the dramatics of Willie Stargell's top-of-the-11th three-run homer. Robinson walked Johnny Bench to load the bases, then struck out Ray Knight, the winning run, to end the rally, earning his first postseason save.

The next evening the Caveman came into a similar mess in the bottom of the ninth with the score tied at two, and Dave Collins on second with one out. Robinson promptly struck out Dave Concepcion and forced George Foster to ground out to Phil Garner to end the threat. Pittsburgh scored in the top of the tenth as Robinson completed the victory with a 1-2-3 bottom of the tenth.

Robinson got an opportunity to pitch in his inaugural Fall Classic early on, tossing two hitless innings in game one, and giving up only a lead-off walk to Ken Singleton in the seventh inning of the 5–4 loss to the Orioles.

After three almost perfect performances, Mountain Man Don was not at his best in game two, but he would battle through his wildness to win the contest in the Bucs' 3–2 victory to tie the series up at one. Robinson entered the game in the seventh inning and showed a penchant for being both wild and dominant at the same time. With one out, he walked Rick Dempsey and Pat Kelly and then struck out Al Bumbry. He then proceeded to walk the bases full, giving up a free pass to Terry Crowley, before mowing down Singleton on strikes. In the eighth the first two batters got aboard, but Robby bore down, getting John Lowenstien to ground out into a double play and pushing Billy Smith into an inning-ending ground out.

Robinson's perfect postseason came to disappointing end in game four. The West Virginian gave up eighth inning leadoff singles to Kiko Garcia and Singleton and loading the bases on a walk to Doug DeCinces. Kent Tekulve came in and allowed base-clearing doubles to Lowenstein and Crowley, erasing a 6–3 Pirate lead; three runs would be charged to Robinson.

The Caveman got one last chance to pitch in the Fall Classic, this time in the fifth inning of the all-important seventh game. With the Pirates down 1–0, manager Chuck Tanner had decided to pinch hit for starter Jim Bibby. He went to the 6-4 Robinson, who still struggled, allowing a lead-off single to DeCinces and then walking pitcher Scott McGregor with two outs. Tanner then tabbed lefty Grant Jackson, who, unlike Tekulve in game four, got out of the jam.

Overall, Robinson gave up three runs in seven innings of work, winning two of the Bucs' seven postseason victories. It was not a bad performance for a man who had suffered with a sore shoulder all season.

Post-1979. Through the rest of Don Robinson's career, injuries would plague him constantly. He had shoulder surgery following the conclusion of the world championship season in 1979, and responded with a 7–10 mark in 1980 after being on the disabled list until May 1. As tough as that season was, during the year the Caveman did show ability for something that he would be known for the rest of his career. Robinson hit .333 in 57 at-bats, including his first major league home run.

He only appeared in 16 games in an injury-marred 1981 campaign, but rebounded by winning a career high 15 games in 1982, despite giving up an NL high 26 homeruns. Mountain Man Don also smacked two homers with 16 RBIs and a .282 average that year. He was named to the *Sporting News'* NL Silver Slugger Team.

Injuries still dogged the tall hurler, limiting him to nine games in '83 before being converted to the bullpen almost full time in 1984. It had been feared that Robinson's arm would not allow him to continue to pitch, but he was such a good hitter that the Pirates made contingency plans for him to go to the minors to learn to play the outfield if his days as a pitcher were over. In fact, he appeared as an outfielder in the last game of the year.[96] Robby remained in the pen until 1987, saving 39 games for Pittsburgh. He struggled with a knee problem in 1986; the Bucs dealt him to San Francisco in the middle of the campaign for Mackey Sasser. Before the deal, Robinson gave up Mike Schmidt's 500th home run on April 18 at Three Rivers Stadium. Following the trade, Robinson caught fire with the Giants, going 5–1 to boost his total output in 1987 to a league leading 11 wins in relief. He saved seven games in San Francisco's run for the NL West title. He won the pennant clinching game against San Diego, also hitting a game-winning homer to break a 4–4 tie.[97]

With the Giants, the Caveman regained his role as a starter with 19 starts in '88 (that season he finished seventh in the NL with a 2.45 ERA) and 57 more over the next two seasons. Injuries, as always, took their toll as Robinson, who once boasted he had taken 150–200 cortisone shots in his knee throughout his career, kept going on.[98]

The year 1991 would be his last season in the bay before he was declared a free agent and signed with the California Angels. Before he left, Robinson became the first pitcher in 19 years to hit a pinch-hit homer, smacking one against Bruce Hurst and the Padres in June of 1990.

The Caveman was released after seven games in Anaheim. He signed on with Philadelphia in May of 1992, where he finished his career with a 1–4 mark and a 6.18 ERA in eight starts.

Year	Team	W	L	PCT	CG	IP	H	BB	SO	ERA
1978	Pirates	14	6	.700	9	228.1	203	57	135	3.47
1979	Pirates	8	8	.500	4	160.2	171	52	96	3.87
1980	Pirates	7	10	.412	3	160.1	157	45	103	3.99
1981	Pirates	0	3	.000	0	38.1	47	23	17	5.87
1982	Pirates	15	13	.536	6	227	213	103	165	4.28
1983	Pirates	2	2	.500	0	36.1	43	21	28	4.46
1984	Pirates	5	6	.455	0	122	99	49	110	3.02
1985	Pirates	5	11	.313	0	95.1	95	42	65	3.87
1986	Pirates	3	4	.429	0	69.1	61	27	53	3.38
1987	Pirates	6	6	.500	0	65.1	66	22	53	3.86
	Giants	5	1	.833	0	42.2	39	18	26	2.74
	Totals	11	7	.611	0	108	105	40	79	3.42
1988	Giants	10	5	.667	3	176.2	152	49	122	2.45
1989	Giants	12	11	.522	5	197	184	37	96	3.43
1990	Giants	10	7	.588	4	157.2	173	41	78	4.57
1991	Giants	5	9	.357	0	121.1	123	50	78	4.38
1992	Angels	1	0	1.000	0	16.1	19	3	9	2.20
	Phillies	1	4	.200	0	43.2	49	4	17	6.18
	Totals	2	4	.333	0	60	68	7	26	5.10
	Totals	109	106	.507	34	1958.1	1894	643	1251	3.79
	Lg Average	109	109	.500	37	1958.1	1925	705	1158	3.84

#44 Dorian "Doe" Boyland

Pos: PH PR; Age: 24; Batted: Left; Threw: Left; Year in the Major Leagues: 2nd

Pre-1979. Touted as one of the Pirates' top prospects after hitting .330 for AA Shreveport in 1977 and .291 for AAA Columbus in 1978, Boyland was a line drive hitter with good speed. The left-handed batter went 2-for-8 after being called up in September 1978.

1979 Season. Boyland was hurt most of 1979, appearing in just 30 games for the Pirates' AAA team in Portland. Despite hitting just .245, he was recalled on September 1 and went 0-for-3 as a pinch hitter, appearing in a fourth game as a pinch runner.

1979 Postseason. Boyland was ineligible for postseason play.

Post-1979. Boyland hit .281 with a minor league career–high 14 homeruns and 67 RBIs for Portland in 1980. He also stole 26 bases, but he was not recalled by the Pirates. The Bucs apparently did not believe Boyland was going to be the answer to the question of who would replace Willie Stargell at first base. After he went 0-for-8 with Pittsburgh in 1981, they traded him to the San Francisco Giants for journeyman pitcher Tom Griffin at the end of spring training, 1982. Boyland never appeared in another major league game.

Year	Team	AB	R	HR	RBI	BB	SO	SB	AVG	OBP
1978	Pirates	8	1	0	1	0	1	0	.250	.500
1979	Pirates	3	0	0	0	0	2	0	.000	.000
1981	Pirates	8	0	0	0	1	3	0	.000	.111
	Totals	19	1	0	1	1	6	0	.105	.255
	Lg Average	21	3	0	2	2	3	0	.262	.710
	Pos Average	8	1	0	1	1	1	0	.268	.748

#45   John "The Candy Man" Candelaria

Pos: P; Age: 25; Batted: Left; Threw: Left; Year in Major Leagues: 5th

Pre-1979. Candelaria was signed by the Bucs as a free agent in Puerto Rico in 1972. There, he not only was trying out for the Puerto Rican National Basketball Team, but had met the great Roberto Clemente, who advised him not to sign with the club for the original $13,000 they offered him. He held out for an eventual $40,000.[99]

John Candelaria broke into the majors in a big way in 1975 at the young age of 21.

The Candy Man was called up from the Bucs' AAA club in Charleston, where he had been 7–1 in eight starts with a miniscule 1.78 ERA, and went 8–6 that first season. Probably his most memorable moment that year, after winning his initial major league game against the Mets on June 20, was being on the winning end of a 22–0 score in Chicago's Wrigley Field. The game not only marked the record setting 7-for-7 performance by second baseman Rennie Stennett, but was also the most lopsided shutout in the 20th century. The season was only a prelude to one of the most legendary postseason performances in Pirates history, when the Puerto Rican mowed down 14 members of the Big Red Machine (including seven of the first ten), in game three of the NLCS, while giving up only three hits in 7⅔ innings. Unfortunately, the last two were in the eighth inning: a homer by Pete Rose to put Cincinnati up 3–2, and a double by Joe Morgan; then Bucs manager Danny Murtaugh pulled the rookie from the game.

His showing in '75 was no fluke; the Candy Man finished the following campaign with a 16–7 mark, while tossing another gem to his ever growing resume, a no-hitter against the Los Angeles Dodgers on National TV. "I'm positive my Mother's drunk by now. I imagine all my friends are going wild," the excited second-year hurler exclaimed, after tossing the sixth no-hitter in Pirates history and the first at home since 1907.[100]

The Brooklyn native's career year came in 1977, which was also one of the greatest seasons a pitcher ever enjoyed in the history of the Pirates. Since Vern Law in 1960, no Pittsburgh hurler had won 20 games in a season, while no southpaw had eclipsed that total in 53 years. The 17-year barren stretch ended on September 30 when the Cubs' Manny Trillo lofted a fly ball to Al Oliver, ending the game. The tall lefty hurled a complete game seven-hitter en route to his 20th win of the season. He finished the season with a bang. Coming into August, Candelaria had an 11–4 mark, a good record, but with only two months left in the campaign he had little chance of getting 20 wins. Candy went on a roll, winning nine of his last ten decisions to finish the year 20–5 with a 2.34 ERA.

While he didn't win the Cy Young Award, finishing only fifth behind Steve Carlton, Tommy John, Rick Reuschel and Tom Seaver, arguments could be made that Candelaria was superior to all of them in 1977. He led the league in ERA and winning percentage, becoming the first major league pitcher to win both titles and accumulate 20 wins in a season since Sandy Koufax 12 years before him. He also finished fifth in the circuit, giving up only 7.69 hits per nine innings while giving an NL-low 1.95 walks a game. John was rewarded for his efforts by being selected to his first and only All-Star Game that season.

John Candelaria (courtesy of the Topps Company, Inc.).

Following his masterpiece campaign, a sore back emerged that would affect him the rest of his career. To go with his lower back pain, Candy also developed arm troubles that limited him to only 11 starts after July 4 in a disappointing 12–11 1978 campaign.

1979. While the Candy Man did not suffer from arm troubles in 1979, his back problems continued to plague him as the season went on. After hurling only five innings in a losing effort to the Mets on September 16, Candelaria was all but shut down for the remainder of the regular season. He appeared in only one more game, and that in relief, the rest of the year, a poor third of an inning against the Cardinals on the 27th, when he gave up three hits and two runs facing only four batters.

Through all the pain, the Brooklyn native still led the club in victories with 14, compiling a fine 14–9 mark with a 3.22 ERA, the 12th lowest figure in the league. He also finished second in the NL in walks per nine innings with a 1.78 rate, while yielding a senior circuit sixth-best 10.52 base runners per game.

1979 Postseason. Despite all the pain in his career, Candelaria proved to be as tough a competitor as there was. This fact was never more evident than in the 1979 postseason. Playing postseason ball in the east brings with it cold weather, not exactly the perfect climate for a man with a bad back.

When Chuck Tanner named Candelaria his game one starter in the NLCS, the former basketball player took the mound, feeling incredible pain in almost every pitch. "I don't remember what it's like to pitch without pain," John said after his performance.[101] Despite his problems he gave the Bucs what they needed, seven solid innings, giving up only five hits. He left the game (which Pittsburgh eventually won) with the Reds and Bucs tied up at two runs.

Appearing in his first Fall Classic after the Pirates disposed of Cincinnati in three straight, Tanner once again called on his 6–7 hurler to face the Orioles in game three of the series with the two clubs tied up at one apiece.

The weather was cold and the Candy Man wasn't exactly at his best. He got into trouble in the first, giving up a lead-off double and single, but got out of it unscathed. Then he set down Baltimore in order in the second inning. The Bucs' offense handed him a 3–0 lead going into the top of the third, when the wheels began to come loose. He gave up a two-run shot to Benny Ayala, cutting the O's deficit to one. He came unhinged following a rain delay in the fourth, allowing all five batters he faced to reach base, four on hits and one via a Tim Foli error, en route to a five-run Baltimore outburst. He left the game with his club all but out of the contest. Pittsburgh wound up on the wrong end of the 8–4 outcome.

Pittsburgh of course would lose the next contest, falling behind three games to one. Veteran Jim Rooker turned the tide in game five, sending the 76th Fall Classic back to Baltimore. There, Candelaria would get the opportunity to make up for his game three debacle.

As bad as John was in that forgettable game, he was good in this one, outdueling Hall of Famer Jim Palmer in a 4–0 triumph. Despite giving up a hit in every inning except the second, Candy scattered only six throughout his six innings of work. He only got into trouble in the first, when he gave up singles to Kiko Garcia and Ken Singleton; then he got Eddie Murray to bounce into a 5–3 double play. Candelaria combined for a shutout with relief ace Kent Tekulve for the fourth time in 1979, sending the series to a seventh game and doing his share to earn his only World Series ring.

Post-1979. Candelaria slumped in 1980, with the first losing mark of his career. He missed all but six games of 1981 after he tore his left bicep muscle in the May 10 game against the Cards, suffering severe nerve damage as well.

The gritty eight-year veteran battled back the following season; he had a 5–0 mark in July as he was named the NL pitcher of the month. His 2.94 ERA was sixth best in the league.

After winning 27 games the next two campaigns, the Candy man became the Bucs' closer in 1985, a position he had declined the year before. There he was solid if unspectacular, saving nine games in 31 outings for the slumping Bucs.

By August of 1985, Joe L. Brown had returned to try and fix the sinking ship; he purged the Bucs' veterans in an effort to rebuild the team. Candelaria, who had been disgruntled with the club the past couple of years, calling then-GM Pete Peterson a "Bozo," was one of the casualties. He went to the Angels with the disappointing George Hendrick and Al Holland for Bob Kipper, Pat Clements and Mike Brown.

With the Angels he found a fountain of youth. He came up with a solid 10–2 mark as a starter once again in 1986, winning game three of the ALCS against Boston, a series in which he was 1–1 with a 0.84 ERA. After an outburst with California manager Gene Mauch, Candy was sent home to the Mets, but signed as a free agent with the cross-town Yankees instead of accepting a role in the Mets' bullpen. Candelaria pitched well for George Steinbrenner's team, finishing with a 13–7 record. Unfortunately, knee problems ailed him that year, which turned out to be the last shining season in the Brooklyn native's career.

The Candy Man traveled often afterwards, ending up in Montreal, Minnesota, Toronto and Los Angeles, then returned to Pittsburgh following the 1992 season, signing with the three-time NL East defending champion Pirates. His comeback was short and unspectacular: the Candy Man lost all three decisions with an 8.24 ERA, and was released in July. Candelaria ended his 19-year major league career with 177 victories, 124 with the Pirates.

There's no doubt he was one of the best hurlers in Pittsburgh history, but how does he rate against the best southpaw in the annals of Pirates baseball? He could be argued to be the best lefty ever to wear the Black and Gold. Compared to the all-time list of left handed pitchers, he rates in the top ten of every major category, in a claim that only Lefty Leifield and Wilbur Cooper can also make. Candelaria finished fifth in ERA with a 3.17 mark; fourth in hits per nine innings, 8.47; second in walks per nine innings with a 2.10 mark; ninth in shutouts with nine; third in strikeouts, 1,159; while in the two most important categories, wins and winning percentage, he was second, with 124 and .588 respectively.

Cooper is probably the best southpaw the club has ever produced, as he is the franchise's all-time winningest pitcher, but number two is certainly up for grabs between Candelaria, Leifield and Jesse Tannehill — company that the man from Brooklyn should be proud of.

Year	Team	W	L	PCT	CG	IP	H	BB	SO	ERA
1975	Pirates	8	6	.571	4	120.2	95	36	95	2.76
1976	Pirates	16	7	.696	11	220	173	60	138	3.15
1977	Pirates	20	5	.800	6	230.2	197	50	133	2.34
1978	Pirates	12	11	.522	3	189	191	49	94	3.24
1979	Pirates	14	9	.609	8	207	201	41	101	3.22
1980	Pirates	11	14	.440	7	233.1	246	50	97	4.01
1981	Pirates	2	2	.500	0	40.2	42	11	14	3.54
1982	Pirates	12	7	.632	1	174.2	166	37	133	2.94
1983	Pirates	15	8	.652	2	197.2	191	45	157	3.23
1984	Pirates	12	11	.522	3	185.1	179	34	133	2.72
1985	Pirates	2	4	.333	0	54.1	57	14	47	3.64
	Angels	7	3	.700	1	71	70	24	53	3.80
	Totals	9	7	.563	1	125.1	127	38	100	3.73
1986	Angels	10	2	.833	1	91.2	68	26	81	2.55
1987	Angels	8	6	.571	0	116.2	127	20	74	4.71
	Mets	2	0	1.000	0	12.1	17	3	10	5.84
	Totals	10	6	.625	0	129	144	23	84	4.81
1988	Yankees	13	7	.650	6	157	150	23	121	3.38
1989	Yankees	3	3	.500	1	49	49	12	37	5.14
	Expos	0	2	.000	0	16.1	17	4	14	3.31
	Totals	3	5	.375	1	65.1	66	16	51	4.68
1990	Twins	7	3	.700	0	58.1	55	9	44	3.39
	BlueJays	0	3	.000	0	21.1	32	11	19	5.48
	Totals	7	6	.538	0	79.2	87	20	63	3.95
1991	Dodgers	1	1	.500	0	33.2	31	11	38	3.74
1992	Dodgers	2	5	.286	0	25.1	20	13	23	2.84
1993	Pirates	0	3	.000	0	19.2	25	9	17	8.24
	Totals	177	122	.592	54	2525.2	2399	592	1673	3.33
	Lg Average	141	141	.500	69	2525.2	2494	911	1458	3.84

#46 Rick Jones

Pos: P; Age: 24; Batted: Left; Threw: Left; Year in Major Leagues: 4th

Pre-1979. One of three pitchers called up late in the 1979 season who did not pitch in a game for the Pirates, Rick Jones had been the Boston Red Sox' most talented pitching prospect just a few years earlier. While the residents of Fenway Park were enjoying their ride to the World Series in 1975, Jones combined to win 20 minor league games while pitching against A and AA competition that year. Only 21 years old in 1976, Jones made the defending pennant winners and went 5–3 with a 3.38 ERA, but the Sox, with a line up of All-Stars, were forced to leave him exposed to the expansion draft. The Mariners picked him in the tenth round. Instead of getting a chance to pitch regularly for Seattle, arm problems limited Jones to just ten games in 1977. He spent most of 1978 in AAA as he tried to regain his stuff.

1979. Rick came to the Pirates organization in the Enrique Romo trade in December 1978. He had a solid year for AAA Portland, going 12–8 with a 3.59 ERA and pitching eight complete games before his September recall. Despite his being left-handed and having major league experience, he did not appear in any games for the Family.

1979 Postseason. Jones, of course, was not on the postseason roster.

Post-1979. The hurler went to spring training with the Bucs in 1980 but did not make the club. He never appeared in another major league game.

Year	Team	W	L	PCT	CG	IP	H	BB	SO	ERA
1976	Redsox	5	3	.625	1	104	133	26	45	3.38
1977	Mariners	1	4	.200	0	42	47	37	16	5.14
1978	Mariners	0	2	.000	0	12	17	7	11	6.00
	Totals	6	9	.400	1	158	197	70	72	4.04
	Lg Average	9	9	.500	6	158	154	57	86	3.66

#49   Dave Roberts

Pos: P; Age: 35; Batted: Left; Threw: Left; Year in Major Leagues: 11th

Pre-1979. Dave Roberts was drafted by the Philadelphia Phillies in 1963 and was picked up off waivers by the Bucs a year later. He was a Rule Five selection by Kansas City in November of 1966, but was returned to the Pittsburgh organization in April of '67.

It was in the Bucs' farm system that Roberts excelled, going 14–5 for Asheville in 1966 with a league low 2.61 ERA. In his marquee minor league campaign two years later, he led the International League with 18 wins with an 18–5 mark and had the circuit's best winning percentage (.783) for the 1968 Columbus Jets, perhaps the most fruitful Pirate minor league team of all time.

Unfortunately, it would be 11 more years before the Bucs would reap the benefits of the best statistical pitcher in the Pirates' system; as he was selected in the 39th pick by San Diego in the expansion draft.

For the Padres, it proved to be a very wise choice. Roberts matured by his third major league season, going 14–17 for San Diego in 1971 with a sparkling 2.10 ERA, second in the senior circuit. Despite his losing record, Roberts finished sixth in voting for the Cy Young Award.

Dave was rewarded for his fabulous campaign by being dealt to the Astros following the season for Derrel Thomas, Bill Greif and Mark Schaeffer. He would be a very solid hurler for Houston with a 12–7 mark in 1972. He had his most successful season in 1973, with a 17–11 record with a 2.85 ERA, finishing sixth in the NL in wins and tenth in ERA.

Following a subpar 8–14 mark two years later, the native of Gallipolis,

Dave Roberts (courtesy of the Topps Company, Inc.).

Ohio, was part of a seven-player deal to the Motor City. He won 16 games with the Tigers in 1976, then slipped again with a 4–10 mark in '77 after undergoing surgery to correct an arthritic knee. The less than stellar mark prompted a midseason trade to the Cubs.

Roberts spent a year in Chicago before being signed as a free agent by the Giants before the 1979 campaign.

1979. Beginning the year in San Francisco, Roberts became a full time reliever for the first time since his rookie season in 1969 and responded with a solid 2–0 mark with a fine 2.57 ERA and three saves in 42 innings of work.

It was on June 28th, as the Giants were 37–38, 8½ games out of the lead, that Roberts' fortunes would be changed. He was part of the famous Bill Madlock deal, which turned out to be the final piece of the Bucs' championship puzzle.

While the major part of the deal was Madlock, Roberts proved to be no slouch, with a 5–2 mark. Eleven years after he was let go by the organization, the reliever finally etched his name in Pirates lore on August 25, 1979. On that night, when the Bucs were involved in a classic tussle against the Padres, Roberts faced adversity twice with the bases loaded in extra innings (enduring the taunts of Dave Winfield, who was flashing the choke sign to the 35-year-old hurler) and pitched the Pirates out of trouble both times, leading Pittsburgh to the 4–3, 19-inning victory as he tossed four clutch innings of relief for the win.

1979 Postseason. Roberts pitched to only one batter in the NLCS against the Reds, walking Joe Morgan on four pitches in the ninth inning of game two. It would be the only batter he ever faced in his postseason career, as he was the only one of 25 players not to be used in a game of the 76th World Series against the Orioles.

Post-1979. By 1980, Roberts' career was nearly at an end. After the Bucs sold him to Seattle mid-1980, he lasted only two more seasons, signing on with the Mets in 1981, his last major league season.

Overall, Dave Roberts turned out to be one of the most well traveled players in the game, performing with 11 organizations in his professional career, while competing with eight at the major league level. His frequent moves prompted Roberts to exclaim, "The way I look at it, either I'm a bum or everybody wants me."[102]

Year	Team	W	L	PCT	CG	IP	H	BB	SO	ERA
1969	Padres	0	3	.000	0	48.2	65	19	19	4.81
1970	Padres	8	14	.364	3	181.2	182	43	102	3.81
1971	Padres	14	17	.452	14	269.2	238	61	135	2.10
1972	Astros	12	7	.632	7	192	227	57	111	4.50
1973	Astros	17	11	.607	12	249.1	264	62	119	2.85
1974	Astros	10	12	.455	8	204	216	65	72	3.40
1975	Astros	8	14	.364	7	198.1	182	73	101	4.27
1976	Tigers	16	17	.485	18	252	254	63	79	4.00
1977	Tigers	4	10	.286	5	129.1	143	41	46	5.15
	Cubs	1	1	.500	1	53	55	12	23	3.23
	Totals	5	11	.313	6	182.1	198	53	69	4.59
1978	Cubs	6	8	.429	2	142.1	159	56	54	5.25
1979	Giants	0	2	.000	0	42	42	18	23	2.57
	Pirates	5	2	.714	0	38.2	47	12	15	3.26
	Totals	5	4	.556	0	80.2	89	30	38	2.90
1980	Pirates	0	1	.000	0	2.1	2	1	1	3.86
	Mariners	2	3	.400	0	80.1	86	27	47	4.37
	Totals	2	4	.333	0	82.2	88	28	48	4.35
1981	Mets	0	3	.000	0	15.1	26	5	10	9.39
	Totals	103	125	.452	77	2099	2188	615	957	3.78
	Lg Average	117	117	.500	72	2099	2027	772	1211	3.66

Appendix A: Team Statistics and Awards

> The 1979 Pittsburgh Pirates
> 98–64 / .605
> National League Eastern Division Champions
> National League Champions
> World Champions

Baseball stats are a lifeline for most baseball fans. This section will give a thorough statistical look at the 1979 Pirates. The primary resources for these stats are *Baseball-Reference.com*, *The Baseball Almanac*, the *Sports Illustrated* baseball web site section and *Retrosheet*.

Regular Season Stats[1]

Team Batting

Pos	Player	Ag	G	AB	R	H	2B	3B	HR	RBI	BB	SO	BA	OBP	SLG	SB	CS	GDP	HBP	SH	SF	IBB
C	*Ed Ott	27	117	403	49	110	20	2	7	51	26	62	.273	.314	.385	0	1	8	0	6	4	8
1B	*Willie Stargell	39	126	424	60	119	19	0	32	82	47	105	.281	.352	.552	0	1	10	3	0	6	12
2B	Rennie Stennett	28	108	319	31	76	13	2	0	24	24	25	.238	.289	.292	1	4	11	0	2	3	6
3B	Bill Madlock	28	85	311	48	102	17	3	7	44	34	22	.328	.390	.469	21	8	14	1	2	5	8
SS	Tim Foli	28	133	525	70	153	23	1	1	65	28	14	.291	.335	.345	6	5	7	9	19	6	0
OF	*Omar Moreno	26	162	695	110	196	21	12	8	69	51	104	.282	.333	.381	77	21	7	3	6	2	9
OF	*Dave Parker	28	158	622	109	193	45	7	25	94	67	101	.310	.380	.526	20	4	7	9	0	9	14
OF	Bill Robinson	36	148	421	59	111	17	6	24	75	24	81	.264	.302	.504	13	2	13	6	1	5	11
	Phil Garner	30	150	549	76	161	32	8	11	59	55	74	.293	.359	.441	17	8	6	3	4	2	3
	*John Milner	29	128	326	52	90	9	4	16	60	53	37	.276	.373	.475	3	5	5	1	2	3	15
	Steve Nicosia	23	70	191	22	55	16	0	4	13	23	17	.288	.364	.435	0	2	5	0	1	0	6
	Lee Lacy	31	84	182	17	45	9	3	5	15	22	36	.247	.327	.412	6	1	1	1	0	3	7
	Dale Berra	22	44	123	11	26	5	0	3	15	11	17	.211	.272	.325	0	0	5	0	2	2	2
	Manny Sanguillen	35	56	74	8	17	5	2	1	4	2	5	.230	.247	.351	0	0	6	3	0	1	2
	*Mike Easler	28	55	54	8	15	1	0	2	11	8	13	.278	.371	.444	0	1	0	0	0	0	2
	Frank Taveras	29	11	45	4	11	3	1	0	1	0	2	.244	.244	.311	2	1	2	0	0	0	0
	#Matt Alexander	32	44	13	16	7	0	1	0	1	0	0	.538	.538	.692	13	1	0	0	0	0	0
	*Doe Boyland	24	4	3	0	0	0	0	0	0	0	2	.000	.000	.000	0	0	0	0	0	0	0
	Gary Hargis	22	1	0	0	0	0	0	0	0	0	0	.000	.000	.000	1	0	0	0	0	0	0
	Alberto Lois	23	11	0	6	0	0	0	0	0	0	0	.000	.000	.000	0	1	0	0	0	0	0
	Bert Blyleven	28	38	70	1	9	1	0	0	3	0	33	.129	.129	.143	0	0	2	0	15	0	0
	*John Candelaria	25	33	68	0	9	4	0	0	6	1	18	.132	.145	.191	0	0	4	0	8	0	0
	Bruce Kison	29	37	55	6	8	2	0	1	6	1	19	.145	.161	.236	0	0	2	0	7	0	0
	Don Robinson	22	29	49	4	10	0	0	0	3	3	9	.204	.250	.204	0	0	0	0	4	0	0
	Jim Bibby	34	34	45	3	8	1	0	2	5	0	25	.178	.196	.333	0	0	0	1	6	0	0
	Jim Rooker	36	19	33	1	4	0	0	0	0	1	13	.121	.147	.121	0	0	1	0	2	0	0
	Kent Tekulve	32	94	15	3	2	0	0	0	1	1	8	.133	.187	.133	0	0	0	0	1	0	0

	Ag	G	GS	SV	L	W										
Ed Whitson	24	19	13	1	0	0	0	0	0	1	5	.000	.071	0	0	4	0	0
Enrique Romo	31	84	12	0	2	0	0	0	1	0	2	.167	.167	0	0	4	0	0
#Grant Jackson	36	72	9	0	0	0	0	0	1	0	2	.000	.000	0	0	0	0	0
Joe Coleman	32	10	5	1	1	0	0	0	0	0	3	.200	.400	0	0	0	1	0
*Dave Roberts	34	21	5	0	0	0	0	0	1	0	1	.000	.000	0	0	0	0	0
#Dock Ellis	34	3	1	0	0	0	0	0	0	0	0	.000	.000	0	0	0	0	0
Rick Rhoden	26	1	1	0	0	0	0	0	0	0	0	1.000	1.000	0	0	0	0	0
TOTAL team age	29.5	163	5661	775	1541	264	52	148	710	483	855	.272	.329	.416	180	113	66	32	98	56

*— bats left-handed, #— switch hits, ?— unknown, else — bats right-handed

Team Pitching

	Player	Ag	G	ERA	W	L	SV	GS	GF	CG	SHO	IP	H	R	ER	BB	HR	SO	BFP	WP	HBP	BK	IB
SP	Bert Blyleven	28	37	3.60	12	5	0	37	0	4	0	237.3	238	102	95	92	21	172	1018	9	6	0	0
SP	*John Candelaria	25	33	3.22	14	9	0	30	2	8	0	207.0	201	83	74	41	25	101	850	2	3	0	0
SP	Bruce Kison	29	33	3.19	13	7	0	25	2	3	1	172.3	157	70	61	45	13	105	704	5	4	0	0
SP	Don Robinson	22	29	3.87	8	8	0	25	1	4	0	160.7	171	74	69	52	12	96	684	6	4	1	0
SP	*Jim Rooker	36	19	4.60	4	7	0	17	0	1	0	103.7	106	58	53	39	11	44	444	6	0	0	0
CL	Kent Tekulve	32	94	2.75	10	8	31	0	67	0	0	134.3	109	46	41	49	5	75	550	4	2	0	0
RP	Enrique Romo	31	84	2.99	10	5	5	0	25	0	0	129.3	122	50	43	43	11	106	537	6	3	6	0
RP	*Grant Jackson	36	72	2.96	8	5	14	0	29	0	0	82.0	67	32	27	35	9	39	339	3	2	1	0
RP	*Dave Roberts	34	21	3.26	5	2	1	3	5	0	0	38.7	47	18	14	12	1	15	170	0	1	0	0
RP	Jim Bibby	34	34	2.81	12	4	0	17	2	4	1	137.7	110	51	43	47	9	103	562	5	4	0	0
	Ed Whitson	24	19	4.37	2	3	1	7	4	0	0	57.7	53	36	28	36	6	31	263	2	1	1	0
	Joe Coleman	32	10	6.10	0	0	0	0	2	0	0	20.7	29	17	14	9	1	14	101	3	1	0	0
	Dock Ellis	34	3	2.57	0	0	0	1	0	0	0	7.0	9	2	2	2	1	1	29	1	0	0	0
	Rick Rhoden	26	1	7.20	0	1	0	1	0	0	0	5.0	5	4	4	2	0	2	21	0	0	0	0
	TOTAL team age	29.7	163	3.41	98	64	52	163	139	24	7	1493.0	1424	643	565	504	125	904	6272	52	31	9	

*— throws left-handed, ?— unknown, else — throws right-handed

Team Fielding

Catchers	G	PO	A	E	DP	FP	PB
EOtt	116	612	53	4	6	.994	7
SNicosia	65	320	25	3	4	.991	2
MSanguillen	8	32	4	2	0	.947	1
Team Total	163	964	82	9	10	.991	10

First Base	G	PO	A	E	DP	FP	
						.992	8.59
WStargell	113	949	47	3	102	.997	8.81
JMilner	48	255	18	3	27	.989	5.69
BRobinson	28	233	13	0	18	1.000	8.79
MSanguillen	5	35	2	0	3	1.000	7.40
Team Total	163	1472	80	6	150	.996	9.36

Second Base	G	PO	A	E	DP	FP	
						.979	4.55
RStennett	102	172	282	12	63	.974	4.45
PGarner	83	175	234	8	58	.981	4.93
LLacy	5	7	5	1	1	.923	2.40
Team Total	163	354	521	21	122	.977	5.27

Third Base	G	PO	A	E	DP	FP	
						.951	2.50
BMadlock	85	63	153	7	12	.969	2.54
PGarner	78	47	144	13	16	.936	2.45
DBerra	22	18	33	7	3	.879	2.32
BRobinson	3	0	0	0	0	.000	0.00
Team Total	163	128	330	27	31	.944	2.76

Shortstop	G	PO	A	E	DP	FP	
						.965	4.51
TFoli	132	255	404	15	97	.978	4.99
DBerra	22	25	53	5	11	.940	3.55
PGarner	14	12	18	1	8	.968	2.14
FTaveras	11	17	26	3	4	.935	3.91
MAlexander	1	0	0	0	0	.000	0.00
Team Total	163	309	501	24	120	.971	4.88

Outfield	G	PO	A	E	DP			LF	CF	RF
						.979	2.00			
OMoreno	162	490	11	13	3	.975	3.09	0	162	0
DParker	158	341	15	15	1	.960	2.25	0	0	158
BRobinson	125	161	6	3	0	.982	1.34	119	0	6
JMilner	64	112	2	5	1	.958	1.78	64	0	0
LLacy	41	70	3	2	0	.973	1.78	41	0	0
MAlexander	11	8	1	0	0	1.000	0.82	6	3	3
MEasler	4	0	0	0	0	.000	0.00	2	0	2
KTekulve	1	1	0	0	0	1.000	1.00	1	0	0
Team Total	163	1183	38	38	5	.970	2.45	163	163	163

Team Statistics and Awards

Pitchers	G	PO	A	E	DP	.951	1.80
BBlyleven	37	14	20	0	0	1.000	1.29
JCandelaria	33	2	36	0	3	1.000	1.65
BKison	33	10	30	1	2	.976	2.09
DRobinson	29	7	10	2	1	.895	0.95
JBibby	34	5	12	0	1	1.000	1.11
KTekulve	94	7	28	1	0	.972	2.35
ERomo	84	10	25	1	3	.972	2.44
JRooker	19	8	13	2	1	.913	1.82
GJackson	72	2	9	0	0	1.000	1.21
EWhitson	19	2	6	0	1	1.000	1.25
DRoberts	21	1	9	1	1	.909	2.33
JColeman	10	1	0	1	0	.500	0.43
DEllis	3	0	1	0	0	1.000	1.29
RRhoden	1	1	1	0	0	1.000	3.60
Team Total	163	70	200	9	13	.968	1.63

1979 NLCS Stats[2]

Pittsburgh Pirates

Player	G	AB	R	H	2B	3B	HR	RBI	BB	SO	BA	OBP	SLG	SB	AB	H	HR	BA	OPS	SB
						Series Stats												Regular Season		
#Matt Alexander	1	0	1	0	0	0	0	0	0	0	.000	.000	.000	0	13	7	0	.538	1.231	13
Jim Bibby	1	0	0	0	0	0	0	0	1	0	.000	1.000	.000	0	45	8	2	.178	.529	0
Bert Blyleven	1	3	1	1	0	0	0	0	0	1	.333	.333	.333	0	70	9	0	.129	.271	0
*John Candelaria	1	3	0	0	0	0	0	0	0	2	.000	.000	.000	0	68	9	0	.132	.336	0
*Mike Easler	1	1	0	0	0	0	0	0	0	0	.000	.000	.000	0	54	15	2	.278	.815	0
Tim Foli	3	12	1	4	1	0	0	0	0	0	.333	.333	.417	0	+532	153	1	.288	.671	6
Phil Garner	3	12	4	5	0	1	1	3	1	0	.417	.462	.833	0	549	161	11	.293	.800	17
#Grant Jackson	2	1	0	0	0	0	0	0	0	0	.000	.000	.000	0	9	0	0	.000	.000	0
Bill Madlock	3	12	1	3	0	0	1	2	2	0	.250	.357	.500	2	+560	167	14	.298	.792	32
*John Milner	3	9	0	0	0	0	0	0	2	2	.000	.182	.000	0	326	90	16	.276	.849	3
*Omar Moreno	3	12	3	3	0	1	0	0	2	2	.250	.357	.417	1	695	196	8	.282	.714	77
*Ed Ott	3	13	0	3	0	0	0	2	0	2	.231	.231	.231	0	403	110	7	.273	.699	0
*Dave Parker	3	12	2	4	0	0	0	2	2	3	.333	.429	.333	1	622	193	25	.310	.906	20
*Dave Roberts	1	0	0	0	0	0	0	0	0	0	.000	.000	.000	0	+10	0	0	.000	.000	0
Bill Robinson	3	3	0	0	0	0	0	0	0	0	.000	.000	.000	0	421	111	24	.264	.805	13
Don Robinson	2	0	0	0	0	0	0	0	0	0	.000	.000	.000	0	49	10	0	.204	.454	0
Enrique Romo	2	0	0	0	0	0	0	0	0	0	.000	.000	.000	0	12	2	0	.167	.333	0
*Willie Stargell	3	11	2	5	2	0	2	6	3	2	.455	.571	1.182	0	424	119	32	.281	.904	0
Rennie Stennett	1	0	0	0	0	0	0	0	0	0	.000	.000	.000	0	319	76	0	.238	.581	1
Kent Tekulve	2	1	0	0	0	0	0	0	0	1	.000	.000	.000	0	15	2	0	.133	.321	0
Total	3	105	15	28	3	2	4	14	13	13	.267	.347	.448	4		148		.272	.745	180

*—bats left-handed, #—switch hits, ?—unknown, else—bats right-handed
A + before season totals indicates the player was with multiple teams this year.

Series Pitching Stats
Pittsburgh Pirates

Player	G	ERA	W-L	SV	CG	IP	H	ER	BB	SO	W-L	IP	ERA	WHIP	SO	SV
			Series Stats										Regular Season			
Bert Blyleven	1	1.00	1-0	0	1	9.0	8	1	0	9	12-5	237	3.60	1.391	172	
Jim Bibby	1	1.29	0-0	0	0	7.0	4	1	4	5	12-4	138	2.81	1.140	103	
*John Candelaria	1	2.57	0-0	0	0	7.0	5	2	1	4	14-9	207	3.22	1.169	101	
Kent Tekulve	2	3.00	0-0	0	0	3.0	2	1	2	2	10-8	134	2.75	1.176	75	31
*Grant Jackson	2	0.00	1-0	0	0	2.0	1	0	1	2	8-5	82	2.96	1.244	39	14
Don Robinson	2	0.00	1-0	1	0	2.0	0	0	1	3	8-8	161	3.86	1.388	96	
Enrique Romo	2	0.00	0-0	0	0	0.3	3	0	1	1	10-5	129	2.99	1.276	106	5
*Dave Roberts	1	inf	0-0	0	0	0.0	0	0	1	0	+5-4	81	2.90	1.475	38	4
Total		1.48	3-0	1	1	30.3	23	5	11	26			3.41	1.290		

*— throws left-handed, ?— unknown, else — throws right-handed
A + before season totals indicates the player was with multiple teams this year.

1979 World Series Stats[3]

Pittsburgh Pirates

Player	G	AB	R	H	2B	3B	HR	RBI	BB	SO	BA	OBP	SLG	SB	AB	H	HR	BA	OPS	SB
#Matt Alexander	1	0	0	0	0	0	0	0	0	0	.000	.000	.000	0	13	7	0	.538	1.231	13
Jim Bibby	2	4	0	0	0	0	0	0	0	1	.000	.000	.000	0	45	8	2	.178	.529	0
Bert Blyleven	2	3	0	0	0	0	0	0	0	0	.000	.000	.000	0	70	9	0	.129	.271	0
*John Candelaria	2	3	0	1	0	0	0	0	0	2	.333	.333	.333	0	68	9	0	.132	.336	0
*Mike Easler	2	1	0	0	0	0	0	0	1	0	.000	.500	.000	0	54	15	2	.278	.815	0
Tim Foli	7	30	6	10	1	0	0	3	2	0	.333	.375	.433	0	+532	153	1	.288	.671	6
Phil Garner	7	24	4	12	4	0	0	5	3	1	.500	.556	.667	0	549	161	11	.293	.800	17
#Grant Jackson	4	1	0	0	0	0	0	0	0	0	.000	.000	.000	0	9	0	0	.000	.000	0
Lee Lacy	4	4	0	1	0	0	0	0	0	1	.250	.250	.250	0	182	45	5	.247	.739	6
Bill Madlock	7	24	2	9	1	0	0	3	5	1	.375	.483	.417	0	+560	167	14	.298	.792	32
*John Milner	3	9	2	3	1	0	0	1	2	0	.333	.455	.444	0	326	90	16	.276	.849	3
*Omar Moreno	7	33	4	11	2	0	0	3	1	7	.333	.353	.394	0	695	196	8	.282	.714	77
Steve Nicosia	4	16	1	1	0	0	0	0	0	2	.062	.062	.062	0	191	55	4	.288	.799	0
*Ed Ott	3	12	2	4	1	0	0	3	0	2	.333	.333	.417	0	403	110	7	.273	.699	0
*Dave Parker	7	29	2	10	3	0	0	4	2	7	.345	.387	.448	0	622	193	25	.310	.906	20
Bill Robinson	7	19	2	5	1	0	0	2	0	4	.263	.263	.316	0	421	111	24	.264	.805	13
Enrique Romo	2	1	0	0	0	0	0	0	0	0	.000	.000	.000	0	12	2	0	.167	.333	0
Jim Rooker	2	2	0	0	0	0	0	0	0	1	.000	.000	.000	0	33	4	0	.121	.268	0
Manny Sanguillen	3	3	0	1	0	0	0	1	0	0	.333	.333	.333	0	74	17	0	.230	.598	0
*Willie Stargell	7	30	7	12	4	0	3	7	0	6	.400	.400	.833	0	424	119	32	.281	.904	0
Rennie Stennett	1	1	0	1	0	0	0	0	0	0	1.000	1.000	1.000	0	319	76	0	.238	.581	1
Kent Tekulve	5	2	0	0	0	0	0	0	0	0	.000	.000	.000	0	15	2	0	.133	.321	0
Total	7	251	32	81	18	1	3	32	16	35	.323	.363	.438	0	148	.272	.745	180		

*— bats left-handed, #— switch hits, ?— unknown, else — bats right-handed
A + before season totals indicates the player was with multiple teams this year.

Pittsburgh Pirates

				Series Stats										Regular Season			
Player	G	ERA	W-L	SV	CG	IP	H	ER	BB	SO	W-L	IP	ERA	WHIP	SO	SV
Jim Bibby	2	2.61	0-0	0	0	10.3	10	3	2	10	12-4	138	2.81	1.140	103	
Bert Blyleven	2	1.80	1-0	0	0	10.0	8	2	3	4	12-5	237	3.60	1.391	172	
Kent Tekulve	5	2.89	0-1	3	0	9.3	4	3	3	10	10-8	134	2.75	1.176	75	31
*John Candelaria	2	5.00	1-1	0	0	9.0	14	5	2	4	14-9	207	3.22	1.169	101	
*Jim Rooker	2	1.04	0-0	0	0	8.7	5	1	3	4	4-7	104	4.60	1.398	44	
Don Robinson	4	5.40	1-0	0	0	5.0	4	3	6	3	8-8	161	3.86	1.388	96	
Enrique Romo	2	3.86	0-0	0	0	4.7	5	2	3	4	10-5	129	2.99	1.276	106	5
*Grant Jackson	4	0.00	1-0	0	0	4.7	1	0	2	2	8-5	82	2.96	1.244	39	14
Bruce Kison	1	108.00	0-1	0	0	0.3	3	4	2	0	13-7	172	3.19	1.172	105	
Total		3.34	4-3	3	0	62.0	54	23	26	41			3.41	1.290		

*— throws left-handed, ?— unknown, else — throws right-handed
A + before season totals indicates the player was with multiple teams this year.

1979 Pirates Awards

1979 National League MVP: Willie Stargell (tied with the Cardinals' Keith Hernandez)

1979 *Sports Illustrated* Man of the Year: Willie Stargell (awarded with the Steelers' Terry Bradshaw)

1979 *Sporting News* Man of the Year: Willie Stargell

Right fielder Dave Parker hoists the World Series trophy as he and manager Chuck Tanner exit the plane at Pittsburgh International Airport. (Courtesy of the Pittsburgh Pirates.)

1979 *Sporting News* Major League Player of the Year: Willie Stargell

1979 Roberto Clemente Award (presented by the Pittsburgh Chapter of the BWAA): Willie Stargell

1979 NLCS MVP: Willie Stargell

1979 World Series MVP: Willie Stargell

1979 National League Players of the Week:

4/15/79 — John Milner —.571 — 2 HR — 8 RBIs

7/22/79 — Phil Garner —.409 — 3 HR — 7 RBIs

1979 Lou Brock Award (league leader in stolen bases): Omar Moreno

1979 Gold Glove Award: Dave Parker — Right Field

1979 All-Star Game Representative from the Pirates: Dave Parker

1979 All-Star Game MVP: Dave Parker

Appendix B: 1979 Pirates Day by Day[4]

Date #	Opponent	Result	Winning Pitcher	Losing Pitcher	Save
4-6-1979	Vs MON N	L 2-3 (10)	Sosa (1-0)	Tekulve (0-1)	
4-7-1979	Vs MON N	W 7-6	Jackson (1-0)	Sosa (1-1)	Palmer (1)
4-8-1979	Vs MON N	L 4-5	May (1-0)	Romo (0-1)	
4-10-1979	At PHI N	L 3-7	Ruthven (1-0)	Romo (0-2)	
4-11-1979	At PHI N	L 4-5	Carlton (1-1)	Blyleven (0-1)	
4-12-1979	Vs STL N	W 3-1	D. Robinson (1-0)	Demny (1-1)	
4-13-1979	Vs STL N	W 7-6	Bibby (1-0)	Schultz (0-1)	Jackson (1)
4-14-1979	Vs STL N	W 7-4	Whitson (1-0)	Forsch (0-1)	Jackson (2)
4-15-1979	Vs STL N	L 4-9 (10)	Littell (1-0)	Tekulve (0-2)	
4-17-1979	Vs PHI N	L 2-13	Carlton (2-1)	Blyleven (0-2)	
4-18-1979	Vs PHI N	L 2-3	Lerch (1-1)	D. Robinson (1-1)	
4-20-1979	At HOU N	L 4-5 (10)	Sambito (1-0)	Bibby (1-1)	
4-21-1979	At HOU N	L 4-5 (10)	Andujar (2-0)	Tekulve (0-3)	
4-22-1979	At HOU N	L 2-3	Andujar (3-0)	Candelaria (0-1)	Sambito (2)
4-24-1979	At CIN N	W 9-2	D. Robinson (2-1)	Pastore (0-2)	
4-25-1979	At CIN N	W 3-2 (11)	Tekulve (1-3)	Tomlin (0-1)	
4-27-1979	Vs HOU N	L 8-9 (11)	Riccelli (1-0)	Whitson (1-1)	
4-29-1979	Vs HOU N	W 10-5	Kison (1-0)	Niekro (1-2)	Jackson (3)
5-1-1979	Vs ATL N	L 2-5	Niekro (3-4)	Tekulve (1-4)	
5-2-1979	Vs ATL N	W 10-2	Candelaria (1-1)	M. Mahler (0-2)	
5-4-1979	At STL N	L 3-4	Sykes (2-2)	D. Robinson (2-2)	Schultz (2)
5-5-1979	At STL N	W 6-5	Jackson (2-0)	Vuckovich (2-2)	Whitson (1)
5-6-1979	At STL N	L 2-4	Martinez (1-1)	Kison (1-1)	Knowles (2)
5-7-1979	At ATL N	W 4-2	Candelaria (2-1)	M. Mahler (0-3)	Tekulve (1)
5-8-1979	At ATL N	L 1-4	Solomon (2-1)	Rhoden (0-1)	
5-9-1979	At ATL N	W 17-9	Bibby (2-1)	Garber (1-5)	Tekulve (2)
5-11-1979	Vs CIN N	L 4-8	Tomlin (1-1)	Whitson (1-2)	Bair (6)
5-13-1979	Vs CIN N	W 3-2	Bibby (3-1)	Pastore (1-3)	Jackson (4)
5-15-1979	Vs CIN N	L 3-7	LaCoss (4-0)	Candelaria (2-2)	
5-15-1979	Vs NY N	L 0-3	Swan (4-3)	D. Robinson (2-3)	Lockwood (6)
5-16-1979	Vs NY N	W 4-3 (13)	Romo (1-2)	Lockwood (0-5)	
5-17-1979	Vs NY N	W 6-5	Tekulve (2-4)	Orosco (1-2)	

Date	Opp	Result	Pitcher 1	Pitcher 2	Save
5-18-1979	At CHI N	W 9-5	Candelaria (3-2)	Holtzman (3-3)	Jackson (5)
5-19-1979	At CHI N	W 3-0	Rooker (1-0)	Krukow (1-3)	Tekulve (3)
5-20-1979	At CHI N	W 6-5	D. Robinson (3-3)	McGlothen (5-5)	Tekulve (4)
5-21-1979	At MON N	W 4-2	Blyleven (1-2)	Sanderson (2-3)	Fryman (2)
5-22-1979	At MON N	L 3-6	Grimsley (4-2)	Whitson (1-3)	
5-23-1979	At MON N	L 0-3	Rogers (4-2)	Candelaria (3-3)	
5-25-1979	At NY N	T 3-3 (11)			
5-26-1979	At NY N	L 8-10	Lockwood (1-5)	Tekulve (2-5)	
5-27-1979	At NY N	W 2-1	Jackson (3-0)	Murray (2-5)	
5-28-1979	At NY N	W 6-1	Candelaria (4-3)	Falcone (0-5)	Jackson (6)
5-29-1979	Vs CHI N	W 8-0	D. Robinson (4-3)	Holtzman (4-4)	
5-30-1979	Vs CHI N	W 9-2	Rooker (2-0)	McGlothen (6-6)	
5-31-1979	Vs CHI N	W 4-3 (10)	Kison (2-1)	Sutter (1-2)	
6-1-1979	Vs SD N	W 9-8	Tekulve (3-5)	Shirley (2-5)	
6-2-1979	Vs SD N	L 1-3	Perry (5-4)	Candelaria (4-4)	
6-3-1979	Vs SD N	W 7-0	Kison (3-1)	Owchinko (2-2)	
6-4-1979	Vs LA N	L 2-4	Sutcliffe (6-3)	Rooker (2-1)	
6-5-1979	Vs LA N	W 3-1	Blyleven (2-2)	Sutton (6-5)	Tekulve (5)
6-6-1979	Vs LA N	W 5-4	Romo (2-2)	Welch (4-3)	Tekulve (6)
6-8-1979	Vs SF N	W 3-2	Romo (3-2)	Curtis (1-3)	Jackson (7)
6-9-1979	Vs SF N	L 2-6	Blue (7-6)	Kison (3-2)	
6-10-1979	Vs SF N	L 4-7	Lavelle (4-2)	Romo (3-3)	
6-12-1979	At SD N	L 3-6	Perry (6-4)	Candelaria (4-5)	
6-13-1979	At SD N	L 2-3	Owchinko (3-2)	Kison (3-3)	
6-14-1979	At SD N	L 1-2 (14)	D'Acquisto (3-4)	Candelaria (4-6)	Fingers (9)
6-15-1979	At LA N	W 6-2	Blyleven (3-2)	Sutton (6-7)	Tekulve (7)
6-16-1979	At LA N	W 6-3	D. Robinson (5-3)	Welch (4-4)	
6-17-1979	At LA N	W 5-1	Whitson (2-3)	Reuss (2-5)	Tekulve (8)
6-19-1979	At SF N	W 9-4	Candelaria (5-6)	Montefusco (1-3)	Romo (1)
6-20-1979	At SF N	W 8-5	Jackson (4-0)	Lavelle (5-4)	Tekulve (9)
6-22-1979	Vs CHI N	W 7-2	Blyleven (4-2)	Holtzman (5-6)	
6-23-1979	Vs CHI N	L 3-4	Krukow (4-5)	D. Robinson (5-4)	Sutter (17)
6-24-1979	Vs CHI N	L 0-5	Reuschel (6-5)	Kison (3-4)	

Date	Opponent	Result	Pitcher 1	Pitcher 2	Save
6-25-1979 1	At NY N	W 8-1	Candelaria (6-6)	Swan (7-6)	
6-25-1979 2	At NY N	L 0-4	Falcone (1-5)	Rooker (2-2)	
6-26-1979	At NY N	W 2-1	Blyleven (5-2)	Hausman (0-3)	Jackson (8)
6-27-1979	At NY N	L 9-12	Twitchell (2-0)	Jackson (4-1)	
6-28-1979	Vs NY N	L 2-3	Allen (2-5)	Bibby (3-2)	
6-29-1979	Vs MON N	W 6-5	Kison (4-4)	Lee (7-5)	Glynn (3)
6-30-1979	Vs MON N	L 3-5	Sanderson (5-4)	Blyleven (5-3)	Tekulve (10)
7-2-1979	At STL N	W 5-4	Romo (4-3)	Knowles (2-4)	Fryman (5)
7-3-1979	At STL N	W 4-1	Candelaria (7-6)	Forsch (3-9)	Jackson (9)
7-4-1979	At STL N	W 6-4	Blyleven (6-3)	Vuckovich (7-5)	Romo (2)
7-5-1979	At STL N	L 0-2	Fulgham (2-1)	Rooker (2-3)	
7-6-1979	At CIN N	L 1-2	Bair (5-4)	Jackson (4-2)	Jackson (10)
7-7-1979	At CIN N	L 2-6	Moskau (5-3)	D. Robinson (5-5)	
7-8-1979 1	At CIN N	L 2-4	Norman (5-7)	Candelaria (7-7)	
7-8-1979 2	At CIN N	W 2-1	Jackson (5-2)	Tomlin (2-2)	Tekulve (11)
7-10-1979	At HOU N	W 4-3	Bibby (4-2)	Andujar (10-5)	Tekulve (12)
7-11-1979	At HOU N	W 5-1	Kison (5-4)	Richard (7-9)	
7-12-1979	At HOU N	W 5-3	Blyleven (7-3)	Niekro (13-4)	Tekulve (13)
7-13-1979	At ATL N	L 4-13	Niekro (12-11)	Rooker (2-4)	
7-14-1979	At ATL N	W 5-1	Candelaria (8-7)	Matula (6-6)	
7-15-1979	At ATL N	W 7-3	Bibby (5-2)	Solomon (4-6)	
7-19-1979 1	Vs HOU N	W 9-5	Roberts (1-2)	Forsch (5-6)	Jackson (11)
7-19-1979 2	Vs HOU N	W 4-2	Kison (6-4)	Niekro (13-5)	Tekulve (14)
7-20-1979	Vs HOU N	W 9-3	Candelaria (9-7)	Richard (7-11)	Tekulve (15)
7-21-1979	Vs HOU N	W 6-5	Romo (5-3)	Sambito (4-3)	Tekulve (16)
7-22-1979 1	Vs ATL N	W 5-4	D. Robinson (6-5)	Solomon (4-7)	
7-22-1979 2	Vs ATL N	W 3-2	Bibby (6-2)	M. Mahler (2-9)	
7-23-1979 1	Vs ATL N	W 7-1	Blyleven (8-3)	Hanna (0-1)	
7-23-1979 2	Vs ATL N	L 0-8	Niekro (14-11)	Rooker (2-5)	
7-24-1979	Vs CIN N	L 5-6	Norman (7-8)	Kison (6-5)	Bair (14)
7-25-1979	Vs CIN N	L 5-6 (10)	Bair (6-5)	Tekulve (3-6)	Hume (3)
7-26-1979	Vs CIN N	L 7-9	Soto (1-2)	Roberts (1-3)	Romo (3)
7-27-1979 1	At MON N	W 5-4	Tekulve (4-6)	Sosa (5-6)	

Date	Location	Result	Pitcher 1	Pitcher 2	Save
7-27-1979 2	At MON N	W 9-1	Blyleven (9-3)	Sanderson (6-6)	
7-28-1979	At MON N	W 5-3	Bibby (7-2)	Schatzeder (5-4)	Tekulve (17)
7-29-1979	At MON N	L 3-5	Rogers (10-6)	Kison (6-6)	
7-30-1979	Vs NY N	W 8-5	Jackson (6-2)	Bernard (0-2)	Tekulve (18)
7-31-1979	Vs NY N	L 1-2	Twitchell (5-2)	Blyleven (9-4)	Glynn (6)
8-1-1979	Vs STL N	W 4-3	Romo (6-3)	Forsch (4-10)	Tekulve (19)
8-2-1979	Vs STL N	L 4-5	Frazier (2-2)	Jackson (6-3)	Knowles (6)
8-3-1979 1	Vs PHI N	W 6-3	Romo (7-3)	McGraw (3-2)	
8-3-1979 2	Vs PHI N	W 5-1	Bibby (8-2)	Christenson (2-7)	
8-4-1979	Vs PHI N	W 4-0	Candelaria (10-7)	Espinosa (11-9)	
8-5-1979 1	Vs PHI N	W 12-8	Tekulve (5-6)	Eastwick (1-2)	
8-5-1979 2	Vs PHI N	W 5-2	Romo (8-3)	Noles (3-3)	Tekulve (20)
8-7-1979	At CHI N	L 2-15	Reuschel (11-7)	Rooker (2-6)	
8-8-1979	At CHI N	W 5-2 (10)	Tekulve (6-6)	Tidrow (8-3)	
8-9-1979	At CHI N	L 3-11	Lamp (8-7)	Candelaria (10-8)	
8-10-1979 1	At PHI N	L 3-4 (12)	Eastwick (2-2)	Jackson (6-4)	
8-10-1979 2	At PHI N	W 3-2	Kison (7-6)	Lerch (6-11)	Tekulve (21)
8-11-1979	At PHI N	W 14-11	Romo (9-3)	Eastwick (2-3)	Tekulve (22)
8-13-1979	At PHI N	W 9-1	Bibby (9-2)	Christenson (3-8)	
8-14-1979	Vs SD N	W 7-1	Candelaria (11-8)	D'Acquisto (8-10)	
8-15-1979	Vs SD N	W 5-1	Blyleven (10-4)	Jones (9-8)	
8-16-1979	Vs SD N	W 5-4	Kison (8-6)	Perry (10-10)	Romo (4)
8-17-1979	Vs LA N	L 6-7	Patterson (3-0)	Bibby (9-3)	Castillo (1)
8-18-1979	Vs LA N	L 1-5	Reuss (4-10)	D. Robinson (6-6)	
8-19-1979	Vs LA N	W 2-0	Tekulve (7-6)	Hooton (11-9)	
8-20-1979	Vs SF N	W 6-5	Romo (10-3)	Lavelle (7-7)	Tekulve (23)
8-21-1979	Vs SF N	L 1-6	Knepper (9-8)	Kison (8-7)	
8-22-1979	Vs SF N	W 8-6	Tekulve (8-6)	Lavelle (7-8)	
8-24-1979	At SD N	L 2-3	Jones (10-9)	Romo (10-4)	Lee (3)
8-25-1979	At SD N	W 4-3 (19)	Roberts (2-3)	D'Acquisto (8-12)	
8-26-1979	At SD N	W 9-2	Kison (9-7)	Shirley (6-13)	
8-27-1979	At LA N	L 2-4	Brett (4-3)	Tekulve (8-7)	
8-28-1979	At LA N	W 4-1	Candelaria (12-8)	Hough (4-5)	

Date	Location	Result	Pitcher	Opp. Pitcher	Save
8-29-1979	At LA N	W 4-1	Blyleven (11-4)	Reuss (4-12)	Tekulve (24)
8-31-1979	At SF N	W 6-4	D. Robinson (7-6)	Curtis (9-9)	Jackson (12)
9-1-1979 1	At SF N	W 5-3	Kison (10-7)	Montefusco (3-6)	Jackson (13)
9-1-1979 2	At SF N	W 7-2	Bibby (10-3)	Knepper (9-10)	
9-2-1979	At SF N	W 5-3	Candelaria (13-8)	Blue (10-13)	
9-3-1979 1	Vs PHI N	L 0-2	Carlton (14-11)	Blyleven (11-5)	McGraw (14)
9-3-1979 2	Vs PHI N	W 7-3	Rooker (3-6)	Lerch (7-12)	Tekulve (25)
9-5-1979	At STL N	W 7-5 (11)	Roberts (3-3)	Thomas (3-3)	Tekulve (26)
9-6-1979	At STL N	L 6-8	Martinez (13-7)	Bibby (10-4)	McEnaney (2)
9-7-1979	At NY N	W 6-4 (14)	Jackson (7-4)	Allen (4-9)	
9-8-1979	At NY N	L 2-3 (15)	Ellis (3-7)	Rooker (3-7)	
9-9-1979	At NY N	W 6-5	Tekulve (9-7)	Glynn (1-3)	
9-11-1979	Vs STL N	W 7-3	Roberts (4-3)	Denny (7-11)	Tekulve (27)
9-12-1979	Vs STL N	W 2-0	Candelaria (14-8)	Forsch (9-11)	Tekulve (28)
9-15-1979	Vs NY N	W 5-4	Roberts (5-3)	Glynn (1-4)	Allen (7)
9-16-1979	Vs NY N	L 0-3	Falcone (6-13)	Candelaria (14-9)	
9-17-1979	At MON N	W 2-1	D. Robinson (8-6)	Rogers (13-10)	Roberts (4)
9-18-1979	At MON N	W 5-3 (11)	Jackson (8-4)	Murray (4-9)	Jackson (14)
9-19-1979 1	At PHI N	W 9-6	Tekulve (10-7)	Eastwick (3-5)	Saucier (1)
9-19-1979 2	At PHI N	L 5-6	Kucek (1-0)	Romo (10-5)	
9-20-1979	At PHI N	L 1-2	Lerch (10-12)	Tekulve (10-8)	
9-21-1979	At CHI N	L 0-2	McGlothen (12-13)	D. Robinson (8-7)	
9-22-1979	At CHI N	W 4-1	Kison (11-7)	Riley (0-1)	Tekulve (29)
9-23-1979	At CHI N	W 6-0	Bibby (11-4)	Reuschel (18-11)	
9-24-1979 1	Vs MON N	W 5-2	Blyleven (12-5)	Schatzeder (10-5)	Tekulve (30)
9-24-1979 2	Vs MON N	L 6-7	Grimsley (10-9)	Jackson (8-5)	Sosa (18)
9-25-1979	Vs MON N	W 10-4	Rooker (4-7)	Sanderson (9-8)	Romo (5)
9-26-1979	Vs MON N	W 10-1	Kison (12-7)	Rogers (13-11)	
9-27-1979	Vs STL N	L 5-9	Forsch (11-11)	Roberts (5-4)	
9-28-1979	Vs CHI N	W 6-1	Bibby (12-4)	Reuschel (18-12)	Littell (13)
9-29-1979	Vs CHI N	L 6-7 (13)	Caudill (1-7)	D. Robinson (8-8)	
9-30-1979	Vs CHI N	W 5-3	Kison (13-7)	McGlothen (13-14)	Tekulve (31)

Notes

1. Prelude to a Championship

1. David Neft, Richard Cohen and Michael Neft, *The Baseball Encyclopedia 2000* (New York: St. Martin's Griffin, 2000), 350.
2. *The Baseball Encyclopedia* (New York: Macmillan, 1996), 2724, 2534.
3. David Finoli and Bill Ranier, *The Pittsburgh Pirates Encyclopedia* (Champaign, Ill.: Sports Publishing, 2003), 154–155.
4. Finoli and Ranier, *Pittsburgh Pirates Encyclopedia*, 470.
5. *The Baseball Online Library*, www.baseballlibrary.com.
6. *Baseball Encyclopedia*, 2724, 2684.

2. The Regular Season

1. Charley Feeney, *The Sporting News*, December 10, 1978.
2. Dan Donovan, *Pittsburgh Press*, March 1, 1979.
3. Pittsburgh Pirates, *1979 Pittsburgh Pirates Media Guide*, 5.
4. *1979 Pittsburgh Pirates Media Guide*, 75.
5. Accounts of game results were obtained from multiple local newspapers, including *The Pittsburgh Press, The Pittsburgh Post-Gazette, The Greensburg Tribune-Review,* and *The Standard-Observer,* as well as the *1980 Pittsburgh Pirates Media Guide*.
6. Lou Sahadi, *The Pirates: "We Are Family"* (New York: Times Books, 1979), 86.
7. Donovan, *Pittsburgh Press*, May 8, 1979.
8. Donovan, *Pittsburgh Press*, May 9, 1979.
9. Ibid.
10. Donovan, *Pittsburgh Press*, May 18, 1979.
11. Donovan, *Pittsburgh Press*, June 1, 1979.
12. *Pittsburgh Press*, June 1, 1979.
13. Donovan, *Pittsburgh Press*, June 4, 1979.
14. Donovan, *Pittsburgh Press*, June 16, 1979.
15. Donovan, *Pittsburgh Press*, July 13, 1979.
16. *Pittsburgh Press*.
17. *Jeannette News-Dispatch* (UPI wire story), July 18, 1979.
18. *Greensburg Tribune-Review* (UPI wire story), July 19, 1979.
19. Donovan, *Pittsburgh Press*, July 22, 1979.
20. *1980 Pittsburgh Pirates Media Guide*.
21. Donovan, *Pittsburgh Press*, July 28, 1979.

22. Donovan, *Pittsburgh Press*, August 4, 1979.
23. Ibid.
24. Donovan, *Pittsburgh Press*, August 6, 1979.
25. *Greensburg Tribune-Review* (UPI wire story), August 8, 1979.
26. Donovan, *Pittsburgh Press*, August 12, 1979.
27. *Greensburg Tribune-Review* (UPI), August 17, 1979.
28. *Greensburg Tribune-Review* (UPI), September 2, 1979.
29. Morris Eckhouse and Carl Mastracola, *This Date in Pittsburgh Pirate History* (Briarcliff Manor, N.Y.: Scarborough Publishers, 1980).
30. Donovan, *Pittsburgh Press*, September 11, 1979.
31. *Pittsburgh Press* (UPI wire story), September 14, 1979.
32. *Standard Observer* (AP wire story), September 22, 1979.
33. Ibid.
34. Donovan, *Pittsburgh Press*, September 25, 1979.
35. Sahadi, *The Pirates*.

3. The Post-Season

1. *The Baseball Online Library*, www.baseballlibrary.com.
2. Joseph Durso, *New York Times*, October 3, 1979.
3. Durso, *New York Times*, October 4, 1979.
4. Dan Donovan, *Pittsburgh Press*, October 4, 1979.
5. Ibid.
6. *Retrosheet*, www.retrosheet.org.
7. *Pittsburgh Press*, October 6, 1979.
8. Durso, *New York Times*, October 6, 1979.
9. Murray Chase, *New York Times*, October 11, 1979.
10. Durso, *New York Times*, October 11, 1979.
11. David Finoli and Bill Ranier, *The Pittsburgh Pirates Encyclopedia* (Champaign, Ill.: Sports Publishing, 2003), 519.
12. *Washington Post*, October 11, 1979.
13. Chase, *New York Times*, October 11, 1979.
14. Chase, *New York Times*, October 12, 1979.
15. Ibid.
16. John Feinstein, *Washington Post*, October 12, 1979.
17. Durso, *New York Times*, October 12, 1979.
18. Byron Rosen, *Washington Post*, October 13, 1979.
19. Ibid.
20. Durso, *New York Times*, October 13, 1979.
21. Durso, *New York Times*, October 14, 1979.
22. *Pittsburgh Press*, October 14, 1979.
23. Durso, *New York Times*, October 14, 1979.
24. Ibid.
25. Dave Kindred, *Washington Post*, October 14, 1979.
26. Kindred, *Washington Post*, October 14, 1979.
27. Durso, *New York Times*, October 14, 1979.
28. Dave Anderson, *New York Times*, October 16, 1979.
29. *Pittsburgh Press*, October 11, 1979.
30. *Pittsburgh Press*, October 15, 1979.
31. Ibid.
32. Feinstein, *Washington Post*, October 17, 1979.
33. Ibid.
34. Chase, *New York Times*, October 18, 1979.
35. Durso, *New York Times*, October 18, 1979.
36. Ibid.

4. The Fall of the Family

1. Zander Hollander, *The Complete Handbook of Baseball* (New York: Signet Books, 1980), 217.
2. *The Pocket Book of Baseball* (New York: Pocket Books, 1981), 197.
3. *The Baseball Online Library*, www.baseballlibrary.com.

4. *The Baseball Online Library*, www.baseballlibrary.com
5. Pittsburgh Pirates, *1984 Pittsburgh Pirates Media Guide*, 39.
6. David Finoli and Bill Ranier, *The Pittsburgh Pirates Encyclopedia* (Champaign, Ill.: Sports Publishing, 2003), 408.
7. Ibid., 192.
8. Ibid., 193.
9. Ibid., 302.
10. Ibid., 192.
11. Ibid., 302.

5. The Members of the Family

1. David Finoli and Bill Ranier, *The Pittsburgh Pirates Encyclopedia* (Champaign, Ill.: Sports Publishing, 2003), 351.
2. Pittsburgh Pirates, *1979 Pittsburgh Pirates Media Guide*.
3. Bill James, *The New Bill James Historical Baseball Abstract* (New York: The Free Press, 2001), 512.
4. Lou Sahadi, *The Pirates: "We Are Family"* (New York: Times Books, 1979), 92.
5. Bob Smizik, Pittsburgh Press, July 6, 1980.
6. Harvey Frommer and Frederic J. Frommer, *The Baseball Online Library*, http://www.baseballlibrary.com/baseballlibrary/excerpts/growing_up_baseball.stm
7. *1980 Pittsburgh Pirates Media Guide* (1980), 41.
8. Sahadi, *The Pirates*, 90.
9. Ibid.
10. Sahadi, *The Pirates*, 90.
11. Russ Franke, *Pittsburgh Press*, October 15, 1979.
12. Bill James, *The New Bill James Historical Baseball Abstract* (New York: The Free Press, 2001), 567; David Pietrusza, Matthew Silverman and Michael Gershman, eds., *Baseball: The Biographical Encyclopedia* (New York: Total Sports, 2000), 696.
13. *1984 Pittsburgh Pirates Media Guide* (1984), 39.
14. *1985 Pittsburgh Pirates Media Guide* (1985), 41.
15. Pietrusza et al., eds., *Baseball: The Biographical Encyclopedia*, 1082.
16. *1980 Pittsburgh Pirates Media Guide* (1980), 60.
17. *Pittsburgh Post-Gazette*, July 16, 1970.
18. Finoli and Ranier, *Pittsburgh Pirates Encyclopedia*, 593–595.
19. Pietrusza et al., eds., *Baseball: The Biographical Encyclopedia*, 366.
20. Sahadi, *The Pirates*, 86.
21. Ibid.
22. Vic Ketchman, *Standard Observer*, April 20, 1979.
23. Ibid.
24. *1980 Pittsburgh Pirates Media Guide*.
25. Ibid.
26. Finoli and Ranier, *Pittsburgh Pirate Encyclopedia*, 414.
27. Pietrusza, et al., eds., *Baseball: The Biographical Encyclopedia*, 1112.
28. Pietrusza, et al., eds., *Baseball: The Biographical Encyclopedia*, 331.
29. *Standard Observer* (AP story), September 22, 1979.
30. Smizik, *Pittsburgh Press*, December 12, 1975.
31. Ed Eagle, MLB.Com, http://www.mlb.com/NASApp/mlb/mlb/news/mlb_leftfield.jsp?ymd=20030519&content_id=327884&vkey=leftfield&fext=.jsp
32. Sahadi, *The Pirates*, 94.
33. Sahadi, *The Pirates*, 95.
34. Ed Eagle, MLB.Com, http://www.mlb.com/NASApp/mlb/mlb/news/mlb_leftfield.jsp?ymd=20030519&content_id=327884&vkey=leftfield&fext=.jsp
35. Finoli and Ranier, *Pittsburgh Pirates Encyclopedia*, 409.
36. *1979 Pittsburgh Pirates Media Guide*, 49.
37. *1980 Pittsburgh Pirates Media Guide*, 55.
38. Dan Donovan, *Pittsburgh Press*, October 15, 1979.
39. *1980 Pittsburgh Pirates Media Guide*, 9.
40. Ibid.
41. *1978 Pittsburgh Pirates Media Guide*, 26.

42. Smizik, *Pittsburgh Press*, March 2, 1977.
43. *1980 Pittsburgh Pirates Media Guide*, 9.
44. Sahadi, *The Pirates*, 107.
45. *1980 Pittsburgh Pirates Media Guide*, 43.
46. Russ Franke, *Pittsburgh Press*, December 11, 1982.
47. Pietrusza, et al., eds., *Baseball: The Biographical Encyclopedia*, 967.
48. Sahadi, *The Pirates*, 180.
49. *1979 Pittsburgh Pirates Media Guide*, 24.
50. Finoli and Ranier, *Pittsburgh Pirates Encyclopedia*, 371.
51. Pietrusza, et al., eds., *Baseball: The Biographical Encyclopedia*, 99.
52. Finoli and Ranier, *The Pittsburgh Pirates Encyclopedia*, 371.
53. *1980 Pittsburgh Pirates Media Guide*, 4–5.
54. *1981 Pittsburgh Pirates Media Guide*, 4–5.
55. Rob Neyer, *Rob Neyer's Big Book of Baseball Lineups* (New York: Fireside, 2003), 137–138.
56. James, *New Bill James Historical Baseball Abstract*, 870–871.
57. Ibid.
58. Franke, *Pittsburgh Press*, October 17, 1979.
59. Sahadi, *The Pirates*, 129.
60. Ibid.
61. Pietrusza, et al., eds., *Baseball: The Biographical Encyclopedia*, 547.
62. Sahadi, *The Pirates*, 112.
63. Donovan, *Pittsburgh Press*, March 16, 1979.
64. Ibid.
65. Donovan, *Pittsburgh Press*, October 17, 1979.
66. Pietrusza, et al., eds., *Baseball: The Biographical Encyclopedia*, 1114.
67. Sahadi, *The Pirates*, 122.
68. Pietrusza, et al., eds., *Baseball: The Biographical Encyclopedia*, 952.
69. Steve Novotney, *The Pirates Report*, January 2004.
70. Ibid.
71. Sahadi, *The Pirates*, 97.
72. Robert Dvorchak, *Pittsburgh Post Gazette*, October 19, 2003.
73. *1979 Pittsburgh Pirates Media Guide*, 59.
74. Pietrusza, et al., eds., *Baseball: The Biographical Encyclopedia*, 1224.
75. *Greensburg Tribune-Review* (AP story), November 11, 1992.
76. Ibid.
77. *1980 Pittsburgh Pirates Media Guide*.
78. Ibid.
79. *1983 Pittsburgh Pirates Media Guide*.
80. Vic Caso, "The Year of the Catcher" in *Team!* (New York: Film and Venture Group, August 1973).
81. Finoli and Ranier, *Pittsburgh Pirates Encyclopedia*, 297.
82. Caso, "The Year of the Catcher."
83. *1980 Pittsburgh Pirates Media Guide*, 20.
84. Peitrusza, et al., eds., *Baseball: The Biographical Encyclopedia*, 1202.
85. Peitrusza, et al., eds., *Baseball: The Biographical Encyclopedia*, 866.
86. Sahadi, *The Pirates*, 53.
87. Sahadi, *The Pirates*, 35.
88. Dvorchak, *Pittsburgh Post Gazette*, March 3, 2004.
89. Bill James, *Whatever Happened to the Hall of Fame?* (New York: Simon and Schuster, 1995), 365.
90. Paul White, *The Baseball Online Library*, http://www.baseballlibrary.com/baseballlibrary/submit/White_Paul12.stm.
91. Scott Miller, *CBS Sportsline*, http://cbs.sportsline.com/mlb/story/6966023.
92. Ed Eagle, *The Pirates*, http://pittsburgh.pirates.mlb.com/NASApp/mlb/pit/news/pit_news.jsp?ymd=20040102&content_id=621405&vkey=news_pit&fext=.jsp.
93. *Greensburg Tribune-Review* (UPI wire story), July 17, 1979.
94. Pietrusza, et al., eds., *Baseball: The Biographical Encyclopedia*, 928.
95. Sahadi, *The Pirates*, 117.
96. Pietrusza, et al., eds., *Baseball: The Biographical Encyclopedia*, 954.
97. *The Baseball Online Library*, www.baseballlibrary.com.
98. Henry Schulman, SF Gate.com, www.sfgate.com, May 23, 1997.

99. Sahadi, *The Pirates*, 108.
100. Ibid.
101. Ibid.
102. *The Baseball Online Library*, www.baseballlibrary.com.

Appendix: The 1979 Pittsburgh Pirates

1. Sean L. Forman, "1979 Pittsburgh Pirates Statistics," on *Baseball-Reference.com*, http://www.baseball-reference.com/, January 30, 2004.

2. Sean L. Forman, "1979 NL Championship Series — PIT vs CIN," on *Baseball-Reference.com*, http://www.baseball-reference.com/, January 30, 2004.

3. Sean L. Forman, "1979 World Series — PIT vs BAL," on *Baseball-Reference.com*, http://www.baseball-reference.com/, January 30, 2004.

4. Mark, Pankin. *Retrosheet.org*, *www.retrosheet.org*, January 30, 2004. This information was obtained free of charge from and is copyrighted by *Retrosheet*. Interested parties may contact *Retrosheet* at 20 Sunset Rd., Newark, Delaware, 19711.

Bibliography

Books

The Baseball Encyclopedia, 10th ed. Jeanine Bucek, ed. dir. New York: Macmillan, 1996.
Cohen, Richard, and David Neft, eds. *The World Series*. New York: St. Martin's, 1990.
_____, _____, and Michael Neft, eds. *The Baseball Encyclopedia 2000*, 20th ed. New York: St. Martin's, 2000.
Eckhouse, Morris, and Carl Mastrocola. *This Day in Pittsburgh Pirates History*. Briarcliff Manor, N.Y.: Scarborough Books, 1980.
Finoli, David, and Bill Ranier. *The Pittsburgh Pirate Encyclopedia*. Champaign, Ill.: Sports Publishing, 2003.
Gillette, Gary, and Pete Palmer, eds. *The Baseball Encyclopedia*, 1st ed. New York: Barnes and Noble Books, 2004.
James, Bill. *Whatever Happened to the Hall of Fame?* New York: Simon and Schuster, 1995.
_____. *The New Bill James Historical Baseball Abstract*, 2nd ed. New York: Free Press, 2001.
Neyer, Rob. *The Big Book of Baseball Line-ups*. New York: Fireside Books, 2003.
Pietrusza, David, Matthew Silverman, and Michael Gershman, eds. *Baseball: The Biographical Encyclopedia*. New York: Total Sports, 2000.
Sahadi, Lou. *The Pirates: "We Are Family."* New York: Times Books, 1980.

Guides

Pittsburgh Pirates. *The Complete Handbook of Baseball*. Pittsburgh: Pittsburgh Pirates. 1980–1982.
Pittsburgh Pirates. *Pittsburgh Pirates Media Guide*. Pittsburgh: Pittsburgh Pirates. 1978–1985, 2003.
Liss, Howard, and John Devaney, eds. *The Pocket Book of Baseball*. New York: Pocket Books, 1981.

The Sporting News Register. St. Louis: The Sporting News, 1975.

Periodicals

Team! 1979.
The Pittsburgh Press, 1978–1979.
The Pittsburgh Post-Gazette, 1979.
The Greensburg Tribune Review, 1979.
The New York Times, 1979.
The Washington Times, 1979.
The Los Angeles Times, 1979.
The Sporting News, 1979.
The Pirates Report, 2003–2004.
The Standard Observer, 1979.

Web Sites

Retrosheet. www.retrosheet.org
The Pirate Web Site. www.pittsburghpirates.com
The Baseball Online Library. www.baseballlibrary,com
Baseball-Reference.com. www.baseball-reference.com
The Sports Illustrated web site. www.cnnsi.com
The Baseball Almanac. www.baseballalmanac.com
The Society of American Baseball Research. www.sabr.org
SF Gate.com. www.sfgate.com
MLB.com. www.mlb.com

Index

Aaron, Hank 138, 139, 140
Adams, Babe 166
Alexander, Gary 121, 170
Alexander, Matt 13, 20, 25, 29, 34, 36, 38, 64, 207, 208
Allen, Dick 34
Alley, Gene 7
Alou, Matty 161, 162
Alston, Walter 158
Altobelli, Joe 123, 198
Anderson, Sparky 46, 148
Andujar, Joaquin 28
Armas, Tony 9, 105, 109, 121
Ayala, Benny 59, 67, 68, 76, 85, 226

Bailey, Bob 5
Bair, Doug 9, 109, 121
Baker, Dusty 38
Baldwin, Reggie 28
Batton, Chris 109, 122
Baylor, Don 59, 170, 179
Belanger, Mark 57, 59, 60, 61, 67
Bell, Derek 160
Bell, Jay 170
Bench, Johnny 45, 48, 50, 51, 52, 55, 152, 169, 188, 204, 221
Berra, Dale 15, 23, 24, 37, 38, 94, 95, 113, 114, 125, 126, 144
Berra, Yogi 38, 95, 205
Bibby, Jim 9, 11, 13, 22, 23, 28, 30, 31, 32, 34, 38, 41, 50, 51, 70, 71, 84, 91, 101, 102, 105, 109, 110, 148, 182, 183, 184, 185, 186, 221

Biitner, Larry 43
Blass, Steve 6, 7, 58, 166, 204
Blue, Vida 24, 38, 172, 207
Blyleven, Bert 3, 9, 13, 17, 19, 20, 22, 23, 24, 25, 28, 29, 30, 31, 34, 41, 54, 55, 63, 77, 100, 101, 102, 103, 109, 111, 112, 137, 167, 168, 169, 170, 171, 172, 173, 178, 184, 185, 188, 201, 202, 206
Bonds, Barry 153
Boone, Bob 33
Bowa, Larry 143, 144
Boyer, Clete 191
Boyer, Ken 17
Boyland, Doe 37, 105, 113, 223
Bream, Sid 130
Breining, Fred 23, 111
Briles, Nellie 166
Brock, Lou 17, 204
Brown, Joe L. 5, 6, 7, 8, 9, 105, 107, 108, 133, 164, 227
Brown, Mike 227
Brusstar, Warren 16
Buckner, Bill 17, 22, 214
Buhner, Jay 113, 114, 126
Bumbry, Al 59, 60, 67, 68, 71, 72, 85, 221
Bunning, Jim 5
Burgess, Smoky 118

Camacho, Ernie 112
Candelaria, John 8, 13, 23, 26, 28, 29, 31, 32, 34, 36, 37, 39, 40, 41, 47, 67,

259

68, 80, 81, 100, 101, 102, 103, 168, 169, 185, 224, 225, 226, 227
Candiotti, Tom 173
Carey, Max 146, 163
Carlton, Steve 16, 17, 32, 38, 42, 225
Carter, Gary 16, 19
Carter, Jimmy 1
Casek, Craig 105
Cash, Dave 42, 132
Castillo, Bobby 34
Caudill, Bill 42
Cepeda, Orlando 138, 139
Cey, Ron 25
Chapman, Kelvin 142
Christensen, Larry 16
Clark, Jack 128, 188
Clemens, Pat 227
Clemens, Roger 171, 173
Clemente, Roberto 1, 5, 7, 8, 28, 29, 58, 60, 65, 83, 135, 136, 138, 179, 205, 210, 211, 224
Coleman, Joe 29, 33, 38, 41, 105, 185, 216, 217
Collins, Dave 45, 47, 51, 52, 55, 188, 221
Concepcion, Dave 45, 47, 48, 50, 51, 52, 55, 144, 188, 221
Cooper, Wilbur 227
Cosell, Howard 116
Cox, Bobby 30
Craig, Roger 23, 36
Crawford, Jerry 129
Cromartie, Warren 16
Crowley, Terry 59, 72, 85, 189, 221
Cruz, Heity 52, 188
Cruz, Victor 112, 170
Curtis, John 24

DalCanton, Bruce 6
D'Aquisto, John 3, 4, 23, 36
Dauer, Rich 59, 67, 68, 77, 81, 84, 176, 185
Davalillo, Vic 176
Davis, Dick 113, 194
Dawson, Andre 16, 214
DeCinces, Doug 59, 60, 61, 64, 68, 71, 77, 82, 84, 86, 105, 221
DeLeon, Jose 172
Demery, Larry 13
Dempsey, Rick 59, 60, 64, 65, 68, 77, 81, 152, 175, 208, 221
Denny, John 17

Dilone, Miguel 9, 110, 160, 161, 205
DiMaggio, Joe 191
Dixon, Tom 125
Donovan, Dan 24, 52
Downing, Brian 29, 212
Drabek, Doug 196
Dreissen, Dan 45, 50, 51, 52
Dyer, Duffy 206

Easler, Mike 16, 22, 30, 31, 33, 39, 48, 64, 93, 97, 110, 113, 178, 179, 203
Easley, Logan 196
Eastwick, Rawley 16, 32
Edwards, Mike 110, 205
Ellis, Dock 6, 40, 41, 105, 112, 147, 148, 149, 150, 185, 217
Espinosa, Nino 16
Evans, Barry 24, 181
Evans, Darrell 38, 128, 139, 188

Face, Roy 5, 190
Fahey, Bill 4, 36
Field, Greg 19, 145
Fingers, Rollie 23, 36, 187
Finley, Charlie 207
Fisher, Brian 196
Flanagan, Mike 58, 60, 61, 76, 77, 134, 193, 212
Flood, Curt 128
Flynn, Doug 142
Foli, Tim 3, 19, 20, 23, 24, 26, 28, 30, 31, 32, 33, 35, 36, 37, 41, 42, 48, 51, 52, 55, 60, 68, 71, 77, 80, 81, 84, 94, 95, 98, 111, 113, 114, 118, 126, 137, 141, 142, 143, 144, 145, 147, 208, 213, 226
Forsch, Bob 17
Forster, Terry 9, 115, 175
Foster, George 7, 45, 47, 48, 50, 51, 52, 55, 152, 178, 211, 221
Frattare, Lanny 124
Friend, Bob 5
Frobel, Doug 159
Fryman, Woody 5, 17, 26

Gagne, Eric 190
Galbreath family 11, 12, 211
Garber, Gene 6, 21, 30, 164, 190
Garcia, Kiko 59, 68, 71, 72, 76, 81, 84, 221, 226
Garner, Phil 9, 14, 15, 20, 23, 24, 25, 26, 28, 29, 31, 32, 33, 36, 38, 39, 40,

41, 42, 47, 48, 51, 55, 60, 61, 64, 67, 68, 70, 71, 73, 77, 84, 85, 93, 94, 98, 109, 112, 121, 122, 123, 124, 131, 134, 137, 142, 153, 156, 176, 181, 192, 213, 221, 243
Garvey, Steve 25, 168
Gaston, Cito 217
Gentry, Gary 183
Geronimo, Cesar 45, 51, 55
Giusti, Dave 6, 8, 9, 109, 122, 190
Glynn, Ed 31
Gorman, Lou 12
Gossage, Rich "Goose" 9, 11, 52, 115, 187, 190
Graham, Moonlight 120
Green, Dick 121
Greif, Bill 229
Griffey, Ken 45, 128
Griffin, Frankie 114
Griffin, Tom 113, 114, 223
Griffith, Calvin 168
Groat, Dick 145
Guerrero, Mario 197
Gullett, Don 11
Gwynn, Tony 158

Haak, Howie 52, 132, 210
Haddix, Harvey 5, 13, 118, 119
Hamilton, Milo 21
Hargis, Gary 37, 120, 121
Harper, Brian 113, 143
Harper, Terry 185
Harris, Bucky 163
Hausman, Tom 31
Hebner, Rich 6, 9, 16, 121, 161
Helms, Tommy 109, 122
Henderson, Ken 201
Hendrick, George 17, 26, 113, 159, 227
Hernandez, Keith 17, 162
Higuera, Teddy 173
Hill, George 110, 178
Hoak, Don 118
Hobbs, Roy 186
Holland, Al 26, 95, 111, 114, 227, 189
Hollander, Zander 91
Holtzman, Ken 25
Hooton, Burt 34
Hough, Charlie 173
Howe, Art 20
Hull, Richard 184
Hume, Tom 48, 137, 138

Hunter, Catfish 172
Hurst, Bruce 222

Ivie, Mike 38, 188

Jackson, Grant 9, 14, 22, 23, 26, 27, 31, 34, 38, 48, 52, 57, 61, 71, 84, 103, 104, 105, 108, 113, 116, 174, 175, 176, 177, 185, 188, 189, 200, 221
Jackson, Reggie 11, 181
James, Bill 171, 214, 215
John, Tommy 225
Johnson, Bart 13
Johnson, Randy 171, 217
Johnstone, Jay 4, 36
Jones, Odell 12, 110
Jones, Randy 35
Jones, Rick 13, 37, 105, 110, 111, 195, 228, 229

Kaat, Jim 16, 167
Kelly, Pat 59, 77, 86, 176, 221
Kemp, Steve 114, 144, 126
Kendall, Fred 36
Kendall, Jason 138
Key, Jimmy 173
Killebrew, Harmon 139, 171
Kimm, Bruce 43
Kingery, Mike 160
Kingman, Dave 17, 42, 43, 139
Kipper, Bob 227
Kison, Bruce 7, 13, 17, 20, 22, 23, 24, 28, 29, 33, 36, 38, 40, 41, 42, 57, 60, 76, 100, 102, 136, 165, 170 180, 181, 182, 184, 185, 188
Knepper, Bob 34
Knight, Ray 45, 48, 51, 52, 221
Knowles, Darold 38
Koosman, Jerry 183
Koufax, Sandy 225
Kranepool, Ed 39
Kuhn, Bowie 60
Kuiper, Duane 199

LaCoss, Mike 55
Lacy, Lee 9, 13, 15, 16, 20, 23, 25, 28, 32, 36, 38, 39, 57, 77, 81, 93, 96, 97, 157, 158, 159, 205
Langford, Rick 9
Langston, Mark 173
Lasorda, Tommy 29, 34, 36

Index

Lavelle, Gary 24, 25, 34
Law, Vance 13
Law, Vern 5, 166, 224
Lee, Bill 17
Lee, Mark 36
LeFlore, Ron 163
Leifield, Lefty 227
Lerch, Randy 16
Lockwood, Skip 22
Lois, Alberto 34, 209
Lolich, Mickey 172
Lonborg, Jim 16
Long, Dale 22
Lonnett, Joe 13, 70, 120, 153
Lopes, Davey 158
Lowenstein, John 59, 60, 64, 67, 72, 84, 189, 221
Luzinski, Greg 19, 32, 33, 211

Madlock, Bill 3, 26, 28, 32, 34, 36, 39, 40, 41, 42, 43, 51, 55, 61, 63, 64, 68, 70, 71, 72, 76, 77, 81, 84, 93, 95, 96, 105, 108, 111, 115, 122, 125, 127, 128, 129, 130, 131, 137, 177, 217, 230
Mahler, Mickey 112, 153
Mantle, Mickey 8, 214
Marino, Dan 1
Marshall, Mike 158
Martin, Billy 199
Martin, Pepper 123
Martinez, Dennis 58, 70, 71, 85
Martinez, Silvio 17
Martinez, Tippy 58, 77, 193
Matlack, Jon 183, 201
Mauch, Gene 118, 227
May, Dave 217
May, Jerry 204
May, Lee 57, 59, 85
May, Milt 7, 113, 218
May, Rudy 17
Mays, Willie 138, 139, 140
Mazeroski, Bill 5, 123, 137
McBean, Al 36
McCaskill, Kirk 173
McClain, Denny 216
McCovey, Willie 24, 137
McDonald, Joe 142
McGlothlin, Lynn 40, 42
McGraw, Tug 16, 32, 33, 152, 183
McGregor, Scott 58, 67, 68, 69, 84, 85, 156, 174, 193, 221

McNamara, John 21, 55, 118
Medich, George "Doc" 9, 109, 122, 149
Mendoza, Mario 12, 110, 111
Messersmith, Andy 172
Michael, Gene 5
Millan, Felix 15, 151
Miller, Scott 215
Milner, John 9, 15, 19, 20, 26, 28, 31, 32, 34, 36, 42, 51, 57, 63, 70, 71, 80, 81, 86, 92, 96, 97, 109, 112, 131, 152, 179, 192, 193, 201, 202, 203, 243
Mizell, Vinegar Bend 5
Monchak, Al 13, 119
Money, Don 5
Montanez, Willie 112, 201, 203
Moore, Barry 191
Moose, Bob 2, 7, 45, 181
Moreland, Keith 42
Moreno, Omar 4, 8, 14, 15, 20, 21, 23, 24, 25, 28, 32, 33, 40, 41, 42, 47, 48, 51, 52, 55, 64, 67, 71, 72, 77, 80, 81, 84, 85, 86, 97, 98, 116, 131, 143, 146, 147, 152, 160, 161, 162, 163, 212, 213, 243
Morgan, Joe 21, 22, 45, 47, 50, 51, 52, 181, 224, 230
Morris, Jack 173
Munson, Thurman 31
Mura, Steve 203
Murcer, Bobby 128
Murray, Eddie 59, 60, 63, 64, 65, 68, 71, 82, 84, 85, 189, 226
Murtaugh, Danny 7, 8, 9, 57, 108, 115, 146, 148, 149, 180, 205, 224

Nelson, Bob 21
Nettles, Greg 29, 212
Nicosia, Steve 15, 22, 32, 61, 67, 68, 84, 99, 100, 113, 152, 156, 157
Niekro, Joe 28, 29
Niekro, Phil 20, 28, 30
Niemann, Randy 112, 123
NLCS Box Score Game 1 48, 49, 50
NLCS Box Score Game 2 52, 53, 54
NLCS Box Score Game 3 55, 56, 57
Nordhagen, Wayne 113, 194
Norman, Fred 55, 129
Norman, Nelson 9, 109, 202

Office, Roland 21
Oliva, Tony 171

Oliver, Al 6, 102, 105, 161, 192, 202, 206, 214, 225
O'Neil, Buck 207
Ontaveris, Steve 41, 128
Orosco, Jesse 22, 190
Otis, Amos 159
Ott, Ed 8, 15, 25, 33, 34, 39, 51, 63, 64, 65, 70, 71, 72, 76, 81, 82, 99, 100, 110, 112, 152, 152, 153, 156, 170, 206
Owchinko, Bob 112, 170
Ozark, Dan 32

Pafko, Andy 176
Pagan, Jose 57, 132
Page, Mitchell 9, 109, 121
Pagliaroni, Jim 204
Palmer, David 17
Palmer, Jim 57, 58, 63, 64, 80, 81, 171, 226
Parker, Dave 8, 10, 11, 12, 15, 17, 19, 20, 21, 22, 23, 24, 26, 28, 29, 31, 32, 35, 36, 37, 38, 39, 42, 48, 50, 51, 52, 55, 60, 61, 64, 67, 71, 77, 80, 81, 85, 87, 98, 99, 105, 129, 131, 133, 137, 184, 189, 193, 203, 206, 209, 210, 211, 212, 213, 214, 215, 243
Parrish, Larry 16, 42
Pastore, Frank 21, 50, 51
Patek, Fred 6
Patterson, Dave 34
Pena, Tony 100, 113
Perez, Tony 16, 45, 139, 181
Peterson, Harding "Pete" 3, 8, 9, 10, 11, 12, 16, 17, 21, 25, 34, 37, 40, 64, 95, 105, 106, 107, 108, 109, 111, 112, 114, 116, 126, 132, 133, 142, 144, 145, 154, 163, 170, 178, 194, 196, 203, 205, 210, 211, 217, 219, 227
Perry, Gaylord 3, 23, 34, 36, 183
Phelps, Ken 177
Pinella, Lou 199
Pinson, Vada 158, 214
Pirates NLCS statistics 238, 239
Pirates Regular Season Day-by-Day 246, 247, 248, 249
Pirates Regular Season statistics 234, 235, 236, 237
Pirates World Series statistics 240, 241
Puhl, Terry 20
Pulido, Alfonso 113, 114, 126, 144
Pulli, Frank 51

Randle, Lenny 26, 111, 127, 217
Rasmussen, Eric 139
Ray, Johnny 112
Reed, Ron 16
Reich, Tom 163
Reuschal, Rick 17, 25, 225
Reuss, Jerry 13, 24, 34, 36, 111, 185, 195, 218, 219
Reynolds, Craig 9, 108, 175
Reynolds, R.J. 130
Rhoden, Rick 17, 20, 22, 101, 103, 111, 195, 196, 219
Rice, Jim 29, 212
Richard, J.R. 28
Rickey, Branch 5
Rijo, Jose 214
Ripken, Cal, Sr. 64
Rivas, Marty 110, 178
Roberts, Dave 3, 4, 6, 26, 29, 36, 39, 41, 52, 103, 105, 111, 125, 127, 175, 185, 217, 229, 231
Robertson, Bob 6, 8
Robinson, Bill 8, 9, 13, 15, 20, 22, 23, 25, 28, 29, 31, 32, 36, 38, 39, 40, 41, 43, 60, 61, 64, 68, 76, 77, 81, 85, 92, 96, 97, 113, 130, 131, 156, 191, 192, 193, 194, 202
Robinson, Brooks 67
Robinson, Don 19, 20, 22, 23, 25, 30, 31, 33, 36, 37, 39, 40, 48, 52, 55, 61, 64, 71, 72, 84, 100, 101, 102, 102, 103, 105, 115, 134, 155, 176, 182, 184, 185, 220, 221, 222
Robinson, Frank 67, 139, 158, 184
Robinson, Jackie 214
Rodriguez, Jerry 191
Roenicke, Gary 59, 67, 77, 81, 86, 165
Rogers, Steve 17, 31 39
Romo, Enrique 12, 13, 14, 19, 20, 22, 26, 28, 32, 33, 34, 37, 41, 47, 51, 52, 61, 68, 103, 104, 105, 110, 111, 112, 116, 154, 155, 176, 228
Rooker, Jim 13, 22, 23, 28, 30, 31, 33, 34, 37, 38, 40, 41, 60, 61, 63, 76, 77, 80, 101, 102, 103, 116, 157, 164, 165, 166, 167, 216, 226
Rose, Pete 12, 16, 45, 132, 134, 140, 212, 224
Ruthven, Dick 16
Ryan, Nolan 183

Saberhagen, Brent 173
Sacier, Kevin 32, 40
Sadecki, Ray 183
Sadek, Mike 34
Saferight, Harry 37, 194, 195
Sambito, Joe 29
Sanderson, Scott 17
Sanguillen, Manny 6, 8, 9, 15, 25, 32, 40, 57, 64, 65, 100, 108, 110, 112, 115, 116, 158, 160, 161, 204, 205, 206
Santarone, Pat 59
Santo, Ron 127
Sasser, Mackey 222
Schaeffer, Mark 229
Schatzader, Dan 17
Schmidt, Mike 136, 222
Scurry, Rod 37, 104, 105, 195, 200, 201
Seaver, Tom 45, 47, 50, 122, 225
Sexton, Jimmy 9, 108, 175
Sheckard, Jimmy 122
Shirley, Bob 23
Shore, Ray 129
Simmons, Ted 17
Simpson, Wayne 8, 192
Singleton, Ken 59, 63, 64, 65, 68, 71, 72, 81, 82, 85, 156, 189, 221, 226
Skaggs, Dave 72
Skinner, Bob 13, 117, 118, 142, 143
Smail, Harry 21, 22
Smith, Billy 67, 72, 82, 189, 221
Smith, Ozzie 36, 45
Solomon, Eddie 22, 30, 101, 103, 105
Sosa, Elias 17, 19, 110, 205
Speier, Chris 142
Stanhouse, Don 59, 64, 116, 206
Stargell, Willie 3, 5, 8, 10, 15, 16, 17, 19, 21, 22, 23, 24, 26, 27, 28, 29, 31, 34, 36, 38, 39, 40, 41, 42, 43, 47, 48, 51, 55, 57, 60, 61, 63, 67, 68, 70, 71, 77, 80, 81, 83, 84, 85, 86, 87, 91, 92, 115, 123, 130, 131, 134, 135, 136, 137, 138, 139, 140, 144, 145, 189, 193, 194, 202, 203, 206, 212, 214, 221, 242, 243
Staub, Rusty 29, 37, 39, 141, 214
Stearnes, John 39
Steinbrenner, George 227
Stennett, Rennie 7, 14, 15, 20, 24, 26, 57, 93, 94, 122, 133, 134, 159, 224
Stewart, Dave 173

Stewart, Sammy 71
Stoddard, Tim 58, 72, 77
Stone, Steve 58, 71
Sutcliffe, Rick 24
Sutter, Bruce 17, 23, 104
Sutton, Don 24
Sykes, Bob 17

Tannehill, Jesse 227
Tanner, Chuck 3, 9, 10, 11, 13, 14, 15, 20, 21, 22, 23, 24, 25, 26, 29, 30, 31, 32, 33, 34, 35, 37, 38, 39, 40, 41, 42, 44, 47, 50, 52, 55, 57, 64, 68, 71, 72, 76, 77, 80, 81, 84, 85, 103, 105, 108, 111, 114, 115, 116, 117, 119, 121, 128, 130, 134, 136, 144, 152, 154, 155, 161, 163, 165, 168, 169, 172, 173, 175, 176, 177, 181, 183, 184, 188, 189, 192, 198, 200, 202, 203, 206, 208, 216, 221, 226
Tavaras, Frank 14, 15, 17, 19, 39, 94, 111, 131, 142, 143, 144, 145, 146, 147, 161
Tekulve, Kent 8, 10, 14, 19, 20, 21, 23, 24, 25, 28, 30, 31, 32, 33, 34, 38, 39, 40, 41, 42, 43, 48, 52, 65, 72, 80, 82, 85, 86, 103, 104, 105, 114, 115, 137, 154, 176, 177, 184, 185, 186, 187, 188, 189, 190, 212, 221, 226
Templeton, Gary 14, 17
Terrell, Walt 160
Thomas, Derrel 229
Thompson, Jason 112, 137, 153
Thrift, Syd 196
Tiant, Luis 172
Tidrow, Dick 42
Torre, Joe 142
Traynor, Pie 214
Trevino, Alex 38
Trillo, Manny 16, 123, 225
Tudor, John 113
Turner, Jerry 4, 36
Twitchell, Wayne 31, 169

Unser, Del 33

Valentine, Ellis 16, 41
Vazquez, Rafael 13, 110, 112
Viola, Frank 173
Virdon, Bill 7, 29, 205
Vukovich, Pete 17

Wagner, Honus 146, 163

Walk, Bob 208
Walker, Harry 14, 116, 161, 162
Walker, Luke 102, 180
Walling, Denny 123
Washington, Herb 207, 208
Weaver, Earl 4, 57, 58, 59, 61, 64, 67, 68, 71, 72, 77, 82, 84, 85, 116, 174, 184, 189
White, Paul 215
Whitson, Ed 14, 19, 22, 23, 25, 26, 95, 104, 105, 111, 185, 198, 199
Wilhelm, Hoyt 190
Williams, Billy 22
Williams, Dick 16, 17
Williams, Mike 59
Willoughby, Jim 37, 195, 196, 197
Wills, Maury 5, 65
Winfield, Dave 4, 36, 230
Witt, Mike 173
Wood, Wilbur 172
World Series Box Score Game 1 61, 62, 63
World Series Box Score Game 2 65, 66
World Series Box Score Game 3 69, 70
World Series Box Score Game 4 73, 74
World Series Box Score Game 5 78, 79, 80
World Series Box Score Game 6 82, 83
World Series Box Score Game 7 88, 89, 90

Yastremski, Carl 139
Young, Cy 172
Youngblood, Joel 22, 25

Zisk, Richie 7, 8, 9, 105

www.ingramcontent.com/pod-product-compliance
Lightning Source LLC
Chambersburg PA
CBHW021342230426
43666CB00006B/377